DARK
PLACES

⊰ OF THE ⊱

EARTH

THE VOYAGE OF THE
SLAVE SHIP ANTELOPE

JONATHAN M. BRYANT

Liveright Publishing Corporation
A Division of W. W. Norton & Company
New York • London

For information about permission to reproduce selections from this book,
write to Permissions, Liveright Publishing Corporation, a division of
W. W. Norton & Company, Inc., 500 Fifth Avenue, New York, NY 10110

For information about special discounts for bulk purchases, please contact
W. W. Norton Special Sales at specialsales@wwnorton.com or 800-233-4830

Manufacturing by RR Donnelley, Harrisonburg
Book design by Lisa Buckley Design
Production manager: Devon Zahn

ISBN: 978-0-87140-675-0

Liveright Publishing Corporation, 500 Fifth Avenue, New York, NY 10110
www.wwnorton.com

W. W. Norton & Company Ltd., Castle House, 75/76 Wells Street, London W1T 3QT

1 2 3 4 5 6 7 8 9 0

"And this also," said Marlow suddenly,
"has been one of the dark places of the earth."

Joseph Conrad, *Heart of Darkness*

———————————————————

NORTH
AMERICA

*ATLANTIC
OCEAN*

Baltimore •

Savannah •
• Amelia Island
• St. Augustine

—— *Providence Passage*

Havana •

St. Martin
St. Barts •

Caribbean Sea

Suriname

*Wreck of the
Arraganta*
x

BRAZIL

SOUTH
AMERICA

*PACIFIC
OCEAN*

EUROPE

Cape
Verde
Islands

AFRICA

Freetown
New Georgia

Cabinda
Antelope captured

ATLANTIC

OCEAN

CONTENTS

Prologue *xi*

Part One / Sea

Chapter 1   3

Chapter 2   16

Chapter 3   30

Chapter 4   44

Chapter 5   59

Part Two / Savannah

Chapter 6   77

Chapter 7   98

Chapter 8   111

Chapter 9   123

Chapter 10   139

Chapter 11   153

Part Three / Washington, D.C.

Chapter 12   175

Chapter 13   193

Chapter 14   207

Chapter 15   227

Chapter 16   240

Chapter 17   257

Part Four / Legacies

Chapter 18   277

Epilogue   295

Notes   307

Acknowledgments   355

Credits   359

Index   361

PROLOGUE

"The Africans are parties to the cause,
at least such of them as are free."

Attorney General William Wirt The Antelope, 23 U.S. 66, 106 (1825)

O n the morning of February 28, 1825, attorney John Macpherson Berrien prepared to open his case. This was the second of what would be five days of argument before the United States Supreme Court, and Berrien faced a formidable challenge. Just two days earlier, on Saturday, Francis Scott Key had opened for the federal government in the case of the *Antelope*. Key had not yet been relegated to textbooks as the pious author of "The Star-Spangled Banner." In 1825 he was a lawyer at his peak: rich, well connected, and influential. He was also a superb speaker—some put him on par with Daniel Webster. Key had unleashed all of his rhetorical weapons on Saturday; this was a case he believed in and had worked personally to bring before the Supreme Court. The *Antelope* was a Spanish slave ship that had been captured by privateers and then seized by a United States Revenue Marine cutter off the coast of Florida. Using clear precedent, poetic language, and appeals to morality, Francis Scott Key argued that the hundreds of African captives found aboard the *Antelope* should be returned to Africa and freedom. United States law demanded it, he said. The law of nations demanded it, he said. Even the law of nature demanded it. Key looked into the eyes of the six justices sitting for the case, four of whom were slave owners, and announced that "by the law of nature, all men are free."[1]

The dim Supreme Court chamber in the basement of the Capitol was packed, and many spectators were impressed by Key's argument. Henry S. Foote wrote that Key "greatly surpassed the expectations of his most admiring friends. . . . [and] he closed with a thrilling and even electrifying picture of the horrors connected with the African slave trade." Most startling of all, Key argued that assuming all Africans were slaves, while declaring that all men were created equal, was philosophical and constitutional hypocrisy. If the United States had captured a ship full of white captives, Key asked, would not our courts assume them to be free? How could it be any different simply because the captives were black? Key knew that such disputes over slavery, race, and the meaning of the Constitution were not new, but in the 1820s, they'd begun to divide the nation. Just a few years earlier, from 1819 to 1821, conflict over the expansion of slavery into Missouri had torn Congress, and almost the nation, apart. Slavery was a dangerously hot subject, but Francis Scott Key stepped deliberately into the fire.[2]

The city of Washington had all of Sunday to discuss and consider Key's argument. On Monday morning there was great anticipation surrounding John M. Berrien's rebuttal. Again the Supreme Court chamber was crowded, and Berrien knew that the spectators expected fireworks. He was a newly elected United States senator from Georgia and wanted to make a strong impression, but fireworks were not his style. Berrien was a man who focused on logic and details, on clear and forceful argumentation. His command of the details of the case was unrivaled, since he had been involved with it from the beginning: so involved, in fact, that he and several friends had substantial financial interest in the outcome. There were professional implications as well; his client was Santiago de la Cuesta y Manzanal, a Spanish nobleman living in Cuba. A ruthless, wealthy, and powerful man, Santiago de la Cuesta stood to lose as much as $100,000 if Berrien failed. By comparison, the annual salary of a Supreme Court justice in 1825 was $4,500. A fortune was at stake, as was John Macpherson Berrien's rising reputation.[3]

Berrien was a highly respected attorney and judge in Georgia, but his work at home was service in the far provinces in comparison to pleading before the Supreme Court. Not that this was his first time; he had argued before the Supreme Court seven years before. Francis Scott Key, in contrast, had argued before the Court every year for the past seventeen years, a total of forty-two cases thus far. U.S. Attorney General William Wirt, Key's co-counsel, had appeared before the Court more than seventy times by 1825. In experience alone Berrien's adversaries were overwhelming, and they also looked the part. Key "was tall, erect, and of admirable physical proportions." Wirt was also tall, broad-chested, and graceful, with piercing blue eyes. Berrien was none of those, and he had a big nose to boot. Berrien also lacked the poetics and the gracious behavior of Francis Scott Key. While a polished and devastating debater, Berrien had a bitter and sometimes cruel wit that emerged even when he fought to control it. He had to restrain himself; one scored points before the Supreme Court with logic and the law, not with clever quips. The hour came; Berrien stood and began his argument.[4]

Slavery and the slave trade had haunted the United States from its beginning, and in 1775, every North American colony was entangled in the system. Many of the Revolutionary generation believed that rebellion against Great Britain included rebellion against the colonial system of slavery. The preamble to the Declaration of Independence asserted inalienable rights of life, liberty, and the pursuit of happiness. Slavery was clearly antithetical to these rights. Thomas Jefferson had gone further in his draft of the Declaration, which famously included a powerful complaint against the king that was struck from the final document. The king, Jefferson wrote:

> has waged cruel war against human nature itself, violating
> its most sacred rights of life & liberty in the persons of a dis-

tant people who never offended him, captivating & carrying
them into slavery in another hemisphere, or to incur miserable
death in their transportation thither. This piratical warfare, the
opprobrium of *infidel* powers, is the warfare of the CHRIS-
TIAN king of Great Britain. Determined to keep open a market where MEN should be bought & sold, . . .[5]

As part of their resistance to Great Britain, the revolutionary states
ended their participation in the African slave trade, even as they condemned British offers of freedom to slaves who enlisted to fight for
the king. This reflected a developing tension in the new nation, as
Americans struggled to accommodate slavery in a society asserting
equality for all. The tension was especially apparent at the 1787 Constitutional Convention in Philadelphia, where conflicts arose over taxation, representation, and, inevitably, slavery. James Madison reported
in his notes on the convention that compromise after compromise followed, until a final document was hammered out in September 1787.
Slavery was never mentioned by name in the final version, but the
Constitution engaged the issue. As John Quincy Adams explained, in
the famous *Amistad* case, "The words slave and slavery are studiously
excluded from the Constitution. Circumlocutions are the fig-leaves
under which these parts of the body politic are decently concealed."[6]

The new system of government counted three-fifths of slaves for
purposes of representation and taxation; required the return of fugitive slaves; and, most directly of all, prohibited any regulation of the
Atlantic slave trade by the federal government until January 1, 1808.
Southern planters, especially in Georgia and South Carolina, had lost
tens of thousands of slaves during the Revolution. They insisted upon
a chance to rebuild their stock of slaves through the direct African
slave trade. Twenty years was the compromise with regard to how
long direct trade would be allowed; most delegates assumed that after
twenty years, the international slave trade would end. Delegates, however, also generally agreed that the new Constitution gave the federal government no power to regulate or control slavery in the states.

This fit the federalist conception of the new government; it had power over international commerce, including the slave trade, but no power over domestic institutions within the states themselves. In a seemingly unconnected area, the Constitution also gave the federal judiciary control of "all Cases of admiralty and maritime Jurisdiction." Federal courts, not state courts, would enforce any future federal laws respecting the seaborne slave trade.[7]

Americans of the Revolutionary generation were torn by the issue of slavery. While many decried it, slavery seemed inescapably integrated into American society. Thomas Jefferson explained this terrible dilemma in a letter to John Holmes in April of 1820, writing, "but, as it is, we have the wolf by the ear, and we can neither hold him, nor safely let him go." Several states adopted plans for emancipation, but these were very gradual plans lasting decades, and were adopted in states where slavery was not central to the economy. There were others, however, who saw slavery not just as the cost of union but as a force maintaining union. Following this line of reasoning, in the *Antelope* case John Macpherson Berrien argued before the Supreme Court concerning slaves:

> The principle by which you continue to enjoy them, is protected by that constitution, forms a basis for your representatives, is infused into your laws, and mingles itself with all the sources of authority. . . . Paradoxical as it may appear, they [slaves] constitute the very bond of your union. The shield of your constitution protects them from your touch.[8]

The slave trade, however, was understood as being different from slavery. It was a commercial practice, not a domestic institution, and so could be regulated and controlled by rational individuals. Its horrors and abuses were well known, and educated citizens condemned it in public. By 1798, every American state had outlawed the international slave trade, though South Carolina reopened it in 1803. In December of 1806, President Thomas Jefferson called upon the United States

Congress for a law prohibiting the international slave trade at the earliest time allowed by the Constitution. By the end of February 1807, Congress had sent An Act to Prohibit the Importation of Slaves to the president for his signature. This law made it illegal for Americans to participate in the international slave trade, and illegal for anyone to import slaves into the United States after January 1, 1808. At almost the same time in Great Britain, in March 1807, after more than two decades of political struggle by abolitionists, Parliament passed An Act for the Abolition of the Slave Trade. Under this law, British participation in any aspect of the slave trade was unlawful, as was the importation of slaves to any British possessions after May 1, 1807.[9]

It was one thing to outlaw the international slave trade; it was something else to put that law into effect. In 1808, the United States had little in the way of a meaningful navy, and did no more than try to control ships bringing slaves to American shores. Great Britain, engaged in a titanic war with Napoleon's France, went much further and empowered its vast navy to suppress the slave trade. The impact of the laws and British action was immediate. From 1800 through 1807, documented voyages delivered almost 80,000 slaves to the Americas each year. In 1807, the number of slaves from documented voyages arriving in the New World totaled 86,343. In 1808, that fell to less than 33,000, and in 1809, less than 31,000. Clearly law and the British assumption of a wartime power to stop and search any vessel on the high seas had a significant effect upon the extent of the international slave trade, even when only one nation was engaged in the effort.[10]

Despite these successes, the slave trade continued. The vibrant and growing plantations of Spanish Cuba and Brazil demanded more enslaved workers, and slavers in Africa continued to offer captives at prices that kept the slave traders' profits high. With the end of the Napoleonic Wars in 1815, the number of slaving voyages and slaves delivered to the Americas began to rise significantly. Slavers learned to use the flags of various nations to protect their ships, especially those of Spain, Portugal, and, increasingly, the United States. British reluctance to stop and search American ships after 1815 conferred significant immunity upon vessels flying the American flag legitimately or illegitimately. Much of the financing for these voyages also came from the United States. This was especially true for slaving voyages to Cuba. Finally, many American citizens were involved as sailors and officers in these ventures.[11]

Partly in response to these and other political issues, in March 1819, Congress passed An Act in Addition to the Acts to Prohibit the Importation of Slaves. This law increased the penalties for Americans engaged in the international slave trade, and for the first time provided money to support implementation of the law. Most importantly for the case of the *Antelope*, the 1819 Slave Trade Act provided that captives brought into the United States illegally would come under the authority of the president of the United States. The president would then arrange as soon as possible to return the captives to Africa. Congress also revised American piracy law in May of 1820. Americans engaged in the slave trade were deemed pirates and, as such, were subject to the death penalty. At a time when the United States was torn over the admission of Missouri as a slave state, and divided on the issue of the westward expansion of slavery, the congressional votes on the 1819 Slave Trade Act and the 1820 Piracy Act suggested a significant commitment to strong laws for suppression of the international slave trade.[12]

The arrival of the *Antelope* tested that commitment. The ship was a Spanish slaver from Cuba, captured off the coast of Africa by a revolutionary privateer. An American revenue cutter later captured the *Antelope* off the coast of Spanish Florida. Found aboard were 281 living captives. The seven years of legal conflict over the captives that followed revealed much of the dark underside of law and commerce in the young Republic. The conflict over freedom for the captives forced the Supreme Court to address a number of important questions. Were the natural rights of liberty more important than the rights of property? Was the Constitution a source of first principles for the American legal system, or simply a legal text providing only limited powers? How was international law shaped, and what role did it have in American law? Did African captives have the same rights as other human beings in the American legal system, or did race limit their rights before the courts? Most importantly, the case forced the Supreme Court to the very precipice on the issue of slavery. If natural rights to liberty made the *Antelope* captives free, did natural rights make all slaves free?

The Antelope is not commonly considered an important Supreme Court case. It is long— more than seventeen thousand words, and complex. It was an admiralty law case, with arcane procedures and different rules of evidence than those of common law. It did not boldly highlight a groundbreaking change in the powers of federal governance. In many ways the case has simply been overlooked. If asked about important Supreme Court cases on slavery, most historians would name *Dred Scott*, or perhaps *Prigg v. Pennsylvania*.[13] Thanks to Steven Spielberg, members of the public would most likely mention the *Amistad*. The *Antelope* is crucial, however, because in it Chief Justice John Marshall and the Supreme Court established precedents—in international law, property law, and the Court's cognizance of natural rights—that influenced future decisions on slavery. As Marshall explained early in his *Antelope* opinion:

> In examining claims of this momentous importance; claims
> in which the sacred rights of liberty and of property come in
> conflict with each other; . . . this Court must not yield to feel-
> ings which might seduce it from the path of duty, and must
> obey the mandate of the law.[14]

By refusing to be "seduced" from the path of duty and by affirming that while slaves might be human beings, at law slaves were property, John Marshall's Court shaped American jurisprudence on these issues for the next thirty-five years. The Court also buttressed the claims of slave owners in looming struggles over fugitive slaves and the westward expansion of slavery. Whether or not the Constitution is a pro-slavery document is much debated among historians, but without question it is a pro-property document. If slaves are property, and nothing else, then a pro-property Constitution will inevitably be pro-slavery. Thus, in many ways John Marshall's opinion in the *Antelope* reinforced the divisions that would tear the nation apart.

John Macpherson Berrien could not see the future, but as a plantation master he understood the importance of slaves remaining property at law. He began his argument by summarizing Key's address, and then highlighted the implications. If the Court accepted Key's assertions, Berrien argued, then "we are bound, prima facie, to hold that there can be no property in a human being." He let that hang for a moment. Then he moved to the logical destruction of Key's presentation, ticking off point by point from a numbered list. Berrien mocked Key's ethical arguments, asking, "[W]ould it become the United States to assume . . . the character of censors of the morals of the world . . . ?" He continued, "We have no pretense, then, to enforce against others our own peculiar notions of morality. The standard of morality, by which Courts of justice must be guided, is that which the law prescribes." Berrien's presentation was masterful, biting, sardonic, and brilliant. Unfortunately for the *Antelope* captives, and for the nation, several justices found it convincing.[15]

Key, Berrien, and Marshall are just three of many voices in this story, a sweeping tale that took eight years to resolve and directly involved hundreds of people and the equivalent of many millions of dollars. Individual voices do not necessarily yield the truth, but a multiplicity of voices from different points of view can serve to sharpen and improve the focus of a story, perhaps moving it toward truth. Sometimes, however, there are no voices; certain points of view remain silent. That is the case here. Only one child's voice from all the hundreds of captives aboard the *Antelope* has survived, and it tells only the story of being kidnapped and sold as a slave. No more voices have been found, although many captives could speak English within a year after arriving in Savannah. Court documents reveal that a translator was hired several times, but not once do the documents mention anything said by an *Antelope* captive. The voices that dominate this story are those of white men, mostly wealthy, and mostly from the South. That in itself tells something of the truth. Thankfully, even without their voices, there are ways to learn about the captives. Accountings, bills, lists, observations by others, and even the names given or chosen by them all tell us bits of the story. These things must now speak for the African captives, for their voices will never be heard.[16]

This is very different from the well-known *Amistad* case. During 1840 and 1841, the *Amistad* captives gave interviews and with the help of supporters used the press to become a national story. As many as 2,500 newspaper articles were written about the *Amistad*, giving voice to the *Amistad* captives, allowing some to emerge by name as participants in their fate. By comparison, fifteen years earlier the national press was tiny, and most information about the *Antelope* spread through newspapers printing a single report. Of original newspaper articles about the *Antelope* there were perhaps a dozen. The *Antelope* predated the nationally coordinated and vocal abolitionist organizations that would emerge out of the growing conflict over slavery during the 1820s and 1830s. There were no abolitionist journals to feature the *Antelope* case, no artists painting the brave captives, no publication of pamphlets calling for justice. The *Antelope* captives, instead of sitting in jail only a day's journey from New York, were hard at work in homes and on plantations in farthest Georgia. Isolated and indistinguishable from the enslaved people working with them, the *Antelope* captives had no bevy of abolitionists building support for their cause. Instead, they depended on help from just one torn man, United States Attorney for the District of Georgia Richard Wylly Habersham. Habersham fought for the captives, and until the last moment possible sought their freedom. Without his actions there would have been no extended legal battle and no cases before the Supreme Court. Like so many caught in the American system of slavery, the *Antelope* captives would have faded into the mists of history.[17]

Justice is a human creation, and requires human action. This is a tale of both justice and injustice, of freedom and oppression, a story of human aspirations, even if constrained by place and time. The result, partial justice for the African captives, was followed by terrible suffering even among those who were the most fortunate. This story is not a condemnation of the founding fathers, the president, the members of the Supreme Court, the inhabitants of Savannah, Washington, Cabinda, or Havana. It is a story of its time, told as clearly as possible based on the chaotic nature of the evidence that has survived almost two hundred years. It is a story to be enjoyed, a tale of exciting battles at sea, of lies and legal conflict, of corruption, money, and failure. It is a story that reveals something of humanity, the good and bad that humans can do. It is an important story, and it should be told—even if it cannot hope to fairly represent all of its players.

Joseph Conrad's great novella *Heart of Darkness* begins with a group of men telling yarns on a yacht anchored at the mouth of the Thames. Marlow, the storyteller, tells his friends that the England around them "has been one of the dark places of the earth." Marlow points to one dark time, that of the Roman conquest of Britain. "Their administration was merely a squeeze," he said, "nothing more . . . robbery with violence, aggravated murder on a great scale." Britain itself, nineteen hundred years before, was a dark place; so too was the vaunted Roman Empire. To a British audience schooled in the classics, this was an unexpected assertion; perhaps even a shocking assertion. There were many dark places in Conrad's story: the "whited sepulcher" of Brussels, the offices of the "trading concern," the great Congo River itself. *Heart of Darkness* is as anticolonial a story as one can imagine for 1899, a story that exposes empire itself as the source of savagery and barbarism.[18]

So, too, in the story of the *Antelope*, there are many dark places: the hold of a slave ship, the deck of a privateer, the slave pens at Cabinda, the plantations of Georgia, the courthouse in Savannah, even the chamber of the United States Supreme Court. These dark places were not of themselves evil, but became so through humans' dark acts. Together they tell one of the most dramatic, important, and unjustly forgotten stories from slavery's tragic history.

PART ONE

SEA

The African slave-trade—slaves taken from a dhow captured by the H.M.S. *Undine*.

CHAPTER 1

"That the course of opinion on the slave trade should be unsettled ought to excite no surprise."

Chief Justice John Marshall *The Antelope*, 23 U.S. 66, 114 (1825)

I n 1819, Santiago de la Cuesta y Manzanal was one of the richest men in Havana, Cuba. This did not mean he could avoid ridicule. A fellow merchant described him as a giant of a man, "so large he looks as if he kept all his money within himself." The fashions of the day would not have helped. They were designed for slim young men, not middle-aged businessmen like Santiago de la Cuesta. Nonetheless, his standing in society required that he dress well: tight pantaloons, a cutaway coat with a tall collar, white linen shirt, and a silk cravat tied in a loose bow. Even if he looked like a fat turtle, no one dared to say so in his presence. In 1819, being one of the wealthiest men in Havana meant something. With a population of 100,000, Havana was the third largest city in North America, behind only Mexico City and New York. Philadelphia had about 65,000 inhabitants, Charleston about 25,000, and Savannah, Georgia, had fewer than 8,000 perma-nent residents. Santiago de la Cuesta's wealth, however, was new. The firm of Cuesta Manzanal y Hermano had begun as a small merchant house in 1802, selling groceries and sundries. By 1819, the business

was engaged in trans-Atlantic commerce, merchant banking, shipping, and sugar plantations. Santiago de la Cuesta followed every
aspect of his firm, and involved himself in each investment. Sometime
during the summer of 1819, he would have visited one of his current
business ventures, the brig *Antelope*.[1]

To visit the ship Santiago de la Cuesta probably rose early to avoid
the traffic and congestion of the narrow streets inside Havana's old city
walls. He was wealthy and could afford a coach-and-six, but visiting the
docks was best done in a smaller volante. This was a small coach with
two huge wheels to ride easily over potholes and only one horse to draw
it. A volante was nimble enough for the teeming city streets. Tides did
not significantly flush Havana harbor, so the smells of birds and fish,
as well as human sewage, greeted De la Cuesta when he arrived at the
waterfront. Wharves lined the eastern edge of the old city, and there he
would have examined the *Antelope*. She was not a particularly impressive vessel: a brig, meaning she had only two masts for square sails rather
than a ship rig's three masts. This helped cut costs in the merchant trade
because it required fewer crewmen. She was registered as being 121
toneladas, or Spanish tons burthen, but this was probably a deliberate
underestimate to reduce port fees and taxes; other records list her as significantly larger. Yet the *Antelope* was small, no more than 80 feet long
on deck, and less than 30 feet broad, or at most four lanes in a twenty-
five-yard-long swimming pool. In April of 1816, Domino Pendergast
had sold her to C. H. Bustamante and Co. in Cádiz, Spain, for $7,700.
Bustamante and Co. registered their new brig as the *Antelope*, formerly
the *Fenix de Cádiz*. They still owned the ship, but management of it
was in the hands of Cuesta Manzanal y Hermano. In 1817, under Captain José Manuel Roche, the *Antelope* had sailed from Cádiz to Africa
and then delivered 234 slaves to Havana. After the ship's safe arrival a
new captain, Nicolas Lopez de Castro, obtained a Spanish Royal passport for another voyage to the African coast. The *Antelope* sailed for
Africa under Lopez de Castro in April 1818 to buy "*negros bozales*." This
meant literally "wild" or "untamed" blacks—newly enslaved Africans
for Cuba's burgeoning plantation system.[2]

The *Antelope* returned from Luanda in 1819 with 217 living slaves. Captain Lopez de Castro did not return at all. The African trade was rough business, often as dangerous for the officers and crew of a slaver as for the slaves themselves. Accident, violence, or disease could have felled Captain de Castro, but no record described his end; the firm of Cuesta Manzanal y Hermano recorded only financial matters, not the fate of employees. Back in Havana in the summer of 1819, the *Antelope* began to prepare for yet another voyage; of these costs the firm of Cuesta Manzanal y Hermano kept meticulous records. A new captain was needed for the ship, and the firm found Don Vicente de Llovio, an unemployed Spanish naval officer. Captain de Llovio would be paid 100 silver pesos per month, and his first duty was to see that the *Antelope* was properly prepared for sea. This included repairing the hull, hiring crew, loading cargo, buying supplies, and organizing the ship's hold and deck to carry hundreds of captives.[3]

The brig *Antelope* was one small part of a vast worldwide trading system that was centered on the Atlantic basin. This thriving trade system had developed during the seventeenth and eighteenth centuries, and the great profits from Atlantic trade led to expansion, bringing in products from around the world. Silver, sugar, coffee, and rum came from the Americas. Gold, ivory, dyewoods, and palm oil came from Africa. Europe provided iron, guns, textiles, and brandy. Cotton cloth, silk, tea, and spices were brought from Asia. Slaves were the linchpin of colonial production in this worldwide trading system, and the slave trade was the key to economic expansion. Wealth from the colonies poured into the hands of a few, including merchants and planters around the Atlantic rim, as well as bankers and financiers based in Amsterdam, Paris, and London. Santiago de la Cuesta combined all three roles: He was a merchant, a financier, and, as his wealth grew, increasingly a planter and slave owner. In 1824, because of his great wealth and service, and, of course, following a large monetary contribution to the Spanish Crown, Santiago was made a count of Spain. Santiago de la Cuesta y Manzanal was one of the fortunate few who profited wildly from the Atlantic system. The slaves he imported on ships like the *Antelope* were some of the many who suffered so that he might profit.[4]

Direct slaving voyages to Africa like those made by the *Antelope* were relatively new ventures for Cuban merchant firms. Before 1790, despite almost three hundred years of European occupation, fewer than one hundred thousand slaves had been brought to Cuba. These imported slaves were taken to Cuba almost entirely in the ships of other nations. The first legal, direct slaving voyage from Cuba to Africa did not sail until 1792. After that, the floodgates opened. Between 1792 and 1820, less than thirty years, more than three hundred thousand new slaves arrived in Cuba. This rapid growth in slave imports had dramatic effects upon Cuban society and its economy, but it also reflected a great contradiction. The Enlightenment of the eighteenth and early nineteenth centuries is usually seen as a progressive scientific, philosophical, and political movement that produced Newton's physics, Rousseau's *Social Contract*, and the Declaration of Independence. As the Marquis de Condorcet wrote, the new openness to ideas and the increased availability of trustworthy information meant that all people could acquire "the necessary enlightenment to conduct themselves in accordance with their own reason."[5]

The ideas developed by the Enlightenment physiocrats and refined in classical economics saw free trade and rational self-interest as more natural and normal forms of economic relations than the economic regulations of mercantilism. Of course, these ideas had already been embraced by many merchants. Free and unregulated trade, they argued, combined with the self-interest of rational economic actors competing in the market, could produce an efficient economic system. Ignoring Adam Smith's concerns about the "dreadful misfortunes" this system had already produced for the inhabitants of the East and West Indies, they instead claimed him as their prophet. Under their reasoning, if the greatest good was the greatest profit, then plantations in the Indies should use the most easily obtained and productive system of labor available. Slavery was that system. Through the eighteenth century there followed a dramatic expansion of the slave trade to the Caribbean, even as the philosophical critique of slavery grew. Immanuel Kant understood this paradox, observing that he lived in "an age of enlightenment . . . not yet an enlightened age." In one of the horrible ironies of history, the Cuban slave trade boomed in part due to Enlightenment reforms led by one of Spain's greatest monarchs.[6]

In 1761 Anton Raphael Mengs painted a brilliant portrait of Charles III, Spain's new king. Mengs depicted Charles in the glory of his military accoutrements, wearing a golden sword, black armor, and a rich sash decorated with medals. In his right hand he grasped the staff of imperial authority, a reminder that Spain still ruled a huge worldwide empire. But Charles couldn't quite carry it off, or perhaps he chose not to, for the man himself peeked through the martial image. There was a glimpse of Charles's natural hair beneath the powdered wig, and with his left hand he gestured as if to invite the viewer into the room. Bright, open eyes and a genial smile completed the image of a man ready to sit down and talk about ideas, policy, perhaps even family. Charles III was a monarch of the Enlightenment, and he already had twenty-five years' experience as the leader of reform in Naples and Sicily. As king of Spain, Charles intended to bring sweeping reform and rationalization to the empire. Prophetically, the king's large, long, bulbous nose dominated Mengs's image of him; it was a nose that colonial officials and bureaucrats from Manila to Mexico City would soon feel had been thrust into their business.[7]

But all that would have to wait; in 1761 the Spanish empire was in crisis. Despite Spain's neutrality in the ongoing Seven Years' War, British victories over French forces in Canada and at sea now threatened Spanish colonies in the Americas. Worst of all, the British refused to give assurances that they would respect neutral Spain's financial lifeline: silver from Mexico and Peru. Charles had grand plans for enlightened reform, but those plans depended upon the riches from Spanish colonies. The king and his advisors concluded from the long history of relations between Great Britain and Spain that the British could not be trusted. Before he could lead reform, King Charles had first to prepare for war.[8]

Key to the Spanish position in the New World was Cuba. The products of Cuba in 1761 were not that important: modest amounts of tobacco and sugar, and cowhides. The city of Havana, however, played crucial logistical and commercial roles in the Spanish system; it was the imperial way station for silver and other colonial products on their way to Spain. Over the previous two centuries, imperial treasure ships and merchant vessels from all of Spain's American colonies gathered every spring in Havana. Then, under watchful military escort and following strict bureaucratic rules, the combined fleet made the journey across the Atlantic to Cádiz. This large convoy was virtually immune to the English, French, and Dutch pirates who harassed Spanish ships in other parts of the world, ensuring the safe transport of American silver and plantation products to Spain. With war looming, Charles dispatched ships and soldiers to defend Havana, but it was too little, too late. In June of 1762, a massive British fleet arrived off Havana, part of a preemptive strike by Britain against neutral Spain. Greatly outnumbered, the besieged Spanish could only hope that yellow fever or a hurricane would destroy the British forces. They hoped in vain, and in August of 1762, Havana fell to the British.[9]

Since the sixteenth century, administrators in Seville and Madrid had imposed strict mercantilist regulation on trade within the Spanish empire. The British invaders ignored those regulations during their eleven-month occupation of Havana. Import and export businesses boomed, and Havana's harbor was crowded with ships bringing a variety of goods to the island. Wealthy Cubans enjoyed this taste of free trade and unrestricted access to goods from across the Atlantic world. Among the regulations ignored by the British was the Asiento: the legal privilege to trade in slaves to the Spanish empire. Through a contract system, the Asiento had strictly controlled the number, price, and destination of slaves within the empire. Prior to the capture of Havana, Cuba's allotment of slaves under the Asiento was less than a thousand slaves per year. As a result, in 1760, a total of perhaps thirty-five thousand slaves lived on the entire island. During the British occupation of 1762–1763, however, the limits on slaving were ignored, and ships brought in four thousand new slaves. This increased the number of slaves in Cuba by more than 10 percent, and sugar production leapt.[10]

The Spanish regained control of Havana after the peace in 1763. Some Cubans and Spaniards had profited from the chaotic commercial boom during the British occupation, and as Charles III launched the Bourbon reforms, these men called for an end to mercantilist regulation. Charles, however, proceeded slowly and carefully with his reforms. An intendant was appointed for Cuba, bypassing the ossified imperial bureaucracy and reporting directly to the king. Along with greater administrative efficiency came new policies intended to promote Cuban commerce. These included opening direct merchant trade to ports throughout the empire, decreasing regulations and taxes on that trade, and improving port facilities and fortifications in Havana itself. In some ways King Charles and his advisors intended to use Cuba as an experiment. By finding which financial and trade reforms worked best in Cuba, the successful policies could then be adapted for the rest of the vast Spanish empire.[11]

General Alejandro O'Reilly was sent by the Spanish king in 1763 to study Cuban affairs. Among his interests was the neighboring French colony of Saint-Domingue, later known as Haiti. It was considered the most valuable colony in the Caribbean because of its rapidly growing sugar and coffee production. Saint-Domingue lay just across the Windward Passage east of Cuba. The only difference between Cuba and Saint-Domingue, O'Reilly argued, was that in Cuba slaves were scarce and expensive. "It can be stated as an absolute principle," he argued, "that the prosperity of this Island depends mainly on the import of African slaves. . . . The King will derive much more revenue from the taxes on sugar produced by slaves than he will obtain from the import duties on the slaves themselves."[12]

At first, however, this idea fell on deaf ears. Too many important people benefited financially from the Asiento system for it to be so easily challenged. Planters in Cuba, however, having briefly enjoyed "free trade" under British occupation, began to complain about the high prices and limited supply of slaves. They petitioned for the allocation of greater numbers of slaves to Cuba. They begged for liberalization of the rules controlling the slave trade. Despite their petitions, the prices of slaves brought in by the *asentistas* continued to be much higher than those offered by merchants in the French and British West Indies. Cuban planters learned that, while limited liberal experiments were acceptable, discarding the entire mercantilist edifice of Spanish imperial trade was not.[13]

As a result, the smuggling of slaves into Cuba increased. This smuggling was not always surreptitious. Putting the right money into the right hands allowed "smugglers," usually French or British ships, to land slaves in Havana itself. The labor of these smuggled slaves and the slaves delivered under the yearly Asiento allotment generated a modest Cuban sugar and coffee boom, though much smaller than the boom in nearby Saint-Domingue. Cuba's sugar production increased from an average of thirteen thousand boxes of sugar per year in 1760–1763 to an average of over eighty thousand boxes a year during the period 1778–1788. Profits soared, and planters clamored for more slaves. Finally, in October of 1788, just two month before the death of King Charles III, the dam broke. The Crown issued new regulations that ended the Asiento system and opened the slave trade to both Spanish and foreign shippers.[14]

Santiago de la Cuesta y Manzanal arrived in Cuba at just the right time. Born about 1778 in the Val de San Lorenzo in the mountains of northern Leon in Spain, in the 1790s he accompanied his brother, Pedro, to Cuba, where they acted as the agents of several Spanish merchant firms and soon opened their own grocery business. Benefiting from his Spanish birth and connections to merchant firms in Seville, Santiago rose quickly in Cuban society. He entered Havana's merchant trade himself, where he proved aggressive and ruthless, quickly accumulating a fortune. In 1806 his social and financial success was confirmed by his marriage to the daughter of Bonifacio Gonzáles Larrinaga, one of Havana's leading bankers. Santiago de la Cuesta had climbed to the top of Havana's heap.[15]

Meanwhile, the nature of the slave trade changed dramatically. In the 1790s, first rebellion and then revolution broke out among the free blacks and slaves of Saint-Domingue. In response, new Cuban regulations in 1796 barred trading for Saint-Domingue slaves, and in 1804, a royal decree forbade trading with any other Caribbean island for slaves. The Spanish and Cuban administrators worried that ideas of equality and republicanism, raised by the Haitian and French revolutions, might slip in among West Indian slaves. So, after 1804, all slave trading had to be for *bozales*, or new slaves brought directly from Africa, where they presumably knew nothing of equality. Three years later, in 1807, both the United States and Great Britain passed laws prohibiting their citizens' involvement in the Atlantic slave trade. Then, in 1808, French armies under Napoleon invaded Spain, and Spain and her colonies were at war with France. Slave imports to Cuba, which had been carried almost entirely in British, American, and French vessels, diminished to a trickle. Wealthy, well connected, and successful, Santiago de la Cuesta saw opportunity in this development.[16]

In 1809 Santiago de la Cuesta y Manzanal joined two other merchants in sending a ship to London to buy trade goods for use in Africa. Through his wife's banking family he had connections in London and access to large amounts of capital. Soon after, Santiago and his partners dispatched the ship *Zaragoza* to the Loango coast in west central Africa, and the *Junta Central* to Calabar in the Bight of Biafra to trade for slaves. Both voyages were successful, and the firm's involvement in the slave trade grew quickly. Cuesta Manzanal y Hermano usually did not own the ships it used for the slave trade, apparently leasing or engaging in joint ventures with other shipowners. In 1811, for example, the French privateer *Superbe* captured 134 slaves belonging to Cuesta Manzanal y Hermano. Those slaves, however, were carried on a ship, interestingly named the *Juan*, that flew the flag of the

United States. Since the prohibition of the African trade under British and American law, slave trading had become a complex business of flags of convenience and foreign registration, with ships of uncertain provenance often carrying false flags and registrations. British naval officers called these ships "mongrel," and such mongrel vessels began to dominate the slave trade after 1808. This caused endless complications and legal problems for British naval vessels attempting to suppress the trade. Cuesta Manzanal y Hermano learned to play this game early, as did others.[17]

Cuban participation in the African slave trade grew dramatically after 1809, and then exploded with the end of the Napoleonic Wars in 1815. The firm of Cuesta Manzanal y Hermano participated in this boom, and through it Santiago de la Cuesta became one of the wealthiest merchants in Cuba. By 1819 there were 22 active slave-trading firms in Havana, and Cuesta Manzanal y Hermano was probably the largest. In five years, from 1816 to 1820, these 22 firms together legally imported 95,817 slaves to Havana alone. One report from Havana explained that from January through July of 1819, some 713 ships entered the port of Havana. Not all were slavers, but in the month of July alone, 1,728 slaves came into Havana, and prime new slaves were selling at between $450 and $500. Thus, in this one month slaves worth about $700,000 (more than $13 million today) came into Havana. This was big business, and the profits were huge.[18]

In 1819, Santiago de la Cuesta and his brother received royal permission to import 1,664 slaves to Cuba. The *Antelope* was just one of several slaving ventures Cuesta Manzanal y Hermano conducted that year. The trade was risky, and it was wise to put the eggs in a variety of baskets. The chances for success, however, could be improved by investing in quality ships and maintaining them properly. Sailing tropical waters such as those of Cuba and Africa resulted in the growth of weed and marine animals on a wooden hull, greatly slowing a vessel. A clean and fast hull was important for a slave trader. Worse, *Teredo navalis*, the dreaded shipworm, thrived in tropical waters. It could destroy a ship quickly by burrowing into the wooden planks and frame of the hull. In 1819, the best known solution to marine growth and ship-worm was sheathing the entire hull in copper below the waterline. Coppering was expensive and used only by naval vessels and valuable merchant ships. During the summer of 1819, the *Antelope* was freshly coppered, or her copper sheathing was significantly repaired; Cuesta Manzanal y Hermano bought a large number of copper sheets and nails for her hull. The *Antelope* had delivered as many as 961 slaves to Havana over the previous four years, producing what today would be millions of dollars in profits. Such a prodigious moneymaker as the *Antelope* required good care.[19]

During July and August of 1819, a new crew was assembled for the *Antelope*. Captain and Pilot Vicente de Llovio was joined by First Mate Fernando Maguibel and Second Mate Domingo Grondona. Grondona was an experienced slave trader and knew something of the Kikongo languages of the west central coast of Africa. Cuesta Manzanal y Hermano made an additional individual contract with Grondona, giving him specific duties to properly care for and feed the captives taken aboard. In return, he would earn one and a half pesos for each slave brought alive to Havana. As the voyage expected to acquire 350 new slaves in Africa, Grondona could earn a bonus of more than $500, the equivalent of seven months' wages. The crew also included a boat-swain, a guardian, a caulker, a surgeon, and a cook. The boatswain, Thomas Ximenes, had been with the *Antelope* for five years and knew the ship and the slave trade well. Sixteen *marineros,* or able seamen, and twelve *mozos*, or ship's boys, rounded out the crew. The seamen averaged thirty-five years of age and the boys twenty-one, suggest-ing an experienced group. Carlos Cuesta was simply listed among the boys in the crew list, but in the Havana port captain's clearance papers "Charlie Cuesta" was listed as a slave. Thirty-three men, one possibly a slave, would take the *Antelope* to Africa.[20]

The *Antelope*'s load for this voyage was carefully enumerated; food and trade goods used in slaving traveled duty-free. Loading ship was arduous, the sailors timing their work with mariners' chanteys, or work songs. In Havana the work-song leaders often kept the beat by striking together *clavijas*, or wooden shipbuilding pegs, the rhythm varying with the type of work being done. Huge casks weighing hundreds or even thousands of pounds were lifted by sailors heaving in a slow, regular rhythm on lines run through a series of blocks, or pulleys, to produce sufficient mechanical advantage. The casks were then swung over the hold and lowered into the proper and safe place for the correct trim of the vessel. It was a complex, difficult, and dangerous process; a mistake could damage the ship or kill a man. The *Antelope* loaded 4,000 pounds of hardtack, 6,000 pounds of rice, and 5,000 pounds of beans. She also loaded 140 casks of salt beef, each weighing about 500 pounds, for a total of 70,000 pounds of salted beef. This reflected the large cattle production of Cuba; the *Antelope* loaded only six casks of salt pork. Finally, a quarter-ton of dried cod, casks of chickpeas, vinegar, and lard went aboard. All of this was for feeding slaves, and while these supplies were not sufficient for the entire voyage, they greatly reduced the risk of not finding enough food on the African coast. Food for the crew, perhaps of a better quality, perhaps not, was also loaded. One hundred and seven butts of water, each weighing more than a thousand pounds, were carefully swung aboard and positioned below. The water butts were not only terribly heavy, they had to be stored in such a fashion as to stabilize the ship and yet be accessible during the voyage in a sequence that would not upset the vessel's trim. This puzzle required great skill. In total, the *Antelope* carried a bit more than 13,000 gallons of water, enough to last 350 people on strict rations about 70 days in tropical heat. This proved a crucial limit later in the voyage.[21]

For trade the *Antelope* carried eighteen pipes, or 2,250 gallons, of *aguardiente de caña*, inexpensive rumlike firewater that was virtually a by-product of sugar refining. She also carried 15,000 pounds of gunpowder for trade, which, combined with the firewater, promised only more woe for the recipients. Headed to Africa, she shipped five large chests containing 135 bolts of blue Guinea cloth. This finely woven, indigo-dyed cotton textile mimicked some of the highest-quality cloth produced in west Africa. In some parts of Africa, cloth functioned as money, and blue Guinea cloth was worth perhaps three or even four times as much as lesser-quality cloth. The *Antelope* also carried four 8-pound cannons, twelve muskets, and twelve cutlasses, though none of these would prove very useful. Finally, she carried 25,000 silver Spanish dollars; this was changed into gold for ease of handling prior to departure. While slaves were seldom sold for gold on the African coast, trade goods, food, and other items could be purchased with gold. In total, Cuesta Manzanal y Hermano invested $56,273 in the voyage, not counting the value of the *Antelope* itself.[22]

The plan for the voyage was simple: acquire 350 new slaves on the coast of Africa and bring them back to Cuba. If successful, and the ship returned with at least 300 slaves worth $400 each, the voyage would earn more than $120,000. This would be a return on investment in excess of 100 percent. If unsuccessful, all could be lost. Great risk was required, but the potential returns were also great. As fully prepared as possible, on August 24, 1819, the *Antelope* sailed from Havana, passing the Morro Castle, never to return.[23]

CHAPTER 2

"That Americans and others . . . carry on this criminal and inhuman
traffic under the flags of other countries is a fact of such general
notoriety that courts of admiralty may act upon it."

Chief Justice John Marshall *The Antelope,* 23 U.S. 66, 130 (1825)

I n the fall of 1819, a dark and dangerous-looking vessel sailed into the
port of Baltimore. She was the *Columbia,* a brig about 100 feet long
and 250 tons burthen. Following the most recent designs, her hull
was long and lean, with little sheer, a sharp bow, and no elevation to
her bowsprit. She was painted black, had the two masts of a brig, and
wore a hermaphrodite rig. At the time this was an unconventional sail
plan that set traditional square sails on *Columbia*'s foremast while using
the fore and aft sails of a schooner on her mainmast. So rigged and
managed with skill, the *Columbia* could sail faster to windward than
a traditional square-rigged ship, but she was still able to run directly
downwind with the advantage of square sails. It was the rig of a pred-
ator, and any sailor watching as she tied up alongside a wharf in Fell's
Point would have known her for what she was—a privateer.[1]

The *Columbia* was sailing under a commission from Admiral Luis
Brión of Venezuela. Privateers like her were privately owned warships

commissioned by governments to prey on an enemy's commerce. The *Columbia*'s purpose was simple: capture the merchant ships of Venezuela's enemies and sell them for profit. The *Columbia* was not a pirate, not quite, as long as her predation was confined to the ships of Spain and she followed the law of nations in her treatment of captured ships. The *Antelope*, sailing from Cuba under the Spanish flag, was one of those ships that could legally be preyed upon by the *Columbia*. Ships from nations other than Spain were not legal prey for the *Columbia*, because Venezuela was engaged in a war for independence only with Spain. Ships such as the *Columbia* were spoken of as "Patriot privateers" and "Patriot" ships, drawing an explicit connection between the Latin American revolutionaries and the Patriots of the American Revolution.

Since 1810, independence movements had developed across Spanish America, and the resulting revolutionary regimes posed a thorny problem for the United States government. The United States was engaged in negotiations to buy Spanish Florida and to establish a clear border between the Louisiana Purchase and Spanish Mexico. President James Monroe and his secretary of state, John Quincy Adams, needed good relations with Spain to facilitate these talks. Any official show of support for the Spanish American revolutionaries could ruin the negotiations. Yet, many in the United States imagined the Latin American revolutionaries to be philosophical allies, fellow republicans, deserving of support. Others saw these new countries as business opportunities if they were separated from Spanish rule and Spanish commercial regulations. In either case, there was substantial popular interest in supporting the rebels and in recognizing the independence of these Patriots. Not wishing to offend Spain, but pressured by public opinion in the United States, James Monroe's administration concluded that the official U.S. position had to be one of neutrality. This was governed by strict Neutrality Acts, the most recent of which had passed in 1818. Under the Neutrality Acts, ships such as the *Columbia* had to remain foreign vessels, with no connection whatsoever to American citizens as investors, owners, or crew.[2]

In Baltimore, however, dodgy ships such as the *Columbia* were an essential part of local commerce. Baltimore was a seaport town and had developed as a key shipping point for wheat and flour needed in Europe and the West Indies. It also became a center for the transshipment of cargo from Europe to the rest of the United States. Business was good, and so were profits, in part because Baltimore's merchants and captains were known to have few scruples and take risks. Baltimorean ships had plied the Spanish Main, even though such trade without official permission was illegal under Spanish law. Baltimore merchants traded surreptitiously with other parts of the Caribbean as well. Fast, narrow vessels with sharp bows built for speed were developed for this trade. "Baltimore clippers," regardless of where they were actually built, were identified with the city and her merchant trade. These fast vessels were particularly useful for smuggling or, under the right conditions, for commerce raiding.[3]

The United States had struggled throughout the first decade of the nineteenth century to avoid entanglement in the Napoleonic Wars. The Embargo Act of December 1807 was part of this effort, forbidding American maritime trade with the warring European powers or their colonies. At almost the same time, on January 1, 1808, An Act to Prohibit the Importation of Slaves went into effect, officially closing the slave trade to American sailors and ships. Responding to these new laws, Baltimore's captains and shipowners pitched in the way they knew best: subterfuge. Baltimorean ships continued to trade throughout the Atlantic, using false papers, flags of convenience, and in the final extremity the speed of their vessels to circumvent the Embargo Act. Shipowners from Baltimore joined those from Rhode Island and New York in making straw man sales to merchants in Spain, Cuba, and Brazil so that their ships could continue carrying slaves from Africa to the Americas, just under a different flag. In fact, the *Antelope* and other ships used by Cuesta Manzanal y Hermano in the slave trade may have been sold to Spanish owners as part of such straw man exchanges. These practices continued under the various Neutrality Acts that followed the expiration of the embargo.[4]

Even in 1812, when war broke out again between the United States and Great Britain, Baltimore merchants did their best to continue their Atlantic trade. They had dealt with war before. During the American Revolution, Baltimore's shipowners and merchants had simply continued their maritime trade. The risks were great, but so too were the profits. This trade brought some merchants fortunes, and others bankruptcy. Wise investors were cautious. William Patterson, a wealthy merchant newly arrived in Baltimore during the Revolution, invested only half his capital in shipping. He called it "a hazardous and desperate game of chance." Patterson invested the rest of his fortune in sensible real estate.[5]

Others in Baltimore played it differently. If great risk was required, why not truly cast the dice? While war increased investment risk, it also created investment opportunities not available in peace. In Baltimore, that opportunity was a privateering commission. Earlier in English law these commissions had been called letters of marque. A long struggle during the fifteenth, sixteenth, and seventeenth centuries had established privateering as legitimate among Europeans. By the eighteenth century, most European nations recognized the privateering commissions given by other nations during war. Privateers were privately owned vessels commissioned by their government to capture or destroy the state's enemies, whereas piracy was raiding at sea without such a commission. Pirates robbed vessels indiscriminately regardless of nationality and states of war. Captured pirates were criminals to be hanged; captured privateers were prisoners of war. This distinction, and the subsequent international war against piracy in the early eighteenth century, laid the foundations for the modern system of international law.[6]

Under a letter of marque, or commission, private vessels could attack and capture the vessels of a nation's enemy. Vessels and cargoes captured were brought into the commissioning nation's admiralty courts, where they could be condemned as "prizes." This meant that the captured ships and cargo legally belonged to the capturing vessel's owners. With title to the ship and cargo, the new owner could then sell the prize. Some of the proceeds from the sale of captured vessels and cargo went as fees to the court and lawyers, but the lion's share went to the investors and to the men aboard the privateer. These distributions of money were made in proportions laid out in the Articles of Agreement, a contract signed by all participants at the beginning of a voyage. Typically, the crew of a privateer sailed for no pay, instead anticipating shares of the prize money.[7]

When war was declared against Great Britain in June of 1812, Baltimore's shipowners, investors, and captains began to equip privateers. Within a month of the declaration of war, eight privateers had cleared out of Baltimore to attack British shipping. By December 1812, more than forty vessels had departed Baltimore as privateers. Of the eleven hundred or so privateering commissions issued by the federal government during the War of 1812, three-quarters were issued at the Baltimore Customs House. By that time in the early nineteenth century, sailors spoke of two types of private armed vessels. Letter of marque traders were armed merchant vessels engaged in normal trade that could, if given the right opportunity, snatch up a prize. Commissioned privateers were not engaged in trade, being wholly devoted to finding and capturing enemy prizes. Privateering ships were a considerable investment, requiring some $40,000 or more to purchase, equip, and crew. As in previous privateering campaigns, the results during the War of 1812 were mixed. Many shipowners and investors lost everything in this risky business, and many sailors lost their lives. Successful ships and captains, however, brought home fortunes and became the stuff of legend.[8]

With the end of the War of 1812, merchant shipowners and investors hoped for a return to the lucrative commerce they had enjoyed before the war. American shipping had dominated the oceans during the almost two decades of European war before 1812, benefiting from America's neutrality and the lower costs of ships built in North America. The British, French, and Spanish navies had swept the seas of their enemies' merchant ships, so that goods and food carried by neutral Americans were needed by all sides during the wars. War's end in

1815 meant French, Spanish, Dutch, and British merchant ships could for the first time in years safely sail the seas. European ships began to carry sugar from the Caribbean to Europe, take manufactured goods to the Americas, or trade for slaves in Africa. There was no longer a need for the neutrality of American ships to protect the cargoes. In April 1815, *Niles' Weekly Register* published on its front page a sober assessment of what this meant, under the title "Trade and Commerce: As They Were, and As They Will Be." Expectations should not be based on trade before 1812, explained the editor. Instead, expectations should be based on trade before 1793, when there was general European peace. Competition was greater then, and the prices of commodities had been much lower. As a result, before the French Revolution and Napoleonic Wars, maritime trade had been less lucrative. If peace continued, argued the author, "we shall lose the markets for our food almost wholly, or consent to sell to Europeans cheaper than they can supply themselves."[9]

At the same time that there was more competition, the value of cargoes declined along with the profits. During 1816, the price of sugar fell in Baltimore from $26 per hundredweight to $12.50. Probably due to the cold weather and the disastrous harvests of 1816, Baltimore flour prices stayed high until 1818. After that, flour prices collapsed, from above $10 a barrel to less than $5 in 1820. Increased competition and declining commodity prices meant that efficiency in carriage was more important than ever before. The long and narrow Baltimore clippers, so useful when a fast ship was needed, were not efficient carriers of bulk cargo. Shippers did better with traditional fat, slow merchantmen with their cavernous holds. Many firms in Baltimore couldn't sell clipper ships for anything close to their value. In this environment, the heady returns from shipping during a world war and the profits from privateering must have seemed a distant dream.[10]

That dream, however, was not out of reach. As wars of independence raged throughout Spanish America, revolutionary governments sought every means possible to strike at Spain. Privateers were one such means. In 1815, the United Provinces of La Plata, a predecessor to modern Argentina, began issuing privateering commissions. In 1816, the Banda Oriental, a rival of the United Provinces and a predecessor to modern Uruguay, established a capital at Montevideo on the eastern shore of the Río de la Plata and began issuing commissions. The same year, Venezuelan revolutionary forces opened a secure port on the Isla de Margarita in the Caribbean, where they, too, issued privateer commissions. All three revolutionary nations created prize courts for the condemnation and sale of captured ships and cargo, and made privateering commissions available. In some cases they provided commissions in blank to agents in the United States, the names of the commander and ship to be filled in when the commission was purchased and bonded. Privateers with commissions from Venezuela or the United Provinces could prey on Spanish shipping. The beleaguered Banda Oriental, commonly called the Oriental Republic, was under attack from Spain, Portugal, Portuguese Brazil, and ultimately even the revolutionaries of the United Provinces of La Plata. Ironically, privateers with commissions from the leader of the Banda Oriental, José Artigas, benefited from this. With a commission from the Oriental Republic they could prey on ships from a smorgasbord of nations.[11]

The *Columbia*'s master, Simon Metcalf, went to Baltimore in the fall of 1819 seeking financial support and crew for a new privateering voyage. Metcalf was an experienced and successful privateer who had developed a specialty: capturing slave ships. Already his pursuit of slavers had produced remarkable, if unintended, consequences. In 1817, commanding the privateer *Successor,* Metcalf captured the Spanish slave ship *Isabelita* near Cuba and took her into Amelia Island, Florida. There a short-lived revolutionary junta, the Republic of the Floridas, had established a prize court at Fernandina on Amelia Island. Metcalf sold the *Isabelita* and her cargo of slaves, and the buyer smuggled the slaves through the Creek Nation into Georgia. At the U.S. Indian Mission on the Flint River some of the smuggled slaves were discovered. Authorities from Georgia confiscated the slaves, and sold some for more than $36,000. A cascade of consequences followed, including two Supreme Court cases, political ruin for former Georgia governor David Mitchell, and popular support for American military occupation of Amelia Island. The case also influenced new federal legislation concerning the illegal slave trade. Metcalf's raiding and capture of slaves had created problems for a host of people, but he was already involved in new schemes.[12]

In 1818, Simon Metcalf commanded the privateer *Constantia* with a commission from the Banda Oriental at Montevideo. He was wildly successful, capturing one ship with 640 slaves aboard, another with 240 slaves, and a brig with 250 slaves. Even allowing for some exaggeration by correspondents, a thousand slaves at a low price of $300 per slave meant Metcalf had captured $300,000 worth of slaves. This was an incredible fortune, but then his ship and his prizes were captured by Venezuelan vessels and taken into Isla de Margarita. There is no evidence of whether some sort of comity, that is, the recognition of other jurisdictions' laws, existed in the Venezuelan prize court. Did they recognize commissions from the Banda Oriental? Could Metcalf sell his prizes there, or were he and his ships prizes to a Venezuelan privateer? All that's known is that in the fall of 1819, Metcalf returned to the United States commanding a 250-ton armed brig with a Venezuelan privateering commission. Apparently, something went right in Venezuela.[13]

Metcalf needed financial backers, but the fall of 1819 was a tough time to find them. Following the Panic of 1819, the United States had fallen into its first nationwide economic depression. Money was tight, and more than one hundred mercantile and trading firms went bankrupt in Baltimore that summer and fall. Among the bankrupt was the city's leading mercantile and shipping firm of Smith and Buchanan. Samuel Smith, who had invested in privateers in the past, wrote of his finances in October 1819, "[N]ever was a ruin more complete. I have not a dollar left." The unpaid debts of his firm totaled more than $280,000. Other merchants saw the value of their ships and real estate fall so low that they could not get credit to continue their operations. As if things weren't bad enough, in September of 1819, *Niles' Weekly Register* announced that there was yellow fever in the city. The journal made weekly reports on the epidemic, assuring readers that the contagion was confined to the Fell's Point area. It did not help: Thousands fled Baltimore. The disease ran its course by the end of October, but it had only added to Baltimore's economic woes.[14]

There were firms, however, that did not fail during these hard times. Isaac McKim, Joseph Patterson, George Brown, and others continued to prosper. All was not lost if you knew the right people, and apparently Metcalf did. By December of 1819, he was ready for a new voyage.

Metcalf tried to follow the form of American neutrality laws while in port. He did not "augment his force" while there, meaning he did not add cannons, weapons, or ammunition to the ship. He didn't need to; the *Columbia* already had a long twenty-four-pound cannon mounted on a pivot amidships. A massive gun, usually found only on the largest warships, the pivot allowed it to fire across either side of the vessel. There were also six smaller cannon stored in the hold along with plenty of small arms. Metcalf began to recruit crew, and insisted that all men who wanted to sign on first swear before a justice of the peace that they were not American citizens. John Morrison, who swore that he was Welsh and a British subject, remembered that after swearing, he went with about forty men to a house in Baltimore, presumably that of an investor. There, he explained, all the men "shipped"—that is, they signed the articles of agreement, on December 6, 1819. The crew and officers understood that they were joining a cruise in an armed vessel under the flag of Venezuelan admiral Luis Brión. There would be no pay; they shipped for shares of future prize money alone. After signing the articles, each man was given an advance against his share. Morrison was given $15. He did not go aboard the *Columbia* until December 9, giving him plenty of time and money to enjoy his last days in port.[15]

John Smith joined the *Columbia* as first mate. Born in New York,

Smith was twenty-nine years old and had been at sea since at least 1811. He was an experienced privateer, having served aboard an American privateer during the War of 1812. He was captured and imprisoned by the British but somehow escaped to France in 1814. Smith returned to the United States, but he was truly a man of the Atlantic world: a sailor who lived most of his life at sea. He sailed throughout the Americas, and on two occasions served as captain of sailing vessels. In 1818, he commanded the *Athenian*, which took part in an extraordinarily successful privateering venture from Baltimore. Apparently at loose ends in Baltimore, the *Columbia* commanded by the successful Metcalf must have seemed a good opportunity for John Smith. Smith surely did not imagine the dangers that awaited him.[16]

On December 19, 1819, the *Columbia* sailed. Raymond Arrivas, a "passenger" aboard the ship, assumed the name of Blake and cleared the vessel out of Baltimore. There was no reason to attract attention by having the well-known privateer Captain Metcalf take her out. There were already influential voices in the city speaking against the privateers. "It is a disgrace," wrote Baltimore-based Hezekiah Niles in his *Weekly Register*, "[that] American citizens . . . prostitute themselves in nefarious acts of robbery and plunder under the mask of assisting the Spanish patriots of South America." Meanwhile, Secretary of State John Quincy Adams pressured James McCulloch, the collector for the Port of Baltimore, to do more to control the privateers. If "Blake" clearing the vessel out of port was an effort to escape notice by the authorities, it failed. A revenue cutter intercepted the *Columbia* as soon as she entered the Chesapeake Bay. Officials boarded the privateer and examined the ship's commission and the papers of the crew. Under the neutrality laws, American citizens could not serve aboard the privateers of foreign governments. The *Columbia*'s commission must have seemed authentic, and most of the crew must have been convincingly foreign. Only four of *Columbia*'s crew of thirty-eight were taken off the ship. The revenue cutter then escorted the *Columbia* to sea, ensuring she did not rendezvous with another vessel or anchor in some small cove to take on additional crew or equipment. About Christmas Eve she passed Cape Henry and entered the Atlantic Ocean.[17]

The Atlantic world into which the *Columbia* sailed was a wild and lawless place. Since 1793, the Atlantic had seen general European war, colonial conflict, and revolution. This was, of course, not new. Since the late sixteenth century, ships in the Atlantic had faced not just the dangers of the sea but a nightmare of unknown warships, privateers, and pirates. With no radio, no telegraphs, no reliable system of communication, mariners lacked essential information at every turn. News traveled slowly, and each encounter with another vessel raised the same concerns: Had war erupted? Might that be a pirate ship? Why is that vessel approaching so quickly? Mariners faced a Hobbesian world of "all against all," in which no sail on the horizon or flag on the mizzen gaff could be trusted. The result, surprisingly, was the creation of much of modern finance capitalism. New forms of business organization, innovative funding schemes, and increasingly efficient underwriting of insurance allowed European merchants to mitigate the risks posed by Atlantic voyages. Such a heavily hedged system, however, needed enormous profits to function. The "plantation complex," using the inexpensive labor of slaves, produced most of those profits. Simon Metcalf, the commander of the *Columbia,* intended to steal some of those profits that had been invested in the purchase of slaves.[18]

A few days after Christmas, the *Columbia* boarded the schooner *Hope*, out of Liverpool, bound for Baltimore. The *Columbia*'s crew later claimed to have stolen nothing. They then chased a brig but failed to capture her, and boarded another schooner but again claimed that they took nothing. At São Vicente in the Cape Verde Islands they took on water and supplies and then sailed to nearby São Tiago, where they exchanged cannon fire with the Portuguese fort. Thomas Nicholson, a member of the ship's crew, explained later that he "knew not the object except amusement." Metcalf's idea of amusement was apparently not shared by all, and there were some murmurings among the crew. One crew member, Thomas Morrison, testified later that he had signed up for a voyage to the Caribbean and Venezuela, not Africa. Thomas Bradshaw, another crewman, said much the same. It is possible that both men supported Venezuelan independence, expected to fight against Spain, and were not happy with the ship's attack on Portuguese islands. It is also possible that they lied, worried about criminal charges for engaging in the slave trade. Whatever the attitude of the crew, Captain Metcalf's voyage grew increasingly violent.[19]

Leaving the Cape Verde Islands, the *Columbia* "bore away for the coast of Africa." Along the way she boarded an American ship from Nantucket and took two barrels of beer. She boarded a French schooner and forced the crew aboard the *Columbia*, where they were imprisoned belowdecks for sixteen hours. They stole stores from the schooner: rope, pitch, tar, sails, as well as a deck awning and a new four-inch hawser. The next day they returned the French crew to their ship and released them. Following this, the *Columbia* set a course for one of the most notorious centers of the slave trade, the Gallinas River on the coast of west Africa. There they could expect to find large numbers of prey.[20]

On January 21, 1820, Captain Metcalf announced a significant change to their voyage. The ship no longer sailed under a Venezuelan commission. It now sailed under a new commission from the Banda Oriental, signed by José Artigas, who held the title Protector of the Eastern Shore. Under this commission they were at war with both Spain and Portugal, the world's leading slave traders in 1819. Ships from both nations were now their prey and should be found in abundance along the African coast. Metcalf also announced that as a result of the new commission the ship had a new name. The *Columbia* had become the *Arraganta*.[21]

The Gallinas River is near the border between present-day Liberia and Sierra Leone. Close by are two smaller rivers, the Salinas and the Manna, all of which create a chain of difficult entrances, small islands, and mangrove swamps along a stretch of coast long noted for slaving. Ships had to anchor offshore and use boats to reach the islands and the lagoons behind them. Crossing the bar in front of these rivers was very dangerous due to shifting sandbars, river currents, and high surf. Six miles to the southeast of the Gallinas lay the mouth of the Manna River. There, on the morning of January 30, 1820, the *Arraganta* found six slave ships anchored offshore under both American and Spanish flags. She immediately launched an attack. First, the *Arraganta*'s crew boarded a schooner that turned out to be an American slaver, the *Endymion*. They took nothing from her. Then the *Arraganta* fired on a Spanish schooner, wounding two men, one of whom later died. This was the *Anna Maria* out of Matanzas, Cuba, a schooner of 140 tons loaded with trade goods but no slaves. Captain Metcalf put First Mate John Smith aboard as prize master. By that time the wind had begun to die, so the ships' maneuvers became a slow-motion dance taking several hours. Despite the light winds, the *Arraganta* managed to come alongside a third schooner, fired a volley of muskets into her, and boarded. This was the *Del Carmen*, also out of Cuba, preparing to take aboard 200 slaves who waited at Manna Point. The *Del Carmen* was formerly an American vessel, sailing under Spanish colors, but commanded by a man named Wyatt from Rhode Island. The crew was American, one of whom was severely wounded. Second Mate George Ford from the *Arraganta* went aboard the *Del Carmen* as prize master.[22]

Meanwhile, the *Anna Maria* under Prize Master Smith maneuvered toward a brig its crew had seen earlier that day. In the tortuous process of maneuvering in light airs, the captured schooner with its fore and aft rig may have had an advantage over the square-rigged brig. The pursuit was an agonizingly slow process, the crew watching the water for telltale cat's-paws from a puff of wind, trimming the sails to catch as much of the puff as possible, and carefully nudging the rudder so as not to slow the ship. The afternoon passed, and the slow and deadly dance continued. Eventually, the *Anna Maria* closed to within cannon range, and Smith engaged the brig. He fired several shots but was unable to force the brig to surrender; nor could he approach close enough to board. Darkness came on, and the wind died completely. Smith's cannonade, however, had attracted unwanted attention. At about 11:00 p.m., boats loaded with British marines and armed sailors came alongside the *Arraganta* and boarded in a "spirited manner." The *Arraganta* and the two prizes were captured, the officers and crew arrested. All were imprisoned on the slave deck of the *Del Carmen*, accused of piracy.[23]

CHAPTER 3

"No principle of general law is more universally acknowledged than the perfect equality of nations. Russia and Geneva have equal rights. It results from this equality that no one can rightfully impose a rule on another."

Chief Justice John Marshall *The Antelope*, 23 U.S. 66, 122 (1825)

When the *Arraganta* was captured by the British on January 30, 1820, the *Antelope* was on the coast of west central Africa more than 1,700 nautical miles away. Buying more than three hundred slaves was a slow process, and the *Antelope* may have visited several slaving depots in the months since she had left Cuba. Despite the distance between them, a bit more than seven weeks later the *Antelope* and *Arraganta* would meet—violently. This would never have happened had Great Britain not outlawed the African slave trade in 1807, or had the Royal Navy not taken up the task of destroying that trade.

Henry John Leeke played a crucial role in those efforts. In 1835 he would be knighted for his service, a highlight of a sixty-year career in which he rose to full admiral. Leeke first went to sea in 1806, at the age of twelve. By his twentieth year he had attained the rank of commander, a reward for both bravery in battle and for being well connected through an influential godfather. Sadly for Leeke, his promotion came in the summer of 1814, just as the wars against Napoleon wound down. Within a year, Commander Leeke returned to England without a ship and on half-pay. Since he had not been made a post-captain, a high rank in the Royal Navy that essentially created a lifelong sinecure, there was no chance for continued advancement without a ship. Leeke's naval future appeared grim.[1]

Leeke evidently found some consolation ashore; in November 1818 he married Augusta Sophia Dashwood. Soon after, Augusta Sophia was pregnant. Marriage, however, may have been difficult for a man who had lived most of his adult life afloat in the Royal Navy's structured male world. Within months Leeke sought a return to the sea. Again, being well connected paid off. Unlike most of his fellow officers left on the beach after the war, he received orders for a ship in July of 1819. He was to take command of the ship-sloop *Myrmidon*, embark the "Algerine Envoy and suite," and return them to North Africa. After conveying this diplomat and his entourage to Algiers, Leeke would sail to Sierra Leone on the west coast of Africa and there "prevent the illicit traffic in slaves." Leeke was also to gather intelligence concerning the slave trade for the lords of the Admiralty, so that they could seek the "more complete destruction of the Slave Trade north of the Line."[2]

This was dangerous duty. Not only did slave ships often fight back, but west Africa itself was deadly for Europeans. Endemic diseases such as malaria and yellow fever could sweep though entire crews, killing half or more. The west African coast was poorly charted, with few safe harbors and many hostile inhabitants. The currents along the coast were unfavorable, all in an area plagued by unpredictable winds. Conditions aboard the poorly ventilated, crowded, dark-painted warships baking under the tropical sun beggar the imagination. Introduce a few men with dysentery from bad water, and conditions aboard descended to hellish. Despite these dangers and his wife's pregnancy, Leeke put to sea with alacrity.

The *Myrmidon* had been constructed in 1813 during the war with Napoleon, her hull based on the lines of a fast French ship captured by the British. She was 120 feet on deck, had a crew of 135 men, and carried 20 guns. The *Myrmidon* was a fine sailer, and she swiftly delivered the "Algerine Envoy and suite" to North Africa. After all proper ceremony for the envoy, Leeke returned to the Atlantic and sailed for Freetown, Sierra Leone, where he reported to the governor in early December 1819. There was no rest for the weary. Informed at Freetown that slavers were active off the Gallinas River, Captain Leeke sailed immediately to intercept them. Keeping the *Myrmidon* out of sight offshore, he sent his first lieutenant and two boatloads of armed men toward the anchorage where they had spotted several ships. On the evening of December 11, 1819, the boats were able to get alongside the largest ship there and capture her. It was the Spanish schooner *Bella Dora*: 150 tons, bound for Havana with 122 slaves aboard. The other slave ships in the anchorage fled. Each of the five ships fired several wild parting cannon shots at the British captors aboard the *Bella Dora* before slipping away into the darkness. Though only one British sailor was wounded, this was clearly not easy duty.[3]

This difficult duty was also complicated. Along with the orders sending him to the west African coast, Leeke had received copies of treaties with Spain, Portugal, and the Netherlands, as well as detailed procedures to follow when searching Spanish, Portuguese, or Dutch ships. "You are to be careful," warned his orders, "in the whole of your conduct towards such vessels, to be governed by the said Treaties and the Instructions attached to them." In case Leeke had further questions, the packet included copies of all the relevant Acts of Parliament concerning the slave trade. Royal Navy captains on the west coast of Africa faced not just malaria, yellow fever, and the occasional slaver's broadside, they also faced lawyers. The owners of captured ships often contested their condemnation, and in many cases they appealed to the High Court of Admiralty in London. The British decisions resulting from these admiralty cases influenced not just the actions of British officers on the coast of west Africa but the case of the *Antelope*.[4]

The Royal Navy's campaign against the seaborne slave trade began as an outgrowth of the Napoleonic Wars. Since the 1780s, John Clarkson, William Wilberforce, and many others had fought for abolition through law—of the slave trade and, ultimately, slavery. Then, in 1794, the French Republic abolished the slave trade and slavery. Suddenly, slave trade abolition, which had been so close to success, was deemed a dangerous republican and revolutionary idea in Britain. Only in May of 1802, when Napoleon restored slavery and the French slave trade, did the abolitionists devise a new legislative strategy. Goods produced in French colonies supported the French war effort, the abolitionists argued, and the slave trade provided the labor for French colonial production. Cut off the enemy's slave trade, and you would strike a significant blow against the French war economy. In April of 1806, the Foreign Slave Trade Act passed Parliament, prohibiting British subjects' participation in the slave trade to any foreign colonies or colonies captured from Britain's enemies. The abolitionists had their first major legislative success.[5]

By 1807, the slave trade was under attack on both sides of the Atlantic. This resulted in two remarkable laws. In late February 1807, the United States Congress passed An Act to Prohibit the Importation of Slaves. In March 1807, Parliament in Great Britain passed An Act for the Abolition of the Slave Trade. These laws were all the more remarkable because they came with very real economic costs for Great Britain and the United States. Shipping concerns, insurance companies, financiers, and planters in both countries had profited mightily from the slave trade. The slave trade and goods produced and consumed by slaves had played a central role in the expansion of capitalism. By January 1, 1808, however, that slave trade had become illegal for citizens of the United States and Great Britain.[6]

Consumed by the domestic demands of the Embargo and Neutrality Acts, and fearful of the growing conflict with both France and Great Britain over neutral maritime trade, the United States Navy did little at first to enforce the new American slave trade prohibition. The Royal Navy, however, took immediate action. The Admiralty offered a substantial bounty for each slave liberated from illegal traders and instructed its officers to capture ships carrying slaves as if they carried contraband of war. The first ship to do so was the *Derwent*, in January of 1808. She captured two schooners loaded with 167 slaves off the coast near Cape Verde and took them into Sierra Leone. There, Governor Thomas Ludlam had no place to keep the liberated slaves, no vice admiralty court to rule on the prizes, and no money to pay the rescue bounty. So, he improvised. The governor appointed the colony's storekeeper, Alexander Smith, judge of the vice admiralty court in Freetown. Judge Smith, though he had no legal background, then ruled that the prizes were good and that the captives should be turned over to the governor. Forty of the healthiest men were enlisted in the local armed forces, while the remaining eighteen men, fourteen women, and ninety-five children were sold into "apprenticeships" to labor for farmers and merchants in the new colony. The apprenticeship sale raised sufficient money to pay the officers and men of the *Derwent* their bounties and to pay the costs of the court. The governor, no doubt, thought this an elegant solution to a difficult problem.[7]

This elegant solution looked like theft to the American owners of the schooners, and they complained loudly but to no avail. These slave ships were just the first of many condemned by British vice admiralty courts. The government in Great Britain saw this assault upon the international slave trade as a necessary part of economic war against Napoleon's France. Destroying the slave trade would reduce the market for French goods overseas, would starve the French colonies of labor, and would limit the production of colonial products benefiting France. Neutral ships carried most of the slaves and colonial products, so they were inevitably the victims of this economic warfare. The warships of the Royal Navy acted like privateers, snapping up slave ships for profit and the generous bounty of sixty pounds per man, thirty pounds per woman, and ten pounds per child liberated.[8]

This assault on the maritime rights of neutral nations led to conflict between the United States and Great Britain. Even before war began in 1812 to protect what war hawks dubbed "Free Trade and Sailor's Rights," American shippers pushed back. In court, they fought the condemnation and confiscation of their ships. They were joined by others, and numerous appeals from vice admiralty courts made their way up to the Lords Commissioners of the Admiralty in London. A large number of the cases involved ships engaged in the slave trade, so the High Court chose to look first at the case of the *Amedie*. The *Amedie* was a slaver out of Charleston, South Carolina, which had loaded 105 slaves off Bonny, today the coast of Nigeria, in late 1807. Unsure of making it to Charleston before the American slave trade prohibition went into effect on January 1, 1808, the *Amedie* turned toward Cuba. She was captured by British blockaders and taken into Tortola, where the vice admiralty court condemned the ship and her cargo.[9]

The owner of the *Amedie* was Samuel Grove of Charleston, an associate of the famous slave-trading United States senator James D'Wolf. Grove appealed the condemnation, and on July 28, 1810, Master of the Rolls Sir William Grant, sitting as judge of the High Court of Chancery, gave his judgment. It was both startling and revolutionary. Grant ruled that the slave trade was "contrary to the principles of justice and humanity," and "that *prima facie* the trade is altogether illegal." He argued further that the slave trade was contrary to both natural law and the "law of nations," by which he meant the developing system of international law in the early nineteenth century. Because of this, "no claimant can be heard in an application . . . for the restoration of the human beings he carried to another country . . . as slaves." It did not matter that the *Amedie* sailed under a neutral flag; nor did it matter that the voyage had been legal when it departed the United States. The slave trade violated the law of nations. Thus, slavers could be captured and their ships condemned anywhere they were found.[10]

With this decision, Sir William Grant legitimated all the captures that had taken place since 1808, under both British law and the law of nations. Similar appeals by other slave ships that had been captured, the *Africa* and the *Nancy*, both American, were then easily and quickly decided based on the *Amedie*. In the case of the *Anne*, in November of 1810, Sir William Grant summarized his ruling in the *Amedie* a bit differently. "By the judgment in the case of the *Amedie*," he wrote, "the slave trade can have no legitimate existence, except under the particular municipal law of that country to which the claimant belongs." The *Anne* was an American ship, and American municipal law forbade the slave trade, so Grant's formulation worked in that case. The "except," however, would have great importance in the future.[11]

After the *Amedie* decision, the bounty hunt grew more intense. Neutral maritime rights were often completely ignored. The Royal Navy boarded every neutral vessel they could, searching for something amiss in the ship's papers, in the cargo, or among the crew. Ships involved in the slave trade were immediately sent to the nearest vice admiralty court for condemnation. Neutral crew members thought to have been born in England were often "pressed" into the Royal Navy. Slight infractions of the Orders of Council, the executive regulations that grew ever more restrictive from 1807 through 1812, led to innocent neutral ships being detained, confiscated, and sold. This high-handed conduct would in part lead to war with the United States, but it also drove many neutral slaving ships from the seas. The safest course for slavers was a change of flag to that of Spain or Portugal, which were British allies. In other cases slave ships were sold to Spanish and Portuguese purchasers, though there were questions about the sources of capital and ships for these voyages. Then, in 1815, the Napoleonic and American wars ended, and the world changed again.[12]

With the end of war in 1815, ships of all nations put to sea, eager to begin peacetime trade. For the first time in decades even French merchantmen sailed the Atlantic unmolested by British warships. Unmolested, that was, except for ships found on the coast of west Africa. There a squadron of Royal Navy warships, supported by colonial axillaries, continued to fight the slave trade. British warships stopped and searched any suspicious vessel they could catch and continued to bring prizes into the vice admiralty court in Freetown, Sierra Leone. In many cases the British vessels were still bounty-hunting, seeking the prize value of the condemned ships and the generous admiralty bounty given for each rescued African. There were also those in Sierra Leone interested in the "recaptured" Africans themselves, who were often sold into profitable "apprenticeships."

Le Louis, a French slave ship, sailed from Martinique on January 30, 1816, to trade for slaves in Africa. On March 16 she was spotted by the colonial schooner *Queen Charlotte* off Cape Mesurado. *Le Louis* ran, and Commander Robert Hagan of the *Queen Charlotte* pursued. He had unambiguous orders to "seize and prosecute" all slaving vessels, so Hagan opened fire, and a heated battle followed. By the time a British boarding party captured the *Louis*, eight British seamen and nine French sailors were dead. The captured ship had no slaves aboard but was clearly equipped for the slave trade. Bulwarks had been erected to segregate decks, platforms built and fitted with shackles. The ship carried large amounts of food and water, and two prisoners informed their captors that a cargo of slaves awaited at Cape Mesurado. The *Queen Charlotte* took *Le Louis* into Freetown and filed a claim for condemnation for slave trading. The vice admiralty court agreed, condemned the ship, and sold her.[13]

The captain of the *Louis* appealed to the High Court of Admiralty. A number of similar cases were pending before the court. In the five years since the *Amedie* decision, from 1811 through 1816, at least 142 slave trade cases had gone before vice admiralty courts, and many had been appealed. The High Court's decision in *Le Louis* knocked the British anti-slave trade effort back on its heels. First, the judge of the High Court, Sir William Scott, ruled that the Royal Navy had no peacetime "right of search." Only if there was a legitimate suspicion of piracy could British warships stop and search the ships of other nations. Without evidence of piracy, ships could only be stopped and searched if there was a treaty explicitly granting that right. The slave trade, while "reprehensible," wrote Scott, was not piracy. Thus the *Louis* was searched illegally. Second, even if slave trading was a crime under French law, the British navy could not enforce the laws of France. Third, and most importantly, Scott explained that slavery had a long human history, as did the slave trade. Given such a long acceptance of the slave trade by the nations of the Earth, the trade could not be contrary to the law of nations. Scott didn't even respond to assertions by the Crown such as had been made in the case of the *Amedie*, suggesting that the slave trade violated the laws of nature. He even chided the Crown's advocate, lecturing him that "to procure an eminent good by means that are unlawful is as little consonant to private morality as to public justice." Under the *Amedie* decision of seven years before, the *Queen Charlotte*'s conduct had been correct. *Le Louis* swept that case away. The bounty hunt was over.[14]

So, Royal Navy ships needed a treaty granting the right to search, and not just any treaty. In the Treaty of Ghent that ended the War of 1812 between the United States and Great Britain, both nations agreed that "the traffic in slaves is irreconcilable with the principles of humanity and justice." The treaty, however, did not grant either nation the right of search, so the condemnation of the slave trade was essentially hollow. At the Congress of Vienna in 1815, the victors in the Napoleonic Wars declared their desire to end the slave trade, "a scourge, which has so long desolated Africa, degraded Europe, and afflicted humanity. . . ." Despite such high-minded statements, the Great Powers provided no mechanism to carry out this wish, and gave no one the right to stop and search the ships of other nations. Great Britain had little chance of convincing the other nations of Europe to relinquish sovereignty over their ships at sea by allowing the British Navy the right of search. The struggle at Vienna was to balance the power of Great Britain, not to increase it.[15]

There was, however, the possibility of negotiating bilateral treaties with specific countries to provide for the right of search. In 1814, Holland had prohibited the slave trade, but the remnants of the Dutch navy were hardly able to patrol the coasts of Africa. Dutch merchant ships, in violation of Dutch law, continued to carry slaves across the

Atlantic. Thus, the Anglo–Dutch Treaty of May 4, 1817, was the first agreement that promised real action against the slave trade. Under the treaty, both Holland and Great Britain agreed on a mutual right of search. Ships found in violation of the ban on the slave trade by either nation's warships would be brought before a new type of international court, the courts of mixed commission. These courts would be created in Sierra Leone and Suriname, with a judge representing each country. The courts of mixed commission would make the final rulings on the captures and condemnation of slave ships. There was no appeal from the judgment of these courts.[16]

Great Britain made similar bilateral treaties with Portugal and Spain in 1817. Conquered by the French in 1808, Spain and Portugal had become dependent clients of Great Britain, and neither could refuse to sign these treaties. To sweeten the deal, the British gave 300,000 pounds to the Portuguese and 400,000 pounds to Spain. Neither treaty had the sweep of the Dutch treaty. Portugal agreed only to a prohibition of the slave trade north of the equator. Spain agreed to prohibit the slave trade beginning May 30, 1820, with a five-month grace period for any ships at sea. The voyage of the *Antelope* from Havana in August of 1819 was legal under this treaty as long as the ship returned to Havana by the end of October 1820.

Like the Dutch treaty, these treaties created courts of mixed commission for enforcement. In many ways these were the world's first international human rights tribunals, and they rescued tens of thousands of human beings from slavery. Most of the rescued captives were settled in British Sierra Leone, though some ended up in exploitative "apprenticeship" contracts. Courts of mixed commission also created substantial headaches for British naval officers. Spain, Portugal, and Holland had continual problems finding judges willing to serve, delaying judgments months or even years. Even when present, judges were often obstructionist. In cases that went against the captors, the naval officers involved could be assessed financial damages. Nonetheless, haltingly, and with difficulty, these courts of mixed commission began operating in 1819. They opened a new phase in the struggle to suppress the African slave trade.[17]

Like all Royal Navy officers on the coast of Africa, Captain Henry J. Leeke of the *Myrmidon* was required to know the contents and the vagaries of all these treaties. He had to understand and communicate to his officers and crew the strict procedures to be followed in dealing with ships of different nationalities. Leeke was also expected to know and understand the appeals cases involving ships captured in the slave trade. If, despite all his precautions, the courts of mixed commission found his actions in error, like all Royal Navy captains serving on the coast of Africa, Leeke had to be prepared to defend himself against the lawsuits that would follow. These sorts of legal concerns controlled Leeke's next encounter with slavers. After successfully capturing the *Bella Dora*, the *Myrmidon* continued to the southeast, and at first light off Cape Mount "a fleet of schooners hove in sight." Leeke took up the chase, the *Mrymidon*'s speed surprising the schooners' captains. By eleven o'clock the *Myrmidon* forced three schooners to surrender and drop their sails. Two of the schooners had no slaves aboard and had to be released. The third schooner had 140 slaves aboard. Although one paper aboard the ship suggested that she was under contract to Spaniards, she sailed under a French flag with French registry and papers. Just a few years earlier, Leeke and his crew would have celebrated the capture of a Frenchman. Now he had to let her go.[18]

The commander of the African squadron, Admiral Sir George R. Collier, wrote several reports to the Admiralty explaining the problems Leeke and his other captains faced. One of the core obstacles limiting his efforts, Collier grumbled in early 1820, was that "the flags of France and America are now . . . the best cover to illicit Slaving." The Admiralty was well aware of the problem. The British government had lodged several complaints in Washington about the American flag sheltering slavers, and continued to ask for a treaty granting the mutual right of search. The Monroe administration had rebuffed their efforts. The War of 1812 had been fought in part over the right of American ships to sail without interference. A treaty granting Britain the right to stop and search American vessels was politically impossible. The newly reestablished French monarchy also needed to show their independence from Great Britain and refused a similar treaty. The Admiralty had no answer for Collier's complaint.[19]

On January 30, 1820, the *Myrmidon* and the *Morgiana*, along with two slave ships they had captured, sat becalmed on the sea five or six miles south of Cape Mount. In the quiet of dusk they heard cannon firing in the distance. Captain Leeke turned his telescope toward the shore and saw at least three ships off the mouth of the Manna River. More faint cannon fire echoed across the placid water. Leeke decided to send his boats and those of the Morgiana to investigate. Dozens of armed men loaded into the boats and rowed away into the darkness. Leeke waited anxiously, literally blinded by darkness. Two and a half hours later he heard musketry, and he ordered his ships to try to work their way closer to the shore. He soon discovered that his little expedition had captured an "Artigan" privateer called the *Arraganta*, under the command of Simon Metcalf. The boats also captured the slave schooners *Anna Maria* and *Del Carmen*, the *Arraganta*'s prizes from earlier in the day.[20]

Leeke faced a dilemma. Both of the schooners were fitted out as slavers, and prisoners claimed there were slaves waiting ashore. Nevertheless, they flew the Spanish flag and under normal circumstances Leeke could not legally touch them. But this circumstance was not normal, nor was the *Arraganta* a normal capture. Leeke suspected he had captured a pirate. He described the ship as a "patriot privateer Brigantine of 240 tons, one long twenty-four pounder on a sweep a-midships and a complement of forty men." Throughout the night he questioned the prisoners and discovered that the *Arraganta* had fitted out in Baltimore and had not been to any port in South America. In the early morning hours Leeke wrote:

An American complained to me, that the pirate, with Spanish colors hoisted, went alongside an American schooner, and without hailing fired a volley of small arms into her, and I am sorry to add severely wounded one of her crew. I very much fear the above is not the only act of piracy they have been guilty of.

Leeke continued, "I should ill be doing my duty were I not to detain her as a pirate." He moved the crew of the *Arraganta* aboard the schooner *Del Carmen*, where the slave deck provided a convenient, though ironic, place to imprison them. Prize crews took over the three ships, and with the *Myrmidon* and her two previous captures they set sail for Freetown in Sierra Leone. The little fleet arrived eight days later, causing quite a stir.[21]

There were numerous problems posed by Leeke's captures. Because of the *Le Louis* case, the French slaver he captured was sent north to French authorities. Because there was no Portuguese judge in Freetown, a Portuguese slaver he had captured was released. Finally, the *Arraganta* and her two prizes could be condemned if she was truly a pirate, but proving piracy was difficult. Captain Leeke was convinced that the *Arraganta* was a pirate, but others were not so sure. The ship had two privateering commissions, one from Venezuela and the other from José Artigas and the Banda Oriental. If either commission was legitimate, then the *Arraganta* could legally prey upon Spanish shipping. Even though one of the captured schooners appeared to be American with false Spanish papers, it was far too difficult to pierce the veil of fictions as far as registration and nationality was concerned. The ships could be held while inquiries were made in Baltimore, Havana, and Cádiz as to the legitimacy of their papers. These inquiries could take months, perhaps years, and if the papers were legitimate then the British navy at Freetown could be exposed to expensive lawsuits. As Sir George Collier wrote, the entire case "involved so much doubt and uncertainty as to the proof of piracy, and threaten so much difficulty" that he decided not to prosecute. He ordrered the *Arraganta* and the captured Spanish schooners released.[22]

The British gave Simon Metcalf orders "not to cruise south of the line" and freed his ship. South of the line, or the equator, was where Portuguese and Spanish slavers worked the coast of west central Africa without interference from the British. Leaving Sierra Leone, the *Arraganta* inevitably turned south and crossed the equator. Had the "privateer" successfully captured several slavers off the coast of west Africa, the ship would probably have sailed directly to the Americas. There would have been no *Antelope* case. Instead, the *Arraganta* lost the ships she had captured, thanks to the actions of Captain Henry Leeke. As a result, the *Arraganta* began a busy voyage south. First, the privateer captured a Spanish brig, and took from her between three and seven thousand dollars cash, sails, and provisions. Five men aboard the Spanish brig volunteered to join the *Arraganta*. Next they encountered two ships, a large brig with perhaps 18 guns and sailing with it an American schooner. The brig flew Spanish colors, and she and the privateer engaged in an exchange of cannon fire at long distance with no meaningful result. The next morning the *Arraganta* boarded the smaller American schooner. She was the *Exchange*, out of Bristol, Rhode Island, flying an American flag and commanded by Captain Richmond. The raiders took from the schooner twenty-five slaves and then released her. This act was significant, for by stealing slaves from an American vessel the *Arraganta* clearly committed piracy. Now unquestionably a pirate, the *Arraganta* continued south, searching for new victims. Off Cabinda, the *Antelope* waited.[23]

CHAPTER 4

"Slavery, then, has its origin in force . . ."

Chief Justice John Marshall *The Antelope*, 23 U.S. 66, 121 (1825)

I n March of 1820, three ships were anchored in the Bay of Cabinda on the west central coast of Africa. Two of the ships, the *Dolphin* and the *São Panela*, flew the flag of Portugal. The third ship was the *Antelope*. She had been on the coast for some time, trading for slaves. Nothing out of the ordinary had occurred so far, and as Captain Vicente de Llovio accumulated slaves the ship moved ever closer to a successful voyage. One hundred or so slaves were already aboard, and the captain still had plenty of goods to trade and most of the gold the ship had carried from Havana. Cabinda was popular with Spanish slave traders, in part because of the attractive setting. Palms lined the gently curving beach of the bay, while steep bluffs topped by grassy, parklike hills created a green vista to the eastern horizon. This was a very different world than that of the mosquito-infested mangroves and shallow rivers Captain Henry John Leeke contended with far to the north.[1]

The "Black Prince of Tef," Loemba Nkata Kolombo, ruled Cabinda from his family compound atop a hill above the bay. He was the most powerful man in Cabinda, and he may have found the European search for a proper honorific amusing. During the 1820s Loemba was known to English-speaking Europeans as Prince Jack. During the 1830s his title improved to King Jack. In reality, Loemba's position had not changed; he was not a king or a prince. He was of the Woyo people, the *mambouk* of the kingdom of Ngoyo. This meant that he was the principal royal administrator at Cabinda appointed by the king. Cabinda was a welcoming harbor with good trade connections inland in the middle of a long, unwelcoming stretch of west central Africa's coast. Because of increasing trade at Cabinda, the power of the *mambouks* had grown throughout the late eighteenth and early nineteenth centuries. The king of Ngoyo lived in an ancient inland capital, prohibited by law and tradition from approaching the sea. He was dependent upon his *mambouk* to manage affairs at the coast, and the *mambouk* grew rich and powerful as a result.[2]

Loemba's power was not unchallenged. He had succeeded the previous *mambouk*, who was from the rival Npunas, a family still powerful and more closely connected by kinship to the king than Loemba's Nakata Kolombo family. At this time, another family was rising rapidly in wealth and power. In the late eighteenth century Franque Kokelo had rejected the tradition of sending sons to study in Europe. He sent his son, Francisco "Chico" Franque, to study in Brazil instead. After fifteen years abroad Chico had returned. He had adopted Catholicism, European dress, and many European and Brazilian habits. Chico made several more voyages to Brazil, including one in 1812 when he was part of an African delegation that visited the exiled Portuguese court in Rio de Janeiro. Chico Franque's influence was growing, a concern for Loemba.[3]

About that time, British prohibition of the slave trade and the growth of British naval hegemony during the wars with Napoleon meant that Portuguese and Brazilian ships began to dominate the slave trade from Cabinda. Chico Franque used his excellent Portuguese, his connections in Brazil, and his familiarity with the Luso-Atlantic world to become the wealthiest merchant at Cabinda. Loemba, from his family compound on top of Tafe Point, could see Chico Franque's rapidly growing village on the lower slopes. It was positioned above the best landing spot for boats, in an area protected from all but the worst storms. Because of this location, and thanks to the growing Brazilian/Portuguese dominance of the slave trade, Franque's wealth continued to grow. He would become a political challenge for the *mambouk* in the future. In just a few years Franque's village, called Chioua, or fish market, would be renamed Puerto Rico, for reasons obvious to all who lived at Cabinda.[4]

While local power struggles concerned Loemba, there was at least no power struggle with the king. The people at Cabinda, the Woyo, had engaged in regional trade long before the arrival of Europeans. The Portuguese traders who came in the 1500s were simply incorporated into existing trade networks. Most early Cabindan traders sold salt, ivory, and dyewoods, but during the seventeenth century the trade in slaves began to expand. As it did, Ngoyo's kings grew increasingly dependent upon their appointed officials to manage it, as kings could not visit the sea or even glimpse the ocean. The *mambouks* became the most important officials in this trade; they lived on the coast and officially stood next in power to the king.[5]

Extended families formed the basis of society in Ngoyo: not just matrilineal kin but also loyal retainers, adopted children, and even slaves. A large family was one of the visible attributes of prosperity and power, and the "big men" were the recognized leaders of these large kinship groups. The slave trade may have indirectly benefited some of the smaller families along the bay, but without question it made the leading families rich. Slaves had to be acquired in the interior and brought to the coast. Slaves, caravan guards, porters, and ship crews all needed food when they arrived at Cabinda. Baskets and pottery were needed to carry and store the food. Boats and canoes were needed for transport around the harbor and along the coast. Boatmen were needed to navigate, farmers to grow food, and servants for the household. The big men who headed large extended families, such as the Franque, the Npuna, and the Nakata Kolombo, were well placed to meet these demands. As the Atlantic-based world trade system brought wealth to Cabinda, these men claimed most of that wealth. Through taxes and participation in the slave trade, the *mambouk* at Cabinda became so rich and powerful that he essentially operated independently of the king. After 1800, Ngoyo was a kingdom in name only; real power lay with the *mambouk*.[6]

In January of 1826, Captain William Fitz William Owen met the *mambouk* at Cabinda during his survey expedition to west Africa. Soon after Owen's ships anchored, Prince Jack, as the Europeans called Loemba, came aboard for a visit. Having been at sea for quite some time, Owen could not help noting that Prince Jack arrived "accompanied by six of his daughters, who, as specimens of the women of the west coast were rather superior." Owen paid such close attention to the physical attributes of these "well formed" and "highly scented" women that he may have misunderstood the situation. Were the women simply visiting, or were they part of a clever gambit by Prince Jack to distract the British sailor or perhaps even to add a powerful European to the family? Whatever his purposes, Prince Jack and his daughters shared the evening meal with Captain Owen. Owen, an experienced African traveler, was astonished that his guests "behaved at supper with much propriety." He may not have known that many of the elite at Cabinda had visited Europe; some had been educated there. Owen was surprised that Prince Jack, as if he were an upper-class European, drank only wine with the meal instead of the beer or rum typically chosen by Africans. He concluded that Prince Jack must have thought wine "more becoming his rank and importance," something Captain Owen thought an absurd presumption for a black African. As he explained, Prince Jack was "upwards of fifty, possessing much good nature and a great deal of affected dignity, which with a black face almost universally borders on the ridiculous."[7]

Captain Owen's condescension toward Prince Jack was possible only because Owen was not at Cabinda to trade. However ridiculous Owen thought him, Loemba was a very powerful man—a merchant prince and a royal official who controlled access to local trade.

Only with the permission of the *mambouk* could Europeans trade in Cabinda. Only with the permission of the *mambouk* could trade goods be brought ashore. Only with the protection of the *mambouk* would those trade goods be kept safe. To facilitate trade at the various villages along the wide roadstead, the king had also appointed several *mafouks*, lesser officials who functioned as customs agents and brokers under the authority of the *mambouk*. Chico Franque's father had been a *mafouk*, and Chico's brother would soon become a *mafouk* as well. Thanks to these officials, the system of trade at Cabinda was straightforward and simple. When a trading vessel arrived, the *mafouk* from the nearest village would visit the ship to claim a present, the equivalent of harbor dues. That done, the visitors could then come ashore to see the *mambouk* and offer more presents, in essence buying a license to trade. Presuming all went well, the traders could then bring their trade goods ashore. An existing warehouse might be used to store the goods, or a new warehouse would be built for storage.[8]

Europeans had never successfully planted a slave fort at Cabinda. There were no stone prisons, no European soldiers, and no resident officials as there were to the north at Elmina or to the south at Luanda. The English, the Dutch, and twice the Portuguese had attempted to establish forts at Cabinda. All wanted very much to control the local slave trade. All four times, however, through careful diplomacy and alliances with other European powers, the Woyo managed to drive the occupiers away and destroy the forts. As one Cabindan explained to a British naval lieutenant, speaking of the Portuguese, "twice they were our masters—they are now no longer, twice they erected a fort, but the ruins alone remain."[9]

Thus the Woyo at Cabinda controlled local trade. Once the goods were ashore, the next step was the appointment of a broker to handle the trade. These were generally sophisticated men, competent in several languages and familiar with the challenges of cross-cultural exchange. Brokers examined the goods and negotiated the standard mix of items to buy a slave, often called a "bundle." Raffia cloth had long been a preferred item of trade, so prices at Cabinda were denominated in "pieces" of cloth, and each "bundle" was valued at an exact number of "pieces." "Blue Guinea" was perhaps the most valuable cloth, trading for as much as three or four pieces. Slave traders, however, brought much more than cloth. By the early nineteenth century, guns, gunpowder, and alcohol had become so important that they often made up the largest portion of a bundle. Nevertheless, their value was still denominated in cloth pieces. Having established the price of a slave as a particular number of pieces, brokers then worked to attract slave caravans, or even arranged caravans of their own. Sometimes brokers themselves maintained *barracoons*, or slave pens, several miles inland in which they kept slaves for sale, but this was risky, as the arrival of slave ships was unpredictable. Finally, as slaves arrived, the broker saw to the proper distribution of trade goods based on the agreements reached with the Europeans.[10]

When the trade goods went ashore, the *mambouk* took responsibility for their protection. He was well able to do this. In 1784, in the midst of conflict with the Portuguese over their second attempt to build a fort at Cabinda, the *mambouk* offered his French allies eight hundred armed men. Even if that was an extraordinary event, the *mambouk* clearly had sufficient resources to protect trade goods ashore. Maintaining this system and keeping it secure was not just the duty of the *mambouk* but his route to wealth. He received fees for the license to trade and in many cases acted as the broker himself, receiving commissions for his services. When trade concluded, he received another "present," in essence clearance dues for departing the port.[11]

Cabinda's harbor was wide and scenic. It was some forty miles north of the Congo River, ringed with hills, white limestone cliffs, and a profusion of forests and fields. The bay was open to the west and north, but due to prevailing winds and currents from the south, this otherwise exposed anchorage was the best along several hundred miles of coast. Sailors reported that from a distance the cliffs lining the bay resembled the sails of ships. Others compared the cliffs to those of

Dover, though they must have been homesick, for the cliffs at Cabinda were in no way so dramatic. The limestone of the cliffs continued far out to sea, producing to the northwest of the bay a shallow breakwater extending more than a mile. Only in the rare event of swells from the north did the bay become dangerous. Then, towering waves rose on the shallow limestone floor of the bay, the heavy surf pounding the shore. In such weather only a few small vessels could shelter in the inner harbor, protected by a spit of land called Cabinda hook. Other vessels had to anchor far offshore.[12]

A small river, the Lukola, tumbled into the sea at the base of Cabinda Bay, providing clean and healthy water for visiting ships. A long, curving white sand beach lined the anchorage, backed by palm trees. French mariners dubbed Cabinda the "paradise of the coast," though they remarked that a smart captain slept aboard ship at night to avoid fever. Captain Owen found the region around Cabinda enchanting, enthusing over the "lofty cliffs, verdant hills, and deep, luxuriant vales." Inland, he enjoyed the fertile valleys, groves of massive trees, and "a high and sloping ridge of beautiful park-land." Owen described what ecologists call a forest and savannah mosaic, a mix of trees and grassland that when he visited during the rainy season must have glistened with every possible shade of green.[13]

Some twenty to thirty miles inland, however, was the Mayombe, a far less idyllic place. Hills and mountains rose as much as three thousand feet, covered with dense tropical rainforest. The trails across the Mayombe were man-killers: "interminable, wearing, hallucination making." "Huge, shadowy, terrifying," wrote one traveler, "the hostile forests of the Mayombe waylaid us." Yet one had to cross the Mayombe to reach the Congo Basin, one of the most important sources for slaves. Given the difficulty for travelers, one can only imagine the sufferings of slaves driven on foot across the Mayombe on the way to the coast.[14]

That March of 1820, only three ships were anchored in the Bay of Cabinda. The dull trade in a port accustomed to more activity must have worried the *mambouk*. Two of the ships, the *Dolphin* and the

São Panela, were out of Rio de Janeiro and were probably brokered through Chico Franque's family. The third ship was the *Antelope*, and Loemba was engaged as her broker. Captain Vicente de Llovio had sent most of his trade goods ashore, a cargo that weighed more than 35,000 pounds. Happily, the boatmen at Cabinda were highly skilled, and a captain could rely upon their competence. The captain also had thousands of dollars in gold at his disposal, which could be used to purchase additional trade goods and supplies. There is no record of how much Captain de Llovio paid per slave, but with so much alcohol, gunpowder, and blue cloth, he had a fortune to use in trade.[15]

Trading for slaves was a piecemeal business, with captives usually arriving from the interior in small groups: five captives one day, maybe ten the next. Some days there would be no slave trading at all. Ships often took months to accumulate a full cargo, and slaves acquired early in the trading lived aboard ship for a long time. By March of 1820, the *Antelope* had been at sea for more than seven months. The owners of the *Antelope* had anticipated that her voyage would take a full year, allowing at least six months on the coast of Africa acquiring 350 slaves. She may have gone directly to Cabinda, a voyage that with bad luck could have taken as much as four months. More likely the ship had already visited several locations along the coast, not just acquiring slaves but potentially purchasing trade goods along the way. Of the $25,000 in gold she had aboard, Captain de Llovio had spent $3,000.[16]

On March 10, 1820, work began early for the servants of the *mambouk*. More slaves had been bought by Captain Llovio of the *Antelope*, and just after dawn these people were assembled and marched to the beach along Cabinda Bay. There they were loaded into a twelve-oared launch, a large boat owned by the *mambouk*, and taken out to the waiting ship. Additional slaves may have waited their turn ashore. Possibly Loemba watched from his home on Tafe Point as the boat approached the *Antelope* and went alongside. Second Mate Domingo Grondona, who had a special contract to care for the slaves, remembered that before the launch arrived, there were ninety-six slaves aboard the *Antelope*. The two Portuguese slavers, *Dolphin* and *São Panela*, lay anchored nearby. Suddenly, the maintop lookout shouted that a ship was entering the bay.[17]

The new arrival was a felucca-rigged schooner, a vessel common to the Mediterranean, though much associated with Arab pirates. She flew a Spanish merchant flag at her stern. Captain Vicente de Llovio knew better than to trust a flag, and he did what he could to prepare the *Antelope*. The launch, probably still loaded with slaves, was sent ashore. They waited for two long hours as the schooner sailed into the bay. Canoes and boats put off from shore to meet the ship, to direct her to an anchorage, but she ignored them. By now Captain de Llovio and his men saw that the schooner was heavily armed: three cannon on each side and a long twelve-pound cannon on a pivot amidships. Sailing alongside the *Antelope*, the schooner hauled down the Spanish flag and hoisted English naval colors. She fired a cannon shot and hailed, demanding that the captain come aboard with his papers. This was familiar conduct for a British warship on anti-slavery patrol, but the appearance of the ship didn't add up. Most telling was a file of armed black men lining the rail with their muskets leveled. Whether the ship was British or not no longer mattered, for there was no possibility of resistance.[18]

Taken aboard the schooner, Captain de Llovio learned that he was a prisoner of privateers sailing under a commission from revolutionary Venezuela. Having secured the *Antelope*, the privateer then turned on the Portuguese slavers anchored nearby. Boats loaded with armed men assaulted and quickly captured both ships. As Venezuela was only at war with Spain, not with Portugal, this was piracy. For three nights and four days the schooner's crew plundered their captives. From the *Antelope* they stole trade goods, naval stores, and cordage, and even robbed the officers and crew of their personal possessions. They took the four cannon stored in the hold. The captors selected and stole the most valuable slaves aboard. Perhaps to make room on the schooner, they sent back thirty-six slaves of lesser quality. More devastatingly, the captors discovered and stole the $22,000 in gold that was hidden aboard the ship. Several *Antelope* crewmen later testified that while the attacker's crew was from all nations, it was clearly commanded by an American.[19]

When the piratical schooner departed during the night of March 13, it seemed the voyage of the *Antelope* had ended in disaster. Fortunately for Captain Vicente de Llovio, most of his trade goods were in warehouses ashore, and so saved from the depredations of his captors. The captain was able to start trading again almost immediately. He purchased food for his ship and began buying more slaves. Perhaps some slaves were waiting ashore, already paid for. Perhaps several caravans had arrived from the interior with a large number of new slaves, for there were many captives available for sale, and the captain insisted that he would still acquire the planned 350 slaves. Over the next nine days a large number of new slaves were brought aboard. Many were children. While cheaper than teenagers or adults, little children were still valuable in Cuba, especially on coffee plantations, where they were useful picking beans. Suddenly, it looked as if the voyage might be saved.[20]

Who were these captives? In 1790, James Fraser told a British parliamentary committee that "slaves of three nations are brought to Cabinda . . . the *Congues, Majumbas,* and *Madungoes.*" Did these designations reflect the ethnicity of the slaves, that of their captors, or, rather, the places they had traveled through in their journey to the coast? Congues, for example, might mean the Kongo people, or people of various origin along the Congo River, or those who had been captured or sold by the Kongos. Undoubtedly, many slaves sold at Cabinda were probably Kongo in origin, but little more than that can be said. The Majumbas may have come from the town of Mayumba, north of Cabinda, or perhaps were slaves traded by merchants from that area, the well-known Mubiri traders who traveled across all of central Africa. The Madungoes were apparently people from deep in the interior, and many bore heavy tribal facial scars. Perhaps they were from the northeast along the Congo basin, or perhaps victims of the expanding Lunda kingdoms. The potential sources for these captives encompassed a vast area; traders at Cabinda traveled as far as the Great Rift Valley in search of captives.[21]

Years later, Europeans writing about the *Antelope* captives characterized them as being of the "Congo people." The kingdom of Kongo, which had roots as far back as the fourteenth century, dominated a vast area north and east of Angola during the sixteenth and seventeenth centuries. In the 1660s it began to collapse, and much of the former kingdom fell into civil war. The idea of a Kongo kingdom, however, persisted, and in the eighteenth and nineteenth centuries it resembled a failed state, having a clear geographic location with no meaningful sovereignty. The last remnants of Kongo collapsed in the middle nineteenth century. War, banditry, and local power struggles within the territory of the failed kingdom of Kongo produced many captives for the slave trade, quite possibly the captives taken aboard the *Antelope* itself. Sadly, nothing is known about the languages spoken by the captives, which could provide clues to their ethnicity. As they were characterized as "Congos," the captives probably spoke dialects of Kikongo. Kikongo is a Bantu language, and uses tonalities as part of the meanings of words. These tonalities could prove difficult for Europeans to master, especially if they only visited the coast for trade. The people of the coast had been trading with Europeans since the sixteenth century, and a trade language, or pidgin, existed both along the coast and inland. This trade pidgin was probably similar to the Kituba language that is the lingua franca of the modern Congo. If the captives bought by Captain de Llovio of the *Antelope* were Kikongo speakers, perhaps even from what remained of the Kongo kingdom, they probably also understood the trade pidgin as well as their own dialect of Kikongo.[22]

Surveys conducted among slaves in the late eighteenth century and among freed captives in the 1840s found similar causes of enslavement. More than a third were captured in war and another third or so were kidnapped by gangs of bandits. The rest were enslaved as a result of debt or of convictions in judicial proceedings. This suggests an answer to the question, "Why did Africans sell other Africans as slaves?" The key word was "other." The unsettled interior of central Africa in the early nineteenth century, still reeling from the collapse of the Kongo kingdom and the rise of Lunda, had long been a place of warfare and refugees. It was fertile ground for militaristic slavers such as the Lunda, who sent many people they captured to the coast. Fertile ground as well for gangs of bandits, who in some instances were powerful enough to capture entire villages in raids. These captives were then sold to traders and taken to the coast, far from their homes. At the coast these captives were different; sometimes too different to be readily incorporated into existing families and social structures, yet too valuable to be ignored. Sale to European buyers was a simple and profitable way to solve this dilemma. So too was the sale of individuals heavily in debt. Creditors received at least some return on their investment either by enslaving the debtor or selling a "pawn" provided as security by the debtor. Finally, there was the problem faced by every society of what to do with convicted criminals. Sale to Europeans ensured that criminals would be taken away forever. For the people of central Africa, participation in the slave trade was far more than a lucrative activity; it also offered a solution to social problems.[23]

On March 23, 1820, the *Antelope* was anchored at Cabinda about a mile and a half from shore. Second Mate Domingo Grondona claimed that there were 166 captives aboard. Others said the number was less than 50. John Smith, the privateer who would command the *Antelope*, put it firmly at 93. Suddenly, a hail from the maintop reported a sail. As it approached, the lookouts soon made out a hermaphrodite brig running under full sail toward the anchorage. The large black ship flew the Spanish flag but was, of course, the *Arraganta*. The winds were light, so there was no dodging, no maneuvers, just very slow progress over the next four hours as the brig gradually drew ever closer. The situation developed so slowly and was so unnerving that Captain de Llovio sent Second Mate Grondona and four sailors in a boat to "find out what she was." Rowing out to the approaching ship, Grondona and his men saw that armed men were gathered on the deck of the strange ship, but they could not row back to the *Antelope* in time to warn her. Bobbing in their rowboat, Grondona and his men watched in horror as the *Arraganta* sailed straight into the anchorage and crashed aboard the *Antelope* at the bow. Following a musket volley, men armed with swords and guns leapt over the gunwales and onto the deck of the *Antelope*. They swept aside any resistance, and the *Antelope* was quickly captured. The captain and crew were imprisoned belowdecks with the slaves. Grondona and his men, stunned that the *Antelope* had been captured yet again, rowed ashore and waited.[24]

A Portuguese ship anchored nearby was also captured by boats from the *Arraganta*. Simon Metcalf's crew plundered them and brought twenty bales of cloth and the slaves from the Portuguese ship to the *Antelope*. John Smith, the first mate of the *Arraganta,* later swore that there were 93 slaves aboard the *Antelope*, and that the privateers took 183 slaves out of the Portuguese ship. If that was true, then they had just captured 276 slaves worth at least $80,000. It was a fortune, but there was not enough room aboard the *Arraganta* for 276 slaves. The *Antelope*, however, was a well-found brig with a coppered hull and worth some money. The solution was one Metcalf had used in the past. Rather than take the slaves onto his own ship, he would simply steal the *Antelope* in its entirety, slaves and all.[25]

Captain Metcalf put most of the captive crewmen from both vessels ashore in Cabinda. Grondona later said that the *Antelope* crewmen numbered 22, and that he did not know at the time what had happened to the captain. A prize crew, commanded by John Smith, took control of the *Antelope* and renamed it the *General Ramirez*. Captain de Llovio, Boatswain Ximenes, a sailor who was ill, and the black cabin boy Carlos were kept aboard the *Arraganta* as prisoners, along with four sailors from the Portuguese ship. John Stephens, one of the *Antelope*'s crew, deserted his ship and joined the crew of the *Arraganta*. On the evening of March 24, Metcalf's men ran the Portuguese ship aground in Cabinda Bay and set it on fire. As Grondona and his men watched, the *Arraganta* and her prize the *Antelope* sailed out of Cabinda, lit by the flickering light of the burning ship, until they vanished into the night.[26]

Sometime after nine o'clock, when the *Arraganta* and her prize were well out to sea, Captain Metcalf ordered the prisoners into a small boat that was tied alongside. Protesting, Captain de Llovio was forced into the launch with his boatswain, the sick man, and four Portuguese sailors. Carlos, the black cabin boy, was imprisoned among the slaves, while John Stephens had joined privateers. When loaded, the launch was turned adrift with only "two bad oars and a little water in a small barrel." The *Arraganta* and the *Antelope* sailed away, leaving the terrified men in the launch alone on the dark ocean. The boat leaked, was half full of water, and at any moment Captain de Llovio expected to be swamped and to drown in the darkness. Using the broken oars, the men worked their way slowly toward land, struggling all night and into the next day. Incredibly, they landed safely. Two days later Domingo Grondona and the crew at Cabinda received a letter from the captain, revealing he was alive and "about nine leagues distant from the place of capture." The captain soon rejoined his men at Cabinda.[27]

The "Black Prince of Tef" took them in. He gave the castaways food, a kitchen, and a place to sleep in his family compound. There they waited and hoped for a ship that would return them to Cuba. On March 30, ill and worried that he might not live to tell his tale, Captain de Llovio appointed Second Mate Grondona "Temporary Notary." De Llovio then gave his statement of what had occurred, and Grondona wrote it down. Sickness spread and by May six men had died. Of thirty-three men who set out in the *Antelope* for Africa, only nineteen still lived. Finally, two Cuban vessels arrived off Cabinda and agreed to take the survivors home. On May 14, the brig *Timolen* departed

Cabinda with Grondona, Ximenes, and Captain de Llovio aboard. The other surviving members of the crew left in the brig *Paxaro*. The *Timolen* made excellent time and arrived at San Juan, Puerto Rico, on June 21. Captain Vicente de Llovio, however, did not arrive. He died at sea on May 22, 1820, eight days after leaving Cabinda. The *Antelope* had again killed a captain.[28]

CHAPTER 5

"Supposing her to be a pirate or a vessel wishing to smuggle slaves into the United States, Captain Jackson, of the revenue cutter Dallas, went in quest of her."

Chief Justice John Marshall *The Antelope*, 23 U.S. 66, 124-25 (1825)

Even with his success in capturing the *Antelope*, Simon Metcalf did not turn for home. Instead, he took the *Arraganta* and the *Antelope* south, looking for Portuguese slavers sailing out of Angola. He found them. Three days after leaving Cabinda, the *Arraganta* captured a Portuguese schooner carrying slaves. Metcalf loaded the fifteen slaves from the schooner aboard the *Antelope*, imprisoned the officers and crew, and burned the ship. Then he continued the hunt, venturing further south. A week later the *Arraganta* captured two more Portuguese schooners. One schooner carried about fifteen slaves; again these were put aboard the *Antelope*. This time Metcalf loaded the sailors and officers he had captured into the second schooner and released them. The first schooner he burned. Finally, both his ships bursting with slaves, Metcalf turned north and east, steering for the coast of Brazil.[1]

Old salts believed that ships talked—that is, the songs of creaking timbers, straining cordage, vibrating stays, even water bubbling past the hull, could tell an experienced sailor the condition of the ship, what had happened in the past, even what lay in the future. During the twenty-two-day transatlantic passage, the crews of both ships surely listened very hard and tried to discern their fate. In one sense their prospects looked good. The commander of the *Antelope*, John Smith, recalled that his ship had 306 slaves aboard. At least 25 more slaves were aboard the *Arraganta*, as well as 20 bales of trade cloth and many other items looted from Metcalf's victims. The *Antelope* itself was a sound ship worth several thousand dollars. All together this was quite a haul, more than $100,000 of booty. Probably every man aboard the two ships calculated out the value and the amount of his share. Surely they thrilled at the fortune they were bringing home. Home, however, was the problem, and the seas bubbling along the hull offered no answer, for essentially the privateers were homeless.[2]

Metcalf's privateers had captured a fortune, but where to sell the booty posed a problem. The Banda Oriental was still at war, and losing. Montevideo had fallen, and there was no port with a prize court for Artigan privateers. Artigas was also at war with Buenos Aires, so there was no hope the slaves could be landed there. The *Arraganta* had stolen from Portuguese slavers and burned their ships; she would hardly be welcome in Rio de Janeiro. There might have been a chance of smuggling slaves ashore in some isolated location along the Brazilian coast, but that was very dangerous. The largest slave market in the Caribbean was that of the "Ever Faithful Isle" of Cuba, which, unlike so many colonies, had remained loyal to Spain. Cuba would hardly welcome a revolutionary privateer with a captured Spanish/Cuban slave ship. The major colonial powers of the Caribbean, Holland, France, and Great Britain had all outlawed the slave trade. The United States had outlawed the slave trade. The revolutionary regime in Gran Colombia, which included Venezuela, was no longer welcoming new slaves, and would begin a program of compensated emancipation in 1821. The possibilities of finding a market for the slaves in the Caribbean were not good. The two ships carried a fortune, but realizing that fortune would be a challenge.[3]

Samuel Johnson famously quipped that sailing in a ship was like "being in jail, with the chance of being drowned." The captives aboard the *Arraganta* and *Antelope* were literally in jail, and locked below they could easily drown in a disaster. Each gurgle along the hull, each creak of a timber, the hum of vibrating stays, took them further into the unknown. Of immediate concern, the captives were beginning to die. In a voyage that lasted ninety-nine days, at least fifty of the captives perished. These continual deaths only added to the despair of stolen people, while the silent disposal of the bodies overboard increased their dread and horror. Former slave and abolitionist Olaudah Equiano described a similar scene among the captives aboard a slaver:

> The closeness of the place, and the heat of the climate, added to the number in the ship, which was so crowded that each had scarcely room to turn himself, almost suffocated us. This produced copious perspirations, so that the air soon became unfit for respiration, from a variety of loathsome smells, and brought on a sickness among the slaves, of which many died. . . . This wretched situation was aggravated by the galling of the chains, now become insupportable; and the filth of the necessary tubs, into which the children often fell, and were almost suffocated. The shrieks of the women, and the groans of the dying, rendered the whole a scene of horror almost inconceivable.[4]

When they reached the coast of Brazil, further disaster struck. The ships approached to within a few miles of the shore, perhaps seeking a place to surreptitiously sell slaves. The northeast coast of Brazil is treacherous, with numerous small islands, limestone outcroppings, and coral reefs. During a storm to the "southward of Maranhão," the *Arraganta* struck a reef and was wrecked. Eighteen men escaped on a raft and floated ashore. Captain Simon Metcalf, perhaps cursed by the *Antelope* after all, was last seen clinging to a broken spar. Boats from the *Antelope* rescued fourteen men from the wreck, nine of whom were slaves from the American schooner *Exchange*. The rest of the captives aboard the *Arraganta* "died at the pumps" or drowned. The *Antelope* stayed off the coast of Brazil several days but failed to recover Captain Metcalf or any of the men. Finally, John Smith turned the *Antelope* north.[5]

Whatever Metcalf's plans had been for selling the captives, they had vanished with him. John Smith had to devise his own vision for disposing of the plunder. He first headed for Cayenne, but changed his mind and sailed on to Suriname instead. This was a good choice. Since the late seventeenth century the Dutch colony had produced increasing amounts of sugar, coffee, and cotton. There were still great swaths of undeveloped lands suitable for plantation agriculture. British forces had seized Suriname and neighboring Dutch colonies during the war with Napoleon's France. The British kept the neighboring colonies, merging them and renaming them British Guyana, but at the end of the war with France the British returned Suriname to Holland. Dutch planters were desperate to restore and expand their profits by growing more sugar. For that, they needed more slaves, but Holland had outlawed the slave trade in 1814, and in 1817 had entered into a treaty with Great Britain to suppress the slave trade. Official policy, however, was not practice. Slavers commonly found welcoming buyers in Suriname, and local officials were willingly blind to these exchanges if they were kept quiet.[6]

Captain Smith anchored the *Antelope* in the wide mouth of the Suriname River, and sent First Mate George Ford and five men ashore in a boat to search for buyers. Ford soon found customers. When negotiations opened, he offered all the captives aboard the *Antelope*, about 300 slaves, for $80,000. This was a good price, a bit less than $270 each. The potential buyers came back with an offer of $50,000, far too low a price, but at least they were negotiating. The bargaining then came to an abrupt halt when Ford learned that several of his men had deserted and informed a Dutch navy vessel in the harbor of the *Antelope*'s purpose. Ford bolted immediately; the Dutch officials would certainly recover their sight now that the *Ante-*

lope's purpose was public knowledge. Ford and one remaining sailor returned in the rowboat, leaving the four deserters behind. When Ford arrived with the news that they had been betrayed, the *Antelope* hoisted sail and fled.[7]

This was the first clear evidence that all was not well among the crew of the *Antelope*. There had been mention of disgruntled mumblings before this, and some of the crew continued to call their privateer the *Columbia*, apparently rejecting the transfer to an Artigan flag. The crew had signed on for a cruise in the *Columbia*, a Venezuelan privateer. Without consulting the crew, Captain Metcalf had switched to the flag of the Banda Oriental while at sea. This provided the basis for a grievance; the change was not in the articles of agreement signed before the voyage. Worse, now the surviving members of the *Columbia*'s crew no longer served as fighting men aboard a swift privateer. Instead, they tended a wallowing, overloaded slaver that by this point, after months in the tropics with slaves packed onboard, surely reeked. Even worse, it was a slaver without a home, a wanderer without a port. As a result, some men deserted and informed against the ship, probably hoping for a reward to replace their lost share in its cargo.

Fleeing Suriname, the *Antelope* "stood for the five islands," a nickname for the small island of St. Martin/St. Maarten. The island was split between a French side and a Dutch side; the *Antelope* anchored in Simpson Bay on the Dutch side. St. Maarten had for centuries focused on the production of salt, then a bit of tobacco, but in the late eighteenth and early nineteenth centuries the Dutch struggled to increase the production of sugar. Planters needed slaves but were apparently unwilling to buy from the *Antelope*. After several days in Simpson Bay they left and beat upwind some twenty miles to the town of Gustavia on the island of St. Barthélemy. This harbor on St. Barts had a reputation for welcoming all, regardless of their trade. The island was too dry and rocky for meaningful plantation agriculture, though some tried. Far more lucrative was the Swedish colony's role as a neutral free-port, a way station for the trade of the Caribbean. During the Napoleonic Wars, St. Barts had become notorious as a center for shady privateers and perhaps even pirates. It was at St. Barts that Captain Smith welcomed the mysterious Mr. Mason aboard the *Antelope*.[8]

Some of the crew thought that Mr. Mason had owned the *Arraganta* and so now owned the *Antelope*. Others said he was an investor from Baltimore. All agreed that he took captured money from the ship when he left; three bags of coin, perhaps as much as $5,000. Whoever Mr. Mason was, he and John Smith had reached a deal. The next day the *Antelope* left St. Barts and turned north and then west. They were bound for a rendezvous at Hole in the Wall, a natural wonder well known among sailors at the southern end of Great Abaco Island in the Bahamas. There, a large limestone spit thrust south into the ocean, marking the entrance to Providence Channel, the safest deep-water passage through the Bahama Banks. Near the end of the limestone spit, wind and waves had carved a tunnel, through which the sea boiled with every tide. Ships headed north along the East Coast of the United States used the passage because, once through to the other side, the Gulf Stream offered a sure ride north. Ships headed south to the Caribbean often sailed closely alongside the eastern edge of the Bahamas Bank, passing Hole in the Wall, until they caught the trade winds and continued south into the Caribbean or westward to Cuba. It was a busy intersection at sea.[9]

The schooner *Mary*, of Charleston, bound for Cuba, passed near the Hole in the Wall on her voyage south just as the *Antelope* reached it on her voyage north. Flying the Artigan flag, the *Antelope* forced the *Mary* to stop and boarded her. Low on supplies, Smith needed food and water. He took or purchased four casks of rice from the *Mary*. Then, the third mate of the *Antelope*, Raymond Arrivas, from Spanish Florida, who used the alias Blake, recognized one of the passengers aboard the *Mary*. This was Cornelio Coppinger, the son of José María Coppinger, the governor of Spanish East Florida. Arrivas hailed Coppinger as his schoolmate and forced him aboard the *Antelope*. The brig then ordered the schooner to make sail, and the two ships parted. The governor's son had been kidnapped.

John Smith's intentions in taking Coppinger prisoner were unclear.

Niles' Weekly Register wondered if Mr. Coppinger was taken "for a ransom perhaps?" Savannah newspapers left open the possibility that Coppinger was convinced to stay aboard the *Antelope*. According to a report in the *Charleston Times*: "The officer who took Mr. Coppinger is a man of infamous character, and has long ago been disavowed by his family." The newspaper also reported, "The brig appeared to have about 30 men, who had plenty of specie, and the common sailors were gambling on the quarterdeck!" This obvious breakdown of class structure and discipline at sea, as well as the infamous character of an officer, communicated clearly to readers that the brig must be a pirate.[10]

Two days after taking Coppinger prisoner, the *Antelope* came alongside a hermaphrodite brig at the Hole in the Wall. The new ship was under the command of the mysterious Mr. Mason. He sent aboard supplies, ammunition, and four cannon. John Smith never explained why he armed the *Antelope* at this point. Perhaps Smith intended to go privateering in the *Antelope*, but if so, he needed to get rid of his cargo of slaves. Perhaps he armed the ship to placate an unhappy crew; their prisoner Coppinger later described the crew as "mutinous." Perhaps Mr. Mason really was the owner and had decided for his own purposes to arm the ship. Whatever the reason, now armed, and having kidnapped the son of a Spanish governor, the *Antelope* turned west through the Providence Channel toward Florida.[11]

In 1820, one writer described Florida as a land where "government was disregarded." "Adventurers from every country," he continued, "fugitives from justice and run-away slaves found there an undisturbed asylum." Such a place must have been attractive to John Smith, and he may have hoped to sell the *Antelope* captives in Florida. He was not just dreaming; it had happened before. In June of 1817, Gregor McGregor, a mercenary, opportunist, and charlatan, sailed from Charleston, South Carolina, with a small fleet of privateers and a company of fighting men. They landed on Amelia Island, the northernmost part of Spanish East Florida. There the town of Fernandina offered a fine deep-water port and controlled passage north and south on the inland waterway. The Spanish Fort San Carlos at Fernandina had six long eighteen-pound cannon and a company of Cuban soldiers overlooking the harbor and the inland passage. None of the cannon, however, could be trained inland. The rear of the fort was guarded by two wooden blockhouses with loopholes for muskets, nothing more. On June 29, 1817, McGregor's forces landed about six miles south of Fernandina and marched north through the afternoon and into the night. As they approached Fort San Carlos after dark, the Spanish soldiers overestimated McGregor's strength, panicked, and fled. McGregor captured the town without firing a shot.[12]

McGregor claimed to represent the revolutionary republics of Spanish America and proclaimed the establishment of the Republic of the Floridas. He also established a court of admiralty in Fernandina. "John D. Heath, formerly a member of the bar at Charleston, is the judge," reported *Niles' Weekly Register*. A few weeks later Hezekiah Niles concluded that McGregor's purpose, and that of the Louis Aury who displaced McGregor in September, was to establish an "asylum for privateers and . . . a depot for smuggling into the United States." As more privateers and prizes arrived at Amelia Island in the fall of 1817, the most valuable cargoes brought in proved to be slaves. One of the first prizes condemned and sold at Amelia was comprised of "forty African slaves," and soon report after report told of large numbers of slaves coming into Amelia. Among the privateers selling slaves at Fernandina was Simon Metcalf, and a privateering commission from McGregor was later found among John Smith's papers.[13]

Fernandina lay just across the Saint Marys River from Georgia, and Creek territory lay close to the west. Smuggling slaves from Amelia Island into Georgia with its rapidly growing cotton plantation economy or to the expanding and slave-hungry territories to the west was easy. The publisher and editor of *Niles' Weekly Register*, Hezekiah Niles, wrote, "this trade in human flesh is so profitable" that it could not be stopped unless American forces occupied the island. And so they did, just before Christmas of 1817. A United States Navy fleet and a battalion of soldiers took control of Amelia Island, putting to an end seven months of "free trade" on the southern border of the

United States. This occupation, along with Andrew Jackson's invasion of West Florida soon after, demonstrated that James Monroe's government meant to have Florida by any means. In 1821, Florida was ceded by Spain to satisfy American claims against the Spanish government. American soldiers continuously occupied Amelia Island until the transfer of government occurred.[14]

While John Smith probably knew Amelia Island was no longer the haven for slave traders it had once been, he also knew anything was possible in Florida. It was a wild place, poorly administered by a government chronically short of funds. A place where Indians and runaway slaves outnumbered Europeans living in the colony. Someone there might be willing to buy his human cargo. After riding the Gulf Stream north, the *Antelope* came to anchor off the coast at St. Augustine, where she hoisted American colors. No one came out to the ship. By this point in the voyage the stench and the appearance of the brig marked her as a slaver. The *Antelope*'s lookouts spotted a small sloop headed north toward the St. Johns River. They raised sail and chased down the sloop. Terrified, the sloop's captain agreed to supply the *Antelope* with water if they would release him. Smith let him go, but the sloop never returned. He anchored off St. Augustine again, where the water situation became increasingly desperate.

The *Antelope* had carried about a ten- to twelve-weeks' supply of water. In March she surely watered off the coast at Cabinda. She had no chance to water off Brazil or Suriname. Perhaps at St. Maarten or St. Barts she had acquired some water, but the ship did not spend enough time in either place to load the scores of large casks needed for more than three hundred people in the tropics. By the time they reached Hole in the Wall off Great Abaco Island, the ship was short of food as well. Mr. Mason's ship may have given her some water, but with more than 310 captives and crew aboard the ship, large amounts of water were consumed every day. Slave rations were usually two or so quarts a day. Sailors needed more than two quarts to work in the hot sun. Salt beef, the most common food aboard, had to be soaked and boiled in fresh water before it could be eaten. At the least, the

Antelope consumed two hundred or more gallons of water a day. The *Antelope* sat off the coast of Florida in the middle of June, hungry and threatened by thirst. Playing his last card, Smith sent a message to José María Coppinger. He needed water and provisions, Smith explained. If a supply of water and food was sent to the ship, he would release the governor's son.[15]

Governor Coppinger replied "that much as he loved his child, he would not supply them with a mouthful of provisions or a drop of water to save him from the yard arm." He forbade any contact with the pirates by anyone from St. Augustine. Three young men from Charleston were visiting the city during the standoff. They knew the governor's son and feared for his life. Reasoning that U.S. citizens were not under the governor's authority, they borrowed a boat and went out to the *Antelope*. They took with them a cask of water as a gift. To their surprise, Captain Smith received them cordially and brought them aboard. After some discussion, Smith released Cornelio Coppinger, and the young men all returned safely to St. Augustine. These rescuers reported the best details yet printed in American newspapers about the *Antelope*. Not only did they reveal that the ship carried more than 250 slaves, they explained that Captain Smith "was very anxious to dispose of his slaves, and offered them for $100 each." This was far from the price Smith had asked at Suriname, reflecting his growing desperation. He needed to get rid of his dying cargo. Several newspapers up the coast printed reports of this "piratical" vessel off St. Augustine. Despite the new cannon aboard his ship and the kidnapping of the governor's son, Smith was proving a most ineffective pirate.[16]

At St. Marys, Georgia, Captain John Jackson followed reports of the piratical ship with interest. Jackson commanded the revenue cutter *Dallas*, charged with protecting the southernmost point of the United States on the Atlantic Coast. When informants told him that the "piratical vessel" had left St. Augustine and headed north, it seemed clear the pirate would land somewhere along the Georgia coast. Jackson decided to act. The *Dallas* dropped down the St. Marys River with the tide and anchored off the northern point of Amelia Island. Jackson took a ship's boat to Fernandina, where occupying American troops were stationed. He returned two hours later with twelve soldiers armed with muskets and bayonets to bolster his small crew. By 4:00 p.m., the *Dallas* crossed the bar into the Atlantic and turned south in very light winds.[17]

At about 7:00 a.m. the next morning, June 29, 1820, Captain Jackson's crew spotted a sail to the southeast. They made all sail, and closed with the stranger. By 2:00 p.m. the *Dallas* was close enough to make out the brig clearly. At that point, Captain Jackson hoisted the United States Revenue Marine ensign. On seeing the flag, the strange brig immediately turned away to the northeast and began to fly ever more sails: topgallants, staysails, even putting out studding sails to catch as much of the light breeze as possible. Her attempt to escape was in vain. The sleek hull and topsail schooner rig of the revenue cutter proved much faster. By two-thirty the *Dallas* had gained the weather gauge: a position to windward that allowed Captain Jackson to control the engagement. By three o'clock the *Dallas* had so outsailed the brig that she stood just off the starboard quarter of the chase. Suddenly, the brig cleared for battle, took in all the extra sails, and backed the main topsail to stabilize the ship as a gun platform. The Artigan flag broke out over the deck and the crew crouched down behind their cannon. They lit slow matches and made every sign of being ready for combat. The *Dallas* responded, dropping her ports so the pivot gun could bear, crew at quarters, soldiers with their muskets lining the rail. With the men standing "half a pistol shot" apart, only a bit more than a dozen yards, the standoff lasted several minutes. Soon it became clear that the men aboard the brig refused the order to fire. The crew of the *Antelope* had finally mutinied.[18]

Captain Jackson hailed, demanding the brig's identity.

"This is the Patriot brig of war *General Ramirez*," came the reply. Captain Smith had decided to brazen it out.

Captain Jackson sent his first lieutenant and six sailors aboard the brig. The first lieutenant confirmed what Captain Jackson already knew from the stench: There were slaves on board. Jackson demanded that the master come aboard the *Dallas* with his papers. John Smith came aboard with a copy of the Banda Oriental's commission in Spanish and nothing more. Any logbooks, inventories, or business papers had already gone over the side. Smith played the part of the lost mariner out of food and water and headed to the St. Johns River to resupply. Jackson didn't buy the story. The St. Johns River lay far to the south, and the entrance was easily seen from the sea. He had the crew of the *Antelope* brought aboard the *Dallas* as prisoners. Meanwhile, the boarding party counted the cargo: "two hundred and eighty-one African Negroes and the bodies of two others who were dead lying on the deck." Of the 331 people John Smith later said were taken from the African coast, fifty had already died. Smith, who was too kind a man to harm his kidnapped white captive Cornelio Coppinger, was brutal enough to transport African captives in conditions that killed fifty human beings. Those conditions would soon kill even more.[19]

Jackson ordered the prize crew to take the *Antelope* into St. Marys. The light winds of summer made it slow going. The ships did not cross the St. Marys bar until evening of the next day, June 30, and not until July 1 did the *Antelope* drop anchor off the town. Meanwhile, the small cutter did not carry enough water or food to supply the more than 300 people aboard the *Antelope*, its own crew, and the U.S. soldiers. The result was inevitable. Even as they reached the town of St. Marys, Second Lieutenant James Knight remembered that "this day another of the Negroes died." Provisions and water were finally taken to the ship, where, according to Captain Jackson, there were now 280 living captives. After a few days organizing affairs in St. Marys, the *Dallas* left for Savannah on July 4, 1820, with the officers and crew of the *Antelope* as prisoners. The *Antelope* and the captives were left in charge of First Lieutenant William Askwith at St. Marys. The cutter made a swift passage and arrived in Savannah on the evening of July 6, causing quite a stir. The next day the prisoners were examined publicly by the mayor, the examination covered fully by the city's newspapers, and then the prisoners were committed to the city jail.[20]

Captain John Jackson gave a brief account of the capture of the *Antelope* in an affidavit on July 10 in Savannah. He also swore that there were 280 African captives aboard the ship. His second officer, James Knight, gave his account, which was virtually identical except that he swore there were 278 African captives. After several days in Savannah the United States District Attorney for Georgia, Richard Wylly Habersham, ordered John Jackson to bring the *Antelope* and her captives to Savannah. Habersham also wrote his superior, Secretary of State John Quincy Adams, on July 19, reporting that there were "about two hundred and seventy Africans on board" the ship that had been captured. He asked specifically what instructions Adams or President James Monroe had for him regarding the captives. Adams received the letter on July 27, several days after the Africans arrived in Savannah. Instead of replying, he sent it forward to the president.[21]

Meanwhile, the *Dallas* returned to St. Marys and found that the *Antelope* had moved. She was anchored off Point Peter, where there was a U.S. Army fort. It was also a location with easy access to river landings not visible from either the fort or the town. First Lieutenant William Askwith, the prize master of the *Antelope*, had only served on the *Dallas* for a short time. Captain Jackson did not fully trust him. Concerned that the move represented an attempt to land captives surreptitiously, Captain Jackson ordered the *Antelope* to follow him into Cumberland Sound. There they anchored a good distance from shore. Lieutenant Askwith reported that there had been six deaths since the revenue cutter's departure for Savannah. A count of the captives aboard turned up only 261. Askwith could not account for as many as 13 missing captives. He had no bodies, no accounts of their deaths. Perhaps there had been a terrific miscount? Counting sick, dying captives piled in a dark, crowded slave deck while dealing with the stench produced by months of captivity must have been difficult. Even Second Lieutenant Knight and Captain Jackson had differed by two in the numbers they reported. Captain Jackson clearly suspected that Askwith had sold the missing captives as slaves. Jackson would never officially accuse Askwith of this, but Askwith was soon transferred from the *Dallas* and never received his share of prize money. The mystery of the missing captives still unresolved, the two ships sailed for Savannah. Three more captives died during the voyage. Not until July 24, 1820, were the 258 living captives turned over to the U.S. Marshal at Savannah, John H. Morel.[22]

Morel was a slave owner and a planter from a leading Georgia family. He owned 125 acres of rice lands in Chatham County near Savannah, and the lucrative Cottenham plantation, a large tract along the Ogeechee River in Bryan County that was one of the most productive Sea Island cotton plantations in Georgia. Morel had a reputation as a hard man and a harsh slave master. Suddenly taking charge of 258 people in a small city like Savannah would have challenged even a kinder man. Three days after taking responsibility for the captives, Morel wrote to Secretary of State John Quincy Adams, clearly overwhelmed by the demands of the situation. First, he explained that he had received a total of 258 Africans. "Many of them are in bad state of health," Morel wrote, "and when received by me entirely naked and had been on short allowance for some time." Morel then offered a quick list of the emaciated captives:

Captives of the *Antelope*

44	men	supposed	age	from	20 a 40
45	"	"	"	"	10 a 20
82	Boys	"	"	"	5 a 10
23	Women	"	"	"	15 a 20
40	ditto	"	"	"	10 a 15
24	Girls	"	"	"	5 a 10[23]

Marshal Morel was probably not shocked to learn that of the 331 original captives, 22 percent had been lost. Of those, at least sixty persons were known dead, and thirteen were missing. Nor would the starved, sick, naked, and dehydrated state of the captives have surprised anyone familiar with the slave trade. The distribution between male and female among the Africans was not unusual for the slave trade, either; about two-thirds male and one-third female. The sense of shock in the marshal's letter came from the fact that 83 percent of the captives were under twenty years of age. The average age of the captives was about fourteen, maybe younger. Most nauseating of all, 41 percent of the captives, 106 children, were between five and ten years of age. Later records revealed that at least eight of the captives were between two and five years old. The terror of captivity, of sale, of capture at sea by force of arms, of voyage and shipwreck, of deliberate starvation and thirst, and the grisly deaths of at least sixty fellow captives: all this horror had been inflicted upon children.[24]

The captives had survived the first passage—the journey from capture to sale in Africa. They had survived the Middle Passage; the voyage across the Atlantic to the Americas. Free at last from the hold of the *Antelope* and its stench of death, free at last of an increasingly desperate captain and crew, free at last from starvation and thirst, the children were now at the mercy of the people of Savannah.

The long and desperate final passage of the captives had only just begun.

PART TWO

SAVANNAH

EXCHANGE.

Savannah's Exchange building during the 1820s.

CHAPTER 6

"A distinction is taken between men, who are generally free, and goods, which are always property."

Chief Justice John Marshall *The Antelope*, 23 U.S. 66, 122 (1825)

Richard Wylly Habersham was the United States Attorney serving the Federal District Court of Georgia, and would be the federal official in charge of the developing *Antelope* case in Savannah. The illegal slave trade, piracy, and admiralty law were all part of federal jurisdiction, and under the 1819 Slave Trade Act, all illegally imported slaves came under federal control. U.S. Attorney Habersham would have the first say in how these cases proceeded.

Richard W. Habersham bore one of the most distinguished names in the city. His grandfather, a young London merchant named James Habersham, had come to the colony of Georgia with the evangelist George Whitfield in 1738. James Habersham was a devoted Christian, part of the first Great Awakening that shook the British Atlantic world in the mid-eighteenth century. Soon, Habersham ran the Bethesda Orphans Home outside Savannah while Whitfield traveled and preached. Finding that directing the orphanage finances was not so great a burden, in the 1740s, Habersham began a mercantile partnership in Savannah with Francis Harris. Habersham and Harris soon became Savannah's leading merchant house. With the introduction of slavery to Georgia in 1750, Habersham began to buy land and build rice plantations in the region around Savannah. By 1773, James Habersham owned 10,000 acres and 198 slaves and was the president of the Governor's Council. Then, in the midst of growing political conflict, James Habersham died in August of 1775. His will split his three plantations and 200 slaves equally between his three sons.[1]

His eldest son and namesake, James Habersham Jr., enhanced the family investments, even though his father had once had little confidence in the young man. The elder Habersham was worried that James was too much a "Gentleman" to thrive in business. Thinking it was just the thing to improve the boy, he forced James Jr. into a partnership with his hard-headed and business-focused cousin, Joseph Clay. James Jr. was absolutely miserable. He would have much preferred to partner with his good friend Richard Wylly. After his father's death, James Habersham Jr. married Esther Wylly, tying himself to Richard Wylly's successful West Indian merchant family. James Jr. was a patriot during the Revolution, but he did not become famous like his brothers, Joseph and John. While his brothers led troops in battle, James Jr. served as a member of the Georgia General Assembly. He helped finance the rebellion in Georgia and outfitted privateers during the war. When Savannah fell to the British in late 1778, James Jr. fled to Charleston, and when Charleston fell in 1780, he fled to Virginia. He had no interest in collaboration with the British occupiers. After the war he was elected Speaker of the Georgia General Assembly and built the brick Federal style mansion now known as the Pink House on Reynolds Square. James Habersham Jr. died suddenly in 1799, possibly due to suicide in response to either his wife's death or a serious lawsuit facing the family.[2]

His son, Richard Wylly Habersham, was born in Savannah in 1786 and named after his father's good friend. His mother and father died when Richard was thirteen, and soon after he was sent north to attend the College of New Jersey (later known as Princeton University). He graduated in 1805 and returned to Savannah. Richard was supposed to inherit Silk Hope, a plantation on the Ogeechee River about six miles south of the city. In 1798, however, creditors had filed massive lawsuits against his father, and the cases were finally settled about the time Richard finished college. Silk Hope plantation was lost. Instead of a life of ease in Savannah as the master of a large rice plantation, Richard W. Habersham read law and established a law practice. Despite his highly honored name, he led the life of a successful professional, not that of a wealthy heir. While clearly among Savannah's elite, Habersham possessed modest wealth. In 1819, he owned no real property in Savannah, though he did own four slaves. In March of that year he was offered a permanent appointment as the U.S. Attorney for the District of Georgia. He gladly accepted.[3]

During the first thirty-two years of his life, Richard W. Habersham had not been a very notable man. In May of 1820, however, that changed. The case of the *Isabelita*, involving slaves smuggled into Georgia from Amelia Island, had caused political and legal controversy. Many of the smuggled slaves had been captured at the Creek Indian Agency on the Flint River. The Indian Agent there was former Georgia governor David B. Mitchell, a powerful state politician with extensive connections among both the Savannah elite and Creek leaders. Suspicion swirled around Mitchell, and evidence suggested that slave smuggling had occurred numerous times. In May of 1820, the federal circuit court met in Milledgeville, Georgia's tiny frontier capital. U.S. Attorney Richard W. Habersham had received documents and other evidence from John Clark, the sitting governor of Georgia, detailing former governor David Mitchell's complicity in the illegal slave trade. This may have been part of a political ploy; Governor Clark and Mitchell were on opposite sides in an ongoing political struggle between violently warring factions. Regardless, Habersham found the documents convincing.[4]

Habersham went to the grand jury and obtained an indictment against Mitchell for the unlawful introduction of Africans into the United States. After hearing of this indictment, the two federal circuit court judges asked Habersham to join them in their chambers. Neither judge wanted to be entangled in Georgia's wild and violent politics; nor did they think it wise for the U.S. Attorney to get involved. Governor Clark had fought Indians on the frontier, killed a man in a duel, and horsewhipped a political enemy on the streets of the capital. Former governor Mitchell had shot and killed a Federalist opponent in a duel. Both men had powerful and devoted followers. District court judge William Davies and Supreme Court Justice William Johnson suggested to Habersham that it was unwise for him to continue with the indictment. Habersham insisted that he must follow the law. The judges warned him again, and Habersham doggedly insisted that he would continue with the prosecution. If any characteristic stood out during Habersham's career as U.S. Attorney, it was his stubbornness and sense of duty. Habersham saw it as a question of honor.[5]

Returning to the courtroom, the judges took up the indictment and ruled that a two-year statute of limitations on criminal prosecution in the case had passed. "We therefore think it nugatory, and even illegal, to institute prosecutions at this late date," they wrote, and the case was dismissed. Outraged, Habersham dashed off a quick letter of complaint to the Milledgeville newspapers and departed for Savannah in a huff. The confused grand jurors, abandoned in the middle of a term by the U.S. Attorney, struggled for a response. They published a resolution stating that while they did not want to impugn the character of any public servants, "they still feel it their duty to state there [has] been a flagrant violation of the laws of the United States . . . and that the perpetrators of this crime have not been brought to justice." While Habersham's stubbornness did not make him any friends among the judges, the grand jury evidently thought he was right. So, too, did many newspapers across the state. Richard W. Habersham, given his great sense of honor, knew it for certain. This powerful sense of rectitude would shape Habersham's most important work.[6]

On July 6, 1820, the revenue cutter *Dallas* had arrived in Savannah with John Smith and the crew of the *Antelope* aboard as prisoners.

After a night under guard aboard ship, the prisoners were brought before Savannah's mayor in the long room of the City Exchange. Mayor Thomas U. P. Charlton questioned the men, as did the editors of Savannah's two leading newspapers. The *Savannah Georgian* concluded that almost all the prisoners were foreigners, while the *Savannah Republican* decided that almost all were Americans. Clearly, the *Antelope* crewmen were a slippery lot. Why this mattered was made clear the next day. The *Republican* ran a brief account of the voyage, and below it an item entitled "Piracies and Kidnapping." The United States Congress had passed a new law on piracy, the paper noted. The editor summarized the law for his readers: "Citizens seizing negroes on foreign shores, for the slave trade &c., adjudged pirates shall suffer death. Citizens on board foreign vessels [engaged] . . . in the slave trade, [are] declared pirates and to suffer death." While crossing the Atlantic and wandering through the Caribbean searching for a place to sell the captives, the *Antelope*'s crew may have imagined many outcomes, but surely none had imagined that they would face piracy charges for merely trading in slaves. After arriving at Savannah's jail on the common south of the city, what a piracy conviction could mean became very clear to the crew of the *Antelope*.[7]

Smith and his crew were not the only pirates imprisoned in the jail. Ralph Klintock had been first officer on the *Young Spartan*, a smuggling and pirate ship captured by the *Dallas* in June 1818. Klintock was convicted of piracy in Savannah's Federal Court, and the case was appealed to the Supreme Court. The Supreme Court dismissed the objections of Klintock's counsel and sent the case back to Savannah. There Judge William Davies sentenced him to hang. Klintock was one of four pirates given death sentences in Savannah that day. These four were among the forty-five convicted pirates under federal death sentence discussed at a March 1820 cabinet meeting in Washington. As John Quincy Adams, the secretary of state, recalled, "all were cases of privateers under South American colors." The problem of Americans taking up revolutionary privateering commissions as a cover to piracy had grown to a crisis level, and the Caribbean had become a lawless and deadly place. Something had to be done, but President Monroe thought hanging forty-five men in the next month would be excessive. As a result, the cabinet examined the files of the convicted pirates to identify "fit subjects for mercy." Finally, the president decided that "public justice and example required the execution of two in each [of five cities], or a total of ten men." John Furlong and Ralph Klintock were the two men chosen to die at Savannah.[8]

John Furlong was hanged as a pirate on April 28, 1820, on Savannah's common. The "immense crowd" was disappointed when Furlong's neck broke and there was no entertaining struggle at the end of the rope. Ralph Klintock had been scheduled to die that day, too, but the president deferred his hanging for two months, until June 28. On June 22, a second reprieve postponed Klintock's hanging for another two months. President Monroe's uncertainty came down to Ralph Klintock's testimony. He testified that he had worked in concert with two leading citizens of Savannah: the collector of customs, Archibald S. Bulloch, and James S. Bulloch, a wealthy planter, merchant, and lawyer. At trial, Klintock's attorney had submitted documentary evidence, in James S. Bulloch's handwriting, to support these accusations. Somehow, those papers were later lost by the clerk of court. That clerk, John Glen, happened to have a sister who had married into the Bulloch family. John Quincy Adams was convinced that the entire Bulloch clan was involved in the illegal slave trade and other crimes. Adams wrote Monroe that he had seen evidence that the Bullochs were "accessories to the piracy . . . , both before and after the fact." He argued that if James S. Bulloch was not protected by his family connection to Senator John Elliott of Georgia, Bulloch would have been tried for piracy and hanged. Fearing that Klintock's execution might cover up corruption by federal officials, but believing that Klintock deserved to die, President Monroe dithered.[9]

Meanwhile, Ralph Klintock deteriorated in jail, confined in irons, awaiting his turn on the scaffold. In late July, soon after the *Antelope* officers and crew arrived in jail, U.S. Marshal John H. Morel wrote Adams with his concerns about the health of the prisoner. Characterizing his condition as "truly deplorable," he reported that the prison physician believed that unless the irons were removed, Klintock would die. On his own initiative, Morel had removed the irons. "I am fearful he cannot survive the summer," he explained. "He entered prison a hearty man," but after being confined for more than two years in irons he had become "a mere skeleton."[10]

Seeing this "mere skeleton" languishing in the jail, and hearing of Furlong's hanging just two months before, the *Antelope* crew must have wondered about their future. The piracy case against them was already under way. Captain John Jackson and his second officer, James Knight, took a chest confiscated from the *Antelope* to the office of the collector of customs in Savannah. There Jackson and Knight opened the chest and made an inventory of the contents, including sixty pages of John Smith's personal papers. Usually all the papers aboard a captured slaver disappeared. While any inventories, logbooks, and other cargo and voyage-related documents from the *Antelope* had gone over the side, Smith must have thought that the papers in his sea chest were harmless. Most of the papers related to John Smith's life as a merchant ship's officer in the Atlantic world. Included were a bill from a Baltimore tailor for a captain's blue coat with gilt buttons, a privateering commission from Gregor McGregor at Amelia Island, clearance papers from Bahia, and entry papers for Montevideo. These papers also told a bit of Smith's history. He had visited Montevideo in 1817, followed by Bahia, Brazil, and then the island of St. Martin. In May of 1819, he had sailed from St. Thomas to New York.[11]

Two documents, however, revealed something more. The first was a passport issued in France at La Rochelle on July 30, 1814. It read that John Smith, age twenty-three, was a native of New York and an American citizen who had been a prisoner of war of the English. Smith had served on an American privateer during the War of 1812, had been captured, and then somehow escaped a British prison. The passport included a written description: he had black hair, blue eyes, a round chin, and a long face. A second document in the chest had been issued in Philadelphia on January 9, 1811. It attested that John Smith, age twenty, five foot six, with a scar on his left thigh, was a native of the city of New York and an American citizen. This was a sailor's "protection," a document of citizenship intended to protect American sailors from being pressed into the British navy. Presumably, Smith fit both documents' descriptions. The implications were significant. If he was an American citizen, then under the May 15, 1820, Act to . . . Punish the Crime of Piracy, he was, by engaging in the slave trade, a pirate facing death.[12]

As the crew of the *Antelope* marched back and forth from the jail on the south common to three days of meetings with various officials in Savannah, they saw most of the city. It was not impressive. The *Columbia* had departed from Baltimore, which was then the third largest city in the United States, with more than 62,000 inhabitants. Savannah counted only 7,523 people in the 1820 census. About half the city's population was white, and among the whites, 590 were men engaged in commerce. This was twice as large a percentage of men engaged in commerce as was found in Charleston or other southern cities, reflecting Savannah's rapidly growing role in the marketing of cotton. Another 544 of Savannah's white men worked as skilled laborers and mechanics. The 1820 census reported 3,075 slaves and 582 free people of color but did not bother to tally their occupations.[13]

The census numbers were misleading. Savannah's population was not steady; it varied wildly with the seasons. In late fall and winter, people poured in, and Savannah bustled with activity. Scores of small schooners, sloops, and barges arrived from coastal plantations bearing rice and Sea Island cotton for the warehouses. Factors, the commercial men who acted as agents for planters, arranged the sale of these commodities and grew rich from their 2.5 percent commission. Rafts, pole boats, and, by 1820, even steamboats, brought timber, tobacco, and ever increasing amounts of short-staple cotton downriver from the interior. As this cotton commerce grew, so did the income of the factors, bringing great wealth to Savannah. Meanwhile, dockworkers came from the North to load and unload the ships that carried these products throughout the Atlantic world. During the busy winter season, hundreds of sailors and dockworkers sought adventure and release in the taverns and fleshpots of Yamacraw, New Leeds, and Spring Hill on the west side of the city. The wealthy elite celebrated the season with dress balls, gambling, and horse racing. The new Savannah Theatre welcomed rich and poor alike with Shakespeare and lighter fare. In 1821, one resident estimated that the population of Savannah in the winter exceeded 9,000 people.[14]

Summer was the doldrums. The last bags of cotton and barrels of rice were loaded onto the occasional ships that visited the port. Dockworkers departed for work in the North. There was little commerce and less entertainment, just long, hot days plagued by flies and stinging gnats. Night brought no relief from the heat, but it did bring the high-pitched song of mosquitoes. Malaria and other diseases plagued the city, and fever spread. Many of the wealthy left for cooler and more pleasant climes, the theater closed, and the taverns and disorderly houses hosted diminished numbers of truculent men suffering in the heat. Dueling was common in summer, and largely ignored by the authorities. Perhaps as few as 5,000 people lived in Savannah during July and August, though in 1820 the population fell much lower. This sticky, empty city of heat and sickness was what Captain Smith and his men saw as they were shuttled about in July of 1820.[15]

Savannah stood on a forty-foot-high sand and clay bluff that ran in a gentle curve for about a mile along the south side of the Savannah River. Below the bluff lay a beach, though by 1820, most of it was covered with wharves and warehouses. Atop the bluff stood the homes, shops, churches, and public buildings of the town. There citizens were safe from floods and storm surges, but these structures were reachable only by a laborious climb in soft sand. John Smith and his men were first taken for questioning to the City Exchange. Built in 1799, the exchange was the hub of the city and functioned as city hall and a meeting place for civic activities. It stood on the center of the bluff, its steeple and bell towering more than 100 feet above the river. From the steeple, on a clear day, lookouts could see all the way to the Atlantic Ocean. Savannah's unique grid pattern of streets and squares was also visible from the steeple. On each square, house lots stood to the north and south, public buildings or large mansions to the east and west. A city water pump and cistern occupied the center. By 1820 the city had grown to 16 squares, and more were planned.[16]

In 1820, the streets and the ramps down to the river were unpaved. Most residents claimed the sand streets made for a restful quiet, a city free of the cacophony of hooves and wagon wheels on cobblestones. Others disagreed. When Jonathan Mason visited, he wrote that the city had no charms: "It is a wooden town on a sand heap." He likened walking through the deep sand of the streets to wading through snow-drifts in Boston. Another visitor explained, "[O]ne sinks at every step up to the ankles in sand; and in windy weather the eyes, mouth and nostrils are filled with it." Even George Washington commented on the sand streets during his 1791 visit, noting dryly that "walking was disagreeable."[17]

On the east side of downtown the bluff dropped abruptly to marshland. At the last extremity of the bluff, overlooking the river approaches from the sea, stood Fort Wayne. Behind the fort were the old military barracks and Carpenter's Row, and next to them Washington Ward. This area was commonly known as the old fort neighborhood, and it hosted many of Savannah's poor whites and some free blacks. Beginning at Fort Wayne, the remnants of fortifications built during the War of 1812 still ringed the city. These walls, ditches, and redoubts delineated the highest land of the bluff, but they also interfered with the growth of the city. In June of 1820, the Savannah City Council decided to remove them. Instead of appropriating money and hiring workers, it was resolved that the city marshal should "require the service of the free male negroes" to level the old fortifications. There were about two hundred free black men old enough to be part of this draft. "In case of refusal or neglect of any such free male negroe to work as required," the resolution continued, "The Marshall . . . is hereby required to commit the same to gaol." Perhaps no one could sell Savannah's free blacks in 1820, but the council thought the city entitled to their labor.[18]

More than three thousand slaves lived in Savannah, but the city council considered them private property and did not feel entitled to their labor. Nonetheless, the labor of slaves lay at the heart of Savannah's economic growth. Between 1810 and 1819, that growth had been extraordinary. Savannah's population increased by more than 40 percent during that decade, while the value of goods shipped from the city more than doubled. The key factor was increasing short-staple cotton production in the up-country, spurred by high prices and growing demand for cotton in the textile mills of Europe. The high price for cotton also dramatically increased the demand for credit and slaves in the up-country, and Savannah provided both. Slaves, mostly from Maryland and Virginia, passed through Savannah on their way to new plantations. *Niles' Weekly Register*, the closest thing the United States had to a national news journal, commented on the extent of domestic slave trade in the summer of 1817. "The trade has greatly increased in the last two or three years, during which it is thought twenty thousand have been introduced into Georgia alone." The large numbers of slaves passing through Savannah, many handled by factors taking their 2.5 percent commission, only added to the wealth of the city. So too did an associated business, finance.[19]

Planters often borrowed money to buy slaves, and they borrowed money to buy land and expand production. Some of this money flowed from planter's factors, but increasingly banks offered loans. In 1807, the General Assembly had chartered the Planter's Bank of the State of Georgia, and in 1812, that bank moved into James Habersham Jr.'s old mansion in Savannah. By 1815, the Planter's Bank was so profitable that the dividends from the state's stock holdings were enough to pay the salary of every state official. The legislature expected even greater dividends when they chartered the Bank of the State of Georgia in Savannah in December of 1815, retaining a greater share of that bank's stock. To generate the profits needed to meet such dividend expectations, these banks and others made ever more risky loans from 1815 to 1819: loans to planters, slave merchants, businesses, and to develop new real estate in the growing city. Between 1815 and 1820 the newly developed Chippewa and Orleans squares became popular places for Savannah's wealthy to build showplace homes. The young British architect William Jay, fresh from Bath, England, arrived in 1817 to build some of the grandest homes in the city. Savannah was on the road to endless growth and prosperity, or so went the many toasts offered during President James Monroe's visit in May 1819. By then, however, air was already leaking from the bubble. Savannah's exports totaled over $14,000,000 from October 1817 through September 1818. The economic collapse of 1819 was so severe that from October 1818 to September 1819, the value of exports fell to about $9,000,000. From October 1819 through September of 1820, the value of exports fell to only $6,000,000. This was a decline of more than 50 percent in just two years. Cotton prices collapsed, credit grew tight, and endless lawsuits began among Savannah's elite for the repayment of huge debts. The financial disaster of 1819 wiped out some of Savannah's wealthiest citizens, but even greater disasters loomed for the city in 1820.[20]

In the early morning hours of January 11, 1820, a fire broke out in Boon's livery stable on the east side of Franklin Square. A strong northwest wind spread the fire quickly, and efforts to contain it were disrupted by the explosions of two large stores of gunpowder in the Market Square. In some ways the explosions were fortunate—the noise woke everyone in the city. As a result only two people died in the inferno, even though the "wooden town on a sand heap" burned rapidly. In twelve hours it was over. The fire destroyed almost every building between Bay Street to the north and Broughton Street to the south, blown by the wind from Jefferson Street to Abercorn Street. Trying desperately to save anything they could, people had piled possessions in the streets and squares. Many of these piles also burned. The fire burned most of Savannah's commercial and municipal buildings as well as many homes. At least 463 buildings were destroyed, leaving hundreds of people homeless and destroying the business center of the city. "It is impossible to describe their feelings of despair," reported the newspaper. "Many hundreds of families are literally naked in the streets; not even clothing was saved."[21]

The physical damage was probably greater than $5,000,000, and the loss of income was even more. Not all businesses had insurance, but those that did were usually insured by the Phoenix Fire Company of London. Facing claims so huge they could offer payment of only half the value of buildings destroyed, the company was financially ruined. The city's leading mercantile house, Andrew Low and Co., lost their building on Johnson Square and more than $150,000 in merchandise. Low joined many others in petitioning President James Monroe to remit the unpaid duties and bonds on imported goods destroyed by the fire. Months later Congress remitted only one-quarter. The lack of capital, reduced insurance proceeds, and the financial impact of the Panic of 1819 meant that rebuilding went slowly. Losses included the almost finished U.S. Customs and Court building, which had been designed by William Jay. The port collector, Archibald S. Bull-och, had to use a room in a local hotel as the Customs House, later moving to the City Exchange. The post office also relocated to the exchange. U.S. Attorney Richard W. Habersham rented space in the City Exchange for his office. Thus, for several years the exchange functioned as a federal building, though the federal courts were forced to meet in the small and inadequate Chatham County Courthouse on Wright Square.[22]

It was in this small courthouse, in a ravaged city, that much of the *Antelope* case played out. Built of red brick in the 1770s, the building was only 60 by 34 feet. There were no hallways; the entrance from Wright Square opened directly into the courtroom. To the left, raised on a dais, was the judge's bench. In front of the bench sat the clerk's desk, and then a large table for the litigants and their attorneys. Behind this table was the bar, a long wooden railing that separated the participants in the proceedings from the public. In the center of the bar was an English-style prisoner's box where defendants sat during criminal trials. On each side of the room, flanking the judge's bench, were jury boxes. The benches for spectators rose incrementally so that all could have a good view. Upstairs were two small rooms for jury deliberations reached by an outdoor staircase. Also outside, behind the courthouse toward Drayton Street, three wooden buildings served as offices for the court. The *Antelope* case began there, in the clerk of court's office.[23]

On July 15, 1820, John Jackson, captain of the *Dallas*, filed a claim in admiralty against the ship and cargo of the *Antelope*. The claim, called a libel in admiralty law, was for salvage, the award of a portion of the value of a vessel and cargo. Under admiralty law salvage was given to those who saved, rescued, or recovered a ship. Four days later, Richard W. Habersham revealed that he had entered the case when he wrote Secretary of State John Quincy Adams reporting the capture of the *Antelope*. The captain and the crew, he explained, were committed for trial as pirates and in the city jail. Habersham also reported that there was "a cargo of about two hundred and seventy Africans on board" and that the ship and captives were being held in St. Marys. He explained that he had followed the new 1819 Slave Trade Act and instructed Captain Jackson to "deliver the negroes into the hands of the Marshal." They would then be at the disposal of the president. Habersham gave a brief version of the *Arraganta* and *Antelope*'s cruises and explained that he had "libeled the vessel on behalf of the United States, but not the negroes." Habersham wrote that the admiralty claims would be complicated. He expected the Portuguese and Spanish vice consuls to file claims for the captives, Captain Jackson had already filed his claim, and even the captured pirate, John Smith, would probably file a claim.[24]

Then, Habersham made a remarkable statement. The reason he had not made a claim for the captives as cargo was because he intended "to interpose a claim for the United States in order to make them a party before the Court." Habersham saw the captives not as property but as parties in the case. In other words, he saw them as free persons with civil rights. His interposition was intended to halt the admiralty proceedings that treated them as property. Habersham believed he was following the 1819 Slave Trade Act, in which "recaptured Africans" were assumed to be free, under the authority of the president, and the capturing officer was required to "deliver every such negro . . . to the marshal of the district." It said nothing about admiralty proceedings to make this possible; the rescued captives were simply supposed to be sent back to Africa. Congress had appropriated $100,000 so that the president of the United States could pay for the maintenance and return to Africa of "recaptured Africans." In his letter Richard W. Habersham also told John Quincy Adams that he intended to protect the *Antelope* captives and to keep them out of the hands of locals. Given the value of the captives if enslaved, and the history of African captives brought to Savannah over the past few years, Habersham was in for a fight.[25]

When the *Antelope* arrived and Captain Jackson turned the captives over to Marshal Morel on July 24, the people of Savannah got their first look at the 258 surviving Africans. The captives were young, and many were sick, but it was estimated that they were worth at least $300 apiece, or $77,400 altogether. Banker and cotton merchant Richard Richardson's astonishing William Jay–designed mansion on Oglethorpe Square was valued at $25,000 in 1820; it was the most valuable house in Savannah. Shipping merchant William Scarborough's William Jay mansion on West Broad Street and Archibald S. Bulloch's William Jay mansion on Orleans Square were valued at $20,000 each. Thus the captives were worth more than the aggregate value of Savannah's three most impressive and stately homes. The property in the city of the Steamboat Company of Georgia, which maintained wharves, warehouses, and other equipment in Savannah to serve seven steamboats, as well as twenty-eight slaves, was valued at $50,000, or two-thirds of the value of the *Antelope* captives if enslaved. Considering the dire condition of Savannah's economy following the Panic of 1819 and the fire of 1820, the arrival of the *Antelope* captives probably seemed a godsend to the struggling businessmen of Savannah. Most thought they knew what would happen: African captives, or "recaptured Africans" as they were often called, were not new to the city.[26]

During the campaign against the "Patriot" regime on Amelia Island in late 1817, three vessels loaded with recaptured Africans were sent into Savannah. The *Tentativa* with 128 captives aboard, the *Politina* with 109 captives, and the *Syrina* with twenty-four captives: All had been captured by the USS *Saranac* off Amelia Island. Archibald S. Bulloch, the collector of customs at Savannah, wrote Secretary of the Treasury William Crawford about the cases, reporting that "the slaves, by order of the Court, [were] delivered over to the Proctor for the captors and the Collector of this port." This meant that the district court put the captives under the authority of the attorney, or proctor, representing the captain of the *Saranac*, and Bulloch himself. Bulloch explained that the African captives had suffered greatly, and he personally wanted to do something to help. "Under . . . the influence of humanity," Bulloch wrote, "it appears to be my duty to interest myself for the sufferers, and having an estate near the city . . . I have taken possession of forty in number." Reflecting the paternalistic rhetoric justifying slavery that was sweeping the South, Bulloch humanely put forty captives to work on his plantation for no pay.[27]

Four months later, in March 1818, William McIntosh, the collector of customs at Brunswick, Georgia, wrote to Treasury Secretary Crawford expressing his frustration over what was happening on Georgia's frontier with Florida. "It is a painful duty," he wrote, "to express to you . . . that African and West Indian negroes are almost daily illicitly introduced into Georgia." The problem was worse than mere permeable borders; Africans "recently captured by our vessels of war and ordered to Savannah, were illegally bartered by hundreds in that city." He explained how the process of bartering in the cases of the *Tentativa* and *Politina* worked. When the ships arrived in Savannah, the U.S. Marshal, John Eppinger, refused to take charge of the captives. He told the district court that "there was no provision made by law for support and maintenance of the slaves." The proctor for Commander John Elton in the *Tentativa* case, Thomas U. P. Charlton, then moved that he and James S. Bulloch take charge of the captives and bond them out to save the government the costs of maintenance. District court judge William Stephens agreed, and Charlton and Bulloch took 102 captives and gave a $20,000 bond, or less than $200 per captive. The captives were then auctioned on Wright Square in front of the courthouse. All involved understood that those giving bonds had no intention of returning the captives. The bond payment was in essence a purchase price that would be forfeited to Charlton and Bulloch, while Charlton and Bulloch's bond given for the whole was a payment to the court. The difference between the two was the profit made by Charlton and Bulloch. Everyone was happy: the "purchaser" with his new African slave, Bulloch and Charlton with their profits, the court with bond money to pay claimants, costs, and attorneys. As the captives were valued at more than $300 each, this was a pretty profitable deal for Charlton and Bulloch.[28]

This case and similar cases in Savannah convinced Secretary of State John Quincy Adams to clean house in the District of Georgia. He could not do anything about Bulloch, who had family connections to a powerful U.S. senator and fell under the authority of the Treasury Department, headed by Georgian William H. Crawford. However, U.S. Marshal John Eppinger was forced to resign in 1818, replaced by John H. Morel. District court judge William Stephens was old and ill; he was replaced by U.S. Attorney William Davies. Robert W. Habersham was appointed to replace Davies as the U.S. Attorney for the District of Georgia. Adams then ordered Habersham to investigate the case of the *Tentativa*. For six months, from February through August of 1820, Habersham tried to recover the bonded captives. He faced significant impediments. Collector Bulloch was politically untouchable, and Thomas U. P. Charlton was the mayor of Savannah. His investigation went nowhere. In the few cases where he got answers from those who had given bonds, they responded that the captives were dead or had been transported to Spanish Florida. As Habersham could visit neither Spanish Florida nor the realm of the dead, he had no way to determine if these claims were true. Ultimately he wrote

John Quincy Adams: "[t]hat negroes have been introduced into the state, in violation of the law, that such negroes have been sold, and that there has been illegal trafficking . . . are facts of which there can be but little doubt." Some of the captives could be found on a plantation more than 100 miles up the Savannah River, Habersham reported, but the cause of rescuing them was lost. John Quincy Adams's attempt to clean up Savannah had failed, and he blamed Richard W. Habersham. He later wrote, "[T]he District Attorney had shown . . . that he was not the man to grapple with deep and deadly villainy supported by wealth and standing in society." Adams clearly had no idea that he had given Habersham an impossible task.[29]

Richard W. Habersham smarted from his inability to recover the captives from the *Politina* and *Tentativa*. He felt his honor impugned when the court prevented his prosecution of former governor Mitchell for engaging in the illegal slave trade. Perhaps he meant to exert control where he could in a city plagued by both disaster and corruption. Perhaps he simply meant to vindicate himself. Whatever the reason, Richard Wylly Habersham decided that the *Antelope* case would be different. He would not let the captives out of the control of the federal government. There would be no bonding out of captives. The captives would be placed in the hands of the U.S. Marshal and stay there until called for by the president. There would be no more sly frauds, no more captives disappearing into the far interior. Richard W. Habersham intended to control the case of the *Antelope* captives until the president returned them to Africa as free people.

In planning for the captives' arrival, U.S. Marshal John H. Morel expected the captives to walk two miles from the waterfront to Savannah's horse racing track, where they would be housed. The naked, sick, and dying children who emerged from the slave ship could not walk anywhere. Morel had to hire William Richardson, a local teamster, to provide wagons for the journey. Richardson lived near Spring Hill on the western edge of town, and he was known to spend time consorting with free blacks and slaves. In 1818, Richardson had been fined by the city council for gambling with slaves. Morel apparently thought this familiarity made Richardson a good choice to work with the captives, and Richardson remained involved throughout the case. Seeing the dreadful condition of the captives, the marshal also hired Dr. Moses Sheftall to treat cases of dehydration and starvation. Dr. Sheftall "found nearly one half the number of them sick, many of whom were very ill, and that at the time they were destitute of clothes and blankets." Having planned that the captives would build their own shelters, the marshal realized that the captives were too weak and too small to do the work. He had to hire men to build sheds at the racetrack. He had to hire cooks, guards, and nurses to take care of the captives. He had to buy blankets and cloth and hire seamstresses to make clothing. The expenses were mounting, but the marshal handed out receipts, assuring everyone that the federal government would pay their bills. During this time, Marshal Morel may also have realized that the *Antelope* captives offered him a significant opportunity, one that he would make good use of later in the case.[30]

The captives' plight was scrutinized from every direction. Another lawyer besides Habersham had realized the implications of the 1819 Slave Trade Act. It occurred to Judge John Macpherson Berrien that the captives from the *Antelope* could go free under the law. Berrien used this to convince revenue cutter captain John Jackson to hire him to handle the case. Jackson gave Berrien the case. If the Africans were free rather than slaves, Berrien realized, then Jackson's salvage claim against them as property would be worthless. To encourage captures, however, the 1819 Slave Trade Act also provided for a $25 bounty per head for captives rescued. Berrien quickly amended Jackson's original libel, claiming either salvage on the value of the captives of the *Antelope* or, alternatively, the $25 bounty per head for captives rescued from the slave trade. Berrien, ever the shrewd attorney, made certain his client would make money from the case however the winds blew.[31]

Those winds were already blowing. Claimants for the captives quickly emerged, drawn by the high value of the *Antelope*'s cargo.

The Spanish vice consul in Savannah, Charles Mulvey, went after the cargo of the *Antelope* in the name of the king of Spain and the Spanish owners. He had no clue who those owners might be, but he libeled the captives anyway. Mulvey apparently sent word to Havana to inquire about the Cuban ship. Word eventually reached the firm of Cuesta Manzanal y Hermano. Santiago de la Cuesta ordered his employees to begin gathering information about the voyage of the *Antelope*. This information would later play a crucial role in the case. Meanwhile, Mulvey's attorneys, Charles Harris and Thomas U. P. Charlton, filed a libel on August 1, claiming that 150 captives were Spanish property. Harris was the former mayor of Savannah and a former U.S. Attorney; he was highly regarded. Charlton, the sitting mayor of Savannah, had also served as superior court judge. He, of course, had experience dealing with illegally imported captives before. These men were formidable members of the bar and leaders in Savannah society.[32]

On August 12, 1820, a third claimant entered the case. Francis Sorrel, vice consul of Portugal, hired James Morrison and John Nicoll to file a libel claiming 130 of the captives. Both lawyers were leading members of the local bar, and Morrison was a member of the city council. If Vice Consul Sorrel dispatched messengers to Brazil or Portugal to inquire about lost ships or slaves, there was no record of it. Sorrel never named any individual or firm as the claimant, leading to suspicions that he was working secretly with those in Savannah who simply wanted a piece of the *Antelope* plunder. Sorrel may also have had ties to the Baltimore investors involved in financing the privateer *Arraganta*. Both libels reflected the information given by the crew of the *Antelope*, who told of capturing both Spanish and Portuguese slaves. Not surprisingly, the claimants apparently cooperated, divvying up the original 280 captives reported by Captain Jackson, with 150 for Spain and 130 for Portugal.[33]

Richard W. Habersham was a slaveholder in a slave society. While not exceedingly wealthy, by birth and family connections he was a leading man in the city of Savannah. He came from the planter class; slaves helped raise his children and cooked and cleaned in his home.

He had made contributions to the American Colonization Society, an organization that intended to help freed American slaves settle on land of their own in a colony in Africa, and which eventually created the nation of Liberia. While not directly critical of slavery itself, the ACS stood staunchly against the slave trade. A number of leading Georgia slaveholders had given the ACS money, mostly in the hope that transportation to Africa would reduce the number of problematic free blacks in American society. Personal interests aside, Habersham knew the 1819 Slave Trade Act. African captives aboard vessels captured while engaged in the slave trade were to be held safely until the president arranged their return to Africa as free persons. The law suggested that captives like those of the *Antelope* were not slaves, but this part of the act had never before been implemented, and no one knew how it was supposed to work. Habersham had received no response to his request for guidance from the president in the July 19, 1820, report to John Quincy Adams. He knew, however, that enforcing the law was his duty. He was going to stand up to what John Quincy Adams had called "deep and deadly villainy supported by wealth and standing in society." Astonishing the entire bar and the elite of Savannah, on August 16, 1820, Richard W. Habersham filed a claim for the United States, asserting that the captives of the slave ship *Antelope* were free.[34]

CHAPTER 7

"That every man has a natural right to the fruits of his own labor is generally admitted, and that no other person can rightfully deprive him of those fruits and appropriate them against his will seems to be the necessary result of this admission."

Chief Justice John Marshall *The Antelope*, 23 U.S. 66, 120 (1825)

D
r. William R. Waring first noticed the unusual fever in his patient on June 26, 1820, almost a month before the *Antelope* captives arrived in Savannah. During the summer and fall of every year many people in Savannah suffered from what physicians of the day called remittent fever and bilious remittent fever: probably malaria. This was considered normal. Waring had already seen plenty of remittent fever that year, especially in the western Yamacraw district. This new case, in Washington Ward on the northeast side of Savannah near the old fort, was different. The patient's fever did not drop in the regular cycle of remittent fever, and he died after just three days. Dr. Waring could have just ignored the implications of this unusual case. He didn't. Two weeks later another man living in Washington Ward "was attacked with Continuous fever . . . and died on the fourth day with haemorrhages [*sic*] from the nose and bowels."

98

The sclerae of the second victim's eyes had taken on a yellow tinge before death. If that did not clearly reveal the disease, at the same time Patrick Stanton, also living in Washington Ward, was "seized by fever" and died after four days on July 16. Stanton's death was accompanied by black vomit, "el vomito negro," the classic sign of the acute hemorrhagic effects of yellow fever. Waring knew then that the city of Savannah was in trouble.[1]

Yellow fever was a feared and mysterious disease in the nineteenth century. Nothing about it seemed to make sense. It began with the same general symptoms as the remittent fever, yet somehow turned into something very different. The disease was not directly contagious: doctors knew from personal experience that contact with victims, their blood, or even the noxious black vomit did not transmit the disease. Yet the disease was usually confined to limited and identifiable areas. It was a disease of place, and doctors searched for the cause. Physicians knew that the disease usually struck cities, so they looked for the cause in the nature of cities. Some argued that organic filth in streets and alleys was the cause, or that the fever resulted from crowding and poor sanitation, or that it was emitted by newly turned moist earth where building was under way. Others thought that yellow fever was simply a further development of remittent fever, somehow turned more malignant, and thus they dubbed the disease "malignant fever." They connected it to the wet areas, swamps, and marshes that doctors also connected observationally to remittent fever. None of these, or other proposed sources, could be proven as causes. Yellow fever seemed to be a miasma of the air located only in specific places. Of course, in a way, that was right.[2]

Yellow fever is a hemorrhagic viral disease transmitted from person to person by the *Aedes aegypti* mosquito. The virus needs concentrations of both mammal hosts and insect hosts to complete its life cycle, so wet and warm cities are an ideal habitat. *Aedes aegypti* reproduce well in incidental cups and containers of rainwater, a situation commonly found on the roofs of buildings and in urban water cisterns, gutters, refuse, and even flowerpots. Able to fly at only about one mile per hour, *Aedes* do not usually travel far from the place of their birth. Newly hatched females need to feed on an infected human within two to four days. The virus then colonizes the mosquito's gut, and within a week to ten days that mosquito can infect humans. The cycle can continue as long as there are mosquitoes and human hosts. Savannah provided nicely concentrated and easily reached human victims combined with plenty of puddles or containers of fresh water needed for breeding.[3]

Yellow fever itself was terrible and terrifying. It began with shaking chills, fever, and aches. Often liver function failed, and the patient's sclera and even skin turned yellow with jaundice. Sufferers usually began hemorrhaging from the gums, the nose, and the gastrointestinal tract. Sometimes the fever broke, and the patient began to recover. For others, vomit filled with half-digested blood spewed in horrible projectile-spasms, the victim racked by excruciating pain. If the hemorrhaging didn't kill the victim, renal failure soon would. Mortality was as high as 50 to 60 percent, and those who developed the fatal form of yellow fever lasted at most a week in horrible agony. Treatments by doctors were worse than useless, though perhaps the bleeding, blistering, and purging hastened the patients' deaths and so limited their suffering. Family members who cared for the dying were often severely traumatized by the events, and in some cases confessed they had begged God to kill their patients.[4]

The only known prevention was flight. As a result, once yellow fever was recognized, a panicked exodus followed. Yellow fever was both a demographic and economic disaster, bringing entire communities to a halt. Business died, storefronts were abandoned, homes were left empty, and ships leaving the afflicted city were quarantined. The presence of yellow fever was the last thing city leaders would admit, for the panic and isolation that would follow was a sure commercial disaster. Places like Savannah did their utmost to control and prevent mortality from any fever, or at least to control the reporting of such mortality. A variety of laws on "dry culture" and limiting passenger arrivals from ships during the fever months were all regulatory attempts to control fever in Savannah. A reputation as a sickly city hurt business.[5]

The winter of 1819–1820 was mild in Savannah, and by March the weather grew warm. This seemed a blessing given the number of people made homeless by the great fire in January. Beginning in March "there were considerable falls of rain," Dr. Waring reported: nine inches from March through May, ten inches during June and July, and in August alone more than thirteen inches of rain fell. Dr. William C. Daniell observed that because of the fire, many of the poorest people were crowded together in inadequate housing, surrounded by filth. Empty lots and open cellars still dotted the central business district. The garbage and trash in lanes and streets of the overcrowded poor districts such as Washington Ward, combined with heavy rain, provided excellent breeding conditions for *Aedes* mosquitoes. By July, physicians Waring and Daniell began to notice the increased mortality from fever and the signs of yellow fever. Rumors of the sickness spread. Waring was sure on July 16 that yellow fever was in the city, and he began to tell others. On July 18, 1820, the *Georgian* printed the reported deaths in the city in June, probably in response to such rumors. Of thirty deaths reported among white Savannahians, fourteen were due to fever. These were not at all unusual numbers, and many people must have felt relieved. On July 22, the *Georgian* again reported deaths in the city, this report covering the first two weeks of July. Of the twenty-one total deaths, fifteen were from fever. Of the fever deaths, only two were residents, and thirteen were "strangers." Again, these numbers probably reassured Savannah's inhabitants, though it was double the death rate of the previous month.[6]

On July 24, the captives from the *Antelope* arrived in the midst of this developing epidemic and were taken from the ship to the horse racing track west of the city. There they were housed in the stables and hastily constructed sheds. Thirty-nine years later, the elite planter Pierce Butler would sell hundreds of his slaves at what may have been the largest slave sale in American history. Hundreds of enslaved people were housed at the same racetrack for this sale in 1859. A correspondent for the *New York Tribune*, Mortimer Thomson, wrote a fascinating account of conditions for these slaves:

> Immediately upon their arrival, they [the slaves] were taken to the Race-course and there quartered in the sheds erected for the accommodation of the horses. . . Into these sheds they were huddled pell-mell, without any more attention to their comfort than was necessary to prevent their becoming ill and unsalable. . . . In these sheds were the chattels huddled together on the floor, there being no sign of bench or table. They eat [sic] and slept on the bare boards, their food being rice and beans, with occasionally a bit of bacon and corn bread.[7]

Conditions at the racetrack in the summer of 1820 were probably similar, except that the 258 *Antelope* captives averaged fourteen years old and were sick, starved, and naked. On July 25, Morel bought 253 blankets for the captives. Presumably they used these to cover their nakedness until August 8, when Miss Mary Deveara delivered 256 shirts for them. Morel paid rent for the race course and hired from the owners five enslaved men to live at the encampment and help with the captives. He hired cooks to prepare food for more than 250 people each day and paid William Richardson to deliver food and supplies to the encampment. A white man, William Williams, and a white woman, Ann Newton, were also hired for "attendance night and day on the Africans." Marshal Morel later claimed to have visited the encampment three times a day, but presumably Williams and Newton ran things in his absence. Dr. Abraham Sheftall, Dr. Moses Sheftall, and Dr. Jacob De La Motta visited the sick Africans at the encampment numerous times. Among other problems, the doctors began to treat increasing numbers of women and girls for venereal disease, suggesting at least one activity that had occupied sailors aboard the *Antelope*. Despite the medical attention, the rest, and the food, deaths among the captives continued. Meanwhile, the marshal's bills were mounting.[8]

Did yellow fever arrive with the *Antelope* captives? "It was said by some individuals," wrote Dr. Waring later in his report, "to have been brought from the coast of Africa, in a brig called the *Ramirez*, which had on board a cargo of new negroes." Was there a carrier aboard the *Antelope*? Was this, perhaps, some grand cosmic payback for the horrors of the slave trade? Waring's answer was no; the fever could not have come aboard the ship because the timing was wrong. The *Ramirez* arrived after the "fever had grown into considerable extent and severity." He insisted that the ship's crew, which had been brought to the city earlier, was healthy. In fact, despite the immunity many believed Africans had to the fever, the *Antelope* captives began to die in large numbers at the racetrack encampment. No one recorded the causes of death, and many deaths may have been lingering results of the conditions suffered aboard ship. Whatever the causes, Marshal Morel reported that twenty-four of the 258 captives, almost 10 percent, died at the encampment in less than a month. William Richardson began to bill the marshal for providing coffins to the encampment.[9]

Sometime in early August one of the captives escaped. Morel placed an ad in local newspapers reporting that there was "Missing from the African encampment at the race ground . . . an African man, 5ft. 8 or 10 inches high, has his country marks on his face and breast." Thinking the man must have been stolen, Morel offered $400 for his return and conviction of the thief. There may have been no thief. Possibly the runaway found help; there were always groups of runaways hiding on the outskirts of Savannah and in Savannah itself. The missing man was never found. Escape was probably easy from the poorly guarded racetrack on the edge of town; only the poor health and youth of most of the captives explain why more did not run away.[10]

There were good reasons to flee the African encampment. Marshal Morel described the captives as in "a starved and naked condition and the greater part of them sick . . . and mostly children." July was rainy, but beginning August 2, it rained for twelve continuous days. August temperatures were measured as high as 96 degrees. The quarters at the race ground became a steaming, mud-filled horror, inhabited by sick children wearing only blankets. As Marshal Morel wrote to John Quincy Adams, it was "a spectacle painful to humanity." Others viewed this spectacle, however, and saw opportunity. On August 9, the Savannah City Council took up the issue of the captives. Alderman Charles Harris moved that the city "receive any number of Africans now in the custody of the Marshall [sic]." Unstated in the unanimous resolution that followed was the fact that the city intended to put the captives to hard physical labor leveling the old city fortifications and repairing the streets. Just as the aldermen believed that they should require the labor of free black men, clearly they also thought the city entitled to the labor of the *Antelope* captives.[11]

Mayor Thomas U. P. Charlton wrote federal judge William Davies that same day, August 9, saying that he wanted "fifty capable of performing the labor required of them." Judge Davies immediately drew up an order in his own hand "that the Marshal deliver over to the Mayor . . . fifty of said slaves (or more)." Twice in the order Judge Davies referred to the captives as "slaves," though their status at law had not yet been determined. On August 14, the mayor reported:

> That in obedience to a resolution of Council passed at the last extra meeting he has selected and receipted to the Marshall [sic] for fifty-one (51) African slaves lately brought into this Port for adjudication and placed them under the direction and care of Mr. William Richardson until the further pleasure of Council is known. These Africans, are adults and boys and with the Exception of two a girl and a boy capable of performing the labour Council may require of them. The most healthy and athletic of these people have been selected and appear cheerfull and happy under the humane and able management of Mr. Richardson.

The reasons for taking on these captives were also made clear. William Richardson had convinced Mayor Charlton that, using plows, the captives could level the earthen fortifications surrounding the city.

The city had received bids for such work ranging between $6,000 and $8,000. Using the captives would save the city a substantial sum. Work began immediately under the "humane" management of Richardson. There were only forty-three men age twenty or older among the captives, so this draft included older teens. As a result, except for the sick, the captives remaining at the encampment were entirely teens and children.[12]

The day before Judge Davies ordered the fifty captives to work for the city, he took up the admiralty case of the *Antelope* and the piracy case against John Smith. On August 8, even before the Portuguese vice consul had filed his libel in the case, the "interested parties" agreed that the ship and her equipment could be sold. Davies described the ship as "dismantled": Probably the shelves, barricades, and other structures necessary to control and house so many captives on a small vessel had been taken apart and the lumber used to build sheds at the racetrack. Davies ordered that since no one had expressed interest in taking the ship on appraisement, it would be sold by the marshal at a public auction, twenty-five days after notice was given to all parties. The next day in chambers, August 9, as he was ordering fifty-one of the captives to work for the city as prisoners, Judge Davies took up a bail motion for John Smith. Even though Smith would be charged with piracy, a capital crime, the judge set bail at $3,000, and a security bond at $2,000. Though Smith had only $500 in his sea chest, he somehow came up with the money, and walked out of jail into a city ravaged by yellow fever.[13]

On August 11, 1820, the city health committee asked four distinguished doctors to join them in investigating the reports of sickness in the eastern parts of Savannah. The doctors found piles of rubbish and trash and large numbers of poor whites living in overcrowded houses and apartments. While they found sickness in Washington Ward, they concluded that the inhabitants were responsible for their own illnesses. "The diseases were too evidently the effects of individual wants or dissipation to make a subject of alarm," explained the official summary of the report. On August 14, the city council resolved that the jail physician should visit and treat sufferers in Washington Ward. Not everyone found the report reassuring. The *Georgian* wrote, "[A]lthough our Health Committee and Medical Societies are silent upon the subject we are induced to believe that a pestilential disease of no mild character rages to a considerable extent in certain portions of our city." The *Columbian Museum and Savannah Gazette* apparently obtained a copy of the health committee's report and went much further. Quoting from the report, and castigating the city council for keeping the report a secret by publishing "favorable but delusive" excerpts, the *Museum* announced that yellow fever was in Savannah.[14]

The response from Savannah's leadership was swift. The *Savannah Republican* likened the reports by the *Columbian Museum* to an "ignorant fellow" screaming, "[M]ad dog! in the streets." The sickness was local, reported the *Republican*, it was not malignant, and it was under control. There was no cause for alarm. The same day, August 15, Mayor Thomas U. P. Charlton posted a notice at the City Exchange and had it printed in the papers. "I feel myself authorized to announce that no pestilence prevails in this city." The sickness, Charlton maintained, was confined to "strangers and people of intemperate and dissolute habits, and is no more than the ordinary bilious fever of the climate." Others attacked the doctors who tried to warn the community. "Qui Improbat," wrote one correspondent to the *Georgian*, "I dislike to hear Doctors, when they lose a patient, cry out *yellow fever*, because it strikes a panic among the illiterate—but the enlightened know it is only to cover their want of skill."[15]

The attacks in the newspapers upon doctors who reported yellow fever, upon the stories of sickness, upon the newspapers questioning official pronouncements, continued for weeks. The mayor's announcement denying the existence of any pestilence was printed regularly in the newspapers. Savannah had suffered so much, first from the national economic panic, and then from the great fire, surely God would not send a plague? Besides, assertions of an epidemic could always be questioned; the diagnosis of yellow fever was not a sure thing in 1820. Doctors struggled to define the fever they observed afflicting an increasing number of people. According to the city death register, during July, 53 white people had been buried, 39 dying from "fever." In August, 119 white people were buried in Savannah, 110 of whom had "fever" listed as the cause of death. Then the sexton of the city burial ground became ill, complicating the record keeping for reliable numbers of deaths from fever. Meanwhile, the city council and mayor continued to insist that there was no general danger. Local newspapers reported yellow fever in Philadelphia, Charleston, and New Orleans but reported that only one section of Savannah was "unhealthy."[16]

On September 12, the *Republican*, the closest thing to an official newspaper in Savannah, reported that there were sixteen cases of "dangerous fever" in the city. Four of those cases, they revealed, involved black vomit. This was a breakthrough in public recognition of the epidemic. Two days later Mayor Charlton announced that "the character and the type of the fever is of a malignancy, which renders it prudent . . . to remove beyond the city's atmosphere." On September 19, the city health committee finally used the term "yellow fever" and reported that in the previous twenty-six days at least 202 whites had died of it. During August and September, city officials had begun to track where the deaths were occurring. In August the largest number of deaths had been in Washington Ward, the next largest at the Poor House and Hospital. In September the fever began to move, with only three deaths in Washington Ward on the east side; instead, the largest number of deaths was fifty-five, in Oglethorpe Ward on the west side of the city. The second most common location again was the Poor House and Hospital. In September, 232 whites were buried in Savannah. One merchant wrote a Charleston friend in late September, "There are eight new cases today: and they almost without exception terminate fatally in two or three days. God only knows where its ravages will stop." Just as the mayor and council had feared, "No business is doing in consequence of the unprecedented sickness."[17]

Niles' Weekly Register reported that by mid–October, 6,000 people had fled the city and that the white population remaining in the city totaled only 1,404. William B. Bulloch was one of those who fled. In late September he wrote that it was difficult to "recount the affliction of our deserted and ill-fated city." As for the yellow fever, "few escape—old or young, native or stranger." This probably was not true. An excellent study of the 1854 Savannah yellow fever epidemic found significant variations in mortality rates among different groups. The statistics kept for 1820 were not as clear as those for 1854, but some generalities emerge. The 1820 epidemic was first concentrated in Washington Ward, but by September the concentration moved to the west side in Oglethorpe Ward. These were areas of the city with the poorest inhabitants, though every ward suffered some deaths. In August and September, 132 people died of fever at the Poor House and Hospital. Nonresidents died in much larger numbers than residents, though exactly what these terms meant was not made clear. The fever hit people in their twenties the hardest, while children apparently died at a lower rate.[18]

Despite these generalities, there were plenty of deaths among Savannah's white elite who remained in the city. Three of the four doctors asked by the city to investigate the fever died. One of the three who died was Dr. Richard M. Berrien, the half-brother of Judge John M. Berrien. Despite the flight of so many people, in October, 202 more people died of fever. Even Mayor Charlton's family did not escape. On October 16, his wife, Emily, died of the fever. The reassurances he had so glibly given so many times about the health of the city must then have tasted as ashes.[19]

By the end of October the number of deaths began to decline, and in November only 53 people died of fever. In December, it was only 10. Doctors investigating the epidemic later concluded that the fever killed one in five of Savannah's white population. The city death register recorded 642 white deaths due to fever from June through December of 1820. Henry P. Russell created an "Official Register," listing the deaths of 695 whites by name, and in December of 1820 he began selling the register to grieving families. On the last page of the Official Register he estimated that some 200 people of color had died, making a total of 895 deaths in the city. Russell apologized for being unable to print the names of these colored victims. No one had bothered to record the black burials.[20]

Throughout this disaster, in which probably more than nine hundred people died, fifty-one captives from the *Antelope* who worked for the city continued to do so. Richard Habersham reported this to John Quincy Adams at the end of August, saying that the fifty-one were "now well clad and comfortably lodged within the city, and are employed in leveling the streets and other light work." Marshal Morel also wrote Adams four days later to explain the situation further, saying that the fifty-one taken by the city "are now well attended to and to all appearances happy under these circumstances, combining humanity with economy." Of course, the city where these captives were forced to labor was approaching the peak of a yellow fever epidemic, so while the economy of their forced labor was clear, the humanity of it all was less certain.[21]

While many whites assumed that all Africans were immune to yellow fever, immunity poses a confusing issue. If a person suffered yellow fever and survived, that person had a lifelong resistance to that strain of the virus. Children were less likely to die from the fever, and anyone who grew up where yellow fever was endemic often developed a meaningful immunity to the disease. There is no clear medical evidence of any genetic immunity to yellow fever among Africans. Whether they had any resistance to the virus or not, the fifty-one captives taken by the city were forced to labor through the worst of the plague. These captives leveled the fortifications, repaired roads, and cleaned up trash and rubble. It is probable they were also used to collect the dead and dying, even to dig graves for victims. During the epidemic, nine of the fifty-one captives who worked for the city died, but the causes were not recorded.[22]

In mid-August, the marshal decided to move the remaining 184 captives from the race ground encampment. Conditions there were terrible, and, while young, the captives could surely be useful at some sort of work. Alluding to but without speaking of the epidemic, Morel wrote John Quincy Adams that the captives were "at risk of increased disease by the number collected together at this season." "It was suggested," Morel continued, "by persons of the best probity that I had better distribute these Africans, and have them in the hands of humane persons resident in the city or the immediate neighborhood." He assured Adams that the captives would be "clothed, fed, and treated with kindness." He also reminded him, "You will observe that by far the greater part of these people are small, and only fit for work in houses or gardens." Of the captives remaining at the racetrack, half were under ten years old, the other half between ten and twenty years old. On August 20, 1820, Morel parceled out as many of the captives as he could to seventeen "humane persons." For the most part these were wealthy planters or businessmen who already owned slaves. While some captives went to work on plantations close to Savannah, most were moved into domestic service in the city during the height of the yellow fever epidemic. By the end of the year, forty-six captives had died—18 percent mortality during the first six months in Savannah. Less than a year before, in March of 1820, at least 331 captives left Cabinda bound for the New World. By February of 1821, more than a third of those captives were dead.[23]

CHAPTER 8

"If [the slave trade] is consistent with the law of nations, it cannot in itself be piracy."

Chief Justice John Marshall *The Antelope*, 23 U.S. 66, 122 (1825)

Richard Wylly Habersham was a man of principle and honor, but he would be tested in the case of the *Antelope*. As U.S. Attorney, Habersham wore two hats. First, he was the prosecuting attorney in the piracy case against John Smith. Second, he was the proctor for the United States in the admiralty case seeking freedom for the *Antelope* captives. Existing law, reinforced by a recent Supreme Court case, *The Josefa Segunda*, meant that success in one role would almost certainly produce failure in the other. Habersham was on the horns of a very difficult dilemma.

The Josefa Segunda involved the disputed ownership of captives found aboard a slave ship that had been taken by privateers. In many ways the case resembled that of the *Antelope*, and Habersham probably saw it as a guide as well as direct precedent. A Cuban slave ship on its return from Africa, the *Josefa Segunda* was captured off the south coast of Haiti in February of 1818 by a privateer with a Venezuelan commission. The privateer, the *General Arismendi*, voyaged leisurely with her prize to the mouth of the Mississippi River, where the *Josefa*

111

Segunda entered the river and anchored. There she was captured by a revenue officer assisted by some United States soldiers, who found 152 African captives aboard. Taken upriver to New Orleans, the ship and the captives were confiscated by local authorities. At that time, before the March 3, 1819, Slave Trade Act, local law controlled the fate of such captives. Under Louisiana law the surviving captives were sold at public auction. Carricabura, Arieta & Co. in Havana, the Cuban firm that had financed the original slaving voyage, objected to the confiscation and sale of both their ship and the slaves. They sued, lost, and appealed. Their appeal reached the Supreme Court in the winter of 1820.[1]

In March of 1820, Justice Henry Brockholst Livingston delivered the opinion of the Court. While there were a number of issues in the case, the most compelling one was the ownership of the 152 African captives. The Supreme Court ruled that the core consideration in deciding ownership of the captives was whether the captor was a legitimate privateer or a pirate. "It would indeed be unreasonable and unjust to visit upon the innocent owners of this property the sins of a pirate," wrote Livingston. If the captor was indeed a pirate, the "property" should be returned to the owners in Havana. Then, Justice Livingston turned to the facts of the case, asking, "But is it so; was the *General Arismendi* a piratical cruiser?" "The Court thinks not," he answered. "Among the exhibits is a copy of a commission, which is all that in such a case can be expected." He set a very low bar for this commission; its simple existence was enough, even though Venezuela was then a revolutionary republic not formally recognized by the United States. As the *General Arismendi* was a legitimate privateer, the captives were no longer the property of the Havana slave-trading firm. "This capture," explained Livingston, "having been made under a regular commission of the government of Venezuela, the captors acquired thereby a title to the vessel and cargo." The cargo, of course, was 152 human beings.[2]

The implications for the *Antelope* case were clear. If U.S. Attorney Habersham zealously prosecuted John Smith and obtained a conviction for piracy, the captives could be returned as "cargo" to the previous owners, Spanish and Portuguese slavers. As proctor for the United States' claim in admiralty, and believing that under United States law the captives were free, this result was unacceptable to Habersham. The captives in the *Josefa Segunda* were doomed to be slaves either way, but this was not the case for the *Antelope* captives. If John Smith was a commissioned privateer and so had title to the captives as slaves, then based on the *Josefa Segunda* decision and the new 1819 Slave Trade Act, the captives would be returned to Africa and freedom. The captives' best chance of freedom, then, required John Smith's acquittal of piracy. Habersham had to weigh these two outcomes, his duty, his principles, and his honor. His choices can only be inferred from events.[3]

On December 14, 1820, a federal grand jury in Savannah found three true bills against John Smith for piracy. The first indictment charged that Smith had attacked a French ship and stolen, among other items, "one four inch new Hawser" and a "deck awning," the combined value of which was $25. The second indictment was for attacking, looting, and carrying away an unknown Portuguese ship worth $1,000 and a cargo of cloth worth $20. The third indictment was for attacking and carrying away the *Antelope*, valued at $3,000. U.S. Attorney Habersham carefully kept any suggestion that the captives were property that could be stolen out of these indictments. The form of the indictments charged Smith under "An Act to Protect the Commerce of the United States and Punish the Crime of Piracy," enacted March 3, 1819. This law provided that anyone who "shall, upon the high seas, commit the crime of piracy as defined by the law of nations . . . shall . . . be punished by death." Surprisingly, Smith was not charged under any of the federal laws concerning the slave trade; nor was he charged under the law that kept the 1819 piracy law in force. That law, An Act to Continue in Force An Act to Protect the Commerce of the United States and Punish the Crime of Piracy, and Also to Make Further Provisions for Punishing the Crime of Piracy, enacted May 15, 1820, had defined more fully the meaning of piracy. It included piracy on the high seas under the law of nations as well as the robbery of a ship, its crew, or any of its contents while in an estuary or river, all punishable by death. Most importantly, the 1820 Piracy Act made participation by United States citizens in the slave trade piracy also punishable by death. The grand jury's failure to charge under the 1820 Piracy Act raised some significant questions.[4]

When Smith was first brought to Savannah as a prisoner in July of 1820, the *Republican* made clear the general expectation that he and his crew would be charged with piracy under the 1820 Piracy Act. Copies of the text of the new law had arrived just weeks before, so virtually every active attorney would have recently read the new piracy definitions. The president of the United States also knew the new provisions. In July, John Quincy Adams had forwarded Habersham's first report on the *Antelope* to President James Monroe and asked for instructions. In his reply the president wrote that, based on "the act of the 15 of May last, page 102, I am inclined to think that all those concerned in the business who were American citizens . . . will be considered by the Court as pirates." Habersham had received a copy of the president's letter in late August from Adams. The president's comments were the closest thing to instructions Habersham ever received from Washington in the case. The president expected him to prosecute under the 1820 Piracy Act. By the time the president's letter arrived, John Smith had been released on bail, but the actual indictments had not yet been made. Despite the public understandings, despite the president's expectations, in December Smith was not indicted as expected.[5]

There were other puzzling omissions as well. Prosecution witnesses could have provided much evidence concerning the capture of the American schooner *Exchange* and the theft of slaves from that vessel. This was certainly more important than taking an awning from the French ship. Robbing the *Exchange* of its slaves was clearly a piratical act, for neither Venezuela nor the Banda Oriental was at war with the United States. Yet Smith was not indicted for this crime. Nor were there indictments for the *Antelope* detaining and perhaps taking rice from the schooner *Mary* in the Bahamas. Most surprising of all, there was no piracy indictment for the widely reported kidnapping of the governor of Florida's son. The best explanation for these omissions is that they revealed choices made by Habersham on the comparative weight of his contradictory duties.[6]

As a young man, Richard Habersham had struggled to recover financially from the British lawsuit against his father's business. He also became very active in Savannah civic affairs. Politically he sided with the Troupites, the commercially oriented party of Georgia's well-educated elite, which would later become the foundation for the Whig party in Georgia. Bound by a strong sense of duty and rectitude, Habersham gladly risked all when he thought he was right, as was revealed by his conflict with the circuit court in Milledgeville over the slave-trading indictment against former governor David Mitchell. That case also showed that Habersham had no problem persuading a grand jury to indict a powerful man based on questionable evidence. (The John Smith case had very straightforward evidence, and Smith was no more than a cipher in Savannah, so indictments against him would seemingly have had little political cost.) Habersham was also a generous man: an active member of the Union Society, which provided for orphans, an organizer and contributor to the Poor House and Hospital, and, as we have seen, a contributing member of the American Colonization Society. He made clear in his letters to John Quincy Adams that he shared the Colonization Society's disgust with the illegal slave trade. Habersham joined many white southern elites in supporting the society, as it seemed to offer long-term amelioration of the effects of slavery without calling for its abolition. In 1827, in another case, a grateful Georgia House of Representatives resolved that Habersham's conduct rivaled "many of the deeds of Roman virtue." Habersham must have relished that evocation of stoic moral rectitude.

The only convincing explanation of the limited charges against Smith is that Habersham decided to limit them himself. Given his devotion to duty and honor, this choice probably tore Habersham apart, and may have increased his commitment to the cause of the *Antelope* captives' freedom. As he explained later, he proceeded with the case "conscientiously believing . . . that these people are entitled to their freedom."[7]

Habersham may not have expected to have a piracy trial at all. During the yellow fever epidemic, John Smith wisely fled Savannah for Baltimore. If convicted, Smith faced death on the gallows in Savannah. Habersham probably did not expect him to return, and indeed Smith could easily have escaped. Identification was a capricious concept in 1820; this was long before photographs, fingerprints, or even the acceptance of anything beyond direct witness identification as clear proof of identity. Had Smith not appeared, the Court may have assumed he perished during the epidemic and dropped the case. If the Court pursued the case, a search would have been unlikely to find him. Smith could have gone to sea under a new name, or even under his own extraordinarily common name, and that would have been the end of it. Smith could even have simply vanished into the crowded city of Baltimore. Instead, astoundingly, he returned to Savannah in December of 1820. Very powerful forces must have compelled his return, and given Smith's history, it probably did not include personal honor. Other mysteries surrounded John Smith. Where had he gotten $5,000 for bail in August when he had only $500 in his sea chest? How had he afforded to live in Savannah after his release from jail until he left for Baltimore? How did he pay for travel to and from Baltimore? Most mysteriously of all, when his piracy trial began on December 20, how did he have the wherewithal to arrive at the old brick courthouse accompanied by a dream team of lawyers?[8]

Smith's lead attorney was James Moore Wayne, who signed all three indictments. Wayne, an active and wealthy young attorney, was currently the judge of the Court of Common Pleas in Savannah and would later serve many years as a justice of the United States Supreme Court. He was joined at the defense table by John Macpherson Berrien. Over the previous eleven years, Berrien had served as judge of the Superior Court for the Eastern District, and he would later serve as attorney general of the United States. Of three sitting judges in Savannah, then, one occupied the bench during the trial, while Smith had the other two as his defense team. Berrien, Wayne, and prosecuting attorney Richard W. Habersham were all graduates of Princeton University. Wayne and Habersham had been contemporaries while at school. The personal connections went even further: The federal judge on the bench, William Davies, was Berrien's former law partner. In just a few months he would resign his judgeship and again join Berrien in a law partnership. Berrien and Davies were so close that they named sons after each other. All this was astonishingly fortunate for John Smith, but how did he pay for Savannah's preeminent lawyers to defend him?[9]

A year later, in December 1821, the Spanish vice consul paid out some of the proceeds from the sale of the brig *Antelope*. Charles Harris and Thomas U. P. Charlton, as the proctors for the Spanish claimant, each received $300. John M. Berrien was paid $150 from the Spanish vice consul's funds. No explanation was given for the payment to Berrien, raising the possibility that he had done something secretly to benefit the Spanish claim. If so, Berrien had acted unethically against the interests of his client in the admiralty case, Captain John Jackson of the U.S. Revenue Cutter Service. Was it possible that the Spanish vice consul paid Berrien to defend John Smith?[10]

John Macpherson Berrien was no angel, but he was far too shrewd to risk such an obvious violation of legal ethics, especially for so small a sum. Nor would the Spanish claimant have any reason to pay for Berrien's defense of Smith. The Spanish vice consul had every reason to want Smith convicted of piracy. The reason for this unexplained payment was simply the resolution of Captain Jackson's salvage claim against the ship, with the proceeds paid to his attorney, John M. Berrien.[11]

But John Macpherson Berrien and James Moore Wayne did not work for free. If the Spanish claimants did not pay for Smith's defense, who did? Smith himself revealed who when he explained that he came to court on "behalf of himself and others concerned and interested in said vessel and cargo." The only parties not involved in the case with a financial interest in the ship and the cargo were the original investors in the privateer *Columbia*. They had a strong interest in Smith standing trial. If Smith was acquitted of piracy, he could then file a claim in admiralty for restitution of his property as a legitimate privateer. His argument would be that he was captured on the high seas off Spanish Florida, and there was no evidence that he tried to land the *Antelope* slaves in the United States. The argument had some merit, and if successful, Smith's acquittal would offer a chance to turn a disastrous privateering investment into a profit. These investors probably had the financial and legal leverage to compel John Smith to return to Savannah and risk his life at trial. As these investors were essentially engaged in organized crime, it might have been more dangerous for Smith to flee than to stand trial. John Macpherson Berrien and James More Wayne, the future attorney general of the United States and the future justice of the Supreme Court, probably worked for money funneled through Smith from shadowy unnamed investors in Baltimore. The goal was simple: Smith's acquittal. If acquitted, the investors had a chance to recover their illegal investment in privateering and the slave trade.[12]

John Smith was charged with piracy under the law of nations, but even what that meant was controversial. The Constitution granted Congress the power "To define and punish Piracies and Felonies committed on the high Seas, and Offenses against the Law of Nations." In 1790 Congress had acted on this power in the Act for the Punishment of Certain Crimes Against the United States, which included definitions of piracy and the relevant punishments. The 1790 act served until the War of 1812, but as a result of the privateering during that war and the Latin American wars of independence that followed, federal courts were flooded with piracy cases. The definitions under the 1790 law often failed to address these new problems, so Congress responded with An Act to Protect the Commerce of the United States and Punish the Crime of Piracy, approved on March 3, 1819. In this law, piracy, as defined by the law of nations, would be punished by death. To make things clearer, Justice Joseph Story defined piracy under the law of nations to resolve a controversy between Chief Justice John Marshall and federal judge St. George Tucker. Piracy, Story wrote in his decision in early 1820, was "robbery, or forcible depredations, upon the sea, *animo furandi*."[13]

The Latin *animo furandi* means "with the intent to steal." As with many common-law crimes, a charge of piracy under the law of nations required both the commission of the piratical *act* and the *intent* to commit that act by the defendant. This opinion by Justice Story was printed widely in the press because many Americans believed they faced a crisis of privateering and piracy. Richard Habersham was familiar with this case and with Story's definition of piracy under the law of nations. He would have understood that proving *animo furandi*, the intent to steal or rob in a piratical way, was an essential element of proof for a criminal piracy conviction under the law of nations.[14]

On Wednesday, December 20, the Circuit Court for the District of Georgia convened, with William Davies sitting as sole judge. Supreme Court Justice William Johnson did not attend that term of court, but it was permissible for one judge to sit alone. The piracy trial began, and Habersham called five witnesses for the prosecution. The first two, Thomas Bradshaw and William Brunton, had sailed from Baltimore on the privateer *Columbia*, which became the *Arraganta*. The third witness, John Stephens, had been a member of the *Antelope*'s original crew and had remained aboard the ship after it was captured. Habersham used their testimony in a surprising way. As the *Savannah Republican* reported, "the evidence on the part of the prosecution was a history of the cruise of the *Arroganta* [sic]." Bradshaw and Brunton told of sailing from Baltimore, capturing the French schooner, and capturing the *Antelope*, and of the capture and destruction of the Portuguese ship at Cabinda. Finally, they told of the voyage to the coast of Brazil, where the *Arraganta* was wrecked. There was no testimony about the capture of the American schooner *Exchange*, or of taking slaves from that vessel. This was a clearly piratical act, and no secret, as the story had been fully published in several newspapers. Nor was there mention of the kidnapping of Cornelio Coppinger, the son of the governor of Florida, another clearly piratical act. Surely these must have seemed puzzling omissions.[15]

Then John Stephens, a Greek with limited English, testified about his experiences aboard the *Antelope* until the wreck of the *Arraganta*. No testimony was given concerning the attempted sale of the captives in Suriname, or of the voyage through the Caribbean. Nor did Stephens tell of arming the *Antelope*, the boarding of ships in the Bahamas and off the Florida coast, or the kidnapping of Governor Coppinger's son. Again, all these events were widely known and had been published in newspapers. They clearly showed both an attempt to trade slaves and piratical behavior. This evidence, however, was omitted from the prosecution's case. To conclude, Habersham presented both Captain John Jackson of the Treasury cutter *Dallas* and his second officer, James Knight. They described the capture of the *Antelope* and authenticated the documents taken from John Smith's sea chest, including Smith's American citizenship papers. Here Habersham rested the United States' case.[16]

John Smith could not testify. He was a criminal defendant, and under criminal procedure of the day he was barred from testifying in his own defense. James Moore Wayne and John M. Berrien had to use testimony given by other witnesses to set up their two-part defense. First, they acknowledged that John Smith had committed the acts charged in the indictments. Then they turned to consideration of the specific facts of the case, looking first at the robbery from the French schooner. If John Smith had a legitimate privateering commission, they argued, the French schooner carrying munitions for "the enemy" was fair game. In that case the capture and confiscation of the hawser and awning was not theft, it was an act of war, and so not piracy. If, however, the jury believed that this capture was not legal, but "unlawful and piratical," they reminded the jury that John Smith had voiced his opposition to the attack, protesting to Captain Metcalf. Thus, Smith lacked the specific intent to commit piracy. In either case, based on Joseph Story's definition, John Smith could not be guilty of piracy on the French ship under the law of nations.[17]

The defense then turned to the indictments involving the Portuguese and Spanish ships. Using the same reasoning, if John Smith had a legitimate commission from José Artigas and the Oriental Republic, then it was lawful for him to attack, capture, and take property from both vessels because both nations were at war with the Oriental Republic. If, because of his nationality, or some failure of proof, the jury did not believe Smith had a legitimate privateering commission, he was still not guilty of piracy. John Smith *believed* that he held such a commission, they argued, and guided by such good faith belief "if he acted *bona fide*, that is, within the scope of his commission, the acts imputed to him cannot amount to piracy." In other words, because Smith believed he held a valid privateering commission and acted in good faith on that belief, none of the thefts, depredations, or destruction he carried out could be piracy. He lacked the requisite intent, the required *animo furandi*.[18]

In response, Habersham did not attack this facile argument about John Smith's "belief" of legitimacy. Instead, he closed by reviewing the facts of the *Arraganta*'s voyage and nothing more. It had grown dark on Thursday evening when the two days of testimony and argument concluded, but Judge Davies charged the jury anyway. According to the *Republican*, the charge "was brief, but very clear." Davies essentially restated the defense arguments as to the two parts of the law of piracy. He then instructed the jury "that no circumstances of the cruise [of the *Arraganta*] could contaminate the prisoners [*sic*] conduct with the crime of piracy." In other words, the judge told the jury that nothing that happened during the cruise of the *Arraganta* could be used to find Smith guilty. The story of the cruise was, however, the only evidence of piracy presented by the prosecution. With these instructions, at eight o'clock in the evening the jury retired to deliberate. They returned five minutes later with a verdict of not guilty on all three indictments.[19]

So John Smith dodged the hangman's halter. Freed by the court, he obtained an attorney and filed a libel in admiralty, claiming all the *Antelope* captives as his property. Smith continued to live in Savannah, his means of support unclear, until admiralty proceedings began in the case. The failure to convict John Smith of piracy when there was so much evidence of guilt must have rankled the honorable Richard W. Habersham. He could console himself by anticipating the upcoming admiralty case. What was true in the case of the *Josefa Segunda* would have to be true for the *Antelope*. There would be no question about John Smith's having engaged in piracy, for he had been tried on that charge and found not guilty. As he was not a pirate, the Spanish and Portuguese title to the captives had been extinguished when the captives had been taken by Smith, the legitimate privateer. As Smith held clear title to the vessel and cargo, under the 1819 Slave Trade Act, his ship and the captives aboard it were now forfeit to the United States. The Africans would be put under the control of the president, bound for freedom in Africa. While Habersham failed in his duty to convict John Smith, he must have left the old brick courthouse that Thursday night in December with at least a touch of satisfaction, certain he had just freed the captives of the *Antelope*.

CHAPTER 9

"The United States . . . appears in the character of guardian or next friend of these Africans, who . . . insist on their right to freedom."

Chief Justice John Marshall *The Antelope*, 23 U.S. 66, 114 (1825)

Meanwhile, the captives waited. In the *Josefa Segunda* case the captives had been sold three months after their arrival. When the *Politina* was brought into Savannah, the captives aboard were auctioned within a month. Not so the *Antelope* captives. More than six months would pass before the admiralty proceedings that would decide their fate began. The *Antelope* captives were not imprisoned while they waited, but they were treated as slaves and regulated by the same system of laws and customs that controlled slaves. Beginning in August, many of the captives had been distributed to Savannah households, and, as we have seen, fifty-one were put to work leveling the city fortifications. In public and private, they were at the mercy of the white southerners around them. James Thompson, for example, reported in December of 1820 that Marshal Morel had placed three captives in his home. One captive died August 9, one died September 22, and the third died on December 6. The three were not named or identified, nor were causes of death mentioned. Thompson's only responsibility was to report that they had died.[1]

Despite the general disinterest in the identity of captives, some individual names of captives began to emerge in court records, but only after death. George was about twenty-five years old and in the custody of Captain James Smith when he died in October of 1820. Tom and Sophia, both between twelve and fourteen years old, also died in October, and they were joined by Maria, who was just eleven. In November Celia and Fanny, both sixteen years old, died.

In December of 1820, John M. Rupell reported that "the negro Girl, whose african name was Mekiah, and which name was altered by me, by calling her Mariah, strayed from me." He did not mention her age, but Mekiah/Mariah was a child. Rupell advertised for her return in the newspaper and described her. Mekiah was about four feet three inches tall and was swollen by "dropsy in her chest." This was probably anasarca, a heart-damaging edema that often resulted from kidney failure associated with malaria. He wrote she was unable to speak English and was "indolent and slothful." Surely a child suffering from heart-crushing edema who did not speak English was slothful. Rupell later learned that Mekiah had gone to the house of Marshal John H. Morel on Orleans Square. From there she was sent to the home of William Richardson. At Richardson's house Mekiah died.[2]

Captain John Jackson of the revenue cutter *Dallas* waited, too, although in much less dire circumstances. He had captured smugglers and illegal slavers before, and probably a few months' delay did not bother him. If the *Antelope* itself was condemned, half the value of the ship would go to the United States and half to the officers and crew of the *Dallas*. If the captives were freed, Jackson would receive a $25 bounty per captive, or between $6,000 and $7,000, depending upon how the court counted the captives. Would it be the number originally rescued, 281, or the number delivered to the marshal, 258, or the number alive at the time the case was decided? If the captives were ruled property by the court and returned to the claimants as slaves, then Jackson and his crew would earn salvage on their value as property. The amount would vary depending upon the court's valuation and the share awarded, but salvage could easily be double the freedom bounty. Whatever the result, Jackson stood to collect a substantial sum of money.[3]

Admiralty was arguably the most British set of procedures followed by U.S. federal courts in the nineteenth century. The judge sat alone in all but criminal matters: There was no jury. To accommodate the needs of mariners and businessmen, as well as the unpredictability of ship's schedules, cases could proceed in fits and starts over days or even weeks, with the judge considering documents, depositions, oral testimony, and other relevant information. The jurisdiction of a federal court sitting in admiralty was vast. In 1815, Justice Joseph Story ruled in a circuit court opinion that the federal courts' admiralty jurisdiction was at least equal to that of British admiralty jurisdiction. This meant that the jurisdiction extended to all events occurring on waters subject to the ebb and flow of the tide. No one challenged Story's ruling, and in 1825, it would be adopted by the Supreme Court. Under this definition at least half of the commercial litigation in the United States came under admiralty jurisdiction, greatly expanding federal authority.[4]

Civil cases in admiralty usually concerned things (this was jurisdiction *in rem*, "against the thing"), meaning that they required a claim against a specific named piece of property. Typically the thing was a ship, the equipment on the ship, or the cargo of a ship. Admiralty proceedings were not always adversarial; a single claimant could file a libel against a thing, and the judge would consider the merits. In ruling, the judge spoke to each claim, explaining the reasoning for his decisions. If dissatisfied, a claimant in the United States could appeal an admiralty decision from the district court to the circuit court, where both the federal district judge and the Supreme Court justice riding that circuit heard the case. In the case of an appeal from the decision of a district court judge, the Supreme Court justice alone made the ruling. The circuit court decision could also be appealed to the Supreme Court, where the justice who heard it at the circuit court level would be part of the panel considering the appeal. No one seemed to think it strange that the district court judge could be present at the appeal of his decision at the circuit level, or more astonishingly that the Supreme Court justice could hear his own circuit court decision appealed in the Supreme Court and vote on it.[5]

Nor did anyone think it odd that a sitting superior court judge in Georgia maintained an active practice in federal court. During the eleven years he was superior court judge for Georgia's Eastern Circuit, John Macpherson Berrien also continued to practice in the federal courts. He had developed the reputation as Savannah's premier admiralty attorney, and Captain Jackson knew enough about admiralty cases to hire the best. Admiralty law in the United States in the 1820s still depended a great deal on precedents from British admiralty law, so access to an extensive library of British materials was essential for a successful practice. Berrien prided himself on his large law library, and it was probably the best in Savannah. He had also developed a knack for representing the winning side in his legal work. John Jackson's claim for bounty or salvage looked like a sure thing, exactly the sort of case Berrien favored.[6]

In 1820, the *Antelope* was just one of several cases Berrien had in federal court, so initially other attorneys moved the case forward. On November 17, 1820, Thomas U. P. Charlton and Charles Harris, proctors of the Spanish vice consul, went before Judge Davies in the old brick courthouse in Savannah. Domingo Grondona, Thomas Ximenes, and Raymundo Arribas had arrived in Savannah, they explained. The three men had been original crew members of the *Antelope* and had been marooned in Africa after the capture of the ship. Finally rescued, they had arrived in Puerto Rico in June, where they reported the capture of the *Antelope* and made sworn statements about the events. Grondona had then hurried on to Havana, and upon arrival had gone directly to Santiago de la Cuesta's home near the cathedral in the old city and informed him of the *Antelope*'s capture. Now, having heard from the vice consul about the arrival of the *Antelope* in Savannah, Cuesta Manzanal y Hermano had sent the three to testify. They also brought documentary evidence of the firm's investment in the *Antelope*'s voyage. Proctors Charlton and Harris asked that the witnesses be allowed to view the captives and identify them as the firm's property. Judge Davies agreed. November 17 was a Friday, so he ordered the three to report to the clerk of court's office at four o'clock in the afternoon on Monday. "And that in the meantime," his order continued, "the Marshal do conduct the said Witnesses to the places where the slaves are situated."[7]

Judge Davies did not provide for any of the other claimants' proctors to accompany the witnesses on their tour. He did not provide for the marshal to note which particular captives were recognized by the witnesses. He clearly assumed that the captives were already slaves. He gave no directions as to the process, which turned out to be very ad hoc. William Richardson remembered that Marshal Morel and "a gentleman" came to the site where he was directing the work of captives forced to work on the city fortifications. The visitor had clapped his hands as if calling them, and upon seeing him, many captives had gone toward the gentleman. Marshal Morel's version was a bit different. He recalled lining up the captives working for the city, and then Grondona clapped his hands and spoke to the captives in a foreign tongue. Many appeared to recognize the language and approached Grondona. Visiting some of the houses where Morel had placed captives, several other captives seemed to recognize Grondona, and three shook his hand. Much the same happened the next day when Grondona, Ximenes, and Arribas visited Marshal Morel's plantation on the Ogeechee, where he kept more than one hundred of the captives. These, Morel said, were mostly small children and captives not fit for hard labor. According to Morel, many of the captives there also recognized the three men. Surely none of the captives imagined that courtesy and conversation with Grondona, who apparently spoke some words in a Kikongo tongue, or more likely the creole trade language, would be used later to identify them as Spanish slaves.[8]

At 10:00 a.m. on Wednesday, January 17, 1821, oral testimony in the case began. Astonishingly, there were now five parties contending before the court. First, there was Richard W. Habersham representing the United States and, in reality, he argued, the Africans themselves.

Mayor Thomas U. P. Charlton and former mayor Charles Harris represented the Spanish vice consul Charles Mulvey and the claim of the Cuban firm of Cuesta Manzanal y Hermano. The Portuguese vice consul had hired James Morrison and John Nicoll to represent his claim, but unlike the Spanish vice consul, he had not identified any specific claimants. John Macpherson Berrien represented the bounty and salvage claim of the fourth party, Captain John Jackson of the revenue cutter *Dallas*. Finally, there was a fifth party, a new claimant. This was John Smith, the former prize master of the *Antelope* and now an acquitted pirate. He had hired William Law to file a libel for the return of property he now claimed to have captured as a lawful privateer. Who paid for Law's representation of Smith, or whether he worked on a contingency fee arrangement, was not clear. William Law was a well-connected young attorney who had only joined the bar in 1815 but was already on the road to success. He was solicitor general, or prosecutor, for the Eastern District of Georgia Superior Court, which meant he rode circuit and worked closely with Judge John M. Berrien. Interestingly, he had read law with William B. Bulloch, a member of the same Bulloch family that, according to John Quincy Adams, was deeply involved in the illegal slave trade and other criminal activities. Now, Law represented an admitted slave trader.[9]

Richard W. Habersham thought he had a simple case. He needed to show that John Smith and the *Antelope* were engaged in carrying African slaves, which was obvious. He also needed to show that either the *Antelope* had approached the United States with the intent of selling the slaves, or that Smith was an American citizen engaged in any element of the international slave trade. If he showed these things, then the ship would be forfeit to the United States and the captives free and placed under the direction of the president for a return to Africa. The law seemed crystal clear on these issues. John Smith's involvement in the case complicated things, but if he was shown to have violated the law in any way, he would lose his claim.[10]

First up was Captain John Jackson, testifying for the United States. He recounted in great detail the capture of the *Antelope* and testified to the discovery of 280 captives aboard the ship. Jackson repeated information told him by the officers of the ship about the *Arraganta's* and *Antelope's* voyages, including the attempt to sell the captives in Suriname. (What would be considered hearsay in other courts was admissible in admiralty proceedings.) Jackson also explained what he had heard about the 25 captives taken from the American schooner *Exchange*, an issue Habersham had not raised in the piracy trial. Captain Jackson described opening John Smith's sea chest and finding the documents therein, which he identified for the court. Document number 27, he explained, was a sailor's protection from 1811 and convinced Jackson that Smith was an American citizen. Jackson complained that his first lieutenant, William Askwith, had allowed 14 captives to go missing when the *Antelope* waited at St. Marys. Askwith had been commissioned on May 10, 1820, less than two months before the capture of the *Antelope*, and clearly Jackson was unhappy with his first officer's performance. The mystery of the missing 14 was never resolved, but this along with 9 deaths explained why the ship arrived in Savannah with only 258 captives aboard. Organizational matters and Captain Jackson's testimony consumed all of Wednesday, so the court adjourned. On Thursday morning Jackson was back, but this time to file an accounting of his expenses associated with the case. Feeding and watering so many captives for 23 days was expensive, and he submitted a bill of $1,245.96 to the court. U.S. Marshal Morel paid the bill and billed the United States Navy for his cost.[11]

On January 18, the court heard three more witnesses. James D. Knight, the second lieutenant of the *Dallas*, echoed Captain Jackson's testimony. The cutter had intercepted a ship loaded with African captives evidently headed toward the United States. John Smith commanded the ship and possessed documents indicating he was an American citizen. There were 281 captives aboard and two more lying on the deck, dead. He detailed the sufferings of the captives and told of First Mate George Ford's attempt to sell the captives at Suriname. He also testified that three of the *Antelope's* officers, Smith, Price, and Ford, had confessed that they were American citizens. At least one sailor, Nicholson, also identified himself as American. The case was going swimmingly for Habersham at this point. He had both the ship headed toward the United States intending to land slaves, and American citizens in charge of the slaving.[12]

The next witness was John Stephens, who had been part of the *Antelope*'s crew and then joined the privateers. He told of the attempt to sell the captives in Suriname, clear evidence that the *Antelope* was engaged in the slave trade. Then, disturbingly, on cross-examination he testified that in his time aboard the ship after it was captured, he never saw a commission for the *Antelope* as an Artigan privateer. William Brunton, who had been part of the *Antelope* prize crew, testified next and told of taking slaves from Africa and trying to sell them on the *Antelope*'s long voyage. He detailed the capture of the *Exchange*. Twenty-five captives were taken from her, he said, all men except for two boys. This was clearly piracy. He, too, said he never saw a commission for the *Antelope* as the *General Ramirez*. On cross-examination by John Nicoll, proctor for the Portuguese vice consul, Brunton explained that "more slaves were taken out of the Portuguese ship than any other vessel." William Law, for John Smith, asked how many captives were aboard the *Antelope* when the *Arraganta* attacked. Brunton testified that there were "ninety odd slaves aboard" when the *Antelope* was captured.[13]

The direction of the testimony being elicited suggested not just Habersham's strategy but also that of Charlton and Harris for the Spanish vice consul. If John Smith was a legitimate privateer, Cuesta Manzanal y Hermano had little chance of recovering the captives. If, however, Smith had no commission, then he had engaged in piracy. The *Antelope* and the captives could under existing law be returned to the original owners. Besides having Smith convicted of piracy, already a moot point, there was another way to do this, and Charlton laid the groundwork for it on Friday. John Morrison had served on the *Arraganta*, and then as boatswain in the prize crew on the *Antelope*. He told in detail about the taking of twenty-five slaves from the *Exchange*, clear piracy, and stated that he never saw a commission aboard the

Antelope. He described the recruitment of crew in Baltimore. While all the men swore before a notary that they were not American citizens, once in Chesapeake Bay, four men had been taken off the privateer by a revenue cutter because they were discovered to be American citizens. If the *Arraganta* had shipped American citizens, or added to her original crew, she was in violation of the Neutrality Act of April 20, 1818. Everything done by the privateer after that was then illegal under American law, including taking Portuguese or Spanish slaves.[14]

While Habersham wanted to destroy John Smith's claim by showing that he was engaged in the illegal slave trade, Habersham did not want the captives reenslaved. This was a delicate balance: arguing that Smith broke the law but that he was a legitimate privateer. Habersham tried to head off the argument that Smith was a pirate with his final questions to Morrison. Yes, Morrison replied, he knew that there were privateering commissions aboard the *Arraganta* and he had seen them. When they captured the *Antelope*, like any legitimate warship, they were under the proper flag of José Artigas. Most importantly, in his last statement to the court, Morrison explained that "Capt. Smith had a personal Commission as a Lieutenant in the service of the Republic." This was the first direct testimony that Smith held a personal commission in the Artigan service. It also explained why Smith argued that he had expatriated, that is, given up his American citizenship for that of the Banda Oriental. If this was true, it greatly strengthened Habersham's argument that Smith had taken title to the captives.[15]

The Spanish proctors followed with their witnesses. First up was "Thomas Hemanus," otherwise Thomas Ximenes, the original boatswain of the *Antelope*. Boatswains were in charge of maintenance and repairs aboard ship and knew the physical vessel intimately. Ximenes explained through a translator that the *Antelope* and "all the negroes belonged to Spaniards in the Havannah [*sic*]." When asked specifically, he insisted that there were 166 slaves aboard when the *Antelope* was captured. On cross-examination, Habersham asked Ximenes how long he had known the ship, and who owned her. If Habersham could establish that any Americans owned or invested in any part of the voyage, then under the 1819 Slave Trade Act, the ship would be condemned and the captives freed. Ximenes replied that he had known the *Antelope* for five years and she had always been under the Spanish flag. In response to Habersham's follow-up, Ximenes said "that he has no reason to believe that any Americans had an interest in the *Antelope* or the cargo." Here Habersham may have made a classic cross-examination error: asking a question without knowing how the witness will answer. This single answer, from a man who knew the ship intimately for five years, essentially cut off an easy route to victory and freedom for the captives. Habersham had to return to the main path of his argument.[16]

The court, however, would not return to testimony in the case for almost four weeks. There was a great deal of documentary evidence to be considered. During the hiatus, William Law prepared an amended libel for John Smith's claim. Realizing the need to respond to the suggestions that Smith did not possess a privateering commission and that the *Arraganta* had been outfitted illegally in Baltimore, violating the Neutrality Act, the new libel attempted to engage these questions. It was in many ways the desperate gesture of an attorney seeing his case fall apart. In the libel Smith asserted that the privateer had scrupulously followed all American laws while in the port of Baltimore, and that the ship had not "augmented its force" there—that is, they had not brought aboard more weapons or ammunition. The crew that sailed from Baltimore was such as was allowed by law, he insisted. Smith asserted that he "had on board a genuine commission signed Joseph Artigas," and he had "sailed and acted under the authority of said commission." He was no longer a citizen of the United States but had become a citizen of the Oriental Republic. This all may have been true. Then, Smith's libel asserted that the ship and 150 captives he claimed were not legitimately under the jurisdiction of the court and should be returned to him immediately. Finally, he begged for a continuance so that he could obtain more testimony supporting his case. The court's response to this amended libel was silence.[17]

Oral testimony resumed on February 13, 1821, with the second mate of the *Antelope*, Domingo Grondona, testifying for the Spanish vice consul's case. Grondona said he had toured the area and visited many of the captive Africans. He had firmly recognized 144 of the 166 he said had been aboard the *Antelope*. This number probably surprised everyone in the courtroom; in December, Grondona had said he recognized only 40 of the captives. He insisted again that the *Antelope* had 166 slaves aboard when captured by the *Arraganta*. During cross-examination, U.S. Attorney Habersham, most likely in a tone dripping with disbelief, asked how Grondona had identified these 144 captives. Grondona replied that he recognized them by their faces and by the African language they spoke. John Nicoll, for the Portuguese claim, asked that since they were in the process of loading slaves at Cabinda, how could Grondona be so certain there were 166 slaves aboard the *Antelope*? Grondona had another smooth answer, saying he knew because it was his duty to count them twice a day. Asked how many had been aboard when the ship was captured the first time by the unknown felucca, Grondona said 96 captives. William Law asked for more details of the first capture, and Grondona said nothing about slaves being taken from the *Antelope*. Instead, he said that the first ship had taken $22,000 and given 36 slaves in return—in other words, he implied that the *Antelope* had gained slaves through its capture by the first ship. Mocking this improbable development, Law asked if he had recognized the little children, too. Grondona calmly replied that he did not think he could "designate the small negroes."[18]

Thomas Ximenes was brought to the stand again, and this time the court clerk spelled his name correctly. He, too, testified that there were 166 slaves aboard the *Antelope* when it was captured. He knew this because it was his duty to count them twice each day. Challenged, Ximenes was not as smooth as Grondona. It was his duty as boatswain to give the captives their rations, he replied, and count them, he now said, three times each day. Challenged again, he explained that every morning he gave each captive a biscuit, and so once a day he counted them this way. The proctors for the Spanish vice consul hurried Ximenes off the stand after that.[19]

Following Ximenes, John Smith finally testified for his own claim. This sort of testimony by a party would not have been allowed in a normal court of the time, but admiralty made exceptions for parties who had unique knowledge. The *Antelope* was sailing in international waters when captured illegally by the American revenue cutter, Smith argued. His case had been compromised by problems beyond his control. He intended to compel the testimony of the collector of the port of Baltimore to show that no neutrality laws had been violated by the *Columbia*. He even planned to present officials of the Artigan government to testify that his commissions were valid. But because the "prevailing epidemic" had forced him to flee Savannah, and then because of the piracy trial, Smith argued that he had not had time to obtain this evidence. If there was a hint of desperation in his testimony, Smith had good reason to feel desperate. His attorney had surely told him things were not going well. Nor was Smith aware that things had also gone badly for José Artigas. Artigas had been abandoned by his ally General Francisco Ramirez, for whom the *Antelope* had been renamed, and defeated by a Portuguese army that occupied the Banda Oriental in September of 1820. Artigas had fled to Paraguay, and his revolution had collapsed. There would be no Artigan government officials to testify for Smith, nor confirmation of the validity of his commission, for the Artigan government no longer existed.[20]

The next day Smith answered interrogatories from the proctors for the Portuguese vice consul. The questions focused on numbers: how many captives were aboard when the *Antelope* was captured, how many on the Portuguese ships, how many taken from the American schooner? Smith's answers were precise. Taken from the Portuguese ship at Cabinda were 183 captives; 30 more were taken from two Portuguese schooners at sea, and 25 had been taken from the American schooner. The *Antelope,* he said, had 93 captives on board when the ship was captured by the *Arraganta*. According to his testimony, originally there had been 331 captives, meaning at least 50 were lost on the long Middle Passage. No questions were asked about these losses.[21]

That same day, as Smith and his lawyers were answering the interrogatories, a secret deal was cut between the Spanish and Portuguese vice consuls. The Spanish vice consul, representing Cuesta Manzanal y Hermano, had the much stronger case. The Spanish had a concrete claimant, several witnesses, documents showing their investment in the voyage, and clear testimony about the capture of the *Antelope*. Two strong witnesses, however, had already testified that only 90 to 93 captives belonged to the Spanish. Ximenes and Grondona had testified to the number of 166 aboard, but it was possible that the court would accept the lower number and give the majority of the captives to the Portuguese vice consul. The Portuguese vice consul, however, knew he had a much weaker case. While there was plenty of evidence from the testimony of witnesses that most of the captives came from Portuguese vessels, they had no documentary evidence. They had no evidence of ownership of the captives. They did not even have the names of the ships taken. As the U.S. Attorney would point out, this all looked suspicious. Perhaps the Portuguese were not legitimate claimants after all? If the court accepted the Portuguese claim, the lion's share of the captives might go to them. If the court threw out the Portuguese claim, the captives could all go to the Spanish. Both sides feared the worst. In response, they cut a simple deal:

> We agree to unite in defeating the claims of the United States and Captain John Smith to the negroes . . . to bear equally the expense . . . and to divide equally between us the number of Negroes which may be decreed to us or to either of us as Spanish and Portuguese claimants.

This contract was signed by attorneys for each side and hidden away until it was suddenly produced five years later. Because of this deal, the court's struggle to understand how many captives had come from Spanish or Portuguese ships, a struggle that even became an issue before the Supreme Court, was essentially meaningless.[22]

The Portuguese, Spanish, and John Smith's proctors had already made their closing arguments when on February 16, 1821, John

Macpherson Berrien presented the closing argument for his client. The content of his argument can be inferred from Judge Davies's decision. At great personal risk, Berrien argued, Captain John Jackson had managed to capture the *Antelope* and bring the ship into port. Half the value of the captured ship should go to Jackson. As to the captives, if free Jackson should receive twenty-five dollars a head, and if slaves, Jackson should receive a salvage award for restoring them to the claimants. Because of the great risk and difficulty involved, this salvage award should be substantial. Berrien's presentation was short and sweet. Then, U.S. Attorney Richard W. Habersham rose to make the final closing statement.[23]

Habersham began by asserting that the claim of the United States was something new, not a common claim for forfeiture in admiralty. In this case, "the United States are a mere nominal claimant—the Negroes are the actual party." "It must indeed be considered," he continued, "as if the Negroes were before the Court in Habeas Corpus for discharge from illegal imprisonment." Many listeners were probably astonished by Habersham's comparison of the captives' condition as virtual slaves to "illegal imprisonment," but his argument grew even more unusual. "Before the Court will pronounce a decree subjecting them to perpetual slavery, it will require strict proof of property in those who claim title." Most of Habersham's contemporaries looked at the *Antelope* captives, black Africans, and saw slaves. This had not always been the case; the identification of black Africans with slavery was a development of the seventeenth and eighteenth centuries. By 1820, however, the racial identification of slaves was a common assumption in the American South. Habersham suggested instead that the court should assume the captives were free until there was proof that they were someone's property.[24]

Habersham's argument concerning John Smith continued. He explained that "from the moment he took these Negroes into his possession and proceeded in search of a market for them, he became engaged in the slave trade." As an American citizen, this brought Smith under the 1819 Slave Trade Act and meant Smith was engaged in a felony. Habersham had not gotten an indictment against Smith for slave trading under the 1819 Slave Trade Act, but he was more than willing at this point to show that Smith was an American engaged in the slave trade in order to free the captives. Habersham then turned to the more difficult part of his argument.[25]

He began his argument against the Spanish claim by appealing to British admiralty law. There, he argued, the courts held that "the slave trade is altogether illegal." He based this on the 1810 case of the *Amedie* and on the cases that followed. Habersham used the term "*prima facie*" for this illegality, meaning that this was the correct law, the established law of nations, until proven otherwise. To make their case, he argued, the Spanish would have to demonstrate an exception to this law. Thus, the Spanish proctors should have established that slave trading by the *Antelope* was legal under Spanish law. This they failed to do. Then, Habersham argued, the Spanish proctors had to show that the *Antelope* had complied with all elements of the Spanish law. This they had also failed to do. By treaty agreement with the British, Spanish slave ships were required to have a special permit signed by the king in order to trade for slaves in Africa. The evidence showed no such permit; thus the *Antelope* was trading slaves in violation of Spanish law. Habersham claimed that "[i]n the absence of this document the British Courts would condemn." He then went further, suggesting that since the *Antelope* lacked the proper documents, she may have been engaged in the "illicit trade"—as he put it, trade where "the flag is used to cover the property of citizens of other countries." The Spanish failed to prove that they had complied with their own law on the slave trade, and thus they had no property rights in the captives. Without proof of Spanish compliance with the law, Habersham argued, the court cannot "condemn these people to perpetual slavery."[26]

Habersham tore apart the Portuguese claim. Just as in the case of the *Antelope*, there was no proof that the Portuguese followed their own laws regarding the slave trade. Warming to his argument, Habersham asked, "What evidence is there of Portuguese ownership at all?" Only the recollection by the members of a piratical privateer's crew that they saw the "Portuguese flag flying" above vessels they looted. Habersham continued, ridiculing the Portuguese claim.

> But, there is no evidence whatever of Portuguese ownership. The actual claimants are unknown. The names of the vessels unknown. No papers. No documentary evidence. None of the original crew of the Portuguese vessels to give evidence.

> "The absence of all evidence," he concluded, "where evidence ought to have been produced, is itself a circumstance of strong suspicion."[27]

It was a strong and compelling conclusion to a case so important that Habersham was willing to stake his reputation on it. He'd lose.

CHAPTER 10

"The legality of the capture of a vessel engaged in the slave trade depends on the law of the country to which the vessel belongs."

Chief Justice John Marshall *The Antelope*, 23 U.S. 66, 118 (1825)

On Wednesday, February 21, 1821, Judge William Davies read his decision in the *Antelope* case. First, he summarized the claims of others before mentioning that "libels and claims hath also been interposed by the United States claiming the freedom of the Negroes on the ground that some American Citizen was interested or engaged in the transportation from Africa." Richard W. Habersham might have disputed this characterization of his arguments made just five days before, and the libel itself mentioned the 1807, 1818, and 1819 Slave Trade Acts, giving it a much broader context. Judge Davies recited the facts of the case without mentioning John Smith's attempts to sell the captives or his attempts to engage in the slave trade. Turning to the claims, he took up Smith's first and disposed of it quickly. Because the *Columbia* had taken on a crew in Baltimore that included Americans and those of nations other than Venezuela, the ship had violated American neutrality law. This made John Smith a lawbreaker, and he could not acquire title to property obtained as a result of breaking the law. The capture of the *Antelope* could not be recognized in American courts as giving John Smith title to the ship or cargo. Smith's claim was dismissed.[1]

Davies then turned to the libel of the United States and Habersham's claim that the captives should be free under the 1819 Slave Trade Act. First, he ruled that it did not matter that John Smith, an American citizen, had been caught with the captives. Smith had no title to the Africans, because their capture by the *Arraganta* had been illegal. "A variety of decisions in the Supreme Court," Davies continued, "established the principle that upon a piratical or illegal capture the property of the original owners can not be forfeited . . ." He referred specifically to the case of the *Josefa Segunda*, ruling that Smith stood in the position of a pirate, not a privateer. Two months before, Judge Davies had instructed a jury that Smith was a legitimate privateer. Now, in admiralty, he ruled that Smith was essentially a pirate. Smith did not own the captives, Davies reasoned, so the case was not one in which an American was engaged in the slave trade under the 1819 law. The U.S. claim failed on this point even though John Smith was an American citizen.[2]

This remarkable reasoning was followed by more in the same vein. As nothing Smith had done brought the captives under the 1819 Slave Trading Act, the next step was to ask if the Spanish or Portuguese owners had violated that act. "There does not appear in evidence," Davies wrote, "any circumstances connected with the vessel or the Africans found on board previous to the capture . . . which brings the one or the other within the provisions of that act." The captives aboard the *Antelope* when it was taken by the *Arraganta* were still legitimate Spanish property. Judge Davies then turned to the Portuguese claim. That slaves were taken from Portuguese ships was established by several witnesses. That these were ships loaded with slaves off the African coast was enough to establish Portuguese title to those slaves. So, the Portuguese vice consul was in the same situation as the Spanish claimants. The piratical actions of John Smith and the *Arraganta* did not affect the Portuguese title, and the slaves taken from Portuguese ships remained Portuguese property. Francis Sorrel, the Portuguese vice consul, was an appropriate person to claim this property until the true owners could be found. To bring these captives under the 1819 Slave Trade Act, the United States must show that the Portuguese were subject to American law prior to their capture by the pirate John Smith. The United States had presented no such evidence.[3]

Judge Davies rejected utterly Richard Habersham's argument that the "Africans are to be considered free until it is shown they are slaves." No burden of proof fell upon the Spanish or Portuguese claimants to prove that slavery or the slave trade was lawful. Slavery existed, Judge Davies wrote, and the African slave trade continued under the laws of some countries even if others prohibited it. What mattered was whether the captives were possessed by citizens of a government that allowed slavery and the slave trade. In this case they were. The burden of proof lay upon the United States to show that the Spanish conduct was illegal under Spanish law. This they had failed to do. Habersham's argument that the *Antelope* lacked proper documentation under Spanish law to legally engage in the slave trade was rejected; the documents clearing her from Havana harbor were sufficient. Portuguese law controlled the Portuguese slavers, and under their "municipal law" the slave trade was legal. Nor, Davies ruled, was the slave trade contrary to the law of nations. Davies was not even interested in hearing such arguments. Only when Habersham could show that all the "different governments of the civilized world have consented to abolish the trade" would Davies "consider the claims . . . in favor of the Africans."[4]

There was, however, one group of captives that did fall under the 1819 Slave Trade Act. The *Exchange*, Davies wrote, was an American vessel clearly violating American law before the illegal capture by the *Arraganta*. The twenty-five captives taken out of the *Exchange* did come under the 1819 Slave Trade Act. Davies ruled that the survivors among those captives should be turned over to the United States as provided by law, to be returned by the president to Africa. Judge Davies then ordered the clerk of court, George Glen, to divide the surviving captives among the claimants based upon the original numbers reduced by losses since capture. He also ruled that Captain John Jackson should be awarded salvage on the captives returned to the Spanish and Portuguese as slaves, and that he should be paid $25 a head on those captives given to the United States. The U.S. claim, except that part concerning the captives from the *Exchange*, was dismissed. John Smith was ordered to pay costs for the case.[5]

Two days later, on Friday, the district court met at the City Exchange in a special session devoted to divvying up the captives. United States Attorney Richard W. Habersham had already done far more to make his case for the Africans than anyone could have expected. As a result of his hard work, a few of the captives would be given over to the United States and ultimately returned to Africa. When Habersham rose first to speak in this special session, those watching probably assumed he intended to argue about the number of captives awarded to the United States. He had won a partial victory and done everything an honorable man could, and he had one last chance to increase the number of captives freed. Instead, Habersham announced that he took exception to the court's dismissal of the U.S. claim. He also took exception to the court's sustaining the Spanish and Portuguese libels. He would appeal these exceptions, Habersham announced, to the Sixth Circuit Court of the United States. He did not consider the result any sort of victory, and he intended to continue his efforts to free the *Antelope* captives.[6]

The court noted these exceptions and then turned to the exacting business of dividing up the captives. The clerk of court reported that 258 captives had been delivered to the federal marshal in July. Of those, one had escaped from the encampment at the racetrack and was never found. Another captive, Carlos or Charlie Cuesta, the black Cuban sailor who may have been a slave, was discharged by the court as a free man. Forty-four captives had died. There were now 212 captives left of the 331 original captives taken from Africa. Thus, in less than one year the *Antelope*'s participation in the slave trade had killed more than one hundred people. Presumably arguments were offered on numbers and how to calculate the shares, but none were recorded. The clerk finally used the numbers given in John Smith's testimony to decide original shares. Two hundred and thirteen slaves came from the Portuguese ships, ninety-three from the *Antelope*, and twenty-five had come from the American schooner *Exchange*. The overall survival rate of the original 331 captives, now reduced to 212, was about 64 percent, representing a "loss" of 36 percent.[7]

The easiest and most direct way to calculate shares of the captives would have been to multiply the original number by the survival rate of 64 percent. This would have yielded 136 Portuguese captives, 60 Spanish captives, and 16 former captives of the *Exchange* to be turned over to the United States. George Glen, the clerk of court, did not calculate it this way. Perhaps Glen's calculations reflected the arguments of the various lawyers, or anger at Richard W. Habersham for his obstinacy in pursuing the case, or even the instructions of Judge William Davies. Whatever the reason, Glen used this opportunity to limit the number of captives freed. He reduced the original 93 *Antelope* captives by 30, leaving 63 for the Spanish claimant. He favored the Portuguese most, reducing the number by only 71, giving them 142 of the surviving captives. He then wrote of the 25 taken from the *Exchange*, "[I]t appeared by the testimony that 16 had died before the capture by the cutter, leaving 9 to be apportioned." Nine, however, was the number among the 258 captives turned over to the marshal in July. Since then some 17 percent had died, and this figure applied to the nine, and rounded up, allowed the clerk to take away an additional two. So, the U.S. share would be 7 captives. Only 7 would be freed and returned to Africa.[8]

Once the calculation of shares was done—7 captives to the United States, 63 captives to the Spanish, and 142 captives to the Portuguese—the court turned to the next important step: valuation. This process took four more days. It had been almost eight months since the *Antelope* was captured, and the remaining captives had survived the diseases of Savannah and the low country. Called "seasoning," this survival enhanced the value of the captives. A committee of three performed the evaluation for the Court: George Glen and merchants Oliver Sturgis and Henry W. Hill. In their opinion the captives as a group were worth $300 apiece, or a total value of $61,500 for the 205 captives who were Portuguese and Spanish property. This was a relatively low valuation, but it would be used to calculate the value of Captain Jackson's salvage.[9]

There were no established rules for calculating salvage awards. The Spanish and Portuguese captives had been totally lost, and without the actions of the revenue cutter there was little likelihood they would have ever been recaptured. The court asked the same committee of Clerk Glen and the two merchants to determine the salvage award, and the role of the cutter in recapturing the Spanish and Portuguese slaves may have weighed heavily in their decision. At the time, the average salvage award in U.S. admiralty cases was about 15 percent of the property value. Glen, Sturgis, and Hills concluded, "[T]here should be an allowance of one-fourth of said sum [$61,500] to Capt. Jackson, his Officers, and Crew for salvage of the said negroes." This was a bonanza award of 25 percent, or $15,375, to Captain Jackson and his crew. John Jackson's pay as captain of the revenue cutter was $50 a month. The salvage award was for him a fortune.[10]

"To this report exceptions were filed by the Portuguese vice con-sul," blandly wrote Glen. Morrison and Nicoll most likely leapt to their feet and objected the moment they heard the scale of the salvage award. They, or their clients, whoever they might have been, would owe more than $10,000 in salvage to Jackson. Morrison and Nicoll immediately recorded their exceptions, arguing that the salvage award was excessive and not warranted by Jackson's services. More interest-ingly, they argued that the salvage award "ought to be regulated by the Act of Congress in relation to the compensation given in cases where the slave has been decreed to be delivered to the United States." They wanted salvage to be the same as the bounty provided under the 1819 Slave Trade Act, or $25 a head, not $75, as the court clerk provided.[11]

As a result of Judge Davies's decisions in the case, U.S. Attorney Habersham, the Portuguese proctors Morrison and Nicoll, and the Spanish proctors Harris and Charlton all appealed to the Sixth Cir-cuit Court. Even John Smith appealed the dismissal of his libel. On

March 12, 1821, Habersham wrote John Quincy Adams to ask for an affirmation of his decision to appeal. The marshal's bill of expenses for the maintenance of the captives was already quite large, and the prospect of adding to those expenses caused Habersham to hesitate before appealing the district court decree, he explained. But the decision to give so many captives to the Portuguese when they had produced no owner was the last straw. Something was wrong. To help Adams understand his decision, he enclosed copies of his argument in the case, and of Judge Davies's ruling. These items would show how suspicious the Portuguese claim was and let Adams judge for himself whether Habersham had taken the correct action. If the government decided to withdraw the appeal, Habersham agreed that he would do so and be satisfied with the few captives he had managed to free. Habersham heard nothing from Adams.[12]

The Portuguese award in admiralty was not the only suspicious activity in Savannah during February and March of 1821. In early February, John Macpherson Berrien resigned after eleven years as superior court judge. Berrien had political ambitions that he could not seek while a judge, but there may have been more to this decision than political ambition. On March 6, 1821, Judge Davies confirmed the large salvage award for Captain John Jackson, Berrien's client. Three days later, on March 9, William Davies sent his resignation as federal district judge to John Quincy Adams. On March 13, a notice appeared in the *Savannah Daily Georgian* that Berrien and Davies had "reunited their professional interests in the practice of law" and had opened an office on Johnson Square in the center of Savannah's banking and business district. Later documents showed that Berrien received half of Captain Jackson's final salvage award as his contingency fee. If that was the fee arrangement at this stage of the case, then Berrien stood to gain more than $7,500 from Judge Davies's liberal salvage award. The nature and structure of their new partnership was never revealed, but the rapid resignations and new partnership with so much money in the offing surely raised some eyebrows.[13]

Still the Africans waited. There were deaths among the captives, though at a lower rate as they became more "seasoned" to living in Savannah. They worked in homes as domestics, as laborers on Marshal John H. Morel's plantation, or on the roads and fortifications of the city. On March 26, 1821, the city council voted to dismiss "the African negroes under the charge of Wm. Richardson, with the Interpreter." They charged the mayor with making the arrangements. Mayor Thomas U. P. Charlton had resigned at the end of February and taken John Macpherson Berrien's place as Georgia superior court judge. The new mayor was James Morrison, Esq., one of the proctors for the Portuguese claim. On April 11, 1821, Morrison turned the surviving men working for the city over to Marshal Morel, who later described them as the "primest of the lot." Morel put them to work with other *Antelope* captives on his plantation on the Ogeechee River, laying the foundation for future conflict that would ultimately reach James Monroe, the president of the United States.[14]

The federal court system divides the United States into a number of federal court districts. These districts are then grouped into federal judicial circuits. Before 1869, a Supreme Court justice was appointed for each circuit. In 1821 there were seven circuits, and so seven justices on the Supreme Court. Each justice had more than just the duty of sitting for sessions of the Supreme Court; justices were also expected to ride circuit—to travel to each federal district in their circuit twice a year to hold circuit court. Circuit courts consisted of the local federal district court judge and the visiting Supreme Court justice sitting together as a panel. These panels heard appeals from the district court decisions, as well as some other matters from that district. In May 1821, there was still no federal district judge for Georgia. William Davies had resigned in March to join his friend John M. Berrien in a partnership. In April a presidential commission appointing Thomas U. P. Charlton as federal district judge arrived in Savannah, but Charlton had already accepted the position as state superior court judge and refused to accept the federal appointment. Of course, as a state judge,

Charlton could continue his work as proctor in federal court for the Spanish claim in the lucrative *Antelope* case. Because there was still no federal district judge, when the circuit court assembled in Georgia's capital, Milledgeville, on May 7, 1821, the only judge present was Supreme Court Justice William Johnson.[15]

Justice William Johnson was a South Carolina lawyer and legislator who had been appointed to the Supreme Court by Thomas Jefferson in 1804. Johnson came from a modest background: His father was a successful blacksmith who was able to arrange for young William to attend the College of New Jersey. Returning to Charleston, Johnson read law and began an active practice in the 1790s. His vociferous opposition to Jay's Treaty in 1795 marked him as a devoted Jeffersonian, and he became involved in South Carolina politics. Johnson rose quickly, moving from politics to the bench in 1799, where he built a solid reputation while maintaining his political ties to Thomas Jefferson. In 1804, just thirty-three years old, he was the first Supreme Court appointment made by President Jefferson. The president hoped that Johnson would counter the influence of Federalists on the Court, especially the influence of the man Jefferson considered the arch-Federalist, Chief Justice John Marshall. Johnson did provide a Republican voice on the Court, but soon mutual respect bound Johnson and Marshall together as colleagues, if not as friends. Johnson had no qualms about disagreeing with Marshall, writing dissents, even at times offering a quixotic voice from the Court. He believed in the need for a powerful federal government and Union but supported the idea of significant state powers as well. To reconcile these ideas, he argued that power was held "concurrently" by both federal and state governments, seeing no reason for there to be exclusive sovereignty by one or the other.[16]

Johnson's apparent unpredictability and occasional partisanship disturbed some. John Quincy Adams, who sought a predictable and orderly world, struggled to understand Johnson. In March of 1820, Adams wrote in his diary, "This Judge Johnson is a man of considerable talents and law knowledge, but a restless, turbulent, hot-headed politician caballing Judge." When the *Antelope* case came before Johnson in May 1821, the justice was at his peak in both legal knowledge and experience. He had heard many cases involving Latin American revolutionary privateers, admiralty law, and salvage. Johnson seemed an ideal person to hear the multiple appeals in the *Antelope* case. Surprisingly, the opinion he produced in the case would be rambling, combative, and confusing. Perhaps it was too much to ask a slaveholding Jeffersonian from South Carolina, a man already struggling philosophically with the institution of slavery, to decide a case with such obvious and crucial implications. Johnson had personally concluded that slavery was evil, but a necessary evil in an evil world. Slaveholders had a responsibility to deal justly with the enslaved, he believed, but slavery itself was required for southern society to function properly.[17]

On May 7, 1821, Justice Johnson reviewed the papers in the *Antelope* case, and the next day he heard arguments. Charles Harris and Thomas U. P. Charlton appeared for both the Spanish and the Portuguese vice consuls to argue against the size of salvage awarded to Captain Jackson and his crew. John Macpherson Berrien argued for his client Jackson that the Court should sustain the salvage award. Once again, Richard W. Habersham was the outlier. He argued that all of the captives, not just seven, fell under the 1819 Slave Trade Act because John Smith was an American citizen engaged in the slave trade. If the court didn't agree, Habersham made an alternative argument that both the Spanish and Portuguese claimants had given insufficient proof at trial to sustain their claims. In either case, he argued, the captives should be turned over to the United States for return to Africa. John Smith's backers apparently gave up. No one appeared to argue his appeal, it was dismissed, and Smith vanished. As was the practice at the time, three days later, Justice Johnson read his "Reasonings and Holdings" in the *Antelope* case aloud in court.[18]

Johnson began with what he thought was the most important part of the case, Richard W. Habersham's contention that the slave trade violated the law of nations. "A sweeping principle," Johnson wrote, "is for the first time insisted upon in this Court." The slave trade was illegal not only under United States law, Habersham had argued, but also because it was "violative of the laws of nature and humanity." He had offered numerous British admiralty rulings in support of his law of nations argument, so Johnson turned to those opinions. It was true, Johnson wrote, that British admiralty courts had ruled the slave trade illegal under the law of nations. Even so, Johnson asked, should an independent American court follow British law? Habersham "turns our attention toward British decisions with a devotion scarcely consistent with judicial or natural independence." Perhaps Habersham was in "mental subjection" to the British, not an independent Republican and American like Johnson. The British argument that the slave trade violated the law of nations was simply a self-interested "assertion of power." Because of fears raised by the revolution in "St. Domingo," Johnson continued, the British abolished the slave trade. Having done so, it was now in their interest to prevent other nations from following the trade so that their colonies would have no advantage over British colonies. So, based on his own historical analysis, Johnson found that there was no law of nations against the slave trade.[19]

This did not mean that Johnson favored slavery or the slave trade; he wanted it understood that he was a man of sensibility. "That slavery is a national evil no one will deny except him who would maintain that national wealth is the supreme national good." Having established that his personal ethics transcended mere profit, Johnson went on, "However revolting to humanity may be the reflection, the laws of any country on the subject of the slave trade are nothing more . . . than . . . the trade laws of the nation that made them." An American court could hardly enforce American law or British law against Spanish and Portuguese vessels sailing on the high seas. Nor must the Spanish and Portuguese prove in an American court that their ships engaged in the slave trade legally; that was a question under Spanish and Portuguese law and a matter for their courts. The slaves captured by the *Arraganta* from Spanish and Portuguese ships, Johnson ruled, still belonged to their Spanish and Portuguese owners.[20]

That was not the case for the captives taken from the *Exchange*. The captives from the *Exchange* must be freed, Johnson held, but there was a problem. Which of the captives had been aboard the American ship? Of course, he could not ask the captives who had been on the American ship. Johnson instead devised a method to designate the captives that would be handed over to the United States under the 1819 Slave Trade Act. "I would that it were in my power to do perfect justice in their behalf," Johnson wrote, but there was no way to identify the specific individuals who should be freed because we are "not gifted with the power of divination." There was, however, a way the supernatural could still be relied upon to solve this difficulty. To be fair to all "the lot must decide their fate, and the Almighty will direct the hand that acts in the selection."[21]

As to the number of captives who would be freed by this lottery, Johnson was unhappy with Clerk Glen's earlier calculations. He could not agree that the original twenty-five taken from the American schooner should be reduced to only seven. The losses among the captives had to be averaged across the whole, wrote Justice Johnson. Testimony established that those taken from the American schooner were all men and boys, so the lottery would be held only among the males, with sixteen of them chosen by lot for freedom. Johnson ordered that with ten days' notice the marshal should hold the lottery in Savannah, and he provided detailed instructions for how it should be done. As for the Spanish claim, Johnson ruled that the evidence showed there were ninety-three captives aboard the *Antelope* when the ship was captured. That number should be reduced by the average loss of the whole in order to calculate the Spanish share. As for the rest of the captives, he simply could not rule that they should go to the Portuguese consul "without further proof." Though he hated to leave the case open and unresolved, Justice Johnson decided to give the Portuguese an opportunity to present evidence for their claim at the next term of circuit court to be held in Savannah in December. The captives, except for the sixteen given to the United States, would remain in the possession of U.S. Marshal

John Morel until a final order dividing them was given at the next term of court.[22]

There remained the money issue, the question of salvage. In a South Carolina Circuit Court decision in 1819, Justice Johnson had written, "Questions of salvage are always questions of the most disagreeable kind. In vain the mind looks for . . . fixed rules and principles." In the *Antelope* case the award for captives given to the United States was set by statute. Captain Jackson and his crew would get $25 a head for sixteen rescued slaves, a total of $400. This, however, was a bounty, not salvage. The problem lay with the remainder, almost two hundred people. In a confusing and rambling passage, Johnson argued that since American law did not apply to the Portuguese and Spanish slaves, nor to the *Antelope* herself, the seizure and detention of the ship on the high seas by the revenue cutter was not authorized by any statute. John Smith's proctor William Law had made this argument at the district court level, but it was rejected by Judge Davies. Johnson then suggested, in a startling passage, that had a "legal agent of the Venezuelan republic" or John Smith done more than "feebly sustain" his "Artigan commission" claiming the ship and the captives, Johnson would have awarded the ship and cargo to them as a lawful prize. Clearly, Smith's backers should not have given up so easily. None of that happened, however. The court could only engage the claims put before it. "But," Johnson continued, "as a right cannot grow out of a wrong on general principles I will not stand committed to the decision that this is in law a case of salvage." In other words, this case was not a precedent for what constituted legal salvage, and he would only rule on salvage because all the parties still involved had consented to the capture and condemnation of the *Antelope*.[23]

Justice Johnson explained how he reached his decision despite "the difficulties which the case presents." The Spanish and Portuguese owners would not be able to sell the captives in the United States to raise the money needed to pay salvage; they would be required to take them outside the country to whatever place would have them.

Because of this, there was no way to estimate the real value of the captives as slaves. Thus the previous salvage award was too great. "I cannot feel myself justified," wrote Johnson, "in giving to the salvors more than fifty dollars per head on all the negroes that shall finally be actually restored to them from the custody of the law."[24]

This was a devastating blow to John Macpherson Berrien and Captain John Jackson. Not only was the salvage award cut by a third, but Johnson further reduced it by using not the number rescued, nor the number currently living, but the number still alive when transfer to the claimants finally occurred. At the earliest this could not happen until December, at the next term of circuit court, more than seven months away. Captain Jackson had already been transferred to a new ship in New Orleans, another step in what would be a very successful revenue marine career. He would have to leave matters to his attorney, John M. Berrien. The award was impossible to determine. The sickly season was due to begin, and more than forty captives had died during the last season. How many would still be alive in December to be distributed, and salvage calculated, was anyone's guess. Thanks to Justice Johnson's decree, the recovery John Macpherson Berrien and William Davies had thought a sure thing suddenly looked very uncertain.

CHAPTER 11

"That it is contrary to the law of nature will scarcely be denied."

Chief Justice John Marshall *The Antelope*, 23 U.S. 66, 120 (1825)

S lavery in the early nineteenth century was hardly the entrenched institution most Americans imagine today. This was particularly true in Georgia, which had a long and complex history with slavery before 1820. The Georgia colony was founded as a philanthropic trust in 1733, less than ninety years before the *Antelope* case. Slavery was seen as antithetical to the goals of the trustees, so in 1735, slavery was outlawed in the new colony. To some degree this rejection of slavery was based on moral principles. James Oglethorpe wrote to the Georgia Trustees in 1739:

I have wrote already a letter upon the head of Negroes and shall only add that if we allow slaves we act against the very principles by which we associated together, which was to relieve the distressed. Whereas, now we should occasion the misery of thousands in Africa, by setting men upon using arts to buy and bring into perpetual slavery the poor people who now live free . . .

The opposition to slavery, however, was also practical. The Georgia colony was intended to help Britain's worthy poor, to produce needed products such as wine and silk for the empire, and to protect the southern colonial frontier from the Spanish in Florida. To accomplish this, many settlers were sent by the trustees on "charity," given support for a year and fifty acres of land. The idea that criminals and debtors were sent to the colony is false; the trustees were concerned with helping the working poor. A public garden was established to provide the colonists with mulberry trees for silk, *Vitis vinifera* cuttings for wine grapes, and even olive and fruit trees. Allowing slavery, the trustees thought, would result in wealthy planters, not worthy yeomen, dominating the colony. This would create another colony like South Carolina, producing typical plantation products such as rice rather than helping the poor produce unique products. Slavery in the Georgia colony would also reduce, not enhance, security on the southern frontier. Georgia was located close to Spanish Florida. The Spanish often offered runaway slaves their freedom and, more frighteningly, armed and trained them as soldiers. To the trustees in England, slavery in Georgia seemed a very bad idea.[1]

Some settlers in Georgia, however, were convinced that slavery was a necessity. This was particularly true of younger men who came at their own expense. They found life in the colony difficult and saw the trustees' restrictions on land and slaves as attempts to limit their opportunities. These "Malcontents," as they were dubbed, began a campaign, both in the colonies and in Great Britain, to legalize slavery in Georgia. Only Africans could bear to work in the heat, only Africans could bear the disease, went their argument. The defeat of a Spanish invasion of Georgia in 1742, the Malcontents argued, ensured the security of slave plantations on the frontier. Finally, most powerfully, the Malcontents argued that relieving the distressed was less important than generating profits for the empire. Constantly under political attack, in 1750 the trustees gave up. They surrendered the colony to royal control, and in 1755, the royal governor and the Georgia Assembly approved a new slave code modeled on South Carolina's oppressive laws. Over time more laws followed, clamping slaves ever more tightly into their bondage.[2]

According to tradition, during the 1760s and 1770s, Georgia's economy boomed, supposedly as a result of the legalization of slavery and the subsequent rapid growth of plantations. And, the economy did boom, if one measures economic health only by the value of plantation products produced by slaves. Of course, for enslaved laborers the boom meant ever greater work demands and ever more oppressive conditions. For poorer whites the boom meant that wealthy planters increasingly controlled the best land, and the products produced by poorer whites competed with products produced by inexpensive slave labor. A few grew rapidly rich, while most Georgians, white and black, paid a heavy price for those riches. Wealthy members of South Carolina planter families brought capital to Georgia after the legalization of slavery, and they used that capital to build plantations and buy laborers. The number of enslaved blacks in Georgia grew from a few hundred in the early 1750s to more than thirteen thousand in 1773. By then slaves made up almost half the colony's population.[3]

The American Revolution posed not just a philosophical threat to the institution of slavery in Georgia but also a very real military and political threat. In December of 1778, British forces captured Savannah and held it for the rest of the war. Royal government was reestablished, and a number of Georgia's low-country planters reaffirmed their loyalty to the king. Meanwhile, British forces recruited slaves with the promise of freedom, and hundreds of black soldiers joined their cause. Hundreds more escaped the plantations to live in Savannah, where they aided the British, especially during the siege of Savannah in 1779. In 1780, thousands more runaways from South Carolina came to Savannah, seeking the protection of British forces. In the Deep South, enslaved blacks saw the Revolutionary War as an opportunity for freedom—ironically, freedom offered by the British. When Savannah was evacuated by the British in 1782, many Loyalists departed for other British colonies. Between seven thousand and eight thousand slaves were evacuated from Georgia by their loyalist masters. Hundreds more slaves emancipated by the British for their service were sent to New York; many of them would eventually reach freedom in Nova Scotia. An additional unknown number of slaves died during the war, or had run away, often building small maroon communities on the fringes of settlement. Maroons were runaway slaves who constructed viable communities outside of official government authority. They not only stood as a beacon of hope for the enslaved but were often willing to fight to protect their communities. Small maroon communities dotted south Georgia and north Florida. Much larger and more threatening maroon communities developed in Florida, particularly those known as the Black Seminole. As a result, probably two-thirds of Georgia's slaves were gone by 1783, and the plantation system was in shambles.[4]

While some national leaders doubted the future viability of slavery, landowners in Georgia set about rebuilding their plantations on the former model. Loyalist-owned plantations were confiscated by the state and distributed as rewards to Revolutionary leaders such as Nathanael Greene and Anthony Wayne. Patriot veterans were offered free land on Georgia's frontiers, where many intended to build plantations with slaves. Large numbers of new slaves were brought to Georgia from Virginia, the West Indies, and Africa. From the end of the Revolutionary War in 1783, through 1798, when Georgia outlawed the slave trade, more than 8,100 slaves were brought directly from Africa to Savannah. From 1799 to 1808, another 2,000 slaves were brought from Africa, even though the foreign slave trade was illegal both by state law and Georgia constitutional provision. The more than 10,000 slaves brought directly from Africa were dwarfed by the numbers brought into Georgia from other American states. In 1790, Georgia's slave population had more than doubled that of 1773, exceeding 29,000. By 1810, there were more than 105,000 slaves in the state. By 1820, when the *Antelope* captives arrived, Georgia's slave population had grown from 13,000 to 150,000 in less than fifty years.[5]

Despite, or perhaps because of, the growing investment in slave labor, events in the decade before 1820 raised great fears about the vulnerability of slavery. In the early 1800s, Georgia's borders were in flux, and war threatened all. The colonial government of Spanish Florida exercised little authority over much of its territory, and in northern Florida refugee Creeks and other Indians banded together in communities outside the Spanish governor's control. Some of these Indian groups called themselves Seminole, some other names. As they had done for decades, many of these groups welcomed free blacks and runaway slaves. Georgian slave owners understood that these refuge communities undermined their mastery and, worse, threatened armed resistance to the expansion of the plantation system. Thus, two forces, the expanding plantation system of the Deep South and the struggle to make slavery secure, led to almost continuous war on Georgia's borderlands between 1812 and 1818.[6]

In 1812 President James Madison secretly backed an attempt to conquer East Florida by the so-called Patriots so that it could be annexed in much the same way that West Florida had been annexed in 1810. This Patriot army, recruited largely in Georgia by former governor George Matthews, included United States military forces. In March of 1812, the army invaded Florida, capturing Amelia Island and moving south toward St. Augustine. The Patriot War developed into war against the Spanish, free blacks, Indians, and maroons in Florida. Despite their failure to capture St. Augustine, the Patriots demanded that the United States annex East Florida. Patriot leader John H. McIntosh wrote Secretary of War James Monroe, arguing that if the U.S. government failed to support the Patriot revolution, slavery in Georgia would collapse into violence. The result would be "a revolt of the black population of the United States" that would "introduce the horrors of St. Domingo into your Southern country." Despite the warning, Monroe and President James Madison disavowed their support for the Patriots, though subsequent events would show they were greatly concerned about the potential for slave rebellion in the southern borderlands.[7]

Even as the Patriot War degenerated into guerrilla conflict, the United States government declared war on Great Britain in 1812.

Georgia suffered little during this war until the last days of fighting. In early 1815, British forces occupied Cumberland Island and raided southeast Georgia. The British explicitly offered freedom to runaway slaves, and at least 1,500 slaves escaped to British-occupied Cumberland Island and, ultimately, to freedom. Meanwhile, a civil war, often conflated with the War of 1812, broke out among the Creek Confederacy in western Georgia and the eastern Mississippi Territory. United States forces and state militias, including Georgia's, entered this war, fighting against the traditionalist Red Stick Creeks. By mid-1814, under the command of General Andrew Jackson, the Americans and their Creek and Cherokee allies had destroyed most of the Red Stick forces. Jackson then forced upon the Creeks a treaty ceding lands in southern Georgia and what would become Alabama.[8]

The Red Stick survivors fled to refuges in Florida, including the so-called Negro Fort. The Negro Fort was the center of the most powerful maroon community in northern Florida, consisting of more than 250 black runaways. They were joined by hundreds of refugee Red Sticks and Seminole. The fort stood on Prospect Bluff, fifteen miles up Apalachicola River from the Gulf of Mexico. During the War of 1812, British agents had assisted with the construction of the fort and had provided cannon and small arms. During 1815 and 1816, increasing numbers of slaves escaped Georgia, running for the beacon of hope and resistance symbolized by the Negro Fort. Sheltering both Red Stick Creeks and runaway slaves, the fort became an obsession of several prominent Georgians and of General Andrew Jackson. In the summer of 1816, American naval and militia forces invaded Florida and besieged the Negro Fort. During the battle a shot from a navy gunboat produced a spectacular magazine explosion, killing scores of runaways and destroying the fort. The survivors fled to Seminole communities along the Suwannee River and near Tampa Bay. These settlements became the target of another American invasion of Spanish Florida in 1817 and 1818, again led by Andrew Jackson, called by the United States the First Seminole War. As before, this invasion was also an attack upon the threatening maroon communities in Florida,

Spanish protests be damned. The Indians and runaway slaves had to be destroyed. By 1820, when the *Antelope* captives arrived, these direct threats to the institution of slavery in the Deep South had largely been eliminated. Expansion was the order of the day, and as the plantation system expanded rapidly to the south and to the west, it demanded ever more slaves.[9]

On July 15, 1821, Marshal Morel assembled the surviving 204 captives from the Antelope at the home of William Richardson. Some had been brought into Savannah from Morel's Ogeechee plantation, while others were gathered from homes and businesses across the city. William Richardson owned a house on the west side of town near Spring Hill and several undeveloped lots nearby, where the captives waited under guard. Most knew that there was a legal case regarding their captivity; perhaps some even knew that there had been a decision in the case. Michael, "the interpreter," had been hired for $5 to ensure that affairs ran smoothly and that orders were understood and followed by the Africans. This was the lottery decreed by Justice William Johnson. The Spanish and Portuguese vice consuls did not attend, perhaps in protest of any captives being freed, or perhaps because they thought themselves above such chaotic scenes.[10]

The scene in front of Richardson's house was surely chaotic. More than two hundred captives, guards, interested spectators, and government officials all gathered near the busiest intersection of the main road out of town. Communication involved shouting, with pauses for Michael the interpreter to translate what was said into either a Kikongo dialect or more likely a pidgin trade language. Exactly what the captives were told is not recorded, but presumably the confusing opinion and decrees of Justice Johnson were read aloud, leaving many uncertain of just what was happening. Richard W. Habersham and John H. Morel began the lottery after it became clear that the vice consuls would not attend. Habersham chose his cousin, Joseph Habersham, to draw the lots. Only the men and older boys were assigned numbers; according to testimony, all the captives taken out of the *Exchange* had been male. Joseph Habersham drew sixteen numbers. The oldest man drawn was Mingo, age forty. The youngest was Ned, age ten. The average age of the remainder drawn was under seventeen. Among them was twelve-year-old Little Mingo. If he was the son of forty-year-old Mingo, then presumably the Almighty guided Joseph Habersham's hand, as Justice Johnson predicted. Three Johns were among those chosen, joined by Paul, Toney, Billy, Horrace, Jim, Dick, Sawney, January, Boatswain, and Major. These lucky sixteen would be returned to Africa. No one, however, knew how that would be done, or when they would go.[11]

Some of the captives must have been unhappy with the results of the lottery, or simply saw opportunity in the confusion. By the next day, four captives had slipped away. The always helpful William Richardson hunted them down and received a reward of $50 for their return. Finding the runaways may not have been an easy task. As Richard Habersham explained in a letter to the secretary of the navy, "so many of the cargo of the Ramirez are . . . daily about the streets of the city" that it was difficult to distinguish them from the native Creole blacks in Savannah. After a year in the city, many captives spoke English as fluently as the native blacks, "for they so soon learn the language and become assimilated in every respect to the other negroes." The captives were "assimilated," meaning that they not only learned the language of Savannah's enslaved but also knew something of the culture and the everyday experiences of slaves. Because so many captives were children and teenagers, this process of assimilation probably occurred at a very rapid pace.[12]

After the drawing of the lot, the remaining 188 captives were returned to the care of John H. Morel to await the next meeting of the circuit court in December. Supreme Court Justice William Johnson was the first to express concern over what this meant. In a long letter to John Quincy Adams, written in June of 1821, Johnson discussed the *Antelope* and his recent decision in the case. As for the captives, "the sickly summer carried off about 50 of them, and the rest of them are distributed in the neighborhood of Savanna [*sic*], to various individuals under the supervision of the marshal." Johnson clearly knew this was a problem. "God knows how they are treated," he continued, "but we have no other mode of disposing of them; they work for their maintenance." Perhaps Justice Johnson thought that they worked for their maintenance, but not according to Marshal Morel. On the same day the lots were drawn to free the sixteen, Morel drew up a bill for the United States government. It was massive. The bill began with $611.75 for doctors and concluded with a charge of $3,133.44 for subsistence of 204 captives covering the period from April 11 to July 15, 1821. The final total of the bill was $15,144.02 and one-half cent. Marshal Morel expected payment immediately.[13]

John Henry Morel was born in 1780, the oldest son of Peter Henry Morel, a wealthy planter who had inherited one-third of Ossabaw Island. John Henry's mother, Tryphenia, was the daughter of a wealthy Liverpool merchant who was also a member of Parliament. This elite background, however, could not prevent family tragedy. The Morels lived much of their time at Middleplace plantation on Ossabaw, where between 1781 and 1787, four of John H. Morel's five siblings died. When Tryphenia died in 1787, Peter Henry Morel moved his surviving son and daughter to the mainland and put Middleplace plantation up for sale. Living in Savannah, however, did not produce much better results. Peter H. Morel remarried in 1790, and John H. Morel's new stepmother bore twelve children, of whom seven died in infancy. Morel lived a childhood of uncertainty and tragedy.[14]

John H. Morel read law in Savannah and joined the bar, though he also worked as a commission merchant. He had some political success in the first decade of the nineteenth century, serving as an alderman for three terms and as a justice of the Chatham County Inferior Court. Through this he became a part of the Crawford/Troup party, Georgia's version of the Jeffersonian Republicans. In 1803, he married Catherine Waldburg, a widow eight years his senior. Catherine's inheritance from her first husband, Jacob Waldburg Sr., gave Morel control of Cottenham plantation. He came into full ownership of

Cottenham after Catherine died of consumption in 1809. Morel later married another wealthy widow, Sarah Alger, in 1812. That year his father died of fever on his Ogeechee River plantation, leaving John 125 acres of rice land. In 1818, John H. Morel built a fine double house on Orleans Square, a new area for elite family homes. Savannah was a small world for the elite; U.S. Attorney Richard W. Habersham lived across the street from Morel, and the Bullochs built a mansion on the other side of Orleans Square. Despite the Panic of 1819, the tax digests showed Morel's wealth growing throughout the 1820s, unlike that of many others in Savannah. He also accumulated property. One source of his growing wealth lay in his control of the *Antelope* captives.[15]

In August of 1820, after moving the captives from the racetrack, Morel began to work some of them at Cottenham plantation. Cottenham was south of Savannah, on the eastern tip of Bryan Neck, a long peninsula formed by tidewater rivers. The plantation marshlands were too salty for Morel to be able to grow rice on a large scale, but the plantation had hundreds of acres of uplands good for Sea Island cotton. There were also hundreds of acres of pine forest to log. As time passed, Morel grew bolder, putting more and more of the captives to work on his plantation. By November of 1820, when Domingo Grondona visited to identify captives, Morel had one hundred or more captives working for him. Several years later he characterized these as mostly small children and the infirm, but court records indicate that most of the small children were placed in Savannah homes as domestic servants. In April of 1821, when the city of Savannah returned the forty-one surviving captives of the fifty-one they had used for labor on the city fortifications, Morel put them to work on his plantation with the others.[16]

Work on a Sea Island cotton plantation was different from work on the typical up-country cotton plantation. Sea Island cotton was an especially valuable type of cotton that had been bred in the Bahamas and then refined on St. Simons Island in the 1780s. It produced strong, long, silky fibers, quite different from short-staple upland cotton. Liverpool, England, was the dominant cotton market in the world at that time, and Sea Island cotton sold for at least twice as much as upland cotton in the Liverpool market. Most plantations producing Sea Island cotton used the task system of labor; instead of laboring in gangs, each slave was assigned a particular amount of work each day known as a task. A typical daily task would be for an adult to hoe the weeds in a half-acre of Sea Island cotton. An overseer or driver would later check that the task had been completed. At certain times of the year, however, gangs were a more efficient labor system and often used on these plantations. Gangs were especially useful during the winter before planting. Sea Island cotton needed well-drained sandy soil, and the best way to ensure such conditions was to grow the cotton in raised beds or ridges.[17]

Beginning in January, slaves wielding hoes raised a bed four to six feet wide and about two feet high running the length of the field. The slaves then created a gully the same width as the bed, followed by another long bed the length of the field. The raised beds and gullies would alternate for the width of the field. This was grueling work, done for acre after endless acre of cotton land. Then, the fields had to be fertilized. Slaves standing in cold water shoveled marsh mud onto wagons, and forty wagonloads of mud were needed to fertilize each acre. Fertilizer was important, because the well-drained sandy soil needed by Sea Island cotton retained few nutrients from year to year. In late March the beds were ready and planting began. Holes were poked two to four inches deep in the beds, and the shiny oblong black seeds were put into the holes and covered. When the crop first emerged, skilled judgment was needed to thin, or chop, the cotton plants so that they stood the proper distance apart. After that, four to seven workings with a hoe were required to control the weeds and grass and promote good growth.[18]

Sea Island cotton was a large plant, commonly growing six to eight feet tall, clearly showing its derivation from the tree cotton of the Caribbean. Bolls ripened anytime from September through December, and picking was a continuous process for several months. Each day's harvest was carefully spread on a drying floor to let moisture evaporate. The dry cotton was then run through a whipper, a machine that shook the stems, leaves, and sand out of the fibers. Finally, the cotton was ready for ginning. Gins for Sea Island cotton were simpler than the gins used for upland cotton because the seed was more easily removed. Most planters preferred to gin the cotton on their property so that they could control the seed for the next crop. The ginned cotton was packed by hand into hemp bags measuring 7½ feet long and 2½ feet in diameter, until each bag held three hundred pounds of tightly packed cotton. Finally, the huge sausagelike bags of cotton were carried by slaves to the water's edge, where they were loaded onto barges or small schooners and sent to Savannah, and from there shipped to the expanding factories of the British Midlands or the American northeast.[19]

The *Antelope* captives would have learned all these tasks from Morel's slaves, one kind of acculturation. Morel owned one hundred slaves, and with one hundred additional workers he may have doubled his production of Sea Island cotton. The *Antelope* captives would have worked tasks, eaten food, and slept in thatched shacks like the other slaves. The key point of plantation slavery was the extraction of as much labor as possible from each slave. Housing, clothing, and food were kept as cheap as possible and were also used to manipulate and control slaves. Family relationships and sale could also be used to motivate workers, but ultimately violence compelled the slaves to labor. Plantation discipline included not just switches or slaps but also chains, stocks, ropes, paddles, quirts, and whips used to torture or beat people into submission. While the legal status of the captives remained uncertain, working, living, and suffering like slaves on a Georgia plantation was their daily experience.

Their place on the plantation would have been clear: They were the same as slaves, and they were integrated into the community created by the slaves. Captives learned the language and skills of plantation slaves, they made friends, heard stories, sang songs, perhaps even fell in love. Some of the captive women began to bear children during this period, a process that would continue throughout their captivity.

Some of these children may have been the product of rape by white men, but other children came of relationships built by the captives themselves. The average captive was a teenager, after all, with all the desires, drives, and fertility of that age. While this was a world of oppressive labor, boredom, poor food, and poor housing, all with the continual threat of violence, the plantation became a kind of home. People trapped there did their best to build meaningful lives.[20]

Life for captives in Savannah would have been different. There slaves carried out a variety of jobs, dealt with the polyglot population of a growing Atlantic port, and even built their own institutions. Outside observers saw the lives of slaves in Savannah as centrally connected to their churches. In contrast with other southern ports, such as Charleston and Mobile, African Americans in Savannah successfully built independent churches that were owned, run, and controlled by blacks. First African Baptist Church acquired a building in 1790, located in Yamacraw, on the west side of town. By 1812, First African Baptist had almost fifteen hundred members. Founded in 1802, Second African Baptist was located on the east side of town, and by 1832 it had 667 members. The Presbyterian, Methodist, Catholic, and Episcopal churches all welcomed slaves, but those congregations were firmly under the control of white leaders and the majority of Savannah's blacks joined the independent churches. The African Baptist congregations remained independent. Sermons, while aggressively evangelical, focused not on the present condition of slaves but upon personal salvation and the Final Judgment. They offered no overt challenge to the authority of masters or the institution of slavery.[21]

Just as on the plantation, captives' day-to-day lives were dominated by work. The youngest captives were usually put to work as domestic servants, carrying out kitchen tasks, housecleaning, laundry, and personal service of all sorts. As children not yet acculturated, the youngest captives came under the authority of experienced household cooks and maids, learning English and the customs of Savannah, as well as how to perform the tasks that dominated their lives. The "humane persons" given captives by the marshal included some of Savannah's most active and successful merchants, factors, and lawyers, and these captives may have worked in those businesses. As they grew more familiar with the city, captives may have carried messages, made deliveries, and worked at menial tasks in warehouses and offices. Cotton was the driving force of Savannah's remarkable growth, from a tiny commercial appendage of Charleston in 1790 to the leading southern Atlantic port by 1850. Throughout the 1820s, tens of millions of pounds of cotton passed through Savannah each year. Hundreds of slaves labored moving huge bags and bales of cotton through the city, down to the docks, and aboard ships. This involved countless draymen, carters, wagoners, longshoremen, and boatmen. Slaves also moved great amounts of rice, lumber, and other plantation produce. The oldest and strongest captives who were not serving on the marshal's plantation could have been engaged in such labor. Some of the smallest captives may have worked as chimney sweeps, others as gardeners for Savannah's fine homes. All this work, from gardening to cooking to cleaning houses, allowed the elite of Savannah to enjoy their leisure time.[22]

Just as the variety of tasks and jobs given the captives in Savannah provided a far more stimulating world than the drudgery and dirt found on Marshal Morel's plantation, so too did the encounters and social world of a vibrant port. Savannah was hardly more than a large town in 1820, but there were more than 3,000 resident slaves, 500 free blacks, and hundreds more free blacks and slaves passing through town on almost any day. Hundreds of ships from around the world came to Savannah each year. While they worked during the day, by night the captives could meet sailors, servants, and slaves from across the Atlantic world. The taverns, boardinghouses, and brothels of Yamacraw and Oglethorpe Ward often illicitly welcomed slaves, providing gambling, rum, and the chance to meet these exotic visitors to the city. While an official curfew was enforced by a night watch, slaves had their own paths through back alleys and basements to move around the city unseen. The surreptitious movement of slaves, the news and information brought by sailors and other visitors to Savannah, and discussion of these things in the black community constituted a kind of education for the enslaved. The captives would have participated in this world, maybe learned some geography, and perhaps learned, too, that in the United States the international slave trade was illegal. They may even have discussed their own case before the courts.[23]

The captives may have also heard stories of those who escaped. The enslaved people of Savannah and those living on the surrounding plantations certainly knew of these stories. They also knew that opportunities for escape were being choked off. The wars of the previous decade had destroyed most of the maroon communities and driven the Seminole deep into the Florida wilderness. In 1821, Florida became a territory of the United States, ending the official Spanish protection of runaways. Escape to the North was difficult, and in any case New York, Connecticut, and New Jersey were still slave states in 1821. Still, some did escape to those states, although the results were decidedly mixed. While working on the Savannah docks, William Grimes persuaded sailors to hide him among the cotton bales on a ship's deck, and he escaped to New York. A decade later his master located him in Connecticut. Using the courts, the master decimated Grimes's savings by forcing him to pay a self-purchase price of $500. In 1820, Isaac La Roche described his runaway slave Sylvia and her twelve-year-old son, Moses, as "artful and winning," adding that she "will no doubt endeavor to secrete [sic] herself in a vessel for the North, having once succeeded in getting to New York in this way." Evidently, escape to New York was not enough to ensure freedom. As escape was uncertain and rebellion was suicide, most enslaved people in Georgia chose to make the best they could of their lives. The majority of the captives chose to do the same.[24]

Violence was an inescapable part of the captives' lives, something they would have experienced during their march to Cabinda, during the voyage across the Atlantic, and since their arrival in Savannah. Runaway slave William Grimes wrote a fascinating account of his life in Savannah, including the violence. Grimes worked as a stable groom, a coachman, and a plantation laborer. He served a half-dozen different masters, feared witchcraft by fellow slaves, stole, lied, drank with other slaves under the bluff, and had an abiding contempt for the African-born he called "Guinea Negroes." His story also showed that the violence of slavery was not confined to the plantation. One master, Archibald S. Bulloch, deduced that Grimes was trying to manipulate him. He "seized me by the collar, and beat me with his fist most unmercifully; at the same time exclaiming, sell you? yes, you damned son of a bitch. God dam you, I'll sell you; I'll sell you by God; who wants to buy you; God dam you, who wants to buy you?"[25]

Bulloch did nothing illegal; he was legally disciplining his slave. It was Grimes who was locked in the city jail, where the jailor, for a price, would flog him. While taking Grimes to the jail on the south common, Bulloch calmed himself. Grimes was jailed but escaped the whipping to preserve his value for sale. Nonetheless, it was a harrowing experience: "I was compelled to lie there in my solitary cell for the space of three weeks, before any person appeared to buy me. The room in which I was placed, was so foul and full of vermin, it was almost insupportable." Dealing with lice and filth was bearable, however, in contrast with suffering a flogging in Savannah's jail. "As large, stout and athletic a negro as I was ever acquainted with was selected for the purpose of whipping those who were doomed to receive the lash," Grimes explained. "He was compelled to put it on as severely as lay in his power, or take a severe flogging himself." Reuben, a slave belonging to one of Savannah's wealthiest merchants, John Bolton, was flogged in front of Grimes. "This poor man's back was cut up with the lash, until I could compare it to nothing but a field lately ploughed. He was whipped three times in one week, forty stripes, save one, and well put on by this strong athletic fellow."[26]

Apart from violence, the captives would have found the markets in Savannah the most recognizable part of their new home: vibrant, active places, filled with black women selling eggs, rice, vegetables, and other produce. Several marketplaces existed in Savannah in late 1820. A market for fish and seafood was found at the foot of the bluff below the City Exchange. There fishermen, including the ten slaves of free black fisherman Anthony Odingsells, landed their catch for sale. Fish that did not sell on the waterfront would be taken up the bluff to the markets. On South Broad Street the City Council built a new market to replace the Ellis Square market burned in the January 1820 fire. The new market, however, was not as popular as the old market location, where an unofficial market sprang up. Eventually, the city gave in to tradition and built a new markethouse in Ellis Square. The sale of produce in these markets was dominated by black women, both slave and free. Some were legal marketers, possessing a badge from the city that permitted them to sell produce and other items. They brought fresh produce, milk, and meat into the city from surrounding farms, often carrying it in huge bundles on their heads. Sometimes this was plantation produce the master wished to sell. Sometimes it was produce slaves grew in their own gardens. On occasion it was something stolen from the master, and of course the latter received the most attention in local newspapers. Women without market badges risked a fine for selling their own produce, but there were problems with enforcement because Savannah needed the food brought by the unlicensed women, too. Unlicensed women sold their produce to the market women who had badges, or on the outskirts of the market. Some roamed the streets as vendors, creating a cacophony of singing and chanting vendors calling out their wares on Sunday mornings. The similarity to the market women many captives may have seen, known, or even been in Africa must have been striking.[27]

In December of 1821, Marshal John H. Morel's good fortune seemed to have ended. The circuit court, following its order from the previous May, met in Savannah to decree the final division of the captives. The captives Morel worked on his plantation, and who he had been paid by the government for keeping, would be given to the Spanish and Portuguese claimants. On December 28, 1821, the circuit court met at the old brick courthouse in Savannah to take up the case of the *Antelope* one last time. At this session, Supreme Court Justice William Johnson was joined by the new federal district judge for Georgia, Jeremiah La Touche Cuyler. While Cuyler had been brought to Savannah as a child, his practice ranged across the state, and he had a home in Burke County near Augusta. He was a well-connected attorney and another of the Troup party leaders in Georgia. Justice Johnson's decree the previous May in the *Antelope* case had required the Portuguese claimant to provide evidence of Portuguese ownership of the slaves captured by the *Arraganta*. The tone of the May decree suggested that without additional evidence, the Portuguese claim would be dismissed.[28]

The Portuguese vice consul presented no new evidence. Judge Cuyler, however, apparently persuaded Justice Johnson to soften his judgment. The circuit court decreed that even without any evidence of ownership, testimony at trial proved the Portuguese owned some captives, so the court issued a new decree that simply reduced the Portuguese share. Instead of John Smith's number—93 Spanish-owned captives—being used as the base for calculating the Spanish share, the court ruled that Grondona and Ximenes' number, 166 Spanish-owned captives, would be used in calculating shares. The captives would be divided, the court ordered, using 166 for the number of original Spanish captives aboard the *Antelope*, and 130 for the number of original Portuguese captives aboard. This was an error, for the total of 296 original captives was ten short of the 306 captives the court had ruled were carried by the *Antelope*. The specific captives for each share would be chosen by lot. Marshal Morel reported that 185 captives remained in his custody; three had died since May. Using the court's numbers, the Spanish claimant would get 104 captives, the Portuguese claimant 81. The court added another requirement. The captives would be given to the claimants' attorneys upon payment of a bond of $400 a head. This would guarantee the captives' removal from the United States. They were to be removed within six months.[29]

In July, after the May session and decree of the circuit court, Richard W. Habersham had written John Quincy Adams, "I have deemed it not advisable to appeal on behalf of the United States." In the time since, Habersham had received no guidance, instructions, or even confirmation that his report had been received. In the entire course of the case, other than the copy of President Monroe's response to his original report in July of 1820, Habersham had heard nothing from the Monroe administration related to the *Antelope* case. John Quincy Adams had communicated with Habersham on other matters, especially his investigation into the Bulloch family and the fate of illegal captives aboard other vessels brought into Savannah. Adams, however, remained entirely silent on the case of the *Antelope*. Habersham knew he was acting alone, and that any criticism or problems as a result of this case would be laid at his door. He swallowed the bizarre lottery for freedom ordered by Justice Johnson; similar things had happened in the division of estates in Georgia. He swallowed Justice Johnson's ridicule in open court, the caviler dismissal of his argument that the slave trade violated the law of nations, and even his suggestion that Habersham was in thrall to British imperialism. Giving a large number of the captives to the Portuguese vice consul, however, when the vice consul had presented no evidence of ownership or claimant, was too much for Habersham. On January 2, 1822, he appealed the entire decree dividing the captives between the Spanish and Portuguese vice consuls to the United States Supreme Court.[30]

Habersham wrote John Quincy Adams six days later to explain his decision. "Conscientiously believing . . . that these people are entitled to their freedom," he wrote, "I have not waited for instructions from the government respecting the propriety of an appeal but trust that my conduct will meet with the approbation of the President." The tone of this message was as close as Habersham would come to criticism of the Monroe administration for its failure to offer him any guidance. Habersham sent the attorney general, William Wirt, a statement of the case, suggesting that Habersham did not believe Adams would bother to inform the attorney general of his appeal. It was early January, and Habersham expected a quick hearing before the Court, perhaps even a trip to Washington, D.C., to argue the case himself. "I have endeavored," he wrote, "by every means in my power to prepare a case for the final hearing in the approaching term of Court." Several weeks later, on February 21, 1822, the two *Antelope* cases, one appealing the award to the Spanish vice consul, the other the Portuguese vice consul's, were docketed for the 1822 term of the Supreme Court.[31]

This was a lucky break for Marshal John H. Morel. Because of the appeal, the *Antelope* captives remained under his control. Many were sent back to his plantation on the Ogeechee to work for him. Others were distributed to homes in Savannah again. Meanwhile, Morel presented a new bill to the government for the care of the captives. Through December 15, 1821, Marshal Morel billed the United States for $21,556.69, over $6,000 more than the amount of his bill of July. As before, he expected immediate payment.[32]

PART THREE

WASHINGTON, D.C.

Slaves, many torn from their families, march southward past the unfinished United States Capitol during the 1810s.

CHAPTER 12

"These vessels were plundered in March, 1820, and the libel was filed in August of the same year. From that time to this, a period of more than five years ..."

Chief Justice John Marshall *The Antelope*, 23 U.S. 66, 129-130 (1825)

On Tuesday, December 18, 1821, Secretary of State John Quincy Adams went to the White House for a meeting with President James Monroe. There were numerous problems to discuss. The most important was the high-handed behavior of the newly appointed governor of the Florida Territory, Andrew Jackson. Jackson's actions and attitude threatened to poison relations with the Spanish, who were still needed to facilitate a smooth transition in Florida from Spanish to American rule. Another important issue was an ongoing tariff dispute with France. After discussing these issues at length, Monroe and Adams turned to more mundane matters. It was nearing the end of the year, and it was time for the president to appoint a large number of federal officials across the country. Adams handed Monroe a list of the positions requiring appointment. As the president glanced through the list, "the case of the Marshal of Georgia was mentioned." John

H. Morel had written his sponsor, Treasury Secretary William Crawford, asking for reappointment to another term as marshal of the District of Georgia. Crawford had passed Morel's letter on to Adams, who gave it to the president.[1]

While the president considered the letter, Adams reminded him that Georgia governor John Clark, Georgia State Senate president Matthew Talbot, and Speaker of the Georgia House David Adams had all signed a letter in which they opposed the reappointment of John H. Morel. Secretary Adams also mentioned an anonymous letter he had received that alleged Morel had been charged with the "most atrocious murder of a black man, for which he was indicted by a Georgia Grand Jury but acquitted by a jury of trial." On hearing this, President Monroe "said he wished to get rid of the man." Neither Monroe nor Adams mentioned the *Antelope* case, the captives, or Morel's enormous bills for the captive's support. Always the political animal, Adams cautioned the president that the entire affair could be entangled in Georgia's difficult politics; this was a subtle dig at his rival, William Crawford. Perhaps Adams also hoped that a discussion of the moral failings of Marshal Morel would embarrass Crawford; he suggested that the president consult Crawford before making a decision. Four months would pass before President Monroe made that decision.[2]

During his lifetime and after, President James Monroe was often considered the dimmest light of the Virginia Triumvirate. Anyone, however, would seem dim when held up against Thomas Jefferson and James Madison. Monroe was a shrewd and careful politician, successful in most political endeavors, always seeking practical routes to his goals. He strongly believed in a completely unified and harmonious Republic: As he explained in his first inaugural address, "Discord does not belong to our system." A member of the Revolutionary generation who prized unity above all, Monroe sought to build a Republic without destructive factions, or parties that might tear it apart. There should be only one party, he believed, and it would include everyone. By bringing everyone under one big tent, however, the result was continued dispute within. The most frightening conflict broke out in

1819, when Missouri sought statehood and the clash over the westward expansion of slavery tore Congress apart. Two full years of repair work, largely guided by President Monroe, had finally stitched up the wounds. The last thing James Monroe wanted was more "discord" over the issue of slavery. He had no interest in seeing the *Antelope* case come before the Supreme Court.[3]

Many contemporaries thought Secretary of State John Quincy Adams the premier political plotter and schemer of the age. Adams kept detailed diaries, some of the most remarkable documents of American political history, and these diaries reveal that Adams considered himself a straightforward man. He saw himself not as a plotter, not as a politician, but as a man of great virtue and learning. Charles J. Ingersoll, a leading Philadelphia attorney who would play an important role in the *Antelope* case, also kept a diary. Ingersoll thought Adams egotistical and preoccupied by petty matters, and he refused to take him seriously. Ingersoll wrote of attending a ball in January of 1823 in Washington, D.C. The room was filled with music, dancing, and conversation. In the back of the room, John Quincy Adams was playing chess with a federal judge, Buckner Thruston, rather than participating in the social whirl. Henry Clay of Kentucky, Ingersoll wrote, approached the two and said, "Well, Mr. Adams, always playing great games." Adams may not have enjoyed the gibe, but Ingersoll did, and wrote satirically, "Mr. Adams is writing a long answer to the attack."[4]

Clearly, some felt that Adams took himself and his political maneuvers too seriously. That said, while Henry Clay may have ridiculed Adams and his games, Adams later won the presidency, while Clay never did. Adams was a driven man; he worked hard and slept little. An experienced diplomat, he spent a good portion of his childhood and much of his adult life overseas. He was fluent in three languages, competent in several more, and probably no one in America equaled him in knowledge of European politics. Adams loved to walk, and during his career overseas regularly ambled for hours conversing with companions ranging from Tsar Alexander to philosopher Jeremy Bentham. By 1821, his achievements as a diplomat included both the

Treaty of Ghent ending the War of 1812 and the Transcontinental Treaty, winning Spanish recognition of the Louisiana Purchase and the cession of Florida. Some of his contemporaries thought Adams worked hard to prove himself the equal of his father, others that he simply lusted for power and would do anything to get it. Soon after James Monroe's inauguration for a second term in 1821, Adams was planning for the presidential election of 1824. Privately, he found slavery offensive and slaveholders contemptible, but he could not publicly reveal these beliefs and win election as president. Nor did he want a national and potentially destructive debate on slavery, as had happened during the struggle over Missouri's statehood. Like Monroe, Adams had every reason in the world to prevent the *Antelope* case from coming before the Supreme Court.[5]

William Wirt of Virginia was appointed attorney general by his old friend James Monroe in 1817 and served for the next twelve years, the longest tenure of any American attorney general. Wirt probably argued more cases before the Supreme Court than anyone in American history, appearing more than 170 times, successfully arguing cases such as *McCulloch v. Maryland* and *Gibbons v. Ogden*. Wirt was also a successful writer, though he got so carried away in his biography of Patrick Henry that Thomas Jefferson reportedly shelved the book under fiction. Attorney General Wirt maintained a private practice and, conscious of the needs of his family, sought every way possible to increase his income. He had more than enough work as a private attorney, so as the Supreme Court term approached Wirt often suffered his "annual supreme court sickness" due to exhausting overwork. Many friends feared this would kill him. During the winter term of 1822, his "sickness" was the worst yet. That year he was able to argue only one case before the Supreme Court before collapsing with "apoplexy." While he personally may have wanted to argue the *Antelope* as docketed in 1822, William Wirt was physically unable to do so. Substitute attorneys took his place in a number of cases involving the United States, but no one argued the *Antelope*. At the simplest level, then, the *Antelope* case was not argued in the 1822 term because of William Wirt's sickness. Perhaps more importantly, President Monroe and John Quincy Adams did not want the case argued and may have discouraged anyone's taking an interest in the case. Finally, the Supreme Court docket was very crowded; the Court heard and decided thirty-one cases that term, but many more, including the *Antelope*, were carried over to the 1823 term.[6]

A number of important cases involving privateers and admiralty law were argued in the Supreme Court during the 1822 term, but the two most important cases affecting the *Antelope* were argued in lower courts. The Slave Trade Act of 1819 authorized the president to send American naval vessels to the coast of Africa to suppress the slave trade. In 1820, Present Monroe dispatched three warships to Africa. He sent a fourth ship in March of 1821, the new navy schooner *Alligator*, commanded by Lieutenant Robert Stockton. In May 1821, Stockton discovered two schooners at anchor off the Gallinas River, under the French flag, engaged in the slave trade. Stockton captured both vessels and later captured two more ships flying the French flag. *La Jeune Eugenie*, one of the four captured vessels, arrived that summer in Boston under command of a prize crew. Stockton sought condemnation of the vessel and prize money in federal district court. She was an American–built vessel with an American crew engaged in the slave trade. The French flag was a ruse, Stockton believed, as were the papers showing French ownership. The French vice consul in Boston also filed a libel, claiming the ship for its French owners. The French minister in Washington, D.C., wrote an angry letter to John Quincy Adams, protesting this theft of French property, demanding the return of the *Jeune Eugenie*.[7]

Daniel Brent, John Quincy Adams's assistant, wrote to President James Monroe at his Oakhill plantation in Virginia asking for guidance in the case. Monroe replied, "[W]e should declaim all right to seize foreign vessels of any and every nation . . . we ought to give the vessel to the Consul of France . . . it would be a cause of regret, if the

Court of the U.S. at Boston should condemn her." President Monroe wanted to avoid another conflict over slavery. He ordered Brent to share his letters on the case with the entire cabinet, especially Attorney General William Wirt. In September 1821, the federal district court awarded the *Jeune Eugenie* to the French claimants, holding that she was a French vessel and that her movements and actions did not fall under American law on the high seas. Unaware of the president's intentions, and convinced that assertions of French ownership were a sham, the U.S. District Attorney in Boston appealed the case to the circuit court.[8]

Now Monroe and Adams faced a problem. In the circuit court, the case would come before Supreme Court Justice Joseph Story, a staunch critic of slavery and a devoted enemy of the slave trade. In a widely circulated charge to federal grand juries in the fall of 1819, Story had unreservedly condemned slavery. In his charge, he used the image of Americans steeped in the sewage of slavery up to "their very mouths." "The existence of slavery under any shape," Story wrote, "is so repugnant to the natural rights of man and the dictates of justice, that it seems difficult to find for it any adequate justification." John Quincy Adams knew that Story would almost certainly reverse the district court decision and condemn the ship. He also knew that Story would use the opportunity to rule on the legality of the slave trade in international law, and perhaps even on the legality of slavery itself. Both possibilities were dangerous. Adams was in the midst of delicate commercial negotiations with Great Britain, and at the same time he continued to resist British demands for the right to search American ships to more effectively suppress the slave trade. If Adams allowed the British navy to stop and search American vessels, he would sacrifice one of the central principles the United States had fought for in the War of 1812. It was politically impossible to abandon those principles after a war so recently concluded. Yet in the *Jeune Eugenie* Lieutenant Stockton had stopped and searched a French ship, even though we had no treaty with France allowing such searches. To recognize his capture would legitimate the British demand for a right to search, perhaps even embolden them to act unilaterally against American vessels. There was a second fear for Adams, one that he shared with President James Monroe. What if Justice Story ruled on the legality of slavery itself? Story was a highly respected Supreme Court justice and could not be controlled by the administration. If he stirred up sectional conflicts over the expansion of slavery so recently calmed by the Missouri Compromise, it could be a real threat to the quiet political unity Monroe desired and would threaten Adams's presidential ambitions. Adams had to return the vessel to France before the circuit court ruled in the case.[9]

He began one of his "subtle" campaigns, the type of politicking that rivals believed showed Adams was a man without scruples. As he told it in his diary, he met with the French minister, Baron Hyde de Neuville, on November 1, to discuss the case. In that meeting, Adams wrote that the baron mentioned an old Supreme Court case, the *Exchange*, in which the Court ruled that U.S. courts had no jurisdiction over foreign-owned vessels that had violated American law outside of American waters. The executive could order that such vessels, when captured, be returned to their owners. On November 3, Adams adamantly insisted in a cabinet meeting that under the case of the *Exchange* the executive could remove the *Jeune Eugenie* case from circuit court and return the ship to France. Attorney General William Wirt was horrified. Any such action, he said, would result in a breach between the executive and judicial branches of the government. The conflict was not resolved at that meeting. On November 6 and 7, Adams visited Wirt's office for a "conversation" about the case. He began by arguing that "by the law of nature no vessel has the right to board another without its consent." Wirt's riposte was to ask, What, then, should be done with pirates? Trying another tack, Adams insisted on executive power as granted in the case of the *Exchange*. Wirt refused to give in. Two days later, at a second cabinet meeting on the subject, the president suddenly announced that he liked Adams's idea of returning the *Jeune Eugenie* to France. The president agreed that the case of the *Exchange* gave him that power. Finally, at a third cabinet meeting, a worn-down Wirt agreed to provide the president with an opinion that legitimated his returning the ship to the French vice consul under the Supreme Court case of the *Exchange*.[10]

It should have ended there. The ship was no longer under the circuit court's jurisdiction. Justice Story, however, refused to let the case die, and issued his opinion anyway. Arguing that the law of nations could be deduced "from the general principles of right and justice," Story wrote that the law of nations could not countenance the slave trade, because "[n]o nation has the right to infringe the law of nations so as thereby to produce an injury to any other nation." By engaging in the slave trade, the *Jeune Eugenie* had violated the law of nations and injured the interests of the United States. She should be condemned as a prize. Adams was probably surprised that Story did not continue and attack slavery itself, as he had in his charges to the grand juries. Instead, Story appended comments that legitimated returning the ship to France. Even so, the published opinion was embarrassing for the administration and reopened national discussion about the legal status of slavery.[11]

Soon thereafter, another case erupted, this time in New Orleans. John Quincy Adams probably first heard of the slave ship *La Pensee* when the story appeared in Washington, D.C., newspapers on December 27, 1821. The U.S. Navy corvette *Hornet* was returning from the African patrol when off the south coast of Cuba she saw a well-armed privateer attack and capture a brigantine. The *Hornet* discovered that the privateer was the *Centinella,* crewed by Americans but with a privateering commission from revolutionary Colombia. The prize was *La Pensee*, a French slave ship. As France and Colombia were not at war, this looked like piracy, so the *Hornet* took both ships into New Orleans for adjudication. Aboard *La Pensee* were 239 captives from the coast of Africa; by the time they landed in New Orleans, twenty-seven of the captives had died. News about the case reached Washington in January. President Monroe asked Attorney General Wirt if the executive had the power to return *La Pensee* to the French. On January 22, 1822, Wirt sent the president an opinion based on the case of the *Jeune*

Eugenie. Yes, he advised, the president could simply return the vessel to France. Wirt then warned that the "only difficulty" with this sort of executive action "arises from considering the African who enters our country under circumstances like these as standing upon equal ground with the freemen of Europe." In other words, if the African captives were considered free, with human rights, then giving the captives to the foreign claimant as slaves was problematic. Thankfully, there was a clear legal response to this. "The introduction of Africans into our country is expressly forbidden by law," Wirt wrote, and pointed to the 1819 Slave Trade Act's requirement that illegally imported Africans be "re-exported" to Africa. Considering the precedent of the *Jeune Eugenie*, the president could simply hand the slaves and the ship over to the French vice consul and require that he remove them from the country. This must have pleased Monroe: He could both avoid conflict over the slave trade and save the cost of returning the captives to Africa.[12]

Despite the attorney general's opinion, the case of the *Centinella* and *La Pensee* went to admiralty proceedings in March, before district court judge John Dick in New Orleans. In a familiar sequence, the captain of the *Hornet* libeled *La Pensee* and the captives for salvage. The captain and owner of *La Pensee* claimed the vessel and cargo, arguing it was piracy for the Colombian privateer to capture his ship, as France and Colombia were not at war. The owners of the Colombian privateer, the suspiciously American-sounding Kirkland and Cohen, argued that their ship was a legitimate privateer and claimed *La Pensee* as a legitimate prize. Finally, the vice consul of France interposed, demanding the return of the ship and captives. No mention was made of presidential involvement.[13]

In Savannah, the *Georgian* reported the case at length, surely conscious of its similarity to that of the *Antelope*. "The case of 'La Jeune Eugenie,'" explained the *Georgian*, "recently determined by Judge Story, and in which he is said to have decided 'that the slave trade is repugnant to the universal law of nations,' was strongly relied upon at bar in support of . . . the intervention of the French Consul." Judge Dick, however, rejected Story's argument in the *Jeune Eugenie*. He found that the *Centinella* was a lawfully commissioned privateer of Colombia and that there was no evidence of violation of American neutrality law. The seizure of *La Pensee* by the privateer was not piracy, even though France and Colombia were at peace, but a matter for Colombian and French law. "The brig *Centinelle* and the brigantine *La Pensee*, together with everything found on board at the time of their seizure by the *Hornet*, [should] be restored to the libellants and claimants, Kirkland and Cohen." The owners of the privateer were to get everything; there was no salvage for the captain and crew of the *Hornet*.[14]

This was, however, another hollow court decision. Either during the proceedings or just after them, the president ordered that *La Pensee* be turned over to the French, taking her from the jurisdiction of the district court. This was an astonishing assertion of executive power, and Kirkland and Cohen lost their ship as it was taken to France. That summer *La Pensee* was condemned at a tribunal in Bordeaux under the French law forbidding the slave trade. At the time of the condemnation, July 1822, only 160 captives remained alive of the 270 *La Pensee* loaded in Africa. To prevent future cases like these, in 1822 President Monroe halted slave trade patrols off Africa. American anti-slave trade patrols off Africa did not resume until the 1840s. If the administration was willing to trump the federal courts with executive power in these two cases, could there be any mystery why the *Antelope* case remained buried in the dockets of the Supreme Court?[15]

In October 1822, Marshal John H. Morel of Georgia was again a problem for the president. During a cabinet meeting attended by John Quincy Adams, John Calhoun, William Wirt, and the president, Secretary of War Calhoun turned to Adams and asked if Eleazar Early had called on him. Adams replied that he had not. A native of northern Georgia, Early had moved to Savannah in 1806 and built a successful business there. In 1822, he had become postmaster at Savannah. Early had traveled to Washington and visited both Calhoun and President Monroe. He had told each the same disturbing story. Marshal Morel, Early charged, "was now accumulating a fortune of at least thirty-thousand dollars a year by working a number of the African negroes who are now in his possession . . . while at the same time he is making the most enormous charges against the public for the maintenance of the very same negroes." This would have been unsurprising to anyone knowledgeable about the *Antelope* case—certainly Adams and Wirt should have known—but there was more. Early complained that "Morel's cruelty to negroes is universally notorious." Morel had boasted in public that he continued in the position as marshal only because he could make money off the captives. Early reported, Morel "intends to swamp the negroes—that is, to work them to death."[16]

Early found this boast credible because Morel was a vicious man, powerful and wealthy. He had already avoided the consequences of violent crime. Early disclosed that Morel had murdered a black man but was not convicted because the witnesses against him were "spirited away." Adams told the president that Early's account was similar to the information in two anonymous letters that Adams had received. Early also explained that he was of the same political party as Morel, a supporter of William Crawford and George Troup, but was "so horror-struck" by Morel's actions that he had to denounce him. When asked to do this in writing, however, Early refused. The marshal was a desperate man, he said, and "everybody fears him." The only solution Early offered was that the U.S. District Attorney, Richard W. Habersham, and the federal district court judge investigate Marshal Morel.[17]

This was horrifying news about the captives' situation. The marshal of Georgia intended to profit by working the captives to death, all the time billing the government for their "care." In the cabinet discussion William Wirt remained silent, but Calhoun, Adams, and President Monroe believed Early's story: There was too much corroborating evidence to dismiss it. Because Habersham had appealed the *Antelope* case to the Supreme Court, the circuit court had ordered that the marshal continue to keep the captives until the case was resolved. Now that they knew Morel was a threat to the captives, Monroe, Adams, and Wirt had both the reason and the power to take action. The 1819 Slave Trade Act gave the president control over captives taken from illegal slave trading vessels. It was officially at his behest, really due to the lack of any instruction otherwise, that Marshal Morel was in charge of the captives. Under the law, in a less egregious exercise of executive power than in the case of *La Pensee,* the president could have taken the captives from Morel and placed them with someone else. He could have moved them from Georgia altogether, perhaps to Washington or Baltimore, where the attorney general or the secretary of state could see to their care.

Another obvious way to help would have been to prioritize the *Antelope* case docketed for the 1823 term of the Supreme Court. The case could be argued and resolved within four months if moved up in the docket. Given a request from President Monroe the clerk of the Supreme Court could have surely done this and ended the legal limbo of the captives. Astonishingly, the administration did neither of these things.

John Calhoun suggested that Marshal Morel be dismissed from office at once. The president rejected that, saying that Early's refusal to sign a statement meant that there was no avowed accuser, and he could not dismiss a man based on unsupported rumor. Adams commented that he doubted an investigation by the U.S. Attorney for the District of Georgia would result in much. "The District Attorney," Adams wrote later, "had shown in a former case that he was not the man to grapple with deep and deadly villainy supported by wealth and standing in society." He was referring to Habersham's inconclusive investigation of the various Bulloch men, especially Archibald S. Bulloch, whom Adams still considered a slave trader and smuggler. Adams then reminded the president that because of strong support from Georgia congressmen Edward Tattnall and Alfred Cuthbert, he had reappointed John H. Morel as marshal earlier that year. Washing his hands of any responsibility, Adams wrote that he had opposed the reappointment, for "I did believe that the ineffaceable stain of blood was upon [Morel's] hands." Adams had not recorded any clear opposition to reappointment in his diary the previous December. In fact, he had suggested to the president that opposition to Morel's reappointment might simply reflect Georgia's local politics. Now, with a crisis before them, Adams distanced himself from the case and held the president responsible for the worsening situation. John Quincy Adams wanted no connection with or responsibility for the *Antelope* case or the captives. This helps explain his continued failure to respond to Habersham's repeated requests for guidance. Given Adams's personal beliefs about the evils of the slave trade, the only explanation for this silence was his political ambition.[18]

The president decided to postpone any decision about the captives or Marshal Morel to a future date. Meanwhile, he instructed the Navy Department to refuse future bills from Morel for keeping the captives. Like Adams, Monroe chose to avoid the political complexities of a conflict over the dismissal of a man favored by the powerful treasury secretary, William Crawford. To maintain the unity he desired for his government, he needed Crawford to be a happy member of his administration. President Monroe, as a good Jeffersonian, also promoted frugal government. By leaving the captives where they were but refusing to pay the marshal's bills, he saved the government money.

Meanwhile, the sixteen lucky men freed by lot under Justice William Johnson's circuit court order had reached Africa. In July of 1821, soon after Justice Johnson's decision, Marshal Morel had reported to the secretary of the navy that he had the sixteen ready for return to Africa. No action followed; there was no place for them to go. The American Colonization Society had established a struggling, and literally dying, colony on Sherbro Island, near the British colony of Sierra Leone. With things there in disarray, and no U.S. agent to receive them, there was no place to send the captives. While free, the "lucky sixteen" stayed under the charge of Marshal Morel, probably working on his Cottenham plantation. Then, in December 1821, Dr. Eli Ayers and U.S. Navy Lieutenant Robert Stockton compelled a local leader known as King Peter to give them land at Cape Mesurado. One version of the story had Stockton holding a pistol to King Peter's head while he signed the necessary documents. The surviving settlers were moved to Cape Mesurado, and by the spring of 1822, the colony was reported ready for immigrants. The United States Navy hired the sloop *Spartan* to take the lucky sixteen men and boys to Baltimore, there to join the brig *Strong* and sail to the new colony. The *Spartan* cleared out of Savannah on April 26, 1822, with the sixteen from the *Antelope* on board. Two more captives from another ship, the *Lucy*, were also shipped to Baltimore. What these two men, Samuel Benjamin and Emanuel, thought of being shipped to Africa when they were from the West Indies, no one bothered to record.[19]

In Baltimore the new American Colonization Society agent awaited the eighteen "recaptured Africans." His name was Jehudi Ashmun, and he and his wife, Catherine, intended to build a successful new settlement at Cape Mesurado. They wanted to plant Americans of African heritage in Africa as visible missionaries of civilization and the Christian Gospel, and they wanted to show that, removed from the oppressive conditions of living in the United States, people of African heritage could be just as hardworking and successful as people of European descent. The Ashmuns also hoped to establish a local trade in commodities other than slaves and, by doing so, perhaps make a little money for themselves. Thirty-seven colonists were being sent on the *Strong* by the Colonization Society: Jehudi Ashmun, Catherine Grey Ashmun, and thirty-five free blacks. Ashmun was glad to have the additional sixteen *Antelope* captives join the colonists. The lucky sixteen were nearly all young men—potentially strong workers to build the new colony. Upon the captives' arrival in Baltimore in early May, Ashmun tried to discern how much they knew of "civilized" religion. One of the boys told Ashmun that his mistress in Savannah had taught him "to pray to the Good Man above." Ashmun thought this a fine first step. The next day, May 8, 1822, the same "little African boy . . . was drowned." The captives were living aboard ship, and while everyone else was below the little boy, probably either Major or Little Mingo, went on deck and tried to cross to the wharf. He fell, and drowned under the dock. It was an inauspicious beginning.[20]

Samuel Sitgreaves, a young Episcopal minister, became interested in the *Strong* and the colonizing mission to Africa. He wrote to an uncle in Philadelphia about this unique encounter. The colonists, he wrote, "are all very prime people—fellows, stout, hearty, and orderly." He spoke with some of the *Antelope* captives, though he misunderstood the timing of events in their lives, thinking that they had been rescued just three months, not almost two years, before. "They are principally boys, which ages is now only sought for by the slave dealers," he wrote. He continued, "[T]he boys have been here three months only among the English and they now speak it better than most of the blacks in these Southern states." The captives had also learned how to earn money on the docks of Baltimore:

> They dance and sing in their native style, and in the evenings when they assemble together upon the wharf their froliks become gay and obstreporous enough. The money they receive from visitors is laid out with great skill and judgement and is spent principally in procuring Handkerchiefs.[21]

Not understanding the importance of cloth as money in west central Africa, Sitgreaves thought it odd that the captives purchased handkerchiefs and other cloth to take home. One captive, about ten years old, told of being captured in Africa. This was probably Ned, at ten the youngest captive among the lucky sixteen. Ned explained that thieves waited until they saw children away from adult supervision, then rushed them, tied them up, and gagged them. Throwing the children over their shoulders, the thieves slipped away. Ned told how he and his little sister were stolen like this "from the yard of their house situated at one end of a city as large, he says, as Baltimore." Ned's "father . . . was a man of property, owned slaves, and never worked himself." Ten-year-old Ned, who would have been eight years old when he made the Middle Passage, explained that he was going home to his family. He had no idea that Liberia was more than fifteen hundred miles from his home.[22]

On May 20, 1822, the *Strong* left Baltimore. The winds were difficult and contrary on the approach to the Virginia Capes, and then the brig sailed into an eight-day gale, finally reaching the Azores on July 1; clearly she was a very slow sailer. The ship continued on until they reached Cape Mesurado on August 8, after eighty-one days at sea. Ashmun found the colony in complete disorder, with no one in charge. Most of the peninsula of Cape Mesurado was heavily forested. A small clearing with thirty huts and about seventy inhabitants constituted the colony. There were no houses for the new settlers, nor were there storehouses for the supplies on the *Strong*. The colonists were landed over the next several days, all fifty-four crowding into the existing thirty huts. Work began on a storehouse, and then a second building as a dormitory for the recaptured Africans. New huts were built, and within a month everyone was at least sheltered and the supplies safe in a storehouse. By this point the *Antelope* captives had realized that they were far from their home, and that even the local people were culturally and linguistically very different from them. Ashmun ordered that "the fifteen recaptured Africans should form a community by themselves." This was probably at Thompson Town, on the upper part of Cape Mesurado. There they were supervised; the goal was "to regulate their hours, lead them in family devotion, and instruct them in reading, writing, arithmetic, and the principles of Christianity." Thus the first missionary activity of the new settlers was among their fellow new arrivals.[23]

Ashmun also worked to make the colony defensible, building a tower and placing cannon to defend the settlement. He had only thirty-five men capable of bearing arms. Among them were the *Antelope* captives: "[T]hirteen African youths . . . most of whom had never loaded a musket, were enrolled in the Lieutenant's corps and daily exercised in the use of arms." On August 28, Jehudi Ashmun came down with fever, and three days later Catherine contracted it, too. By September 10, all but two of the fifty-four new emigrants, including the *Antelope* captives, suffered from fever. This was certainly malaria, perhaps *P. falciparum*, the most dangerous type. On September 12, 1822, Ashmun wrote in his journal, "Rain falls in floods. The sick all seem better except Mrs. Ashmun. She is speechless, and almost without the use of her reason. There is no rational hope for her recovery." On September 15, Catherine died. Ashmun was devastated, but because his wife had given her life for the colony, he developed an absolute commitment for the rest of his life to what would become Liberia.[24]

The new settlers remained sickly, some for months, but Ashmun forced them to work on improving the colony's defenses. They had warnings of plots to attack the settlement, so Ashmun drove himself and the colonists to prepare. Many were sick with fever, and all worked in driving rain on muddy slopes to build walls, emplace cannon, and construct a meaningful defense, all the while expecting attack at any moment. On November 11, the settlement was attacked for the first time. Ashmun wrote of hundreds of attackers firing muskets and then rushing forward with spears. There were so many attackers, Ashmun reported, that their numbers impeded their advance though a narrow passage. A long nine-pound cannon, the most powerful the colony possessed, was turned on the packed mass of attackers. "Eight hundred men were here pressed shoulder to shoulder," Ashmun wrote, "in so compact a form that a child might easily walk upon their heads from one end of the mass to the other." The cannon was only a few dozen yards from the enemy and began firing directly into the packed mass of men. "Every shot literally spent its force in a solid mass of living human flesh," Ashmun wrote, until the whole host fled. More attacks followed, and the settlers lived on constant alert. In December another large attack simultaneously assaulted different sides of the settlement, complicating the defense. Three bullets passed through Ashmun's clothing that day, but he was not touched. He wrote that he could not even begin to estimate how many of the attackers were killed. Seven men among the defenders died. As the recaptives made up about a third of the defense force, presumably several *Antelope* captives died. By this point, essentially under siege, the settlement was running out of food. The colony was saved by the arrival of the British schooner *Prince Regent*, which landed to investigate the sound of cannon fire heard at sea. Their supplies saved the settlement from starvation.[25]

When the *Spartan* had departed Savannah with the lucky sixteen chosen by lot for freedom, the *Savannah Georgian* had spoken for the captives: "We understand that they were decidedly opposed to the idea of returning to their own country." If the captives were opposed to leaving, perhaps it was because they were not returning to their own country but being sent to a place more than 1,500 miles from their homes. Through information from masters, sailors, and slaves in Savannah the older captives probably knew that they were going to a disease-ridden new colony hacked out of deep forest, where they would be surrounded by hostile people. Once there the captives, young and strong, played an important role in building the new town, and in defending it from attackers who wanted to destroy the colony. Survival alone was a struggle. Had they known more of what they faced before their departure, these captives might have run rather than danced upon the docks of Baltimore.[26]

CHAPTER 13

"The Consuls of Spain and Portugal, respectively, demand these Africans as slaves, who have, in the regular course of legitimate commerce, been acquired as property . . ."

Chief Justice John Marshall The Antelope, 23 U.S. 66, 114 (1825)

At the May term of circuit court in 1822, Supreme Court Justice William Johnson asked the clerk of court to review Marshal Morel's bill of $21,556.69 for the care and maintenance of the captives. The clerk rejected $1,269.71 of the charges, giving a final bill due the marshal of $20,286.98. Justice Johnson signed off on this amount, and by July 17, 1822, the United States Navy had paid the marshal in full from the $100,000 that had been appropriated to support the 1819 Slave Trade Act. Then, after the October 1822 cabinet meeting discussing Eleazar Early's corruption and violence allegations against Morel, either President James Monroe or Secretary of State Adams ordered U.S. Attorney Richard W. Habersham to investigate. The only clear record of this investigation shows that in December 1823, the U.S. Navy paid Richard W. Habersham $431.75 as "Compensation and expenses in the investigation made into the conduct of J. H. Morel . . . in relation to the negroes of the cargo of the *General*

Ramirez." Habersham, of course, was investigating his neighbor who lived across the street and a man he worked with closely in most federal legal matters. Whatever the actual findings of Habersham's report, it resulted in quick action by the administration, something unusual in the *Antelope* case.[1]

The president must have given the results of the investigation to Secretary of the Navy Smith Thompson and to Supreme Court Justice William Johnson in late February or early March of 1823. Despite the busy Supreme Court term, on March 10, 1823, Justice William Johnson found time to terminate Marshal Morel's control of the captives. Morel was ordered to bring them into Savannah. There, the district court would bond them out in the usual way, as had been done before the *Antelope* case. In order to be sure these bonds did not turn into purchases, Johnson set a very high requirement of $800 for adults over the age of fifteen and $500 for children. In Savannah the captives were gathered and bound out to twenty-seven different men. These men all swore to "well and truly maintain the said African Negroes," and to give them "proper and adequate clothing, provisions, and Medical attendance." To keep track of the captives, the court drew up a marvelous document with the "Names of Africans cargo of the Brig Ramiriz [*sic*] collected together and delivered to sundry persons whoes [*sic*] names are here with stated." There followed the name, sex, and sometimes the age of each of the 180 captives still living in Savannah on March 24, 1822, and the name of the person or company bonding each person.[2]

Most captives' names were short and simple, like those used for pets and slaves. These names stripped the bearers of their former identity. Jack, Tom, Jim, Bob, and Ned were among the most commonly used male names. Mary, Lilly, Nancy, Diana, and Cora were all commonly given female names. Months such as July and January were represented, as well as the place-name Boston. There were some oddities. The classically inclined must have named Atticus, Hurculus, Cato, and Titus. Some names were descriptive, such as Cook-boy, Big Jim, and Smart, bestowed upon a twelve-year-old girl. Next to the name Jenny was the descriptor "Preg.," while "Mary & child," "Bina & child," and "Linda & child" designated mothers and their recently born children. Finally, a few names reflected connections to Africa. These may have been versions of the bearers' original names, though the fact that they were rendered by clerks in Savannah resulted in transcription errors. Quaco, MaKinda, and Tippo were men, and Tenna, Tena-girl, and Bina & child were women. While these names have clear west African roots, they do not necessarily connect the bearers to Cabinda or even Kikongo speakers. Odd names such as Mrundy and Jinkiny may have been transcription errors or simply inventions, meant to express exoticism. Of course, there was the inevitable Sambo, in this case a six-year-old boy who would have been three when he arrived on the *Antelope*. For the most part the names reflected the powerlessness of the captives, only enhanced by their youth. Unable to keep their own names, sometimes given names more appropriate to dogs and horses, it was remarkable that a few managed to keep names that reflected their African origins.[3]

The court apparently intended to move the captives out of the marshal's hands and to secure their return and ensure their safety by requiring a large bond. The men giving bonds were mostly planters or owners of substantial enterprises. Thomas Young, one of Savannah's richest men and the owner of Rae's Hall plantation on the Savannah River, bonded the largest number of captives at thirty-five. William Richardson, the marshal's jack-of-all-trades, bonded twelve captives. The Waldburgs took sixteen captives, possibly to use on their St. Catherines Island plantation. Robert Habersham, the wealthy merchant and factor, took twenty-one captives. Not surprisingly, his cousin, U.S. Attorney Richard W. Habersham, did not bond any captives. He believed that they were free.[4]

Those who bonded captives put them to work in their households and businesses, and on their plantations, probably in conditions not very different from those they had suffered under John H. Morel. Those that gave bonds made a pledge enforceable by the court to maintain the captives well, but no court documents show any action to enforce the pledge. Some individuals bonded captives and then hired them out in the same manner as slaves. On May 31, 1823, George Millen hired "one Negro Man named Dick" at "Forty dollars for one year" from Francis Sorrel and Samuel Clark. Perhaps the circumstances at Morel's had been dire enough that this relocation came as a relief, but it is also true that the captives again had no choice in the matter and were split up with no regard for relationships or familial ties. Yet again their daily lives were upended entirely without their consent, all so that others could profit from their labor in the name of saving the government money.[5]

Surprisingly, in spite of his prior threat against the lives of the captives, U.S. Marshal John H. Morel was given twenty captives under bond. Previously, when Morel had made money by controlling the adult captives, he had complained vociferously about having to take care of small children and the infirm. In this new distribution, Morel was given almost entirely small children; the average age was nine years old. Of them, Amos was later noted as "diseased," Mary was later noted as "Stupid," and Isaac was later said to be "deranged." In other words, Morel was stuck with the captives no one else wanted. Perhaps this was a sort of punishment imposed by the court for his previous exploitative behavior, and there was more to come. In May, Marshal Morel submitted additional bills to the navy for *Antelope* captives' expenses, but this time the navy refused to pay. Despite this setback, Morel apparently did well through his use of the captives. Richard Richardson, one of Savannah's wealthiest men, had suffered both financial and personal setbacks following the Panic of 1819. He decided to relocate to New Orleans. He sacrificed his spectacular mansion on Orleans Square to the Bank of the United States to satisfy unpaid loans. In 1823, he also put the elaborate furnishings from his house up for sale. John H. Morel bought the furniture.[6]

John Macpherson Berrien also bonded captives in April of 1823. He took twenty: ten men, five women, three boys, and two girls. Most were probably put to work on his wife's Savannah River plantation, while some of the children may have served in his three-story Federal style mansion on Broughton Street in Savannah. The house had been finished in 1791 for his father, and may have hosted George Washington during his visit to the city that year. John M. Berrien inherited the house upon his father's death but continued to rent it to an elderly former judge and his family. Finally, in 1823, Berrien moved his family into the old house, and he probably put some of the newly bonded captives to work there. Berrien had been involved with the *Antelope* case from the beginning, representing Captain John Jackson and then defending the accused pirate John Smith in court. Now he benefited from the labor of some of the captives. In the future he would benefit more from the case, eventually dominating the entire affair.[7]

In 1778, Major John Berrien, John Macpherson Berrien's father, had traveled north from Georgia to serve in George Washington's army. A year later, Major Berrien resigned his commission and moved to Philadelphia to invest in privateering. The investments did not go well, but in 1780, he met and married Margaret Macpherson, the daughter of a notorious Philadelphia privateer captain. Their son, John Macpherson Berrien, was born in New Jersey in 1781. In 1783, Major Berrien returned to Georgia with his family to take advantage of land bounties offered to veterans. He began rice planting in Liberty County, but the plantation was not a success and brought him personal tragedy as well: In the fall of 1784, Margaret died of fever. Major Berrien moved with his son to Savannah, where he began a lifelong career as a minor politician, speculator, and plunger.[8]

Major Berrien's fortunes waxed and waned repeatedly; as a child John M. Berrien lived in an uncertain financial environment. When he was six years old, his father shipped him off to school in New York, and over the next nine years John M. Berrien visited Georgia once. He did well in school, and in 1793, at the age of twelve, exams placed him in the sophomore class at the College of New Jersey. There Berrien excelled in debate and adopted a style of extreme formality in such contests, in part to control his emotions and wit. This formal behavior often enraged his debate opponents, who saw Berrien's exaggerated courtesy as mocking. Berrien made many acquaintances during his time in college, but, as was true throughout his life, he made few real friends. No mother, a distant father, boarding school from age six, and few if any friends must have made for a very lonely childhood.[9]

While John Macpherson was away at school, his father lurched from investment scheme to investment scheme. Major Berrien also held a variety of minor political offices, the most lucrative of which was state treasurer of Georgia. He'd moved his family to the tiny up-country town of Louisville, Georgia's capital, in order to serve. John Macpherson visited his family there briefly after his graduation from college at age fifteen. Then he headed for Savannah, where he was to read law with one of Georgia's leading lawyers, Joseph Clay Jr. Clay had studied law under George Wythe, a legendary law professor who had also taught Thomas Jefferson, John Marshall, and James Monroe. Clay lived at his plantation on the Savannah River, five miles above the city, and he commuted daily in a longboat rowed by slaves. In September of 1796, soon after John M. Berrien's arrival, Clay was appointed judge of the U.S. District Court of Georgia, a position he would hold until 1801. Berrien lived with Judge Clay in the Savannah River plantation house, where Clay kept his own law library. Reading law with Clay and attending federal district court as both an observer and an assistant to the judge was more than just practical training in law, it was an intellectual apprenticeship that surpassed anything Berrien had experienced in college. During this time he learned how to relate successfully to others. If he was cold and disdainful by nature, it helped that he also came across as learned, well informed, and well spoken. After two years of study under Judge Clay, in 1798, the seventeen-year-old Berrien passed his examination in open court and joined the Georgia Bar.[10]

He moved to Louisville, where his father was still serving as state treasurer, and began to build a law practice. Recalling those days many years later, John M. Berrien offered a glimpse into the filial relationship. In one case, he wrote, he made for his father "an amount nearly equal to the whole expense of my education." Clearly, there had been some discussion of those expenses. Soon, his father's irresponsible and confrontational actions began to derail young Berrien's legal career. Under the Yazoo Act, millions of acres of Georgia state land (present-day Alabama and Mississippi) had been fraudulently sold by the state legislature to investors for a pittance. General James Jackson entered politics to right this wrong. With his supporters he took control of state government, and the Yazoo Act was rescinded. For this righteous action, Jackson was swept into the governor's office with great public support. Governor Jackson used his remarkable popularity to reshape state government; among his achievements was the creation of a new state constitution. The powerful General Jackson and the mercurial Major Berrien were soon at loggerheads.[11]

Major Berrien, as state treasurer, objected to the absence of any audit of the Yazoo monies. The governor refused to allow an audit. He argued that, with the law rescinded, the funds did not belong to the state and could not be audited. Next, Major Berrien objected to the cost and ugliness of large stables Jackson built next to the governor's mansion. Against the governor's wishes, the stables were taken down. Major Berrien then objected to expense accounts turned in by Governor Jackson's friends. The implications of this objection soon brought Major Berrien and the governor's private secretary to the verge of a duel. Even as Major Berrien's conflicts with Governor Jackson escalated, Jackson's statewide influence and power continued to grow. He was reelected governor and began organizing a political party that would become Georgia's Jeffersonian Republicans. Major Berrien, by contrast, was a Federalist, and Jackson wanted him removed from the state government and replaced by a Jeffersonian. In late 1799, the General Assembly received a letter from Governor Jackson alleging that Major Berrien was a thief who had embezzled $10,000 from the Yazoo funds. In the fall of 1800, the lower house of the General Assembly impeached State Treasurer Berrien for the theft of Yazoo funds, and he went on trial before the state senate.[12]

Nineteen-year-old John M. Berrien defended his father in the impeachment trial. Rather than deny the theft, or attack the facts and witnesses, Berrien responded with a clever technical defense. By law, based on the Yazoo Rescinding Act, the Yazoo funds were not state monies. That had been the governor's objection to Major Berrien's auditing the funds two years before. Thus, even if Major Berrien had taken the money, he could not be impeached for it, as it was not an embezzlement of *state* money. Given the way Georgia's statute on embezzlement was written, the younger Berrien was correct. Flummoxed by this argument, the senate postponed the impeachment trial to their next session. Major Berrien resigned from office and put $4,000 into the Yazoo fund, and the issue never came up again. John M. Berrien had saved his father, but at what cost? Governor Jackson had been hoisted with his own petard, and his party was outraged. Young John M. Berrien was now a political pariah. His chances of building a successful law practice in the up-country town were slim, his chances of a political career negligible.[13]

Berrien's mentor, Joseph Clay Jr., became his savior. Judge Clay had been swept up by the religious fervor of the developing Second Great Awakening. He wanted to devote more of his time to evangelical work for Savannah's growing Baptist Church. In late 1801, Clay invited John M. Berrien to take over his extensive law practice in Savannah. In December of that year, in one of his last acts in Louisville, Berrien drafted and obtained approval of articles of incorporation for Savannah's Baptist Church. Then, in early 1802, he moved to Savannah to take up Clay's law practice. Perhaps the best part of this move was that it placed him far away from his father and their political problems in Louisville. Over time, memory of Berrien's role in the political controversy faded, and he built a new career in Savannah.[14]

Berrien developed a reputation as a skilled pleader, constructing logically impenetrable arguments and rarely making mistakes. He rose quickly in the Savannah bar, but not because he was well liked. He was a hard and distant man. Even after his death, eulogizers described a man cold and calculating. His undeniable skills may not have brought him friends, but they attracted work from Savannah's leading merchants.

These merchants appreciated Berrien's hard logic, his sardonic quips, and especially the fact that he was a master at winning the paperwork battles of the law. Berrien was increasingly successful at trial as well. While other attorneys focused on charming jurors, or overwhelming them with bombast, Berrien, with his soft and almost musical voice, invited jurors into his intellectual world. There, he explained his version of the law with such elegantly convincing arguments that jurors' heads were swayed, if not their hearts.[15]

In December of 1803, John M. Berrien married his second cousin Eliza Anciaux. Eliza's father, Colonel Nicholas Anciaux, had served in General Rochambeau's expeditionary force during the American Revolution. After the war he had married Major John Berrien's first cousin and moved to a 1,200-acre plantation along the Ogeechee River in Bulloch County, Georgia, some forty miles inland from Savannah. John M. Berrien had visited these kinfolk a number of times over the years, but Eliza and John Berrien never recorded anything of their courtship. The few surviving letters between them are formal and direct. The marriage, however, was fruitful. By 1820, Eliza had given birth to eight children, one every two years. Along with the births came the usual tragedies of the era: Two of the children died in infancy, and a third, John Macpherson's namesake, was physically and mentally impaired. Eliza also brought more than children to the marriage. Through her, John M. Berrien gained control of Morton Hall, a five-hundred-acre rice plantation with more than forty slaves on the Savannah River above the city. Like his mentor Joseph Clay, Berrien now controlled a Savannah River plantation and dozens of slaves. It was the first of several plantations and other extensive properties he would acquire during his lifetime.[16]

Not long after his marriage, Berrien formalized another relationship. In 1804, he and William Davies formed a law partnership. While Davies did not have Berrien's reputation for hard-headed logic, he was considered a good attorney. More importantly, he was likable. They made a good pair: the brilliant but "stern, cold and proud" John M. Berrien and the affable yet competent William Davies. By 1809, they shared the largest and most lucrative law practice in Savannah. That year, aside from his plantation properties, Berrien owned an $8,000 house in Savannah, two carriages, and six house slaves. He was a leading member of the Independent Presbyterian Church, where he enjoyed the music of composer and organist Lowell Mason. He also helped organize the Savannah Literary Association and was an active member of the Union Society. The death, in 1806, of James Jackson, his father's political nemesis, also made Berrien's political redemption possible. The Federalist Party was dead in Georgia, and political parties in the state resulted from conflicts between two wings of the Jeffersonian Republicans. Bit by bit, Berrien built connections to William Crawford and George Troup, who dominated one wing of Georgia's Republican Party. It paid off. In 1809, Berrien was appointed solicitor of the Eastern Circuit Superior Court, and in 1810, the legislature elected twenty-nine-year-old John Macpherson Berrien superior court judge of the Eastern Circuit.[17]

Over the next eleven years John M. Berrien served as superior court judge, riding the nine (later ten) counties of his circuit twice a year as well as spending several months working in chambers. Typically, in July he and his growing family would leave Savannah, and they would return in October for his circuit duties. During these holidays, Eliza and John often entrusted the children to Eliza's parents on their hot and sandy Bulloch County plantation, where, as one daughter remembered, the kids enjoyed "coarse sand and pine saplings, squash, watermelons, nubbin' corn, and wormy peaches." Meanwhile, John and Eliza would travel to Richmond Baths, a rustic spa with mineral springs west of Augusta, Georgia. They clearly had a successful marriage by the standards of the day. While we know little of their emotional intimacy, their physical intimacy was active enough for Eliza to bear five of Berrien's fifteen children in the eleven years he served as judge.[18]

His service as judge pleased Berrien more than any other accomplishment. For the remainder of his life, even while serving as attorney general or in the United States Senate, he enjoyed being called "Judge Berrien." Judge Berrien's service, however, was not without conflict.

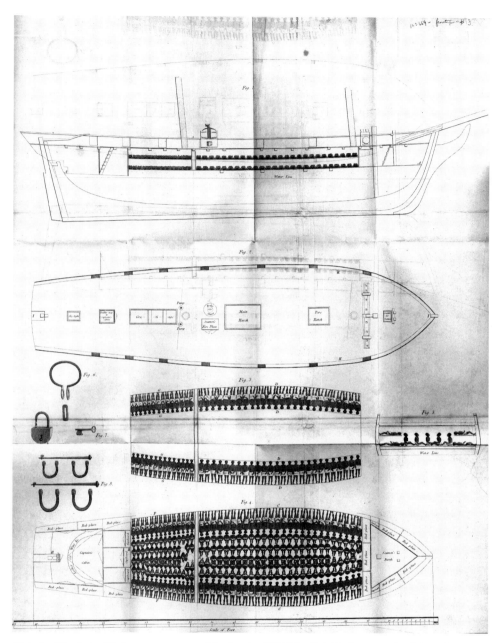

Plate 1   The brig *Vigilante* was captured in April of 1822 by British forces at the River Bonny in what today is Nigeria. At 91 feet long and 22 feet wide on deck and 240 tons, the *Vigilante* was about the same size as the *Antelope*. She had 347 captives aboard, depicted in this illustration.

Engraved by J.C. Buttre from a Daguerreotype

Jn: Macpherson Berrien

OF GEORGIA

Plate 2 Judge John Macpherson Berrien was the alpha and omega of the *Antelope* litigation. He was involved in the case from the first filings of admiralty claims, successfully defended John Smith in his piracy trial, successfully represented the Spanish claimant twice before the Supreme Court, and as a United States senator introduced the legislation that brought the case to a close in 1828. He later served as attorney general of the United States, though his hopes for a seat on the Supreme Court were dashed by the politics of the Jackson administration. This engraving is probably from the late 1840s, when he was again a United States senator.

Plate 3   This map depicts Savannah in 1818. The growth inland with the creation of new squares is clearly visible, along with the fortifications thrown up around the city during the War of 1812. Fifty or fifty-one of the *Antelope* captives were forced to labor leveling the old fortifications from August 1820 until April 1821. These were the strongest of the captives, but nine died while performing the work.

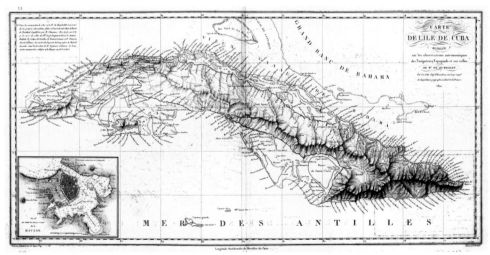

Plate 4   The *Antelope* departed from Havana harbor in August of 1819 to trade for slaves in Africa. The owners, the firm of Cuesta Manzanal y Hermano, expected the ship to return within a year with approximately 350 *bozales*, or fresh slaves.

John Jackson
vs
The Antelope or
General Ramirez
} Libel under Act of Congress 20 April 1818 prohibiting Slave Trade

C. Mulvey Esqr Span: V.C
vs
150 Negroes part Cargo Antelope
} Libel for Restitution

F. Sorrell Porty V. Consul
vs
130 Negroes part sd Cargo
} Libel for Restitution

The Clerk reports that two hundred & fifty eight Negroes were delivered by Capt. Jno Jackson Commander of the Revenue Cutter Dallas to the Marshal of Georgia from on board the General Ramirez. Of that number forty four have died, one is missing, & one discharged by order of Court. The Marshal returns two hundred & twelve Negroes which remain to be apportioned.

Of the Negroes taken from the American Schooner 25 in number it appears by the Testimony that 16 had died before the Capture by the Cutter leaving 9 to be apportioned with reference to the subsequent loss.

American Negroes delivered the Marshal	9	
average loss	2	7
Portuguese Negroes	213.	
average loss	71.	142
Spanish Negroes	93	
Average loss	30	63.
		212

The Clerk therefore reports that there are remaining in the hands of the Marshal seven Negroes taken from the American Schooner. One hundred & forty two from the different Portuguese Vessels & Sixty three from the Antelope. Geo Glen Clk

The Clerk apportioning with

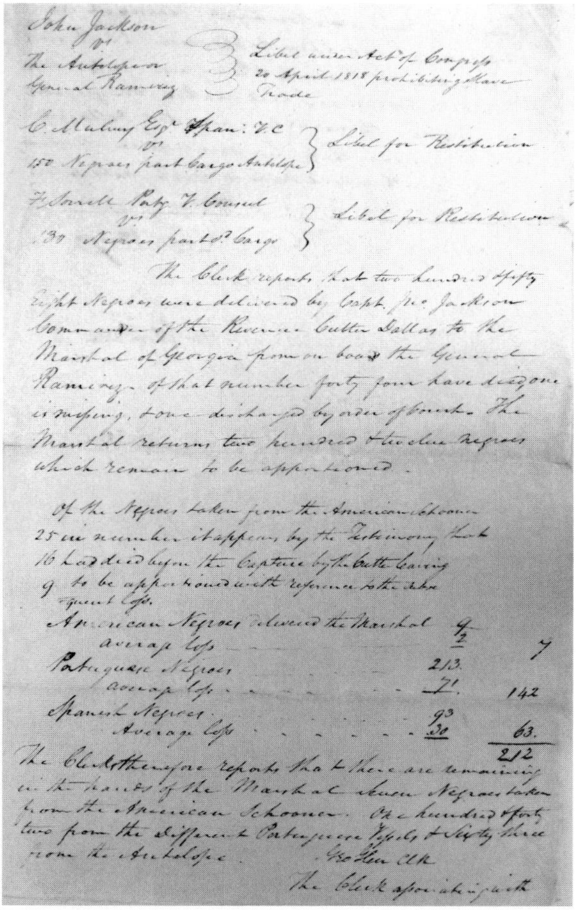

Plate 5 In February of 1821 Judge William Davies accepted the division of the captives performed by Clerk George Glen. Of the 212 captives still living, 142 went to the Portuguese claimant as slaves and 63 to the Spanish claimant as slaves, and 7 were given to the United States for transportation to Africa and freedom. U.S. Attorney Richard W. Habersham appealed from this decree, arguing that all the captives were free and should be returned to Africa. His appeal ultimately led to three decisions by the United States Supreme Court.

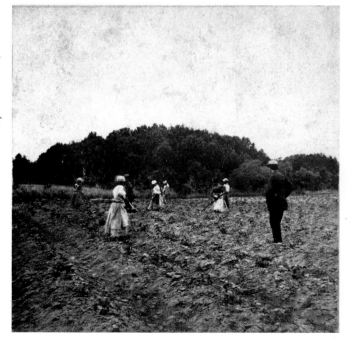

Plate 6 Emergent Sea Island cotton being cultivated by workers with hoes in the 1860s. The *Antelope* captives forced to work on Marshal John H. Morel's Cottingham plantation would have spent most of their time engaged in Sea Island cotton production.

Plate 7   This markethouse was constructed after Savannah's fire of January 1820. Here the *Antelope* captives would have found a bustling trade, often conducted by black women, similar in many ways to that of west central African markets. This was particularly true on Sunday mornings, and the activity became a political issue in Savannah during the 1820s, as slaves appeared to have too much freedom and were sometimes accused of failing to show proper deference.

CAPITOL.
Washington, D.C. 1826

Plate 8   A depiction of the United States Capitol in 1826, with laborers in front. Burned by the British during the War of 1812, its central dome was completed the year the first *Antelope* case was heard. The Supreme Court chamber was behind the ground-floor windows on the right. Someone looking in those windows would see the backs of the justices seated at their desks. This was the only source of natural light in a large chamber some described as a "cellar."

FRANCIS SCOTT KEY.

Plate 9 Francis Scott Key was far more than just the author of "The Star-Spangled Banner." During the 1820s he was a powerful and influential attorney in Washington, D.C., a manager of the American Colonization Society, and a vocal opponent of the African slave trade. He argued for the freedom of the *Antelope* captives twice before the Supreme Court. He hoped that the Supreme Court would assert the primacy of natural rights and rule the African slave trade illegal under international law.

Plate 10 William Wirt was the United States Attorney General during both the James Madison and the John Quincy Adams administrations. Wirt may have argued more cases before the Supreme Court than any attorney in American history. His goals in the 1825 *Antelope* case were more modest than Francis Scott Key's. Wirt hoped to free the captives and see them return to Africa. John Quincy Adams intervened to prevent Wirt from arguing the final *Antelope* case in 1827.

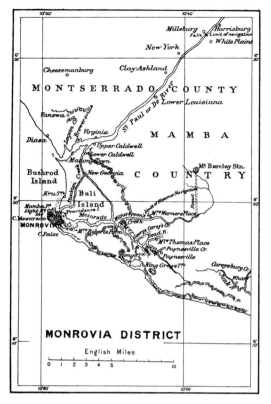

Plate 11   A map of Liberia from the 1830s. Approximately 120 surviving *Antelope* captives arrived in Monrovia in August 1827. In September of 1828, the captives settled along Stockton Creek, creating the town of New Georgia. Life was very hard for the new settlers, and by the census of 1843, when the average captive would have been about thirty-six years old, fewer than thirty were still alive.

Plate 12   Chief Justice of the Supreme Court John Marshall ruled in the *Antelope* case that the positive, or written, law of slavery superseded natural rights to freedom, and thus the property rights of those who owned slaves took precedence over the slaves' natural right to liberty. There was also, the Court ruled, no international law prohibiting the slave trade. As a result, suppressing the African slave trade was made more difficult. The ruling extended the Constitution's strong protection of property rights to slavery, perhaps against the Founders' wishes. The full fruit of this appeared in Roger B. Taney's Dred Scott decision (1857).

Plate 13   The old Supreme Court chamber. It was a dark and gloomy place, lit only by the windows behind the justices and smoky oil lamps on the desks. The *Antelope* cases were considered here three times: in 1825, 1826, and 1827. In 1825, the *Antelope* arguments continued for five days, and the chamber was packed with spectators. The chamber looked the same in 1841, when John Quincy Adams presented his two-day-long argument in the *Amistad* case.

Plate 14   Thirty-seven of the *Antelope* captives were enslaved by the courts. Georgia congressman and literary figure Richard Henry Wilde put them to work on his and Joseph White's Casa Bianca plantation in north Florida. This photo dates from about 1900. Perhaps the black servants were descendants of the *Antelope* captives?

As there were no appellate courts in Georgia until 1846, Berrien used the tradition of holding ad hoc conventions of the state's superior court judges to convene an appellate panel. This panel considered appeals from the superior courts. In 1815, he led this judges' convention further, attempting to establish formal judicial review of statutory law in Georgia. At their meeting, the convention of Georgia's four superior court judges heard arguments on the constitutionality of Georgia's Stay Law. This law blocked the collection of some debts by creditors. Berrien's judicial panel ruled it unconstitutional, presenting an opinion that Berrien had prepared beforehand. While judicial review may have made inroads in the United States Supreme Court, there was no provision in the Georgia Constitution of 1798 for judicial review. The reaction among legislators was immediate. Three of Georgia's four superior court judges were rejected by the legislature the next year. Reflecting his growing status and political influence, only Judge Berrien retained his seat.[19]

Meanwhile, the Georgia General Assembly decided to reform the criminal code. Thomas U. P. Charlton of Savannah was asked to draft a new code. He replaced corporal punishment with prison, limited imprisonment for debt, and reorganized the penitentiary system. The tenor of the whole suggested a movement toward reformation and away from brutality in punishment. The new code passed the legislature, and among its provisions were requirements that superior court judges make regular reports to the General Assembly on the workings of Georgia's legal system. Judge Berrien used his first report, in 1817, to attack Charlton's reformed criminal code. Berrien called for abolishing the penitentiary system, arguing that only public and severe corporal punishment would deter the criminal class. He emphasized the importance of imprisonment for debt, and called for a reduction in the number of pardons and an increase in public executions. Then, on technical grounds he picked Charlton's code apart, item by item, destroying it as a coherent system. Charlton never forgave Berrien for this attack.[20]

Berrien the judge was much like Berrien the lawyer. Deliberate and thoughtful, his seventeen extant written opinions were based deeply in published authorities. Lord Mansfield, the Enlightenment Lord Chief Justice in eighteenth-century Britain, was probably mentioned more often in Berrien's decisions than the statutes of Georgia. As he explained in one case, while some American precedents supported a position, "the current of English authorities is against it." For Berrien, this was enough. He loved his books, and the authorities he relied upon were almost always British. Berrien was no romantic; he considered himself a man of reason, and recorded little if any self-analysis during his lifetime. Reason was the key to good decisions, he believed, and reason saved mankind from chaos. As he lamented in 1818, while sentencing a man to death:

> Alas! What is man? The child of error—the sport of every furious passion—a helpless vessel on the tempestuous ocean of life, without a rudder to guide it from the shoals and quick-sands of vice. Such is the wretched condition of him who madly refuses to yield to reason's guidance.[21]

While Berrien's first role in the *Antelope* case was relatively minor, over time he became a major player. If anyone bore responsibility for the shape and the outcome of the case, it was John Macpherson Berrien.

In creating their partnership following the *Antelope* admiralty trial in February 1821, John Macpherson Berrien and William Davies hoped to profit from the case, but they were motivated by other ambitions as well. Berrien planned to enter politics. William Davies could manage day-to-day affairs in Savannah while Berrien pursued political office. Berrien and Davies soon had active cases in both state courts and in federal court, and by the end of 1821, the law partnership was thriving. Meanwhile, Berrien searched for an issue that would excite Savannah voters. He found that issue in the direct election of the governor.

The first half of the nineteenth century saw the emergence of many popularly based reform movements in the new United States. Among them was a growing demand for a more direct and democratic form of republicanism. In Georgia the governor had always been chosen by the General Assembly, but by the 1820s, the idea that the governor should be directly elected by the voters grew increasingly popular. In 1822, John M. Berrien won election to the state senate on this single issue. The highlight of his first term in the legislature was his speech in support of amending the Georgia Constitution to provide for the direct election of the governor. Berrien argued that the legislature's choosing the governor violated the principle of the separation of powers in government. He drew on not just the *Federalist Papers* but also a quote chosen from Thomas Jefferson's *Notes on the State of Virginia*. Concentrating power in one governmental body, Jefferson argued, "is precisely the definition of despotic government." Allowing so much as the possibility of such concentrated power, Jefferson argued, would inevitably lead even good legislators astray. Thus, John M. Berrien argued, the right to choose a governor must rest with the people alone. In 1822, the amendment was defeated, but this speech created a statewide perception of Berrien as a firm and devoted Jeffersonian.[22]

In 1823, Berrien was reelected to the state senate, and in the legislative session that year the constitutional amendment for the direct election of the governor passed the General Assembly. Berrien broadened his political activities, and as chairman of the Judiciary Committee he proposed more efficient appeals procedures and improved evidence rules. He also built a great deal of support among his fellow legislators both through his extraordinary competence and the skillful use of spoils. When U.S. Senator John Elliott announced his retirement in April of 1824, the first proposed replacement was Thomas U. P. Charlton of Savannah. Charlton was an old and well-connected Republican. He had been close to James Jackson, the founder of the party in Georgia. Charlton also became a confidant of Treasury Secretary William Crawford, a candidate for president in 1824. Charlton had served in the state General Assembly and as mayor of Savannah and had taken Berrien's place as judge of the Eastern Circuit when Berrien resigned in 1821. Despite all this, the Crawford wing of the Republican Party in Georgia soon made it clear that John M. Berrien was the preferred candidate.[23]

Georgia governor George Troup was probably behind this move. William Crawford was in poor health, perhaps the result of a stroke; some said he was unable even to sign his name. While Crawford's supporters tried to minimize the severity of his illness, Troup directed party affairs. George Troup was friends with Thomas U. P. Charlton, but the severely ill William Crawford was Charlton's patron. Berrien and Troup had known each other for years. They were students together at Princeton, where they were separated by only one year. They had both read law in Savannah in the late 1790s, two of only a half dozen young men so engaged. This long acquaintance was enhanced by Troup's respect for Berrien. Troup had learned to depend on John M. Berrien's intelligence and skill at accomplishing difficult tasks. They had worked together on amending the state constitution to allow the direct election of the governor, and Troup was the first beneficiary of this law, winning reelection as governor in the first popular vote in Georgia. While there was some opposition to Berrien based on the argument that he was an insufficiently pure Republican, this opposition evaporated when Georgia's other U.S. senator, Nicholas Ware, died suddenly in October of 1824. The General Assembly now had two U.S. Senate seats to fill and could please everyone. The unblemished, pure Republican Thomas W. Cobb was elected by the General Assembly to one seat, and the less pure but impressively able John Macpherson Berrien was elected to the other. Astonishingly, after just three years in politics, John Macpherson Berrien had become a United States senator.[24]

CHAPTER 14

"[These] claims ... have drawn from the bar a degree of talent and of eloquence, worthy of the questions that have been discussed."

Chief Justice John Marshall The Antelope, 23 U.S. 66, 114 (1825)

James Monroe and John Quincy Adams, arguably the two most powerful politicians in Washington, had shown they did not want the *Antelope* case heard in the Supreme Court. The case not only had the potential to stir up the sectional conflict over slavery, but it could also embarrass the Monroe administration. Monroe and Adams were well acquainted with Marshal Morel's reputation as a violent man, but despite that information the president reappointed Morel as marshal. When additional evidence of Morel's violence, fraud, and exploitation of the captives came before the cabinet, Monroe and Adams neither fired nor prosecuted him. Attorney General William Wirt might have moved the case forward. He did not. The case was not heard in 1822. It was not heard in 1823. It was not heard in 1824. John M. Berrien remembered that Wirt considered abandoning the case. The problem was not that the case involved the slave trade; numerous cases involving slave traders came before the Court during this time. The problem with the *Antelope* was that it raised questions about human rights, international law, and the fate of the captives that were potentially explosive in the 1820s. That Wirt did not abandon this inconvenient case, and the *Antelope* was finally heard in 1825, was the result of work by one man: Francis Scott Key. [1]

On December 21, 1816, a group of influential and well-connected men met in Davis's Hotel on Pennsylvania Avenue in Washington, D.C. Henry Clay of Kentucky, who had risen rapidly to national prominence as Speaker of the House a scant five years before, chaired the meeting. The object, Clay explained, was to consider the idea of a colony for America's free blacks and to organize for that end. If this colony was placed in Africa, the United States could atone for inflicting "evils and sufferings . . . upon the inhabitants of Africa" and "transmit to her the blessings of our arts, our civilization, and our religion." Elias B. Caldwell, the clerk of the Supreme Court, spoke next. Free blacks, he said, "remain a monument of reproach to all those sacred principles of civil liberty." Free blacks could never be given their inalienable rights in the United States, he explained, and this denial of rights contradicted the philosophical foundations of the nation. Free blacks could, however, have full equality in an African colony. John Randolph of Virginia followed, arguing that removing free blacks to a colony in Africa would help "secure the property of every master in the United States." The final comment at the meeting was made by one of the organizers, Francis Scott Key. The resolves of the new American Colonization Society, Key said, should include "an express disclamation of any intention . . . to touch the question of the abolition of slavery."[2]

Key had grown up on the family plantation in Maryland and had always owned slaves. A deeply religious Christian and a conservative man, he struggled to balance his belief in a Christ-like rejection of worldliness and his personal commitment to mastery and wealth. He toyed with the idea of entering the Episcopal priesthood but chose the law instead. In 1814, as British invaders marched on Washington, Key had stood with the militia at the Battle of Bladensburg. The militia panicked and fled. Key ran with them. Washington fell into the hands of conquerors who burned the Capitol and the White House. Perhaps hoping to atone for this failure, Key followed the British forces to Baltimore to plead for the release of a family friend taken prisoner by the British. There, he witnessed the attack on Fort McHenry, and within a few weeks had composed a patriotic song about the battle. "The Star-Spangled Banner" was heard widely after the war, and Key enjoyed a measure of fame as its author. Meanwhile, he enjoyed the money that came from inheriting his uncle Philip Barton Key's substantial law practice in 1815. Over the next decade, Key's wealth increased dramatically. He and his growing family lived in a fine Georgetown home, while Key became a top-drawer lawyer in Washington, D.C.[3]

Still, the need to bring the Jesus of the Sermon on the Mount into his life haunted Key. His open piety either impressed or repelled those who knew him; John Quincy Adams detested Key, but Andrew Jackson trusted him completely. Key's involvement with the American Colonization Society was one way he could engage in Christ-like philanthropy. The purpose of the society was to establish a colony in west Africa for America's free blacks and manumitted slaves. The goals were so broad and so moderate that the Colonization Society attracted both slave owners and abolitionists. While its public pronouncements raised no challenge to the institution of slavery, some members saw its work as a useful challenge to prevailing beliefs about blacks. They believed that in Africa, removed from the oppressive racial climate of the United States, a black colony would flourish. There was an almost utopian hope of illuminating the potential within people of color through the success of an African colony. Others thought the society represented a clever move toward gradual emancipation, or perhaps a route to compensated emancipation. Some slaveholding members believed the society would end demands for emancipation by removing problematic free blacks from American society, others that the colony would provide a dumping ground for elderly or unproductive slaves. Slave owner and Supreme Court Justice Bushrod Washington, the nephew of George Washington, presided over these mixed purposes as president of the society. There were several vice presidents, among them Henry Clay of Kentucky, William Crawford of Georgia, and Andrew Jackson of Tennessee. Francis Scott Key was one of the founding authors of the organizing articles and resolutions, and was named a manager of the society responsible for operations. Key was a devoted Christian paternalist, and the society promised to alleviate suffering without challenging the institution of slavery itself.[4]

The remarkable political firepower amassed by the American Colonization Society came to bear during the congressional session of 1818–19. Henry Clay and others shepherded An Act in Addition to the Acts Prohibiting the Slave Trade through Congress. Approved by President Monroe on March 3, this was the 1819 Slave Trade Act that allowed the president to use U.S. Navy ships to suppress the slave trade. It provided for bounties to the crews of ships that captured slaving vessels, and gave rewards to informants. Most importantly to Francis Scott Key, section two of the law provided:

That the President of the United States be, and he is hereby, authorized to make such regulations and arrangements as he may deem expedient for the safe keeping, support, and removal beyond the limits of the United States, of all such negroes, mulattoes, or persons of colour, as may be so delivered and brought within their jurisdiction: And to appoint a proper person or persons, residing upon the coast of Africa, as agent or agents for receiving the negroes, mulattoes, or persons of colour, delivered from on board vessels, seized in the prosecution of the slave trade, by commanders of the United States' armed vessels.[5]

The law appropriated $100,000 to pay for the support and return of captives to Africa. On March 12, 1819, Francis Scott Key and two other Colonization Society leaders approached Secretary of State John Quincy Adams to convince him to begin implementation of the new law. They wanted federal financial and logistical support for a colony in Africa, the appointment of a federal agent, and an influx of captives freed from slave ships to help the colony grow. Adams disappointed them, telling them that he considered using federal money to establish a colony in Africa unconstitutional. Later, President Monroe would overrule him, and with an opinion by Attorney General William Wirt supporting his action, President Monroe sent agents to Africa and provided navy support for the creation of a colony. After much struggle, by 1824, that colony was stable and needed settlers to grow. The Colonization Society named it Liberia, and the capital, Monrovia, was named to honor the president who had made its creation possible.[6]

The impediment used to prevent the *Antelope* from going before the Court was the desperately overcrowded docket. During the 1820s, there were far too many cases scheduled for the annual six-week term of the Supreme Court. The term could not be extended because it was set by law. The idea was to allow sufficient time for the justices to ride circuit twice a year, some in faraway places like Georgia, Tennessee, or Mississippi. Nor could the Court choose which cases to hear by issuing writs of certiorari; that was a twentieth-century development. In the 1820s, every properly filed appeal that had a right to go to the Supreme Court had to be docketed by the clerk. After 1815, the Marshall Court decided about forty cases each year, but its docket averaged more than one hundred cases per year. At the beginning of the 1825 term, there were 164 cases on the Supreme Court docket. After a "fatiguing session of six weeks," the Court had heard and decided thirty-eight of them. This was a remarkable achievement, but it represented less than a quarter of the cases on the docket. The remaining 126 cases were carried over to the next term and would be joined by whatever new appeals came forward. "The average time for obtaining a decision on appeal to the Supreme Court," reported the *National Intelligencer,* "no matter how urgent, how important, or universal . . . must be *five years.*" In such a situation, it was very easy to keep a case like the *Antelope* buried in the Court's docket, ensuring it would never be heard.[7]

Elias B. Caldwell had served as clerk of the Supreme Court since 1800. Attorney General William Wirt maintained a desk in the Supreme Court chambers, next to the desk of Clerk Caldwell, and they must have discussed the order of the docket. Apparently, Wirt could exercise some influence as well. In 1823, John Quincy Adams wrote to Wirt, asking him to see that the case of the *Apollon* was decided quickly. The *Apollon* was part of an ongoing trade dispute with France, and Adams needed it resolved. It too came from Georgia, was docketed after the *Antelope*, and was heard and decided in early 1824. With no push from John Quincy Adams or President Monroe, with no desire on the part of the attorney general to increase his own workload, and with the political difficulties posed by the case, the *Antelope* had little chance of being heard. The fate of African captives in far-off Georgia could hardy overwhelm these impediments.[8]

John Macpherson Berrien wrote, "The Attorney General had . . . given up the case . . . and . . . it was retained [kept on the docket] at the insistence of a member of the Colonization Society." Chief Justice John Marshall and Justice Bushrod Washington were both members, but Berrien surely would have mentioned if someone as important as a Supreme Court justice had saved the case. It's more likely that Francis Scott Key was responsible for its retention. A founder, promoter, and manager of the American Colonization Society, Key was a strong opponent of the slave trade, in part because he feared that increasing the number of slaves and free blacks in the United States would lead to increasing political conflict or, worse, slave rebellion. Despite positive reports fed to newspapers across the country, the colony had not attracted large numbers of voluntary immigrants. Many members of the society were worried that few settlers wanted to go to the colony, and so they would go to any length necessary to get settlers, even involuntary settlers rescued from the slave trade.[9]

Francis Scott Key probably learned about the *Antelope* case from his first cousin and college friend Savannah's Mayor Thomas U. P. Charlton. Key and Charlton corresponded regularly. In 1824, Charlton sought appointment as United States minister to Mexico. He wrote

Key to ask who could best influence Secretary of State John Quincy Adams on this appointment. "That would depend entirely upon the person that called upon him," Key replied. Referring to Adams's hopes for the upcoming presidential election, Key explained that if the person calling "was a man who could turn a State . . . on the presidential question, the Secretary would try to bend his stiff sinews & soften his hard face, and would be as polite & promising as possible." Key confessed he was not such a man, and so could hardly expect more than a few meaningless monosyllables from Adams. Such a political animal as Adams could only be moved by his political needs.[10]

Perhaps these frank discussions with Charlton led to mention of the *Antelope* case. Regardless of how Key learned of the case, it offered a much-needed opportunity. If the *Antelope* captives won their freedom under the 1819 Slave Trade Law, scores of healthy, young, newly rescued captives could be added to the population of the struggling Liberia colony. Always seeking good press, the Colonization Society could highlight their rescue of hundreds of Africans from the slave trade. Even better, if the Supreme Court found that the slave trade violated the law of nations, then American warships could pursue and capture suspected slavers just as they could pirates. Not only would this deal a severe blow to the continuing slave trade, but it would provide even more rescued captives for settlement in Liberia.

Key may have had no influence with John Quincy Adams, but he had strong connections to Elias B. Caldwell, the clerk of the Supreme Court. He and Key were part of the small group that canvassed Washington's political and religious elite to organize the first meeting of the Colonization Society. At the first full public meeting of the society, Caldwell gave an idealistic speech about the possibilities of an African colony for blacks. He was elected secretary of the society and organized the annual meetings, which were usually held in the Supreme Court chamber. One of the larger settlements in the new colony would later be named Caldwell in his honor. Key convinced Caldwell that the case was important to the Colonization Society, and Caldwell scheduled the case for hearing during the 1825 term of the Supreme Court.

At long last, the captives would have their day in Court. Confronted with arguing this case, Attorney General William Wirt did the logical thing: He asked the man responsible for bringing it before the Court to help argue the case he championed. Francis Scott Key would open the argument for the captives of the *Antelope*.[11]

On Monday, February 7, 1825, the Court was supposed to begin its term. Due to travel difficulties, only four justices were present on that day. Court finally began Wednesday, with six of the seven justices in attendance. Justice Thomas Todd was ill and would miss the entire term. Attorneys arguing before the Court during the 1825 term included Henry Clay, Daniel Webster, and Roger B. Taney. The Court produced decisions with remarkable speed, but attorneys did not always present speedily. Arguments were often long, drawn-out orations that sometimes lacked logical coherence or even a connection to the issues of a case. Charles Jared Ingersoll was a former congressman from Pennsylvania and the current U.S. Attorney for the Eastern District of Pennsylvania who would represent the Portuguese interest in the Antelope case. Ingersoll wrote that public speaking was "really the only public spectacle of Washington," and many lawyers played up the drama. During these showy orations, justices stared at the floor or the wall or could be seen writing. Some suspected that the justices were not taking notes but writing drafts of opinions in other cases, or even letters home. Reflecting on the self-referential bombast often heard in Court, Chief Justice Marshall was purported to have said, "[T]he acme of judicial distinction means the ability to look a lawyer straight in the eyes for two hours and not hear a damned word he says."[12]

The *Antelope* arguments began on Saturday, February 26, 1825. A large audience packed the Supreme Court chamber that morning. Word had spread about this important case. The Supreme Court chamber was on the ground floor of the north wing of the Capitol. It had been destroyed by the British in 1814 and rebuilt under the direction of Benjamin Latrobe. The chamber was semicircular, measuring about seventy-five feet wide by fifty feet deep. Above was a beautiful vaulted ceiling divided into nine lobes. Spectators sat around the perimeter of the semicircle, while attorneys sat at tables in the center of the room facing the bench. Some found the setting impressive, but one visitor in 1824 was not so impressed. Going to the courtroom, which was directly under the Senate chamber, was "like going down a cellar." The room, he wrote, had the aspect "of justice being done in a corner." Francis Scott Key invited friends and Colonization Society supporters to hear his argument that day. Because of the importance and complexity of the case, each of the four attorneys involved argued before the Court for an entire day. On the fifth day they went over everything again. The only windows in the courtroom were on the eastern wall directly behind the justices' desks. The chamber was usually dim during the term in winter, and attorneys were compelled to use lamps at their desks. Smoke from the oil lamps gathered under the low ceiling. The justices became backlit silhouettes glimpsed through smoke, making it difficult for attorneys to read their faces or responses to arguments. Spectators probably had even greater difficulties, and sometimes crowded the justices' bench in an attempt to follow the action.[13]

As was usual, the justices began the day with the presentation of a prior case decision. The *Santa Maria* had been argued on February 19, and Justice Joseph Story read his opinion aloud, as was the practice of the time. It was a complicated admiralty argument that turned on a variety of obscure technical questions. Justice Story gloried in such technicalities, and so he dwelt on the intricacies of his argument. Many in the audience may not have appreciated the complexities of the case, and some surely wondered if they had made a mistake in coming to hear Key's argument. They had expected conflict and entertainment, not the reading of a dense decision.[14]

Francis Scott Key and Attorney General William Wirt represented the United States, the appellant challenging Justice William Johnson's circuit court decree. Following the form of the action below, there were two cases before the Court: *The United States v. Charles Mulvey, Vice Consul of Spain* and *The United States v. Francis Sorrel, Vice Consul of Portugal*. John Macpherson Berrien represented the Spanish vice consul, and Charles Jared Ingersoll spoke for the Portuguese. When the case was called, Attorney General Wirt stood and suggested that the cases "were so blended together" that the two should be heard at the same time. Chief Justice Marshall disagreed. He wanted them kept separate, but he would allow reference in one case to arguments presented in the other. Finally, at about noon, all eyes turned to Francis Scott Key.[15]

Key immediately set the tone of his presentation. "The persons in question are not by our laws to be considered slaves, but as free men," he asserted. "The Spanish and Portuguese claimants demand them as their property. We repel the claim, by asserting their right to liberty." After boldly claiming that the captives had a right to liberty, Key continued, arguing that under the 1819 Slave Trade Act, the captives were free. The Court must enforce the laws of the United States, "not the laws of Spain." The American laws prohibiting the slave trade "constitute a solemn pledge to all nations interested in the suppression of this inhuman traffic, and to Africa herself." "Those human beings who are claimed as property," Key argued, "are to be treated just as if they were thrown upon our shore by a storm." As would be the case with such castaways, the captives of the *Antelope* were free the moment they arrived in the United States. The slave owner Key, speaking to six justices, four of whom owned slaves, then hit his central point. "Depending on the local law they may be the subjects of property and ownership," Key explained, "but by the law of nature all men are free."[16]

While this case was about American law, Key continued, it was also about the larger questions of natural law. Simply because the captives were black Africans did not mean that they were slaves. Had a shipload of white men been cast upon the country's shores, would the Court assume them to be slaves? Why should black men be treated differently? Under natural law all men were free. The Spanish and Portuguese claimants, Key said, must demonstrate how the law of

nations compelled American courts to treat the captives as property
and to take away their natural rights. "The Spanish law is not only
contrary to ours, but inconsistent with the law of nature," Key said.
He turned the burden of proof onto the claimants, arguing that they
must show the Court some positive law of nations, meaning a written
treaty or statutory law generally agreed to by all parties, that made
these people slaves. Otherwise, he argued, the presumption of the law
of nations was that they were free.

What was the positive law in this case? By American positive law
the African slave trade was illegal and rescued captives free. By the
positive law of treaty between Britain and Spain the African slave
trade was illegal, and the rescued captives free. "This trade is now
condemned by the general consent of nations," Key continued, "who
have publicly and solemnly declared it to be unjust, inhuman, and
illegal." Key gestured toward the "great moral and legal revolution"
that was destroying the slave trade. In the African trade, the "enslaved
are clandestinely brought away, under circumstances of extreme cruelty, aggravated by the necessity of concealment, and smuggled into
every country where the cupidity of avarice creates a demand for these
unhappy victims."[17]

Knowing that the Court might not take up his call for moral
action, Key also presented alternative arguments directed to freeing
the captives of the *Antelope*. The claimants asserted that the slave trade
was legal under Spanish and Portuguese law. If so, Key argued, they
must show that their ships off Africa acted correctly and fulfilled their
responsibilities under those laws and treaties. "This they have failed
to do by satisfactory evidence," Key said. Further, even if the claimants acted lawfully under Spanish and Portuguese law and treaty, they
failed to adequately identify their property by providing proof of who
owned which particular captives. The Portuguese lack of proof was
the worst, Key argued:

> As to the Portuguese claim, the owners are still unknown, and
> it is impossible that restitution can be made to the Consul, or
> even to his government, merely upon evidence that the Afri-

cans were taken from a vessel sailing under the Portuguese flag and papers, without any specific proof of the individual proprietary interest.

Finally, Key argued, a lottery to divide the captives between the claimants as ordered by Justice Johnson was unacceptable. One could not substitute a lottery for ordinary legal proof in such an important case when "a claim to freedom conflicts with a claim to property."[18]

Key's presentation was so powerful that almost fifty years later Senator Henry S. Foote wrote about it vividly. As a young lawyer in 1825, Foot was fascinated by Key's "bright ethereality of aspect and a noble audacity of tone and gesture which pleased while it dazzled the beholder." His performance wowed the gallery, and "greatly surpassed the expectations of his most admiring friends." Foote also saw a sincerity in the presentation that made it utterly convincing. While Foote may have been dazzled, others saw the weaknesses in Key's case. Key knew that his argument for prohibition of the slave trade under the law of nations was weak. Joseph Story had declared, in *La Jeune Eugenie*, that the law of nations prohibited the slave trade, but Story's argument had not convinced John Marshall, Bushrod Washington, or William Johnson. Key probably knew this, and backpedaled a bit when he called for a similar declaration, admitting, "No decision [by this Court] has yet gone to that length." Key had presented an enthusiastic, heartfelt, and compelling call for the Court to declare that the law of nature was the law of nations. He could not, however, force the Court to declare that the law of nature eclipsed positive law on slavery.[19]

Key's argument consumed the time allowed on Saturday, and John M. Berrien waited until Monday for his chance to speak. He was an experienced attorney and had argued before the Supreme Court before, in 1818, but the delay must have been nerve-racking. Though his prior appearance before the Supreme Court was apparently forgotten, the expectations for Berrien's argument were high. "Berrien was now making his first public appearance in Washington," wrote

Foote. "His fame, both as a jurist and advocate, had preceded him." Berrien had begun his association with the case representing Captain John Jackson, the commander of the revenue cutter. No records show how he came to represent the Spanish claimant, Santiago de la Cuesta y Manzanal. Charles Mulvey, the Spanish vice consul in Savannah, had died in March of 1823. Harris and Charlton, his attorneys, had received full payment for their services in April 1824. Though the title of the case still bore Mulvey's name, the Cuban firm of Cuesta Manzanal y Hermano stood behind the case. Based on Justice William Johnson's circuit court ruling of December 1821, and the secret deal made with the Portuguese vice consul to split equally all captives recovered, the firm should have recovered over one hundred slaves. Instead, they still had nothing, not even the ship. The *Antelope* had been condemned and sold for a pittance years before. Santiago de la Cuesta wanted the case resolved, and he wanted his share of the captives. Perhaps Savannah's best admiralty lawyer, associated with the case from the beginning, could finally bring it to a close.[20]

On Monday at eleven o'clock Court began, and for once the justices had no opinions to read. Again, the Court chamber was crowded. John Macpherson Berrien began by restating the arguments presented by Key for the U.S. appeal. Taking up Key's assertions concerning natural rights and liberty, Berrien argued:

> One prominent proposition pervades the whole of the opposite argument . . . that all presumptions are in favorem libertatis; and, whatever the laws of other countries may tolerate or ordain, having ourselves declared the slave trade to be contrary to the principles of humanity and justice, we are bound, prima facie, to hold there can be no property in a human being.[21]

"No property in a human being" was not really what Key had argued. By presenting it this way, however, Berrien suggested that Key's case was an attack on slavery itself. This would certainly catch the attention of everyone in the Court chamber, and the attention of the four slave-owning justices. Berrien then turned to a numbered list he had made of responses to Key's argument. First, Berrien argued that the capture of the *Antelope* was illegal. The revenue cutter *Dallas* had no orders authorizing the seizure of a ship on the high seas off the coast of Spanish Florida. U.S. jurisdiction did not extend to such vessels, Berrien argued, and the law did not "authorize the cruisers of the United States to rove the ocean in search of objects on which that jurisdiction may be exercised." The only possible legal ground under which the revenue cutter could seize the *Antelope* was piracy. If John Smith and his crew were pirates, and the seizure of the *Antelope* by the revenue cutter was lawful, then under the 1795 Treaty of San Lorenzo el Real with Spain, the United States must immediately return to the Spanish owners property taken by the pirates.[22]

Berrien then turned to Key's argument that American law on the slave trade constituted a pledge to the world. "The notion of the *pledge*," said Berrien, with a mocking emphasis, "is equally visionary" with the notion of American ships roving the seas to do good. Continuing in this tone, Berrien asked, "[W]ould it become the United States to assume to themselves the character of *censors of the morals of the world* . . . to realize the lofty conception of the adverse counsel, and consider themselves as the ministers of heaven, called to wipe out from among the nations the stain of this iniquity?" His remarks, which mocked Key's moral argument, bordered on the vicious. Other nations would reject any such American pretensions, saying "If the slave trade be robbery, you *were* robbers, and *are yet* clinging to your plunder." The slave trade had been protected for twenty years by the Constitution, and slavery, the foreign nations would observe, is "protected by your Constitution . . . is infused into your laws, and mingles itself with all the sources of authority." Until that was changed, Berrien argued, no nation would take American moral pretensions on the slave trade seriously. The Constitution's protection of slavery could not be changed, for to do so would destroy the bonds of union. "We have no pretence, then," Berrien continued, "to enforce against others our own peculiar notions of morality. The standard of morality, by which the Courts of justice must be guided, is that which the law prescribes."[23]

After this devastating dismissal of Key's call to make the law of nature the law of nations, Berrien turned to additional numbered points to show that the captives were property, and the lottery a legal method to divide property. Even if a lottery was not the correct method of proof, the United States could not question this part of the decree because they had already agreed to it. They had accepted the lucky sixteen drawn by lot and sent them to Africa. They could no longer argue against the lottery. Berrien moved to his next list, a consideration of what law the Spanish had allegedly violated. The slave trade, he argued, was always legal under the law of nations. "Slavery exists, and has from all time existed," Berrien stated. The law of nations had two sources. The first source was long-existing customs and usages. Here Berrien made an analogy to the similar sources of common law. The second source, he argued, was treaty, analogous to statute or positive law. So, "the slave trade is not contrary to the natural law of nations, because, until recently, it was universally tolerated and encouraged. It is not contrary to the positive law of nations; because there is no general compact inhibiting it . . ." The only American case asserting that the slave trade was contrary to the law of nations was that of *La Jeune Eugenie*, and even in that case the property was restored to the French claimants. Berrien could not see how the law of nations prohibited the slave trade unless it was "too occult for the apprehension of a legal mind."[24]

Berrien pointed to one logical inconsistency after another in the U.S. appeal. It was a devastating performance. Francis Scott Key may have put on a show in his opening presentation, but Berrien destroyed it piece by piece. Henry S. Foote remembered it well: Berrien was surrounded by a "vast and eager assemblage." "His voice," Foote wrote, "which I suspect to have been assiduously cultivated . . . was distinct, sonorous, and impressive." Berrien "wandered not a moment from the main points in controversy, he indulged in no flights of fancy . . . attempted no tinseled rhetoric, [and] essayed no pompous declamation." The audience grew utterly silent as the "clear and copious stream of his methodical and well digested logic flowed on . . . like some smooth, majestic river." Much of Key's effort was washed away by Berrien's logic. The core of Berrien's argument was simple: Law was not morality. There was no discernible law of nations against the slave trade. When possessed by the Spanish claimant, the captives were slaves. As slaves they were not persons, but property. The Constitution protected property in slaves, and that protection had made the Constitution possible. To undo the protection of property in slaves would not just contradict the Constitution but perhaps result in its dissolution. Under existing law the circuit court decision was not just legally correct but constitutionally necessary, and the captives should be returned to their Spanish owners.[25]

Charles Jared Ingersoll was a Philadelphia lawyer with a very lucrative practice, and he served as the U.S. Attorney for the Eastern District of Pennsylvania. Ingersoll represented the Portuguese interest but also presented an argument during the Spanish case. His presentation was not as memorable as Key's, because it lacked rhetorical fireworks. It was not as memorable as Berrien's; it lacked Berrien's disciplined structure. Henry S. Foote did not even mention Ingersoll in his recollection of the case. During the third day of argument, however, Ingersoll demonstrated that he was an expert on the law of nations. The law of nations was a delicate thing, Ingersoll explained, and without a treaty there was little more to it than "a body of political ethics." As there was no positive law of nations on this subject, Ingersoll argued, one had to use "the light of reason in determining . . . whether it be contrary to the law of nature as properly applied to the conduct of nations." He provided citations to numerous authorities to support his argument. The history of civil law, he argued, showed that slavery "was an institution established by positive law against the law of nature." Because of this positive law, at common law the correct action for recovering slaves was trover, an action for the recovery of personal property. In 1689, "all the Judges of England . . . concurred in opinion that negroes were 'merchandise.'" Thus positive law made enslaved people property, merchandise that could be bought and sold. In 1772 the Somerset case ruled that there could be no slavery in England, but the case also recognized the existence of slavery by positive law outside of England. Multiple declarations against the slave trade by European conferences and in numerous treaties demonstrated "that the slave trade has not yet been prohibited by anything like the unanimous consent of nations." It would be unconstitutional for the Supreme Court to pronounce or make international law. To do so would require the Court to "exercise the treaty making power," a power reserved for the president and the Senate by the Constitution.[26]

Ingersoll took apart the last shreds of Key's proposal that the Court find that the law of nations prohibited the slave trade. If they did, the Court would not be finding law, Ingersoll argued, they would be making it, and doing so unconstitutionally. Making law would lead the Supreme Court beyond the powers allowed in the Constitution. Here Ingersoll touched on one of the great constitutional conflicts of the early Republic. Was the Constitution a statement of principles and ideals from which Congress, the president, and the Supreme Court could draw to solve problems, or was it a strict collection of rules as to how the government should operate? John Marshall and most of his fellow justices generally sided with the latter understanding, arguing that they were bound by the text of the Constitution as if it were written positive law. While the Court "found" the law in that text, they did not "make" law based on the text. What might seem a self-serving rhetorical distinction today mattered a great deal to John Marshall. The Constitution was not a grab bag of fundamental moral principles from which the Court could draw whatever law it wanted. It was a written text, Marshall argued, one that had to be interpreted, but a text nonetheless. Ingersoll knew his audience, and could not have made a more devastating attack on Key's argument.[27]

On Wednesday, March 2, Attorney General William Wirt began the final argument for the United States. The previous day, the *Washington Daily National Intelligencer* had printed a letter from an unnamed southern congressman. The case of "Charles Malory [*sic*]" concerned whether the slave trade was contrary to the law of nations, explained the congressman. "The argument of the Attorney General will be particularly interesting, as he is a member of the present Cabinet and is understood to be continued by the President elect." William Wirt's argument could "be considered as furnishing a view of the doctrines which the new administration mean to maintain." In February of 1825, just three weeks before the *Antelope* case, John Quincy Adams had been elected president in a confused and contentious contest. For years, Adams's long experience as a diplomat had served him well politically, and he had publicly espoused opinions that made him all things to all men. This congressman, and many others, were concerned about what an Adams presidency would mean for slavery. They looked to Wirt's presentation as an indicator of the new administration's policy.[28]

Attorney General Wirt was the most experienced appellate lawyer in the room, as became clear during his presentation. He began with the positive law. The Slave Trade Act of March 2, 1807, allowed the United States to condemn "*any ship or vessel found hovering on the coast of the United States*, having on board any negro, mulatto, or person of color, for the purpose of selling them as slaves." The revenue cutter's capturing the *Antelope*, Wirth explained, was the correct action under the law, for the law read "any vessel," not just American vessels. Thus the *Antelope* was brought in under United States law, and so only American law should guide the Court. "No person can claim a right to take [the captives] away from the custody of the Court, and carry them away into slavery, but those who can prove them to be slaves." Yet the captives had not been treated as free, said Wirt, and had been claimed as slaves. "The Africans stand before the Court as if brought up before it upon *habeas corpus*," he argued. The standard of proof for the claimants must be as much as was required in a habeas case in the United States. At the very least the claimants must present clear and consistent witnesses supported by documentary evidence that the captives were slaves. This, Wirt said, the Spanish had failed to do.[29]

The Spanish claimants considered the captives "effects" and "merchandise," Wirt continued, and claimed that they must be returned under the 1795 treaty. But could the Court consider them merchandise "under the laws of our country?" Some of the captives were already found to be free, so which of the remainder were truly slaves? The claimants "must prove that they are *property*, and that they are *their* property." The claimants had a heavy burden of proof and had not come close to meeting it.[30]

Wirt then took up the questions surrounding foreign laws, treaties, and the law of nations. Africans aboard a European ship off the coast of Africa were no more presumed to be slaves than Europeans aboard an African ship off the coast of Spain:

> The natives of Africa, however imperfect may be their civilization, compose an independent nation. By the general law of nations, they are as free as the Spaniards, or the Portuguese. Hence, it may be seen, that the mere possession of an African, claiming him as a slave, by a Spanish ship, on the coast of Africa, would no more prove the African a slave, than the possession of a Spaniard, by an African ship on the coast of Spain, would prove the Spaniard a slave.

The law of nations gave no one the legal right to engage in the slave trade, Wirt argued. "Nor does the existence of slavery in the United States form any excuse or palliation for perpetuating and extending the guilt and misery of the slave trade." The Spanish alleged, Wirt continued, that three centuries of slaving meant that the law of nations gave them the right to make slaves of Africans. "The African opens the volume of the law of nations, and shows, that the foundations of that code are laid in justice and humanity." The Spanish and Portuguese could not claim that the law of nations legitimated the slave trade, for "no legitimate right can grow out of a violation of these principles." The enslavement of the captives by the Spanish, Wirt concluded, "derives no support from the law of nations."[31]

Attorney General Wirt had presented a very strong argument on the issue of proof. Though he borrowed Habersham's original argument that this case was similar to a habeas corpus case, he took it much further, arguing that the law of the United States must control the fate of the captives. The claimants must offer meaningful proof that the captives were slaves, and that they had owned these particular slaves. The contradictory testimony presented by the witnesses from the *Antelope* should not be acceptable to the Court. There was no documentary proof regarding the captives and never would be, for surely John Smith tossed overboard all documents regarding the captives as normally occurred when a slaver was captured. Finally, there was no law of nations that said that these captives were slaves. Unlike Key, Wirt did not ask for a sweeping pronouncement that the slave trade was illegal under the law of nations; rather, he argued that there was no law of nations that made these captives slaves. He closed simply, saying, "By the law applicable to this case, these persons are free."[32]

On Thursday, March 3, 1825, all four attorneys returned to argue the case of the Portuguese. As they could refer to the arguments that they had made in the Spanish case, the arguments took much less time. The Court adjourned for the day, and the arguments were over. Friday, March 4, was inauguration day for the new president, John Quincy Adams, and the Supreme Court did not meet. When the six justices who heard the *Antelope* case would reach their decision, no one knew.

CHAPTER 15

"Whether, on this proof, Africans brought into the United States under the various circumstances belonging to this case ought to be restored or not is a question on which much difficulty has been felt."

Chief Justice John Marshall The Antelope, 23 U.S. 66, 126 (1825)

On March 4, 1825, John Macpherson Berrien wrote attorney Charles Harris in Savannah. Berrien had been sworn in as a United States senator that morning and had just attended the inauguration of a controversial president chosen by the House of Representatives, John Quincy Adams. Even with those exciting events to report, Berrien knew what Harris really wanted to hear. His argument in the *Antelope* had gone well, Berrien wrote, though he had no idea which way the case would go. The United States attorneys, Key and Wirt, "have the advantage of a prevailing mania on the subject of slavery, which has reached the Bench." Berrien meant in particular Justice Joseph Story, who, in his circuit court opinion in *La Jeune Eugenie*, had found that the law of nations prohibited the slave trade. Joseph Story, who, in 1819 and 1820, had delivered a famous round of grand jury charges condemning the slave trade and, by implication, slavery itself. Throughout official Washington,

D.C., Berrien wrote, the *Antelope* case had stirred up an "uncommon excitement." Press reports commented on the quality of the arguments and the power of their presentation. A correspondent of the *Boston Advertiser* wrote that he had seen several Englishmen in the courtroom during the arguments. He felt an "honorable pride . . . that so vigorous an effort of intellect was witnessed by foreigners. I have never heard a more interesting case throughout." He added that "Mr. Wirt's argument was worthy of all praise."[1]

Meanwhile, the Court continued at its fatiguing pace. Opinions were presented in the morning, cases argued, and then the justices returned to their boardinghouse to confer and write decisions. The justices were transients, living in Washington, D.C., for only a few weeks, and otherwise riding circuit or at their own homes the rest of the year. It was a demanding job, and because of the heavy case load, the justices were very busy. While they did have social lives, their time in Washington was dominated by work. During an earlier term in Washington, Joseph Story wrote, "I scarcely go to any places of pleasure or fashion." There were no law clerks in those days to help with research or writing, no office space, not even a conference room to work in. The Law Library of Congress did not exist before 1832, so the "library" used in 1825 was limited and largely based on the justices' personal books. At the boardinghouse they shared books, discussed the cases, and engaged in informal conferences. Once a decision had been reached, a justice would either volunteer or be assigned to write the opinion. How the justices divided on an opinion was not usually revealed, for John Marshall had established the practice of presenting opinions as a corporate effort, the opinion of "the Court," not the opinion of individuals. Only occasionally did justices write a dissent, and concurrences were even less common.[2]

On Tuesday morning, March 15, 1825, both Francis Scott Key and William Wirt were in the Supreme Court chamber when the day began. Key was there to finish arguments in a case carried over from the day before, and Wirt was there to argue a case scheduled for that day. John M. Berrien and Charles J. Ingersoll had last been in the

Court on March 12, to argue the case of the *Bank of the United States v. Bank of Georgia*. Allies in the *Antelope* case, in this case they represented opposing sides, and Berrien lost. They were probably not in the Court chamber that morning. Chief Justice John Marshall began the day by reading the Court's opinion in the case of *Cornelius Vanderbilt v. John R. Livingston*, an opinion not reported by Henry Wheaton, editor of the comprehensive *Reports of Cases Argued and Adjudged in the Supreme Court*. This was a case from the New York courts related to the famous steamboat monopoly case of the 1824 term, *Gibbons v. Ogden*. As the issue in the case had already been decided, it had been submitted to the Court without argument by Daniel Webster. The opinion was brief, and it was another victory for Webster. Then, John Marshall picked up his handwritten opinion in the case of the *Antelope*.[3]

The *Antelope* opinion was lengthy and took about forty minutes to read. If Berrien and Ingersoll were nearby, they were surely told that the opinion was being read and may even have hurried into the chamber while the reading was in progress. People circulated in and out of the Supreme Court chamber constantly. Marshall was conscious of the attention given to the case, and the national political context, so he began with statements intended to show the good faith of both parties. "The United States," he read, "appear in the character of guardians, or next friends, of these Africans." Perhaps unconsciously, Marshall gestured to the requirement, in several states, that free blacks have guardians, and he referred to the fact that they could not speak for themselves in court. He continued:

> These Africans . . . insist on their right to freedom, and submit their claim to the laws of the land, and to the tribunals of the nation. The Consuls of Spain and Portugal, demand these Africans as slaves, who have, in the regular course of legitimate commerce, been acquired as property. . . .

In examining claims of this momentous importance; claims in which the sacred rights of liberty and of property come in conflict with each other; which have drawn from the bar a degree of talent and of eloquence, worthy of the questions that have been discussed; this Court must not yield to feelings which might seduce it from the path of duty, and must obey the mandate of the law.[4]

Key and Wirt, while surely flattered by the compliment from Marshall, must have wondered where that "path of duty" might lead. They soon found out. In a passage that at first seemed remarkably general, Marshall revealed a great deal about the behind-the-scenes conflict between the justices. Speaking of the slave trade, Marshall wrote that "the detestation in which it is held is growing daily." He continued:

[I]s it not wonderful that public feeling should march somewhat ahead of strict law, and that opposite opinions should be entertained on the precise cases in which our own laws may control and limit the practice of others. Indeed, we ought not to be surprised, if, on this novel series of cases, even Courts of justice should in some instances have carried the principle of suppression farther than a more deliberate consideration of the subject would justify.[5]

There must have been substantial argument among the justices over this case, and more signs of that would emerge. Reflecting that conflict, Marshall was speaking directly to Joseph Story and of his opinion in *La Jeune Eugenie.* Marshall offered an olive branch, telling Story that, given the emotionally charged issue of the slave trade, it was not surprising he'd made a mistake. On the surface the Court appeared calm, but underneath the waters the *Antelope* had caused great turbulence. The comments also told the listeners that Key and Wirt had lost on the law of nations argument. Whether they realized as much upon hearing it, or only later upon reading it, this had to be discouraging.

Marshall also suggested that differing public opinions on the issues of the slave trade and slavery could all be dealt with happily under a system of laws. Marshall was a nationalist, and he tried to minimize the impact of this case on the growing political and moral conflict in the United States over slavery. Just as the expansion of slavery into Missouri could be accommodated under the Constitution, so too could all "public feelings" on slavery. Those "public feelings," however, were not part of "strict law." One of the accomplishments of the Marshall tenure as chief justice was the transformation of the Constitution from a statement of fundamental principles for government into a legal text that could be interpreted like any other legal text. In 1800, there was still uncertainty about the supremacy of the Constitution and the meaning of the powers given to the federal government. By the time of the *Antelope* decision, those questions had been convincingly engaged by Marshall's Court. In the process, the Marshall Court had transformed the Constitution into a species of supreme positive law. This remarkable accomplishment began with *Marbury v. Madison* (1803), in which the Court asserted its power to rule federal legislation invalid if it contradicted the text of the Constitution. The process then continued in all areas, but most powerfully through cases engaging the contract clause and the commerce clause, until *McCulloch v. Maryland* (1819) and *Gibbons v. Ogden* (1824) firmly established the supremacy of the Constitution's language. Marshall liked "strict law"—in other words, clear textual law that had authority due to its source, not due to its merits. This was a type of legal positivism, and Marshall transformed the text of the Constitution into the most authoritative positive law in the United States. Now he signaled that he would extend these same principles to international law and the slave trade.[6]

The sources for the law of nations were still debated in 1825. Without a sovereign or a legislature to establish law, how could there be a law of nations? The very idea seemed to contradict the growing philosophical emphasis on sovereignty as the authoritative source of law. Yet the law of nations clearly existed. By the early nineteenth century there were two approaches to understanding this. One argued that the source of the law of nations reflected the law of nature. The seventeenth-century Dutch jurist Hugo Grotius had argued this, and the concept was more fully developed by Swiss law professor Jean-Jacques Burlamaqui in the eighteenth century. "It is necessary, therefore, there should be some law among nations, to serve as a rule for mutual commerce," Burlamaqui wrote. "Now, this law can be nothing else but the law of nature itself. . . . Thus, natural law and the law of nations are in reality one and the same thing." There was no need for sovereign authority, because the source of natural law was the essential nature of man and the universe, perhaps even God. During the eighteenth century this approach grew to include the idea of inherent individual natural rights. The law of nations consisted of principles derived from the laws of nature and from the implications of inherent natural rights. Based on principles of justice, natural law, and natural rights, it was forward-looking. It asked what the law of nations should be in a case; this had formed the basis for Joseph Story's ruling that the slave trade violated the law of nations. It was also the heart of the argument against the international slave trade presented by Francis Scott Key in the Antelope.[7]

The other approach to the law of nations was empirical: It focused on what was actually done between states. Jeremy Bentham had ridiculed the concept of natural rights and natural law as "nonsense upon stilts." The empiricist sought rules based upon facts, as shown through the history of international relations. Prescriptive principles had no place in this approach; instead legal scholars looked to the past to discover the law of nations in established customs, court cases, and treaties. The operative question for these scholars was, "What had nations done?," not "What should nations do?" The empirical sources of the law of nations, or what Bentham had dubbed "international law," resembled the sources sought by legal positivists like John Marshall. Treaties and court decisions issued from sovereign authorities, were written texts and subject to interpretation by a court. In some ways Marshall's approach resembled what was later called legal formalism: applying the law strictly regardless of the social or political context or consequences. Marshall, however, was never a strict formalist and often found ways to fit the law into his policy goals.[8]

In his *Antelope* opinion, he looked first to published cases on the slave trade to find the law of nations. The three cases he used were all from the British courts, and out of these decisions he derived the first legal principle that would shape the opinion of the Court. "The principle common to these cases is, that the legality of the capture of a vessel engaged in the slave trade, depends on the law of the country to which the vessel belongs." If the national law of the ship's flag forbade the slave trade, then the ship was a good prize and could be condemned. If not, if the nation allowed the slave trade, then the ship or its value had to be returned to its owners. In either case, the question was not one of natural law but a question of positive law of a particular nation—in this case, the laws of Spain and Portugal.[9]

Another empirical source for the law of nations was long-established custom or practice. Marshall looked to the 1817 British admiralty case of the *Louis* for guidance on this question. The *Louis*, Marshall found, concluded that the right to search at sea was valid only in wartime. This, of course, had been one of the contentions that led to the War of 1812, and Marshall and other American nationalists felt that this principle had been reasserted successfully by the war. The *Louis* also engaged another important matter, the legality of the slave trade under the law of nations. Justice William Scott ruled that based on "general, and ancient, and admitted practice," the slave trade did not violate the law of nations. This, Marshall argued, was where the British admiralty courts stood, and where history stood on the issue. By implication, the rulings of these courts and the interpretation of history that William Scott presented were seen by Marshall as the most authoritative. The records of United States courts, Marshall argued, were less authoritative because "different opinions have been entertained" as to the legality of the slave trade under the law of nations. "The subject is now, for the first time, before this Court," Marshall wrote. He intended to resolve the matter.[10]

He began by discussing the law of nature argument made by Story and Key.

> That [the slave trade] is contrary to the law of nature will scarcely be denied. That every man has a natural right to the fruits of his own labor, is generally admitted; and that no other person can rightfully deprive him of those fruits, and appropriate them against his will, seems to be the necessary result of this admission.

This statement probably went further than anyone in the courtroom expected; Marshall clearly suggested that not just the slave trade, but slavery itself, was "contrary to the law of nature." In other words, he accepted Key's assertion that "by the law of nature all men are free." The law of nature, however, was not the law of nations. "Whatever might be the answer of a moralist to this question, a jurist must search for a legal solution." Because something was morally wrong did not mean that it was legally wrong. The standard used by a court was not what was right but what the law was. "If we resort to this standard as the test of international law, the question, as has already been observed, is decidedly in favor of the legality of the trade." The slave trade was also legal under the laws and treaties of Spain and Portugal at the time the captives were acquired in Africa. Under clear positive law, the captives were property. The natural rights Marshall or others might accord them did not matter. The positive law of property eclipsed natural law and the rights of individuals.[11]

The international slave trade did not violate the law of nations, nor was it piracy. There were powerful implications to this ruling in 1820s America. Since the time of the Declaration of Independence, Americans had never satisfactorily resolved the question of slavery existing in a republic based upon assertions of universal natural law and rights. Marshall's answer was simple: Slavery resulted from positive law, which took precedence over natural law in the courts. He had previously hinted at controversy among the six justices over this case.

Joseph Story must have objected to this evisceration of his carefully argued and widely distributed opinion in *La Jeune Eugenie*. Justice Gabriel Duvall may have objected as well—twelve years earlier, in the sole dissent of his long and largely silent career on the Supreme Court, Duvall had disagreed with Marshall in the case of *Mima Queen and Child, Petitioners for Freedom, v. Hepburn*. Marshall had ruled that hearsay evidence could not be used to overturn the ownership of property. Duvall dissented, and wrote that he would have freed Mima Queen and her child because "the right to freedom is more important than the right of property." Even if Duvall supported Story on the question of whether the captives had a natural right to liberty, a vote of two against four meant that Marshall's argument prevailed. As was the usual practice of Marshall and his Court, Story and Duvall remained silent and joined the whole in presenting a united opinion.[12]

"The general question being disposed of," Marshall continued, "it remains to examine the circumstances of the particular case." Both Key and Wirt were very familiar with Marshall and his Court. While he might find the general law to be one thing, he also often found particular exceptions due to facts in the case, allowing him to render a more just decision. In this manner Marshall escaped the trap of formalism. While the hope for a sweeping declaration against the slave trade under the law of nations had died, there was still hope for the captives' freedom. Marshall restated what he believed were the important facts in the case. The *Antelope* was a Spanish ship loading a cargo of slaves on the coast of Africa when she was captured by the *Arraganta*, a privateer manned in Baltimore. Other ships, "said to be Portuguese," were also robbed, and slaves taken from them were put aboard the *Antelope*. On the coast of Brazil the *Arraganta* wrecked, and the *Antelope* continued on alone, searching for a place to sell the captives. Hovering near the coast of the United States, the *Antelope*

was captured by the revenue cutter *Dallas*. The ship and the captives aboard were libeled, or claimed, in admiralty proceedings. The *Antelope* itself was condemned and sold, but a conflict developed over the captives.[13]

The vice consuls of Spain and Portugal claimed the captives found aboard the *Antelope* were the property of their nationals, while the United States opposed the claims on behalf of the captives and their claim for freedom. The issue, Marshal suggested, was a simple dichotomy. If the captives were legal slaves when loaded onto ships off the coast of Africa, then the laws of Spain and Portugal controlled, and the captives should be restored as slaves to their owners. If they were not legal slaves, then the laws of the United States controlled, and the captives would be transported to Africa and freedom. Who, then, had the burden of proof? Did the Spanish claimants have to prove that the captives were legally slaves, or did the United States have to prove that they were not? Herein lay the solution to the case.[14]

Surprisingly, Marshall wrote that the Court could not rule on this question. The issue of proof "is a question on which much difficulty has been felt." In other words, the justices had disagreed and were unable to resolve this issue. There was no reason "to state the reasons in support of the affirmative or negative . . . because the Court is divided on it." The justices had divided three to three on the crucial question of whether the captives had to be proven legal slaves by the claimants, or proven not to be slaves by the United States. "Consequently, no principle is settled," wrote Marshall, and "the decree of the Circuit Court as directs restitution to the Spanish claimant of the Africans found on board the *Antelope* when she was captured by the *Arraganta*, is affirmed." Berrien's client, Santiago de la Cuesta, had just recovered a portion of the captives, but, Marshall was not finished.[15]

"There is some difficulty in ascertaining their number," he continued, meaning figuring out how many captives belonged to the Spanish claimants. The Spanish libel claimed 150 captives as slaves, the district court had ruled that there were originally 93, and the circuit court had increased that number to 166. Domingo Grondona, the second mate of the *Antelope*, and the boatswain Thomas Ximenes had testified to the number of 166. The Supreme Court did not find that number credible. Ximenes was a weak witness, and Grondona said that he had not counted the captives on the day they were captured by the *Arraganta*. Most telling of all, Marshall wrote, was the improbability of the *Antelope*'s acquiring so many slaves in the ten days between the departure of the first privateer and the second capture by the *Arraganta*. John Smith had testified that there were 93 captives aboard the *Antelope* when it was taken by the *Arraganta*, and William Brunton had said ninety-odd were aboard. While there was a division within the Court on the question of proof as to whether the captives were legal slaves, there was no question that the Spanish had to prove how many slaves were aboard the *Antelope*. Based on the evidence from the district court, "Their proof is not satisfactory beyond ninety-three." Then, crucially, Marshall wrote, "The individuals who compose this number must be designated to the satisfaction of the Circuit Court." This meant that less than a third of the surviving captives would belong to the Spanish claimant. Additionally, the proportion of captives remaining from the original 93 had to be "designated" in the circuit court. This suggested something more than chosen by lottery, as the circuit court had decreed. Marshall then turned so quickly to the next part of the opinion that he failed to make clear the Court's intention.[16]

"We proceed next to consider the libel of the Vice-Consul of Portugal," Marshall read. By this point he had been reading for about half an hour. If John M. Berrien was in the room, he knew about the secret deal between the Spanish and Portuguese vice consuls to split equally all the captives recovered as slaves. The proportion awarded the Spanish claimant of less than a third of the survivors did not matter'; ultimately, they and the Portuguese would split all the survivors. Marshall's listeners followed him to the most startling part of the decision. The Portuguese vice consul had claimed 130 captives as the property of Portuguese owners. First, Marshall asked, How could the Court even know that there were any Portuguese owners? The Spanish had provided attested documents showing their ownership of the *Antelope* and the investment in her voyage. The Portuguese had provided nothing. Several witnesses had testified that slaves were taken from Portuguese ships, Marshall continued, but "it does not appear that their opinions were founded on any other fact than the flag under which the vessel sailed." A flag meant nothing, and there was no other evidence of Portuguese ownership:

These vessels were plundered in March, 1820, and the libel was filed in August of the same year. From that time to this, a period of more than five years, no subject of the crown of Portugal has appeared to assert his title to this property, no individual has been designated as its probable owner. This inattention to a subject of so much real interest, this total disregard of a valuable property, is so contrary to the common course of human action, as to justify serious suspicion that the real owner dares not avow himself.[17]

Despite the district court and the circuit court rulings that scores of slaves belonged to the Portuguese claimant, no claimant had emerged. How could that be, when so much money was at stake?

That Americans and others who cannot use the flag of their own nation carry on this criminal and inhuman traffic under the flags of other countries is a fact of such general notoriety that courts of admiralty may act upon it. It cannot be necessary to take particular depositions to prove a fact which is [a] matter of general and public history. This long, and otherwise unaccountable absence, of any Portuguese claimant, furnishes irresistible testimony, that no such claimant exists and that the real owner belongs to some other nation and feels the necessity of concealment.[18]

"These Africans still remain unclaimed by the owner, or by any person professing to know the owner," Marshall read. Then he went further: "The libel . . . alleges a state of things which is *prima facie* evidence of an intent to violate the laws of the United States, by the commission of an act which, according to those laws, entitles these men to freedom." Perhaps Key and Wirt glanced at each other for confirmation. Had they heard correctly? Had the chief justice just denounced the Portuguese libel as part of a criminal conspiracy? Had the chief justice just declared that the Portuguese captives, the largest share, were actually "men," and free? If Berrien was present, he must have realized with a jolt that this was disaster. Not only had his client been given only a third of the surviving captives, but that number would have to be split with the Portuguese vice consul. The recovery was hardly worth the effort.[19]

There must have been a stir in the courtroom as Marshall finished reading his opinion. The chief justice was up to his old tricks. Having found that there was no prohibition of the international slave trade under the law of nations, and having sustained the circuit court's ruling that the remaining captives of the *Antelope* were slaves, he had turned everything on its head. With one small statement, he had recognized the humanity of the majority of the *Antelope* captives and in the same breath freed tens of thousands of dollars' worth of property. This was John Marshall's version of adhering strictly to the law while punishing those engaged in the illegal slave trade. Surely some shook their heads and smiled at the cleverness of the chief justice. That cleverness, however, would result in the captives' suffering more than two additional years of slavery.

CHAPTER 16

"The Africans of the Antelope being paraded in front of the courthouse, Mr. Richardson was directed by the court to point out and designate, individually, the Africans who had worked on the fortifications, and he designated thirty-four."

Supreme Court Justice Robert Trimble, *The Antelope*, 25 U.S. 546, 553 (1827)

I n Georgia the *Antelope* captives still labored in and around Savannah. On May 30, 1825, William Harrison, the overseer on John M. Berrien's Morton Hall plantation during 1824, swore that at the start of that year he had on the plantation twenty captives as laborers. One of the captives, a woman named Hetty, died in childbirth in August 1824. Thomas Nelson, the overseer on Berrien's plantation for 1825, swore that he began with nineteen "African negroes from the Ramirez" working under him. On March 31, 1825, a woman named Liddy died in childbirth. Even as captives continued to die, a development suggested by the causes of death on Berrien's plantation became evident. Robert Habersham, the wealthy merchant, had hired twenty-two captives from Francis Sorrel. Two of the captives, January and Pay, had died. Two other captives, Nelly and "Eliza called Clarissa," had each given birth to healthy babies. The *Antelope* captives had been in Savannah for five years and now averaged about eighteen or nineteen years old. Increasingly, the young women began to have children. Whether the fathers were fellow captives, local slaves, or white men was not recorded. Then, even as these domestic matters and relationships and the tragedies of life dominated the daily lives of the captives, the *Antelope* case became entangled with Georgia's determination to dispossess the Creek Indians. The result was a threat to the political career of John M. Berrien.[1]

Broken by civil war and dominated by military forces under the command of General Andrew Jackson, the Creek Nation had begun to unravel in 1814. At the site of the former French Fort Toulouse, renamed Fort Jackson in the wake of war, General Andrew Jackson presented terms to his stunned Creek allies. Despite their alliance and support in destroying the Red Stick Creeks, they were forced to accept the Treaty of Fort Jackson. More than one-third of the Creek lands were lost, including a broad strip lining the southern edge of the Creek Nation. The strip separated them both from Spanish and British merchants in Florida and from the Seminole. Thus began the conquest of the Creek Nation by treaty rather than by war. In 1818, more land was ceded to Georgia. In 1821, the first Treaty of Indian Springs ceded over five million acres in Georgia between the Ocmulgee and the Flint rivers. The bulk of the $450,000 given to the Creek for this land went not to Indians but to Georgians with claims against the Indians, mostly for trade debts. William McIntosh, a mestizo Lower Creek leader who helped facilitate the 1821 treaty, was given $40,000 and 1,000 acres surrounding Indian Springs. The land taken from the Creeks was distributed by lottery. Settlers poured into the newly opened lands between the Ocmulgee and Flint rivers, many bringing in slaves to cultivate cotton.[2]

Land hunger in Georgia, driven by the gold mine of expanding cotton production, was not satisfied by this huge cession of territory. Georgia politicians demanded that the federal government force the Creeks off all their remaining lands in the state. Meanwhile, the Creeks adopted laws and resolutions forbidding the transfer of any more land to the

United States or to Georgia under pain of death. When federal treaty commissioners met with Creek leaders at Broken Arrow in December 1824 to ask for more land, they faced an unqualified refusal.[3]

From Milledgeville, Governor George Troup watched this closely, grappling with a new sort of challenge. Earlier, John M. Berrien's legislative success had paved the way for Troup to be elected by popular vote. Troup needed a popular issue for reelection, and that issue was land. Because Georgia used a lottery to distribute land from Indian cessions, any man or widow, no matter how poor or improvident, had a chance to win a parcel of land. If Troup could present the voters with another massive land cession and the promise of a lottery that would benefit thousands of Georgians, his chances for reelection would soar. He also had an ace up his sleeve: His cousin was William McIntosh, the influential and wealthy mestizo Lower Creek leader who had helped arrange the first Treaty of Indian Springs in 1821. McIntosh supported the idea of the Creeks moving to the West, and he was susceptible to suggestion if the result promised to be financially lucrative.[4]

In February of 1825, treaty commissioners invited several carefully chosen Creeks to William McIntosh's Inn at Indian Springs. The result, on February 12, 1825, was the second Treaty of Indian Springs, through which McIntosh and a handful of other village leaders surrendered the remaining Creek lands. Georgia took more than 4.700,000 acres, and three million more acres went to the new state of Alabama. In return, the Creek were to leave their land and move to federal land along the Arkansas River to the west whose acreage equaled that of their former property. They were also given $400,000 for the costs of removal. McIntosh and the other eight signers were given half the money, or $200,000, immediately. McIntosh was also paid $25,000 for his property at Indian Springs. The treaty was quickly sent to Washington and was approved by the Senate on March 3, 1825, the last day of arguments in the *Antelope* case. Newly inaugurated President John Quincy Adams approved the treaty four days later without looking deeply into the matter.[5]

On March 17, 1825, Governor George Troup attended the Hibernian Society's St. Patrick's Day dinner in Savannah. Toasts were offered to St. Patrick, the Republic of the United States, and the "National Guest," the Marquis de Lafayette, who would arrive in Savannah two days later. U.S. Attorney Richard W. Habersham gave a rousing speech on Irish nationalism and the cause of liberty. Governor Troup was toasted for his support of Ireland, as was John Macpherson Berrien, whose "splendid talents have been acknowledged before the Supreme Court, which gives us an earnest [promise] that he will be an able representative of the State in the Senate."[6]

Berrien was still in Washington and missed Governor Troup's visit to Savannah and the fete for General Lafayette. Not until late April did Berrien return home, and soon thereafter he journeyed up to Milledgeville to meet with Governor Troup. Berrien saw this as an informal chat; the governor considered it an official meeting. Berrien had not spent much time outside of Georgia since leaving Princeton in the 1790s, and he had been surprised by the growing vehemence in Washington surrounding the issue of slavery. He talked about the nature of the anti-slavery ideas he encountered. The case of the *Antelope* showed just how powerful the issue had become, he said. John Quincy Adams's administration was no friend of slavery, as was demonstrated by Attorney General William Wirt's arguments in the case. The report of the case would not be published until the fall, but Berrien's characterization of the attorney general's argument touched a nerve with the governor. Berrien suggested to Governor Troup that the Georgia legislature, in cooperation with other southern legislatures, produce a resolution stating that slavery was a matter for the states alone. After the meeting, Berrien returned to Savannah.[7]

On May 15, 1825, President John Quincy Adams arrived at his office to find a delegation of four Creek Indians waiting for him. They were relatives and supporters of William McIntosh, the Creek leader most responsible for the second Treaty of Indian Springs. McIntosh had been murdered, they said, by a force of renegade Creeks setting fire to his home and shooting him as he tried to escape the flames. Of course, other Creeks saw this as an execution for violating the law against ceding more land. The visitors also passed to the president a "ferocious" letter from Georgia Governor Troup about his preparations for war. After attending church, Adams went to Secretary of War James Barbour's house to discuss the matter. Barbour read the letter and called Governor Troup a "madman." Barbour and the president then discussed how they could prevent an Indian war. Over the next few days a flood of ever more bellicose letters arrived from Troup, who made insulting allegations against members of the administration. He wrote that he intended to immediately survey the ceded territory and demanded federal protection for the surveyors. These events and letters, and the demands from a seemingly unhinged governor, set in motion an investigation by the Adams administration into the second Treaty of Indian Springs. By May 20, Adams had concluded that something was rotten. Further investigation would uncover a story of bribery and fraud. The majority of Creek leaders opposed the treaty. Ultimately, it would be disavowed by the administration, and a new treaty would be negotiated with the Creeks.[8]

Perhaps fearing this very result, and hoping to profit politically from his handling of the crisis, Governor Troup called a special session of the Georgia General Assembly for May 23. Most of his message to the General Assembly and the citizens of Georgia on that day dealt with the Creek crisis and the need to survey the new lands. Near the end, however, the governor pointed to another danger, a threat by the federal government itself to the crucial institution of slavery.

> Since your last meeting, our feelings have been again outraged
> by officious and impertinent intermeddlings with our domes-
> tic concerns . . . it is understood that the Attorney-General
> of the United States, who may be presumed to represent his
> Government faithfully, and to speak as its mouth-piece, has
> recently maintained, before the Supreme Court, [destructive]

doctrines on this subject. . . . The moment we cease to be masters, we are slaves. . . . it is not too late, to step forth, and, having exhausted the argument, to stand by your arms.[9]

Troup spoke the language of the men aggressively expanding the cotton empire: "The moment we cease to be masters, we are slaves." This was strong rhetoric, calculated to motivate political support from men on the frontier, but it also sounded like a threat to take up arms against the federal government over the issue of slavery. A correspondent for the *Augusta Chronicle* asked, "Is the intemperate language of these paragraphs in accordance with that spirit of union and harmony?" The *Charleston City Gazette* wrote, "The time certainly has not arrived when 'argument is exhausted,' and there is a necessity for the people 'to stand by their arms.'" Pressured to clarify his comments, on June 7 Troup sent another message to the legislature, in which he made more specific assertions about Wirt. "The Attorney General, representing the United States, says before the Supreme Court, in a ripe and splendid argument, that slavery, being inconsistent with the laws of God and nature, cannot exist." Troup was talking about the *Antelope* case.[10]

Troup also shared his source for the account of Wirt's argument. "The Governor states, that a few days before the meeting of the Legislature, he conversed with the Hon. J. M. Berrien." They had discussed the growing national attacks on slave property, Troup explained. Berrien had said that "the crisis was an awful one, and that no time was to be lost in taking measures of defense." Berrien had then recounted the attorney general's argument in the *Antelope* as an example of the Adams administration's view of slavery. This statement by Governor Troup was published widely and had the potential to destroy John M. Berrien. Suddenly, the *Antelope* case was not just a way for Berrien to make money or showcase his courtroom skills before the elite of Washington; instead it had become an issue in the growing sectional conflict between slave and free states. Politically, Berrien was trapped. He could not insist that Wirt had spoken so about slavery, because the report of the case, soon to be published, would show otherwise. Either Berrien had to admit that he had exaggerated the situation to the governor, or he could call the governor a liar. No matter which course he chose, it could destroy his political career.[11]

Publicly, Berrien remained silent on the case, but at a dinner in Augusta to honor John C. Calhoun, he offered a toast to "John Marshall, Chief Justice of the United States—The mild but steady lustre of the evening of his life is still more grateful than even the splendor of its brilliant morning." Perhaps Berrien had drunk a bit too much at that point, but his public posture was clear. He was a nationalist; he supported the union and its institutions, including the Supreme Court. Privately, Berrien asked several political allies for help.[12]

Among the friends he consulted was a rising star of Georgia politics, Richard Henry Wilde. Wilde was born in Dublin, Ireland, and had come to America as a child. When he was twelve years old his family moved to Augusta. There, in 1809, at age nineteen, Wilde joined the local bar. Like Francis Scott Key, he had a gift for words and compelling argument. His rise in the legal profession was swift. From 1811 through 1813, he served as attorney general for Georgia, and in 1814 he was elected to the House of Representatives. He was not reelected in 1816, instead returning to the practice of law. During this time, he and Judge John M. Berrien became acquaintances and, to the extent that it was possible for Berrien, friends. By the 1820s, the two men corresponded regularly. Wilde dabbled in poetry and hoped to one day compose a meaningful and lasting epic poem. His skill as a writer helped John M. Berrien craft a strong response to the governor.[13]

Berrien went on the attack, angry that the governor had made a private conversation public without asking permission. He had suggested no crisis requiring a call to arms, Berrien said; rather, he had urged "a decisive, but temperate, expression by the legislatures of the Southern states." Now, he was in a quandary. Berrien wrote, "I am unwilling, perhaps unable, at the moment, to shake off the feelings springing from a friendship of more than twenty years." Berrien did not want to injure Troup politically, he said, but Berrien himself felt injured. He tried to explain his recollection of their conversation and the important points he had made.[14]

> I thought that the sentiments which I heard expressed, and those which I understood were expressed in the case of the "Ramirez," and the conversations out of doors, to which the argument of that case gave rise, were calculated to excite a restlessness among our colored population, which might be productive of the most awful consequences. . . . I considered the doctrines advanced, as alarming . . .[15]

Berrien closed with a plea for an explanation from Troup, some sort of admission that he had misstated, misunderstood, or perhaps misattributed the statements. In a world in which political conflict could easily escalate into a duel, it was important to give the other party an easy way out. Berrien also had to clear his name. If he failed to end the conflict honorably, it would "diminish the little prospect which I have of being in any degree useful in the National Councils." In other words, Berrien would be a man without honor, and his political career would be finished.[16]

Governor Troup responded craftily and suggested that Berrien had lied about their conversation. More letters were passed back and forth between Berrien and Troup and between Berrien and Wilde. Berrien was furious and wrote Wilde that he thought Troup irresponsibly violent, something John Quincy Adams and he could have agreed on that summer of 1825. Wilde disagreed, thinking Troup shrewd in the new era of popular politics. Troup played "the game of violence only to attract support from the violent."[17]

The conflict spread to newspapers around the nation, and William Wirt was mortified by the accusations of Governor Troup concerning the *Antelope* arguments. His and Key's arguments had been directed against the slave trade, not against slavery, Wirt wrote to Chief Justice John Marshall; to Justices Smith Thompson, Bushrod Washington, and Gabriel Duvall; and to Henry Wheaton, the Supreme Court reporter. Did I say any such things about slavery? Wirt asked. John Marshall responded, "I have no recollection of your having uttered, in any form, the sentiment imputed to you." The others replied similarly, none with more certainty than the court reporter Wheaton, who had both his own and the chief justice's notes on the case.

> I presume the occasion . . . was the argument of the Antelope . . . I am confident that no such propositions or sentiments . . . were asserted by you, because I listened with great attention to the arguments on both sides, both on account of the interesting nature of the subject, and the power and ability with which it was handled.[18]

On July 21, Wirt showed the letters to President Adams and discussed the situation with him. Adams wrote in his diary that after returning the letters to Wirt, he "advised him to publish them." Wirt did. The letters appeared in papers and magazines across the country. Once again Berrien and the *Antelope* case were in the news, and once again it appeared that Berrien might be a liar. Feeling he had no choice, in early September Berrien released his correspondence with Governor Troup to the newspapers. Troup came across as a hothead, uncertain of his memory, while Berrien seemed reasonable, a man wronged but willing to accept any explanation whatsoever from his friend the governor. Meanwhile, Governor Troup's increasingly frantic letters and pronouncements on the Creek treaty conflict had also been widely published. Anyone who read the whole could only have concluded that Troup was truly a madman. This triumph came at a cost. By releasing these papers, Berrien cut himself off from Troup's party in Georgia. In public the two men maintained formal good relations, but the Troup/Crawford party was through with Berrien. He would be a one-term Republican senator as a result.[19]

The Supreme Court had ruled on the *Antelope* case in March 1825, and the U.S. Circuit Court met in Milledgeville in May of that year. All that remained was for the circuit court to designate the Spanish slaves and turn the remainder of the captives over to the United States. Both Justice Johnson and Judge Cuyler were present in Milledgeville, and Justice Johnson surely had a copy of the Supreme Court order, yet the court did nothing that term. Not until December 1825 did the circuit court in Savannah take up the Supreme Court's decree in the case of the *Antelope*. Of course, this wait meant that the captives continued to work as slaves for their bondholders or for those who had hired them. Marshal Morel had all the captives brought in and counted; there were 177. Morel's count also included the young children and babies born since the captives had arrived in Savannah.

The court, however, faced a problem. The Supreme Court order said that the Spanish slaves "must be designated to the satisfaction of the Circuit Court." What exactly did that mean? On December 20, 1825, Joseph Mulvey, now acting as vice consul in place of Charles Mulvey, who had died in 1823, filed a petition with the circuit court arguing that the Spanish slaves should be determined by drawing lots, as was provided in the original circuit court order. Richard W. Habersham, still fighting to free all the captives, filed an answer the same day. He argued that "it manifestly appears" that the Supreme Court meant for the Spanish claimant to provide "strict proof . . . individual by individual" of ownership. The failure to do so would mean, he argued, that the captives were not properly designated and should be handed over to the United States and freedom.[20]

The court read the petition and the answer and listened to oral arguments by Thomas U. P. Charlton and Habersham. The next day, the two judges discussed the motion. Lotteries were commonly used to divide property in estates or other undifferentiated groups and had still seemed, to Justice Johnson, a sensible solution. Judge Jeremiah Cuyler did not think a lottery was satisfactory. He accepted Habersham's argument that when a case involved human liberty, the proof must be strict. Unable to agree, on December 21, 1825, the two judges drew up a certificate of division for the Supreme Court. The case would have to go back to Washington for another decision by the Court.[21]

Meanwhile, 177 captives were gathered in Savannah, soon increased to 178 by the birth of another infant. Richard W. Habersham made another motion that he thought would help the captives. Most had been hired out, ostensibly by Francis Sorrel, since they were taken away from Marshal Morel at the end of March 1823. Any money these captives had earned should be paid to them, Habersham argued, for they were free people under the ruling of the Supreme Court. At the very least, money earned by hiring out the captives or other activities should be paid to the court to use in caring for them. Berrien's friend Richard Henry Wilde now represented Francis Sorrel, the Portuguese vice consul. Sorrel had taken responsibility for the captives when they were removed from the marshal's care. Wilde responded that Sorrel had agreed to see that the captives were well taken care of and to bond them for their return when demanded by the court, but that he had never agreed to pay to the captives or the court any monies made from their hire.[22]

Judge Jeremiah Cuyler considered both Habersham's motion and Wilde's response. "If these people were held to labor," Cuyler wrote, "every principle of justice requires that they should be entitled to what they have labored for after their expenses are paid." Meanwhile, Marshall Morel reported to the court that he had possession of the captives but no funds for their support, and that the claimants refused to give him any funds. "Here are 178 people . . . what must be done with them?" wrote Judge Cuyler. The judge ordered that Sorrel pay to the court the money earned by the captives minus his costs and a commission for handling the affair. But the future was a problem. The case had gone to the Supreme Court again, and not until the May 1826 term of circuit court could there be a "final disposition of these people." How would they live in the meantime? Judge Cuyler ordered that the captives be "put out until the first day of May, 1826, and thereafter until called for by order of this court, in the same manner as they have been," and under the same conditions as required before. The captives were back to living and working like slaves.[23]

Secretary of the Navy Samuel Southard expected a final division of the captives that spring. He wrote the U.S. agent in Liberia that the recaptured Africans would soon arrive. Timber, tools, and other supplies had been shipped to Cape Mesurado to build shelter for the arriving "recaptives." "The buildings must be finished in the simplest and cheapest manner," wrote Southard. Chief Justice John Marshall was watching as well. On January 1, 1826, he wrote to Southard, "In the case of the Antelope . . . I understood that You had ordered a vessel to be in readiness." He asked if the vessel had taken the freed captives to Africa already. "As the annual meeting of the Auxiliary colonization society at this place approaches some interest will be felt in this augmentation of the colony."

That same day, President John Quincy Adams characterized daily life for his diary. Each day he rose at five or so in the morning and took a four-mile walk under the moon and the stars. "I then make my fire and read three chapters of the Bible, with Scott's and Hewlett's Commentaries." He reflected with amazement on his unusual rise to the presidency. Four candidates stood for the presidency in the election of 1824, and none won a majority of electoral votes. Andrew Jackson had taken 99 electoral votes, John Quincy Adams 84 votes, William Crawford 41 votes, and the young Henry Clay 37 votes. The election then went to the House of Representatives, where, by clever politicking, John Quincy Adams defeated his opponents and was elected president. Adams was very aware that he was a minority president. Elected "not by the unequivocal suffrages of a majority of the people," he wrote, and "with perhaps two-thirds of the whole people adverse to the actual result." Because of this he felt a great responsibility to do good things, the right things, as president. Adams was also increasingly concerned about affairs in Georgia. A new treaty had been negotiated with the Creek, the Treaty of Washington, which displaced the discredited second Treaty of Indian Springs. Georgia Governor Troup continued to howl about federal interference in state matters and found it increased his popularity. Despite this focus on Georgia, Adams mentioned nothing in his diary about the *Antelope* captives.[24]

In late December of 1825, Richard W. Habersham had written to the secretary of the navy explaining the new delay in the *Antelope* case. Southard wrote back, expressing his disappointment. Habersham's letter "created surprise, as it was supposed that the question had been clearly settled by the opinion of the Supreme Court." A certificate of division allowed the Supreme Court to resolve differences between the two judges of the circuit courts. John Marshall's imprecision in ruling that the captives made Spanish slaves "must be designated to the satisfaction of the Circuit Court" lay at the heart of the controversy. The Supreme Court's brief response, given on March 16, 1826, indicated that the justices thought the answer obvious. "The Africans to be delivered must be designated by proof made to the satisfaction of that court." The phrase "designated by proof made" supported Habersham's argument that the Spanish claimant must present evidence of ownership for each person claimed. He felt sure no such evidence existed, and that all the captives would be freed. While Habersham won this second Supreme Court decision, the captives continued to work as slaves in Savannah.[25]

In May of 1826, the circuit court met again in Milledgeville and took up the case of the *Antelope*. The first order of business was to decide how many captives the Spanish claimant would be allowed to designate. The court had found earlier that the original number of captives was 331, and that 93 captives were slaves belonging to Cuesta Manzanal y Hermano. The court calculated that 28 percent of the original cargo belonged to the Spanish, and that Cuesta Manzanal was entitled to that portion of the surviving captives. The last report to the court had counted 178 living captives; 50 captives would be the Spanish share. The Spanish claimant asked for more time, arguing that it was not possible, in Milledgeville, to designate anyone by proof, as the captives were all in Savannah. A motion by Habersham allowed the claimant until the next term of court to designate by proof the Spanish slaves. Habersham also moved that final costs be presented and resolved at the next term of court, bringing the entire affair to an end. The circuit court agreed with both motions, thus putting off a final resolution once more. Meanwhile, the captives continued to labor as slaves.[26]

Samuel Southard was charged with transporting the released captives to Africa. He moved from surprise to outrage at the additional delay, writing to Habersham with barely controlled anger: "Will you be pleased to inform me what has been done . . .?" Southard was particularly concerned about the growing costs in the case. More than $20,000 had already been paid to Marshal Morel, the largest expenditure made by the navy in the entire African colonization project. Southard was right to be worried. When the circuit court assembled in Savannah in November 1826, Marshall Morel submitted a new and final bill to the court. For the period from July 1820, to May 1823, the marshal submitted a charge of $35,775.60. From December 15, 1825, to January 15, 1826, when the captives were assembled for the last attempt to divide them, he submitted a bill for $519.91. Since January 15, 1826, the captives had been hired out by the marshal, earning him $3,349.50, which he was willing to deduct from the final bill. This gave a total of $32,946.01 due the marshal, close to a million dollars today. If the government was unwilling to pay this bill, Morel suggested that payment be divided between the Spanish and Portuguese claimants.[27]

Judge Jeremiah Cuyler had been district court judge in July of 1822, when John H. Morel had received his largest payment from the navy for the care of the captives: $20,286.98, covering the period July 1820–May 1822. Apparently Cuyler did not notice that the newest bill included charges for those dates. Morel was billing twice for more than $20,000. Justice William Johnson must have remembered ordering that the captives be taken away from Morel in March of 1823, in part because of the marshal's financial irregularities, yet he remained silent. Habersham had been paid to investigate Morel's conduct and his bills, and he knew that the marshal had been cut off from payments by the navy as a result of his investigation. He, too, said nothing about Morel's having billed for monies already received. It was not just the officials of the court who said nothing; in a small city like Savannah, many other people must have known about the payments to Morel. The closest anyone in the case came to exposing the marshal was Justice Johnson, who wrote:

> The Court cannot help feeling that the paying of such bills of such an extraordinary amount as those of the Marshal in this case must expose the Court and the administration of justice in this Country to certain imputations. And we do not hesitate to avow that if we could see any ground on which the amount could be reduced we should lay hold of it.[28]

Apparently Justice Johnson, Judge Cuyler, U.S. Attorney Habersham, and clerk of court George Glen—in fact, no one in the old brick courthouse in Savannah—could see any grounds for reducing the marshal's bill. Just as Justice Johnson feared, this failure of memory raises "certain imputations."

The acceptance of the bill raised a new question: How would it be paid? Johnson and Cuyler decided that it should be paid not entirely by the government but also by the claimants, in proportion to the number of captives received. The Portuguese vice consul, thanks to the able representation of Richard Henry Wilde, was excused from paying any costs, as the Portuguese would receive none of the captives. The Spanish share, 28 percent, worked out to about $9,000, payable to Marshal Morel. That left more than $23,000 unpaid. Would the United States have to pay this claim to free the captives? The marshal argued that he held a lien on the captives until the amount was paid. Could he somehow execute the lien and force the sale of free captives as slaves?[29]

The judges split again. One argued that Marshal Morel had a lien on the captives given to the United States, and that the United States would have to pay the balance before they could go free. The other argued that a lien on free men was absurd, and that Morel would have to submit his bill to the Treasury for payment. Again, no one mentioned that the amount that would be due from the United States was very close to the amount the United States had already paid the marshal. Without indicating who supported which position, the judges ordered another certificate of division for the Supreme Court.[30]

The court was not finished. It took up the Supreme Court's order that the Spanish slaves be designated by proof. Morel, Richardson, merchant Henry Haupt, and Dr. John B. Berthelot all gave evidence about the visit of Domingo Grondona in 1821. The Spanish proctor, Thomas U. P. Charlton, argued that any captives who recognized Grondona during this visit must have belonged to the Spanish when the *Antelope* was at anchor off Cabinda. The testimony concerned events from many years before, and at several points the witnesses were uncertain. Richardson remembered having charge of the fifty or so captives working for the city of Savannah. He told the story of Grondona clapping his hands and all fifty men approaching Grondona and speaking to him. On cross-examination by Habersham, Richardson admitted that it was impossible to say which of the men had known Grondona. Marshal Morel testified that he escorted Grondona around the city and countryside to view between 200 and 220 captives. At Haupt's house three captives had recognized Grondona and shook his hand. At Dr. Berthelot's, Grondona recognized a boy named Tom. Visiting Morel's plantation, Grondona had pointed out several captives as ones he recognized. On cross-examination Habersham asked how Grondona identified captives. Morel explained that Grondona would make a sign with his hands, and that those that recognized and returned it were Spanish slaves. What about the more than one hundred captives on Morel's plantation, Habersham asked—had they all recognized Grondona? "No," said the marshal. What about the ones who worked on the city fortifications? All of them had recognized Grondona, Morel said, and they were the "primest."[31]

Then, "The Negroes of the cargo of the Ramirez, being collected in front of the Courthouse, the witness was directed by the Court to designate the individuals of those who had worked under him at the fortifications." Some 170 captives were gathered in Wright Square, much as at monthly sheriff's auctions at which slaves were bought and sold. Just as when slaves were bought and sold, the captives could be separated from each other by the simple motion of a white man's finger. Richardson pointed to thirty-three men as having worked for the city in 1820 and 1821. As these would have been the older captives, they were also the ones most likely to have wives and families. Richardson said he also knew of two more men from the work crew, Joe and Ned, who were in the possession of Ebenezer Jenckes. Jenckes owned a turn-pike and a ferry across the Ogeechee River and had recently begun building the Savannah-Ogeechee Canal. Along with these thirty-five identified by Richardson, Marshal Morel designated the three captives who had been seen shaking Grondona's hand at Henry Haupt's house, and the youngster Tom who had been at Dr. Berthelot's house. With no discussion of the required level of "proof," of the problems with the witnesses' memories, or other questionable elements of this process, Justice Johnson and Judge Cuyler ruled that these thirty-nine captives had been designated by proof, naming thirty-six men, two boys, and one woman as Spanish slaves. Coincidentally, they were among the fittest and most able-bodied of the captives.[32]

Richard Wylly Habersham thought this "designation by proof" a farce, objecting to such weak and self-serving evidence. That same day, Habersham informed the court that he would appeal the division of the captives to the Supreme Court. The next day he expanded his appeal, arguing that the claim by the marshal of a lien on free human beings was absurd and unconstitutional. The unpaid portion of the marshal's bill should be paid by the Portuguese vice consul to pun-ish him for bringing a groundless claim, Habersham argued. Both a certificate of division and the appeal by Habersham were sent off to Washington. For a third time, the captives continued to work as slaves while they awaited a judgment of the Supreme Court.[33]

CHAPTER 17

"It ought not to be forgotten, that . . . it had been established to the satisfaction of this Court, that ninety-three of the Africans brought in with the Antelope, were the property of the Spanish claimants; but as many of the Africans had died, it was the opinion of this Court, that number should be reduced according to the whole number living."

Supreme Court Justice Robert Trimble, *The Antelope*, 25 U.S. 546, 552 (1827)

During the 1827 term of the Supreme Court, Chief Justice John Marshall dissented from an opinion for the first and only time in his career. The case was *Ogden v. Saunders*, and Marshall's dissent argued that under the commerce clause of the Constitution only the federal government could regulate bankruptcies. The majority of the Court disagreed. This was considered the big case of a term that produced forty-seven written opinions, among them a little-noticed third decision in the *Antelope* case.[1]

The Court confronted two issues in the new *Antelope* case. The first was the certificate of division from the judges on how Marshal Morel should be paid, and the second was the U.S. Attorney's exceptions to the method of proof and the marshal's assertion of a lien on the captives given to the United States. The case was scheduled for March 6, 1827, and William Wirt and Francis Scott Key were to argue the case for the United States, just as they had two years earlier. John M. Berrien and Charles J. Ingersoll were both to argue the Spanish interest, and Richard Henry Wilde was there to protect the Portuguese vice consul from being charged anything. No one openly represented John H. Morel's claim of more than $30,000. In December Morel had written Berrien about the case. Berrien responded, promising to look over the record "and see what I can do for you." "I notice what you say in relation to the compensation," Berrien continued, "and shall I presume meet your convenience by drawing upon you at 60 days, which I will do when I know something more of the case." This cryptic comment may have meant nothing, or it may have meant that Berrien was taking money to protect John H. Morel's interests in the case. Either way, the waters were awfully muddy.[2]

William Wirt missed the argument. Early on the morning of March 6, he called on the president to "say he was much engaged with public causes at the Supreme Court" and that he would have to miss the cabinet meeting scheduled later that day. Perhaps John Quincy Adams recalled the furor Governor George Troup had raised over Wirt's arguments two years before. Perhaps Adams did not want Wirt arguing the case again. Perhaps he truly felt he needed Wirt's extensive knowledge and experience at the cabinet meeting. For whatever reason, Adams told Wirt he "could not dispense with his attendance." Wirt would have to miss the Supreme Court argument. Wirt dutifully joined the cabinet meeting, which debated for three hours the wording and strategy of a proclamation in a trade controversy with Great Britain before deciding nothing. Attorney General Wirt was not pleased. He wrote in disgust to a friend, "I am *obliged*—I find to be at the President's at one o'clock. . . . The Court meantime has full employment from the *Antelope*, which I have committed to Mr. Key."[3]

When argument began on March 6, Francis Scott Key alone confronted Richard Henry Wilde, Charles Jared Ingersoll, and John M. Berrien. This time there were seven justices to hear the case, so another split decision was unlikely. Justice Thomas Todd, who had missed the first *Antelope* arguments, had died in February of 1826. His replacement on the Court was Robert Trimble from Kentucky. Trimble had shared circuit court duties with Todd and was a natural replacement. The 1827 term cases were the first Trimble heard as a Supreme Court justice. He wrote three opinions that term, including perhaps his best, a concurring opinion in the lengthy and seemingly unending *Ogden v. Saunders*. Trimble's career as a justice was short. He died in 1828, after only his second term on the Court. Of the seven sitting justices in 1827, he was the only one who had never dealt with the *Antelope* case. Perhaps he was chosen to write the opinion because he was fresh to the case, perhaps because he made the most cogent argument in conference, or perhaps because the other Justices were simply tired of it. Trimble delivered the third *Antelope* opinion on March 10, 1827.[4]

Richard W. Habersham had done his utmost to turn this appeal into another freedom bid for all the captives. The core of his argument was that the Spanish claimants had failed to provide legally sufficient evidence of identity of the *Antelope* captives who were slaves. Francis Scott Key followed his lead, arguing that "there is no credible and compelling evidence to identify them, or any of them." Hearsay testimony from Grondona, hand clapping and hand signals supposedly observed by Morel, were insufficient to prove the case. Perhaps Key referred to the *Mima Queen* case of 1813, in which the Court found that hearsay was not admissible to prove a slave free. Now, would hearsay be admissible to prove that the free were slaves? Key argued, as had Habersham, that the failure to provide adequate proof meant that the captives designated should not be given to the Spanish but handed over to the United States and awarded their freedom.[5]

Trimble's opinion scolded Key for arguing an issue already decided by the Court. "It ought not to be forgotten," Trimble wrote, "that in the original cause, it had been established to the satisfaction of this Court that ninety-three of the Africans brought in with the Antelope were the property of the Spanish claimants." The orders in the last two decisions said only that the Spanish portion had to be identified to the satisfaction of the circuit court. The court said that it was satisfied by the proof from Richardson and Morel's testimony. "We think that under the peculiar and special circumstances of the case," Trimble wrote, "the evidence of identity is competent, credible, and reasonably satisfactory to identify the whole thirty-nine." Key and Habersham had lost their final bid to free all the captives.[6]

As for the marshal's bill, apparently no one informed Trimble that there had been problems before. No one informed him that the navy had paid Morel more than $20,000. Trimble regarded the entire claim as legitimate but concluded that it was absurd for the marshal to claim a lien on free people. "The Africans to be delivered to the United States are neither slaves in contemplation of law nor prisoners of war nor persons charged with crimes," he wrote. "It would indeed be extraordinary if the marshal, who is the servant of the government and holds possession of the Africans merely by its authority, could obstruct the operations of the government by a claim for compensation for his services." Marshal Morel could charge an appropriate share of the costs to the Spanish claimant, but the remainder must be charged to the U.S. Treasury. The 1819 Slave Trade Act had appropriated $100,000 to pay for its enforcement. The marshal could be paid from that fund. No one told Trimble that the $100,000 appropriation had been exhausted.[7]

By 1827, the colony on Cape Mesurado had several hundred inhabitants. It continued to grow. The Rev. Ralph Gurley had drawn up a constitution for its governance, and after some resistance, the Colonization Society had adopted it in May of 1825. Under the leadership of Jehudi Ashmun, during 1825 and 1826 the colony expanded beyond the confines of Cape Mesurado. Ashmun leased, bought, or simply occupied additional land, and now the colony desperately needed more settlers. The society saw its future as bright and expected Liberia to thrive if only enough money could be found to transport and settle a sufficient number of colonists. The U.S. government had joined the cause and now had multiple agents in Liberia to receive Africans rescued from the slave trade. There were high hopes that efforts to suppress the slave trade would produce large numbers of settlers for the colony. Through Key, Marshall, and others, the members of the society were well aware of the *Antelope* case. Believing it had been resolved, in early 1826 the U.S. agency in Liberia prepared to receive the liberated Africans from the *Antelope*. Two large buildings were constructed to house the expected influx of new colonists, and plans were made for their arrival.[8]

A year later, in 1827, Justice Trimble decreed that the circuit court and district court carry out the order of the Supreme Court. The captives not designated as Spanish slaves would "be delivered to the United States absolutely and unconditionally." Once that had happened, the law required that they be transported to the American agency in Africa. In December of 1826, Jehudi Ashmun wrote from Liberia that "a new town for the re-captured Africans has been founded on the Stockton [creek]. . . . It is not yet named." The navy hired the ship *Norfolk* to transport the captives to Liberia. The *Norfolk* departed from the city of that name with twelve additional liberated Africans from a case in New Orleans and arrived in Savannah on May 23, 1827. During the voyage, the U.S. agent traveling with the captives, Dr. John W. Peaco, became ill and died shortly after arriving in Savannah. The ship could not proceed until the United States sent a new agent to accompany the captives to their new home in Africa. Yet again, the *Antelope* captives were stuck.[9]

On the morning of November 30, 1826, Dr. Henry Huntt, a prominent Washington, D.C., physician, visited President John Quincy Adams. "Huntt came, very seriously" Adams wrote, "to put me on my guard against Dr. Todson, the Assistant Surgeon cashiered by sentence of a Court-martial for embezzlement of public stores." Dr. George P. Todson was outraged that Adams had approved his dismissal from the army and was "determined to murder me for revenge," wrote Adams.

The cabinet met to discuss Chesapeake and Ohio canal proposals. Afterward, Adams spoke with another visitor, Col. Randall, who had been Todson's attorney for the court-martial. "Todson had avowed his determination to assassinate me," Adams learned. Randall told the president that this was no idle threat; that Todson was desperate and "perfectly mad." The greatest danger, Col. Randall suggested, would be during Adams's lengthy predawn walks.[10]

Adams thanked Col. Randall for the information and told him that it was impossible "to guard myself against the hand of an assassin." There was no Secret Service or other official protection for the president until after Abraham Lincoln's assassination in1865, so in that sense Adams was correct, but he also seemed to court the danger. The next morning, he walked four and a half miles around the Capitol square, returning to the White House "in time to see the sun rise." The following morning when he went out to walk in the dark, he sprained his foot and hobbled along slowly. A man approached out of the darkness, and the president could not avoid him. It was only Henry Clay, the secretary of state, who walked around the square in the darkness with him. Clay may have done so out of concern for the president. Adams, however, remained publicly unconcerned about the potential threat. He even met with Todson several times over the next six months, eventually concluding that the man's only problem was "the badness of his temper." On May 30, 1827, Dr. Todson again visited Adams to ask for help in getting a federal job. Adams sent him away empty-handed. Then, on June 2, Secretary of the Navy Samuel Southard told Adams the bad news of Dr. Peaco's death in Savannah. The rental of the ship was expensive, and the *Norfolk* had remained idle in Savannah for twenty days, but Southard "did not know whom to employ in the place of Dr. Peaco."[11]

"I mentioned . . . Dr. Todson as a professional surgeon, accustomed to Southern climates, and perhaps as well suited to the service as any person," Adams wrote. Two days later, Todson turned up and, told of the opportunity, excitedly accepted the assignment. Adams may have been trying to redeem a lost soul, or he may have been trying to get rid of a problem; agents to the African colony died with great regularity. What was totally lacking, however, was any consideration of Dr. Todson's interest in the cause of colonization, or the relationships he might have with black Americans and with Africans. On June 12, 1827, he was appointed to the agency. Several days later he boarded the sloop *Florida* bound for Savannah. "On the arrival of Dr. T. in Savannah," reported the newspaper, "he will take passage in the ship *Norfolk* . . . waiting at that port to take the captured Africans to Messurado [*sic*]"[12]

Marshal Morel had gathered the captives in May, and then everyone had waited. The captives had no choice in the matter: They were being sent to Africa. Some reportedly did not want to go. Some may had married local slaves, or had children in Savannah. It didn't matter; wives, husbands, and children would have to be left behind. While they waited, Marshal Morel hired guards to ensure that no captives ran away. Morel would be paid based on the number he loaded aboard the *Norfolk*, and he intended that all should board the vessel. On June 11, 1827, the secretary of the navy wrote Morel instructing him to transfer the "Africans now in your custody" to George P. Todson. This order was not filed with the court in Savannah until July 2, and the captives were finally loaded aboard the *Norfolk* on July 5. Marshal Morel billed the government for the cost of loading 134 captives. In reality, he could have loaded no more than 131. These were not, however, all survivors of the group that had arrived in July of 1820, almost exactly seven years before. Fourteen of those on the *Norfolk* were under ten years old, and by simple distribution, at least 10 must have been born since arriving in Savannah. Probably 120 or 121 of those loaded by the marshal on the *Norfolk* were survivors of the original voyage.

At long last, on July 18, 1827, the *Norfolk* sailed. Given the long delay before departure and the years of captivity suffered by the captives, there may have been some sort of celebration. Todson mentioned none; he wrote only of prayerful and dutiful people. Perhaps that was what he thought the society wanted to hear. The prayerfulness, however, may also have been sadness or terror. Sadness for those left behind, and terror of the unknown ahead. The last shipboard experience of the captives had been the Middle Passage, and now again they were aboard ship bound for a destination no one knew. The captives probably had little information about Liberia, and as Todson had only recently taken the position as agent, he may not have known much more. The lucky sixteen who had been chosen by lot in 1821 and sent to Liberia in 1822 could have told the captives a great deal. They had suffered sickness, rain, mud, and attacks by hostile inhabitants. Such stories would have better prepared the new colonists for the hardship ahead. The lucky sixteen, however, had sent no letters or reports, and there is no evidence that any were even alive in 1827. This alone would have told the new colonists something. The *Norfolk* had an easy voyage and arrived off Monrovia on August 20, 1827. Dr. Todson reported that during the voyage two adults and one child died, while two children were born. Counting the 12 people loaded in Norfolk, Todson delivered 142 recaptured Africans to Jehudi Ashmun in Liberia. In anticipation of their arrival, Ashmun had prepared a settlement for the rescued captives, or recaptives, as they were called. "Situated on the Stockton creek, four miles above Monroe," he wrote, "these lands extend half a mile along the southeast bank of the Stockton, and two miles back." This was fertile and easily cultivated land, and Ashmun expected the captives to do well there.[13]

It would be more than a year before the captives got their land. Most were apprenticed to established settlers, a few were employed at wages, and nineteen women and their small children were put to agency work in Monrovia. No one mentioned whether the captives discovered any survivors of the lucky sixteen sent on the brig *Strong* in 1822. The work arrangements for the captives may have seemed similar to those they had endured in Savannah, except that for the first time some of the men received wages for their work. While the arrangements were worked out, Dr. Todson toured the colony and began to find purpose in Liberia. "I have seen a great number of patients in the most deplorable state, for want of medical and surgical assistance," he wrote. "I have taken great interest and pleasure in endeavoring to be useful." Perhaps President Adams had been correct in concluding that Todson was simply a man in need of a purpose: His work in Liberia truly redeemed him. From a cashiered army surgeon making threats against the president, Todson became a great advocate of the colony. He spent many years in Liberia, at great risk to his own health, serving as the colony's doctor.[14]

Those risks were soon apparent. Dr. Todson came down with the "fever," and suffered for two months before recovering. When the brig *Doris* arrived in January 1828, of 107 passengers, 24 died during the first few weeks in Liberia. Richard Randall wrote in February 1829, "I have at length gotten through this much talked of African fever; and, after all, do not think it any great thing. A Carolina or Georgia Fever is just as bad." Brave words, for Randall died of the fever two months later, in April 1829. As for the captives, "About forty of the whole company from Georgia have been slightly afflicted with intermittents," meaning the regular rise and fall of fever common to malaria. This was a great relief; the seasoning was often very difficult for new arrivals, but only a third of the Georgia captives became ill. The mildness of the malaria suffered by the liberated *Antelope* captives probably reflected previous exposure in both Africa and Georgia. Disease, however, could strike even those who were seasoned. Since 1822, Jehudi Ashmun had become indispensable, expanding the colony, making peace arrangements with local leaders, and regularizing the colony's expenditures. Even he continued to have significant health problems almost every year. He had recovered from a bout of what he called "rheumatic fever" just before the arrival of the *Antelope* captives.[15]

During the first year in Africa, the former captives labored for the most part as apprentices or servants. Observers marveled at what Dr. Todson had called "their propriety of conduct." Ashmun wrote, "These people have proved, far beyond expectation, orderly, peaceable, and industrious." Perhaps seven years living as slaves had taught them to be "orderly, peaceable, and industrious." Only 2 of the 142 new arrivals had died during their first five months in the colony. John Clark died of fever, and on October 10, John Jenkins was bathing in the Mesurado River when he vanished. The official cause of death was listed as drowning, but Ashmun wrote that there was good reason to suppose he had been killed by a crocodile. Five marriages were celebrated among the recaptured Africans, and more than forty had arrived with a "simple and imperfect, but serious and practical knowledge of Christianity."[16]

By February of 1828, Ashmun was too sick to continue his work, suffering extreme swelling and edema as well as pain in the joints. He returned to the United States, where he died that summer. Before leaving Liberia, Ashmun designated the assistant agent, Lott Cary, as his successor. Cary had been born a slave in Virginia in about 1780 and had experienced Christian conversion in 1807, while working in a Richmond tobacco factory. His wife died in 1812, and in 1813 he purchased his and his children's freedom. That same year he became a Baptist minister, and by 1819 he was involved with the American Colonization Society. The society sent him to the colony in 1821, and he had become an essential player in Ashmun's plans for development and expansion. In September 1828, Lott Cary moved most of the *Antelope* captives to their new town behind Halfway Farms on Stockton Creek. When a new agent, sent to replace Cary, visited in December of 1828, he was very impressed by the former captives' accomplishments. "They have been on their lands but three months, and have already have built themselves comfortable houses, enclosed their lots, and have their cassada [sic], plantains, and potatoes growing most luxuriantly," wrote Richard Randall. He though the location healthy—it was removed some distance from the mangroves that lined Stockton creek. Agent Randall decided to name the settlement Carytown to honor his predecessor, but that name never stuck. Instead, the settlement was named New Georgia.[17]

The surnames of the liberated captives also recalled their Georgia captivity, one that had lasted for a biblical seven years. Having been treated as slaves, many captives may not have had any surname before their arrival in Liberia. Most people would have chosen their own last name, either while in Savannah or on arrival in Africa. The most common surname among those who arrived on board the *Norfolk* was Habersham, with twenty-three people, or almost 20 percent of the captives, bearing it. Clearly they were aware of Richard W. Habersham's struggle for their freedom. At fifteen occurrences, the next most common name among the arrivals was Morrell. Most of the captives had spent years working on John H. Morel's plantation, and he had charge of them for most of their captivity. Whether any were aware that Morel had spoken of working them to death will never be known. Nine people took the name Berrien, most likely because twenty captives had worked for him during the endless litigation, and he was a prominent man in Savannah. Two other names stood out among the captives: Tippo Charlton combined an African name with the name of the Savannah lawyer who was mayor when the captives first arrived. But without question, the most expressive name of all the captives who had suffered so long and so much was that of a woman who died in Liberia in 1843. Her name was Despair Hope.[18]

The net proceeds from the sale of the *Antelope* had been only $750 in 1821 and had been distributed by the court. This was surely a bargain price for a vessel that had cost more than ten times as much only five years before and had been valued at $3,000 in the newspaper. In March of 1822, a brig named the *Antelope* began regular runs between Havana, Cuba, and Charleston, South Carolina. It was registered out of Providence, Rhode Island, suggesting that Chief Justice John Marshall's suspicions about the "Portuguese" claimants were correct. The brig seems never to have visited Savannah, traveling only to Charleston and Philadelphia with cargoes of Cuban molasses and coffee. If this was the same ship, it was still a bad luck vessel. In January of 1823, it grounded on the Florida reef off the Keys. The first and second mates, along with two sailors, took the ship's boat and abandoned the vessel, leaving the rest of the crew stranded. The *Antelope* subsequently got free of the reef, and the remaining crew made it safely to Havana. The captain thought that the men deserted to join with the pirates then haunting the Keys. The *Antelope* was still sailing as late as the winter of 1826, even as the captives' case languished in the courts.[19]

The United States Navy handled most of the payments associated with enforcing the 1819 Slave Trade Law. The costs for the *Antelope* case were quite high. From August 26, 1820, to July 17, 1822, the navy paid John H. Morel $20,286.98. John M. Berrien received for John Jackson $5,100 in bounty money on 204 Africans, and Jackson had directly received $400 for bounty on 16 Africans. Richard W. Habersham was paid $431.75 to investigate Marshal Morel. The total direct payments from the navy to these four men in Savannah totaled $26,552.75, but there were other costs. The cost for lease of the *Norfolk* and transportation of the captives to Liberia in 1827 was $6,712.50, making a total of $33,265.25. There was also passage for the lucky sixteen to Baltimore in 1822, which cost $180. U.S. government costs related to the voyage of the *Strong*, which took the fifteen survivors to Africa with supplies for the U.S. agency there, totaled $5,544.16. The result was $38,809.41 paid by the navy for the *Antelope* case alone. This was an astounding amount, none of which was paid in any meaningful way to the captives.[20]

In Savannah, the courts were still clearing up the final costs of the case. During the November 1827 term, Judge Berrien submitted a final bill for $1,250 in fees, Thomas U. P. Charlton a final bill of $800, and John H. Morel, acting as the executor for Charles Harris, who had died, a bill of $500. There was also the issue of Marshal Morel's final bill for the care of the captives. The Supreme Court had ruled that he would have to petition the Treasury for the portion related to the captives who had been given to the United States. The portion related to the thirty-nine captives awarded the Spanish claimant equaled $6,347.00. Surprisingly, at this point Richard W. Habersham entered the case one last time.

Like many Georgians, Habersham was angered by the Adams administration's rejection of the second Treaty of Indian Springs in

1825. Conflict continued even after the new Treaty of Washington was approved by the Senate in 1826, and the older treaty set aside. Governor Troup of Georgia insisted that he would conduct a survey and prepare a land lottery based on the territory grants in the second Treaty of Indian Springs, not the new Treaty of Washington. President John Quincy Adams, with a supporting opinion from Attorney General William Wirt, threatened to have any surveyors or others who entered Creek territory under Troup's order prosecuted in the federal courts. Richard W. Habersham would have to prosecute such trespassers. He refused to do so and resigned as United States Attorney for the District of Georgia in the fall of 1827. In November of 1827, now a private attorney, he returned to federal court as Marshal John H. Morel's proctor. Habersham moved that the Spanish claimant would have to pay their share of the costs, $6,347.00, during the current term of court before the marshal would hand over the thirty-nine slaves. Habersham knew that Cuesta Manzanal y Hermano had no intention of paying this sum of money or the cost of transportation, attorney's costs, and other sundry charges to recover this small group of slaves. Habersham, representing his neighbor Morel, and once again delaying judicial processes so that the captives remained under Morel's control, suggested a disorienting possibility: Was Habersham working with Morel? Had all his appeals and motions been a ploy to delay, and to ensure that the marshal control the captives as long as possible? The answer was in Habersham's motion. If the Spanish claimant failed to pay, he argued, the designated slaves should go free and be returned to Africa. This was Habersham's final gambit to free the remaining captives. Sadly, it was a gambit that failed.[21]

Richard Henry Wilde also entered the case again. He had represented the Portuguese interest since 1826 and protected them during the third Supreme Court case. According to a petition Wilde submitted to the United States Congress, he had become familiar with the *Antelope* case as a result of this work. In their almost eight years of captivity in Savannah, these slaves "had formed connections by marriage, and many of them have children, from whom, if sent out of the country they must be separated." Concerned about the plight of these slaves, when the Cuesta Manzanal agent arrived in Savannah in November to arrange shipment to Cuba, Wilde took action. The slaves, he explained, were unhappy with the idea of going to Cuba. They wanted to remain in the United States with "the language and habits to which they were accustomed; where easy labor was imposed and kind treatment received." So, Wilde purchased the interest of Cuesta Manzanal y Hermano. Following the circuit court order, the Spanish slaves were heavily bonded, requiring their removal from the United States before the end of May 1828. Wilde petitioned Congress to cancel the required exportation bond so that the slaves could stay in the United States.[22]

Wilde offered the slaves to the American Colonization Society if they would reimburse his costs. They declined. On December 26, 1827, he paid Marshal Morel's bill of $6,347 for the thirty-nine captives' support and care, even though two of the thirty-nine had died by that time. Wilde also paid the outstanding attorney bills, and the outstanding court costs, and other expenses in the case. Telling Congress that sending the surviving thirty-seven slaves to Cuba would be cruel and harmful and would also cost him his investment, he asked Congress to pass an act canceling the bond. Then, the slaves could remain in the United States with their families and enjoy the allegedly good treatment they had had experienced so far in Georgia. In response to this plea, John M. Berrien introduced a bill to cancel the bond in the United States Senate.[23]

The story Wilde told in a letter to John M. Berrien was somewhat different from his public account. Berrien knew about the deal that had been made in 1821 to split any captives recovered as slaves equally between the Spanish and Portuguese vice consuls. Wilde wrote that his client, the Portuguese vice consul Francis Sorrel, had no desire to claim his share of the thirty-nine enslaved captives and paying the associated costs. Thus, perhaps in lieu of attorney's fees, Wilde took the one-half interest from Sorrel. "I understood," Wilde wrote, "the Spaniards could not or would not take the negroes upon the terms required of them, in which event they would go to the U.S. &

be free." This was exactly the hope of Richard W. Habersham and explained why he represented the marshal's claim before the court. Wilde discovered that the marshal was trying to cut a secret deal with Cuesta Manzanal y Hermano, which would have given him some of the money he claimed and let them take the slaves. Here Wilde saw an opportunity. He and Joseph White, the congressional delegate from the newly acquired Florida Territory, had plans for creating a plantation together. "I shall at all events buy about 20 slaves shortly," wrote Wilde, "now if I can get these poor devils in consequence of this arrangement somewhat lower than I should buy others, & they will be better off with me than they would in Cuba, I do not see why I should by any sickly fastidiousness neglect at once interest and humanity."[24]

Then, astonishingly, Wilde described his idea in detail, and asked Berrien to join him in what could only be described as a conspiracy.

> My plan is simply this. If the Portuguese title is thus made good & the Spaniards will acknowledge or be bound by a division of the slaves according to it—which you must judge of and arrange for me—I then propose to buy off the Marshal's claim . . . I propose to leave them with you until next winter when their fate would be decided. . . . My plan then is this. I will apply to the Govt. of the U.S. to do one of two things: either reimburse me the actual expenses paid by me & take the Africans, or pass a law cancelling the bonds for exporting them . . . in other words, allowing them to remain as slaves. If they adopt the first alternative, I am only just where I was, at liberty with my money to buy negroes which I do not want at all events until next winter. If the second, I have the slaves I want for my Florida project. . . . But, there are many difficulties in it in which I require your professional, aye & your friendly advice and assistance.[25]

The plan went smoothly. With Berrien's leadership the bill canceling the bond passed quietly through the Senate. The quiet ended when, on Monday, January 7, 1828, the bill came before the House of Representatives. John W. Taylor of New York, who had just stepped down as Speaker of the House, objected to the haste with which the bill was taken up. He moved that it be sent to the Judiciary Committee so that the facts might appear in the form of a report. The bill was tabled. Three days later, on Thursday, it came up again, and John Taylor objected that there had been no report. Taylor had been one of the leaders against the admission of Missouri as a slave state and was one of the most tenacious members of the House. He apparently detected a foul smell, and he began to demand more facts concerning the *Antelope* case. A dramatic debate ensued. Charles Fenton Mercer, a spokesman for the American Colonization Society, explained that the society had eighteen hundred people awaiting transportation to Africa and had no funds to pay for Wilde's captives. The Judiciary Committee, he proposed, should find out exactly how much Wilde had spent on the captives, and then Congress should reimburse Wilde and return the captives to "their native land." That Liberia was some eighteen hundred miles from Cabinda did not factor into his calculations. The house debate devolved into an effort by slavery opponents to amend the bill to provide for purchase of the captives and an insistence by pro-slavery advocates that the bill be passed as written. Like so much of the *Antelope* case, the specifics came to stand for the ever-present, ever-escalating American debate over slavery itself. The Judiciary Committee considered the bill over the weekend and reported it unchanged on Monday, January 14.[26]

The bill was not taken up again by the House until April 26, 1828. Wilde and Berrien must have been worried by this point. The bond on the captives required their exportation by the end of May, and Congress was nearing the end of its session. If the private bill for Wilde did not pass, he could be financially ruined. On April 26, John Taylor of New York proposed an amendment: "That for the purpose of refunding to Richard H. Wilde the amount he has expended in the purchase of thirty-nine Africans the sume [sic] of $11,700 be . . . appropriated." The purchase required that the captives be given to the American

Colonization Society for removal to Liberia. "The motion of Mr. Taylor led to a protracted and warm debate," noted the recorder. The amendment lost. Debate continued for two more days, but ultimately supporters of the bill to cancel the bond wore down their opponents. On April 28, 1828, the bill passed by a vote of 92 for and 82 against. In the view of Congress, Richard Henry Wilde had saved the surviving thirty-seven *Antelope* slaves; they would not be separated from their families and friends and sent to a sugar plantation in Cuba or exiled to a raw frontier in Africa. Richard Henry Wilde, however, did separate them from their family and friends in Georgia, sending then to a prospective sugar and cotton plantation on the raw frontier of Florida.[27]

On May 2, 1828, President John Quincy Adams signed Richard Henry Wilde's private law, canceling the bonds on the thirty-seven surviving *Antelope* slaves. This was the most active role he had played in the entire eight-year odyssey: a signature that ensured thirty-seven human beings would be enslaved.

PART FOUR

LEGACIES

Congressman John Quincy Adams, from a daguerreotype made about the time of the *Amistad* case.

CHAPTER 18

"I concur with you in thinking nothing portends more calamity &
mischief to the Southern states than their slave population; Yet they
seem to cherish the evil."

John Marshall to Timothy Pickering, March 20, 1826[1]

In February of 1828, while the bill to cancel the bond languished
in congressional limbo, Savannah attorneys Robert Campbell and
George B. Cumming sent a memorial, a type of official memo-
randum, to the United States House of Representatives concerning
Wilde's petition. George B. Cumming was an established attorney
in Savannah, part of the large Cumming family involved in the river
traffic in cotton from Augusta. He also owned some undeveloped
Savannah lots in partnership with Robert Campbell. Campbell was
an attorney who also engaged in the mercantile and factorage business
in Savannah. In early 1827, he was named a director of the Savannah
Office of the Bank of the United States, joining Richard W. Habersham, who was already a director. He was also a member of the Pulaski
Monument Association and had donated one hundred dollars to that
cause. That association was led by Richard W. Habersham. Perhaps
Campbell and Cumming were worried about the fate of the captives,

or perhaps Habersham had shared his concern and they became interested in the case. No matter the reason, Campbell and Cumming pled for Congress to save these captives; this was their last chance for freedom.[2]

After a brief history of the *Antelope* case, in which the attorneys noted that "those claimed by the Spaniards were unable to maintain their natural rights," Campbell and Cumming wrote that the thirty-nine enslaved captives were in the "prime of life": "Twenty-five are said to have married; that is, have attached themselves to persons with whom they live as though they were husband and wife." The laws of Georgia did not recognize slave marriages, but the petition called upon Congress to honor those attachments. If the bond was canceled, it would "subject these persons to slavery, under laws much more severe than exist in the Spanish West India colonies." The attorneys detailed how Georgia's laws were more oppressive than the laws of Spanish Cuba. The petition asked that "a sufficient appropriation may be made to relieve the Hon. R. H. Wilde and to carry more perfectly into effect his first benevolent intention, by causing these persons to be restored to freedom and their country, with such members of their families as are desirous of accompanying them and can be redeemed." The petition was referred to the Committee of the Whole House, printed, and distributed. After that it vanished.[3]

While Wilde and Berrien awaited their victory, the enslaved captives remained in the Savannah area through the winter, working, while the bill slowly ripened in the House. Richard Henry Wilde's partner, Joseph White, had meanwhile found another partner to make the dream of vast land holdings in Florida possible. Farish Carter was a wealthy war profiteer, land speculator, and steamboat developer. He had built a cotton plantation empire in middle and north Georgia, and in 1827 he began to expand into the new territory of Florida. He invested with White and Wilde in the creation of Casa Bianca, a 3,500-acre plantation in Jefferson County, Florida. Despite Wilde's plan as explained to John M. Berrien, Casa Bianca was not a sugar plantation but soon became one of the most prosperous cotton plantations in Florida. Wilde's petition had dwelt upon his humanitarian motives for acquiring the slaves, but it hardly reflected his full opinion. In February of 1825, writing to a friend in Georgia, Wilde bemoaned the election of John Quincy Adams as president. "We have fallen upon evil times," he wrote, "there is no hope for the Republic during the next four years." There was a grand conspiracy afoot against the South and slavery, Wilde argued, in the most grandiloquent terms possible. "Rely upon it," he wrote, "we are not far from questions which must rouse Southern feeling. . . . We shall have before long proposals for emancipation." He concluded, "The Southern States are already the Ireland of the Union."[4]

Like so many southern elites in the decades before the Civil War, Wilde felt threatened and under siege, even while slaves and cotton made him rich. In the 1827 Richmond County, Georgia, Tax Digest, Richard H. Wilde owned no slaves and 250 acres of land in Georgia. By 1830, he owned 1,237 acres in Georgia worth $10,000, and 39 slaves in Georgia alone. More questions were raised about the *Antelope* captives in the fall of 1828. The *Savannah Mercury* questioned the propriety of Wilde's obtaining a private law to his benefit. His "imposition upon Congress in the late African transaction, should expose him to the indignation of every honest man." Tongues must have been wagging in Savannah and across the state: Wilde was a sitting member of the House of Representatives. The *Augusta Chronicle* criticized the editor of the *Mercury* for his comments, so the *Mercury* responded in full. The editor quoted the entire Wilde memorial, full of its protestations of genuine concern for the Africans and their families, commenting, "Mr. Wilde here holds out the idea to Congress that his sole object in making the purchase was to prevent the Africans who had formed connections . . . from being separated from their wives and children." Then the editor issued a challenge: "Now, will Mr. Wilde step forward, and tell candidly and frankly what became of these Africans . . . what became of those tender ties, formed during a residence of eight years in Georgia? Where are the wives and children, do they not remain in Bryan county, and have not the husbands, the fathers, been carried to Florida?" These male captives—the "primest of the lot," in Marshal Morel's words—had built relationships with women on Morel's Cottenham plantation in Bryan County. When Wilde had used his position in Congress to obtain the cancelation of the bond, explained the *Mercury*, "it was prostituting the dignity of public legislation to the purposes of private thrift . . . his motives were altogether mercenary."[5]

Mercenary, but fruitful. In 1834, Richard Henry Wilde lost his seat in the House of Representatives. At that point it did not matter. He had made a fortune from the Casa Bianca scheme and his other plantations in Georgia. He sold his interest, and in 1835 he traveled to Europe to pursue what he believed was his true calling: writing literary criticism and poetry. Settling in Florence, Wilde turned to studies of Dante and several other Italian poets. He assisted in the restoration of the Bargello and befriended English and American artists and writers who passed through the city, chief among them Edward Bulwer-Lytton, a popular novelist and playwright of the day. Among Wilde's literary works was an epic poem, *Hesperia*, in which he wrote:

> Slaves still are slaves while raging to be free;
> True desperation has a quiet tone;
> Loud words show little love of Liberty,
> And plots and curses shake no despot's throne.[6]

Wilde, of course, had been one of the despots of Casa Bianca plantation. Perhaps he observed among his own slaves, slaves taken from the *Antelope*, a quiet tone of desperation? By 1843, Wilde had tired of Europe and returned to the United States. He accepted the position of professor of constitutional law at the University of Louisiana at New Orleans, now Tulane University. There Wilde died of yellow fever in 1847.[7]

Four Jacks, three Jims, three Neds, two Toms, two Joes, Sam, Billy, McCoso, John, Titus, Dick, Prince, Sandy, Jean-Pierre, Bob, George,

Dick, McKinda, Boatswain, Sandy, John, Peter, Tony, Quacco, and Simon—all had been identified by William Richardson as Spanish slaves. Henry Haupt identified Sam, Lucy, and a third Joe. John H. Morel identified a third Tom. These were the original thirty-nine designated for slavery, and, unlike the captives transported to Africa, they were not accorded last names. Two died before being taken to Florida. The rest were put to work on Casa Bianca plantation producing cotton for Carter, White, and Wilde. Sadly, as with most of the millions enslaved in the United States, information about these individuals ended with the court case that determined their fate. They were subsumed into that great mass of the enslaved who worked, suffered, and died to build America.[8]

Captain John Jackson of the revenue cutter *Dallas* remained in Savannah until September of 1821. He was then transferred to New Orleans, where he took command of the revenue cutter *Louisiana*. In November of 1821, during an anti-piracy cruise off Cuba, Jackson captured five pirate vessels. He burned two and sent the other three to New Orleans as prizes. While in New Orleans, Jackson was also involved in the case of *La Pensee*, and he wrote later of watching the slaver he had helped escort into port put to sea for its return to France. In 1827 the *Louisiana* captured the Colombian privateer *Bolívar* and took her into New Orleans. Captain Jackson was clearly a superior officer in the revenue marine. After commanding the *Louisiana*, he was transferred to Charleston, where he took command of the exceptional cutter *Marion*. These were described by Treasury Secretary Richard Rush as "the most complete vessels of their class ever produced." Captain Jackson would continue on in command of revenue cutters and would serve in the second Seminole war.[9]

Richard Wylly Habersham remained in Savannah for several more years. He served as a federal commissioner in 1830 to direct the work done to improve the Savannah River channel. He was joined in that commission by William B. Bulloch, who John Quincy Adams thought was involved in the illegal slave trade, and John H. Morel, still U.S. Marshal for the state of Georgia. Habersham had large land-holdings in north Georgia's Habersham County, named for Colonel Joseph Habersham, a Revolutionary War hero and his uncle. By the early 1830s, he concluded that there was more to be gained by living on those lands than by continuing in Savannah, so the family moved, spending most of their time in Clarkesville, Georgia. By that time the Habersham children had largely come of age. Richard Wylly Habersham Jr. was an artist, traveling and studying in Europe. He became friends with Samuel Morse and appears in Morse's *Gallery of the Louvre*, where he is depicted painting a copy of a landscape. His brother Barnard Elliott Habersham became a noted leader of the Episcopal Church in the South. He led his family in the great journey across the plains to Oregon, where he became a leader in the church there. The third son, Alexander Wylly Habersham, joined the navy. He achieved some fame as a chronicler of long voyages along the coasts of Asia. Stephen Elliott Habersham was a successful physician. Daughter Catherine Elliott Habersham married John Milledge Jr., the son of Georgia governor John Milledge and a successful and wealthy planter. Richard W. Habersham was proud of his successful children. Habersham himself never accumulated great riches. While he was wealthy compared to his neighbors in the up-country, it was not riches on the scale of so many in Savannah. He never wrote about his fight for the *Antelope* captives; nor did any of his children. He continued to own slaves, and they were a major component of his wealth in 1840. It was as if the *Antelope* case had never happened.

In 1838, while living in Habersham County, Richard W. Habersham reentered politics. He was elected to the United States Congress as a Whig and, like so many Whigs, tried to occupy the middle ground in American political conflicts. He had resigned his position as U.S. Attorney over the issue of federal interference in Georgia's relations with the Indians, and others surely saw that as a states' rights position. Habersham spoke of asserting state power and limiting the power of the federal government, but compared to many of his peers he was a moderate in Congress. He was elected twice more to Congress, but in December of 1842, at age fifty-five, he died suddenly at his home in Habersham County, surrounded by his family.[10]

John H. Morel continued as United States marshal and in the winter of 1834 was appointed for a fourth successive term. His fine double house, built in 1818 on Orleans Square in Savannah, still stands. No record shows with certainty how much money Morel made from the labor of the *Antelope* captives on his plantation. He bragged that it was $30,000 a year, a huge sum. More realistically, for every one hundred captives working on Cottenham plantation, he probably netted $10,000 or so per year from their work. Morel also received a total of $20,621.98 from the United States Navy and was paid $6,347.00 by Richard Henry Wilde for his lien on the Spanish slaves. While there were some expenses paid out of that money, most of the $26,968.98 Morel received was pure profit. The *Antelope* case must have made him at least $50,000, well over a million dollars today. The 1832 tax digests show a very wealthy man. John H. Morel owned four houses in Savannah, 222 acres in Chatham County, 490 acres in Rabun County, and 4,500 acres of plantation land in Bryan County. He owned 120 slaves, while his wife owned another 268 acres and 33 slaves. In aggregate, Morel's holdings in Georgia were worth more than $100,000 in 1832. He died June 2, 1834, at the age of fifty-three. The Savannah death register recorded the cause as gout, suggesting a very painful passing.[11]

John M. Berrien also did well from the *Antelope* case. Not only did it introduce him to Washington with a bang in 1825, but the money was good. The navy paid Berrien, as Captain John Jackson's proctor, $5,100 in bounties on the free captives rescued by the revenue cutter. Berrien took about one-third of the bounty payment in fees. Jackson was also paid $1,950 in salvage, from which Berrien took about one-third. Berrien's final share was at least $1,770. Berrien was paid $1,850 in fees and $150 from the sale of the *Antelope*. In total, he made at least $3,770.00 from the *Antelope* case. Not as much money as he might have made from the original judgment by his friend, district court judge William Davies, but close. He may have also charged additional fees of John Jackson, and he may have taken secret payments from John H. Morel, but there is no clear evidence for that.[12]

Berrien broke politically with Governor Troup's party in Georgia, though he maintained cordial relations with Troup himself. In Washington, Berrien found a rising star to carry him even higher. Andrew Jackson had been one of five candidates for president in 1824, and when he lost that controversial election, his supporters rejected the Adams presidency as illegitimate. Over the next four years they did their utmost to stall or defeat the Adams administration's wishes in Congress and to undermine the administration in the public eye. Berrien joined this group of Adams haters, criticizing and blocking Adams's initiatives in the Senate, slowing government to a crawl. By doing so he tied himself to Jackson. When Jackson trounced Adams in the 1828 presidential election, he named John Macpherson Berrien as his attorney general.

Berrien was an extraordinarily active attorney general, producing eighty-eight opinions and arguing before the Supreme Court fifteen times during the two years he held the office. Probably his most significant opinion came in December of 1830, in a case involving Sam Houston. Houston, fleeing a failed marriage in Tennessee, had opened a trading post in the Cherokee Nation without a federal license. When sued by the U.S. Attorney, Houston argued that the Cherokee Nation was sovereign and that the United States lacked jurisdiction to require such a license. Berrien's opinion was that the Indian nations were not sovereign. The Cherokee may have held title to lands, but the federal government had sovereignty over the whole. There could be only one sovereign, not many. The Jackson administration found this argument legally compelling and, more importantly, useful. The argument played a significant role in the upcoming case of *Cherokee Nation v. Georgia* and the ultimate forced relocation of southeastern Indians to what would become Oklahoma.[13]

John M. Berrien also dealt with a potential sequel to the *Antelope* case while serving as attorney general. On June 5, 1830, the U.S. Navy schooner *Grampus* captured the Spanish slaver *Fenix*, well-armed, with twenty crew and eighty-two African captives aboard. A prize crew took the *Fenix* into New Orleans. John Slidell, the U.S. Attorney in New Orleans, libeled the schooner under the 1819 Slave Trade Act. He really did not know what to do, and, as he wrote to Secretary of State Martin Van Buren, he was "much embarrassed as regards the course to be pursued with the slaves found onboard." Seventy-four captives were still alive and had been claimed by their Spanish owner. Slidell mentioned the *Antelope* case and observed that there were several differences between that case and this one, particularly that the laws of Spain now forbade the slave trade, as did treaties with Spain. The reasoning of the *Antelope* case for returning the slaves no longer seemed to apply. Attorney General Berrien wrote his opinion in the case on August 18, 1830. He argued that the case was of such difficulty that it probably should go to the Supreme Court. This would allow the Court to decide the issues still remaining.

> The great question [in the case of the *Antelope*] on which the court divided was whether our judicial tribunals were bound to restore [such property]. . . . these Africans cannot with propriety be delivered up to any person claiming property in them until the validity of such claim and our obligation to deliver them, shall have been affirmed by the Supreme Court of the United States.[14]

Berrien warned the district court and the U.S. Marshal to prepare for great expenses in keeping the captives alive until the issue could be resolved. He did not suggest that they could arrange to profit from the situation.

Contemporaries debated the reasons John M. Berrien accepted the position of attorney general in the Jackson administration. Many concluded that Berrien took the position because he was promised a seat on the U.S. Supreme Court. No seat had opened up, however, before the John and Peggy Eaton conflict tore the administration apart. John Eaton was a longtime supporter whom Andrew Jackson named secretary of war. Peggy, his wife, had been married before. She was suspected of sexual improprieties before, during, and after her first marriage. Because of this, many women refused to socialize with her, and she became a pariah. Andrew Jackson obsessively defended her, perhaps remembering the destructive allegations of sexual impropriety made against his own late wife, Rachel. John M. Berrien's first wife, Eliza Anciaux, had died in the summer of 1828, and his household in Washington was managed by his two unmarried daughters. Joining with many other households in Washington, Berrien's daughters refused to receive the morally suspect Peggy Eaton at their home. The conflict grew and festered, entangled with a struggle for power within the president's circle. Ultimately, Jackson required his entire cabinet to resign, and the cabinet was remade. In June of 1831, John Macpherson Berrien resigned as attorney general. He was not invited to be part of the new cabinet. His place was taken by the Maryland attorney general, Roger B. Taney. A bit more than four years later, Roger B. Taney would be named chief justice of the Supreme Court. The thought had to have occurred to John M. Berrien that had he welcomed Peggy Eaton into his home, he might have been chief justice.[15]

Berrien returned to Savannah. While his law practice brought in a good income and he benefited from a partnership with attorney and railroad promoter Richard R. Cuyler, Berrien's political career seemed to have ended. This was made clear in January of 1835, when President Jackson appointed James Moore Wayne to the United States Supreme Court. Wayne had in many ways been mentored by Berrien, and being passed over for a younger man must have rankled. Berrien turned to his other interests. In 1833, he married Eliza Hunter; she was twenty-three, he was fifty-two. In less than a year, he fathered the first of six children with her. He also focused on developing his planting interests. In 1836, he expanded his Morton Hall plantation on the Savannah River by buying the bordering Oakgrove plantation of seven hundred acres.

Almost inevitably, Berrien became involved with Savannah's greatest project of the 1830s, helping create what would become the Central of Georgia Railroad. He obtained a charter for the railroad granting banking privileges, helping to fund its construction. He invested his own money in the railroad. Through these efforts, Berrien began to associate with a number of other men working on "internal improvements," men who would lead the creation of Georgia's Whig Party. In 1840, he openly supported the Whig candidate William Henry Harrison for president. As Whig influence grew in Georgia, the party chose the respected former attorney general as their candidate for the United States Senate. In December of 1840, the Georgia General Assembly elected John M. Berrien U.S. senator for the second time. He would serve two terms, replaced in 1852 by fire-eater Robert Tombs. On January 1, 1856, at age seventy-four, John M. Berrien died.

"On the left bank of Stockton Creek, and near the settlement on Bushrod Island, the recaptured Africans are located," wrote one visitor to New Georgia in March of 1830. He reported that of the 400 people in the settlement, 250 had been transported to Liberia by the federal government, while 150 were captives taken from Spanish slave factories on the west African coast near the Gallinas River. Visitors to the colony always wanted to see the settlement of the recaptured Africans; it was clear evidence both of the benevolent intentions behind the colony and of United States support. It was also unique, inhabited by people who literally occupied a middle ground between the American blacks settled near Monrovia and the native Africans inland.[16]

In March of 1830, the *Antelope* captives living at New Georgia were joined by a group of captives rescued in the Florida Keys. On December 19, 1827, the British warship *Nimble* on anti-slavery patrol off Cuba in the Florida Straits spotted a suspicious vessel. It was the Spanish slaver *Guerrero*, loaded with 561 captives. The *Guerrero* ran; it was a large and fast ship, while the *Nimble* was smaller and slower. The chase continued for more than five hours. A front was pushing

through, and the weather worsened as the chase continued. By evening the *Nimble* had outsailed the *Guerrero* and was close enough to
open fire. A running battle ensued. They were close to the shores of
Key Largo, and the *Guerrero* was tearing along at 10 knots when she
struck the reef. The hull tore open; the masts tumbled over the sides.
The screams of the captives, crushed and drowning, "were heard two
miles away by the crew of the *Nimble*." The *Nimble* tried to turn, but
she too hit the reef. All efforts turned then to rescue.[17]

Early the next morning a group of wreckers arrived at the *Guerrero*. The captives had spent the night in darkness on a ship filled with
water, turned on its side, heaving with the seas upon the reef. Eventually, many had climbed into the rigging to avoid the seas that were
sweeping over the ship. As they looked upon the scene of horror,
the wreckers were astonished to find the Spanish captain climbing
aboard one of their ships. He insisted that his ship was not a British
prize and would pay salvage to any wrecker who saved the ship and
cargo. Amazingly, some 510 captives were still alive, as well as more
than 80 Spanish crew. In a complex story of conflict and deceit, over
the next several days the Spanish hijacked two wreckers' ships and
took almost 400 captives to Cuba. The remaining 121 captives were
taken to Key West. There followed another legal odyssey, in which
the captives were bonded out around St. Augustine while the courts
decided their fate. Finally, in late 1829, the surviving captives began
a terrifying five-month voyage from Fernandina on Amelia Island to
Liberia. Ninety-one survived to reach Monrovia in March of 1830.[18]

These ninety-one captives were Igbo, taken from Old Calabar
by the *Guerrero*. They were soon settled at New Georgia, among the
Kongo *Antelope* survivors and the people of other ethnicities rescued
from along the coast. There were difficulties, but in promotional letters printed in the United States the conflicts were minimized. Visitors to New Georgia saw that the town was segregated by ethnicity.
The survivors of the *Antelope* had arrived with both the advantage
of knowing English and experience with American ways of work.
The newly arrived rescued captives did not have those advantages.

Not all the conflict, however, was between those of different ethnicities, or even within the colony. In early 1832, conflict broke out with the local Dei people over runaway slaves who "took shelter with our recaptured Africans." Fighting broke out, and the Igbo and Kongo fought side by side.[19]

While war is often spoken of as a unifying force for a society, the town of New Georgia remained very much divided. Residents even differed in marriage patterns. The Kongos from the *Antelope* married only within the colony, while the newly arrived "Ebo [Igbo] and Pessa . . . were in the habit of procuring wives from the adjacent tribes." This greatly concerned the U.S. agent, Joseph Mechlin, and he forced couples to marry in church or at least before the clerk of court. In July 1832 the divisions in New Georgia became even clearer. Mechlin wrote:

> [It is] their urgent request that I should be present at, and superintend their election for a chief. Both the Eboes and Congoes had several times attempted to choose a chief, but always without success. The principle difficulty arose from those in the minority refusing to acknowledge the person chosen by the majority. . . . I had the election held in my presence, and as soon as it was concluded made some remarks on the necessity . . . of submitting to the will of the majority.[20]

Turning to a description of New Georgia for the managers, Mechlin wrote, "These people occupy two very neat and well-built villages near the east bank of Stockton Creek . . . a small rivulet separates that of the Eboes from the Congo village." The farms looked rich, he said, with more than 150 acres planted in cassava, Indian corn, sweet potatoes, and vegetables. New Georgia not only fed itself, it produced enough to help feed the colony. "Each tribe have built by voluntary subscription and joint labor, a house of worship and a town or palaver house." When not farming, the inhabitants of New Georgia produced lumber and shingles for building. Speaking of the former

Antelope captives, Mechlin wrote "Many of the Congo tribe can read and have established a Sunday school, which is regularly attended by both children and adults." He concluded, "These people are decidedly the most contented and independent of any in the colony." Others agreed. "New Georgia—Our recaptives of the Congo tribe, have progressed so far in civilization that . . . through the whole village, there reigns so much neatness and comfort that we have seen few spots to surpass it," commented the *Liberia Herald*.[21]

But all was not perfect. Some black American colonists thought that the recaptives were a bit too proud of their accomplishments. One wrote, in 1833, that "our recaptured Africans seem somewhat presumptuous at times." The American colonists assumed that they were superior to the local indigenous people. In their developing social construct for Liberia, the recaptives fell between the free black immigrants from America and the local people. This was expressed in comments about marriage. "A large number of the recaptured Africans settled at New Georgia," reported the *African Repository*, "have intermarried with the female emigrants from the United States, and in this way civilization is extending a little into the interior of the country." The recaptives might produce food and lumber for the entire colony, they might fight to defend the colony, but in the eyes of those from the United States they were not yet truly civilized.[22]

By 1840, the inhabitants of New Georgia felt much more secure about their place in the colony. One visitor reported that the recaptives referred to themselves as "Americans" and "feel greatly superior to the natives around them." How many of these people were survivors from the *Antelope* was never clear. For all the quaintness of the town of New Georgia, the square blocks with streets "as smooth and clear as the best swept sidewalks in Philadelphia," in truth Liberia was a deathtrap. Many immigrants did not live long after their arrival. Even though two-thirds of the *Antelope* captives escaped the initial severe suffering and deaths from malaria, they were still in danger. May other diseases swept the colony, the nearby indigenous people launched occasional attacks, and daily work scratching a living from the African forest could itself be deadly. In September of 1843, the U.S. government took a census in the colony of Liberia. It included a breakdown of arrivals by ship. None of the lucky sixteen sent on the *Strong* in 1822 were listed in the document; presumably all were dead. The town of New Georgia had a population of 263, but very few were original settlers. Of the 143 people sent on the *Norfolk* who had arrived in Liberia in August 1827, only 33 were alive in 1843. A few of the captives had moved to Caldwell or Monrovia, but most had stayed in New Georgia. This was a survival rate of 23 percent among people who had averaged twenty-one years old upon arrival. If 121 original captives from the *Antelope* had boarded the *Norfolk* in Savannah, sixteen years later only 28 survived.[23]

The Antelope case lived on much longer than the captives who voyaged to Liberia. The Marshall Court's decision made explicit several important principles. First, that the written, positive laws on slavery superseded the natural rights of individuals. Positive law establishing and regulating slavery made slaves property, and property had no rights. It was not much of a stretch from this to Justice Roger B. Taney writing about black Africans in the Dred Scott decision:

> They had for more than a century before been regarded as beings of an inferior order, and altogether unfit to associate with the white race, either in social or political relations; and so far inferior, that they had no rights which the white man was bound to respect; and that the negro might justly and lawfully be reduced to slavery for his benefit. He was bought and sold, and treated as an ordinary article of merchandise and traffic, whenever a profit could be made by it.[24]

As property, bought and sold like ordinary articles of merchandise, what rights could slaves have? Morality is not the law, John Macpherson Berrien had told the Court, and the *Antelope* decision proved him absolutely correct. By the 1830s, even abolitionists had embraced this reasoning. As Theodore Dwight Weld wrote in 1838, property in slaves could exist "only by positive legislative acts, forcibly setting aside the law of nature." This conception of law and slavery lies at the heart of the antebellum Supreme Court cases on slavery; all are tied to Marshall's search "for a legal solution."[25]

Second, while the Court decried the slave trade in the harshest possible terms, the justices concluded that they had no choice but to follow the law of nations permitting the trade. American law condemned slave traders as pirates, and by law enslaved captives from Africa should be confiscated by the president and freed in Africa. Despite the clear intent of these laws, the Court rejected the application of American law to a ship crewed by Americans headed toward American shores. The Court was compelled, Marshall argued, to follow Spanish and Portuguese law on the slave trade, even while they announced that they could not enforce the criminal laws of other countries. Marshall's tone was one of regret, as if he felt trapped, compelled by the law to return the Spanish captives as slaves against his own wishes. He was trapped by the rule that formal, textual law superseded natural rights and natural law. Marshall presented himself as unable to do otherwise. Francis Scott Key thought differently. He thought that the Supreme Court had the power to make the rules. Marshall argued that he could only find the rules and follow them. This sort of legal formalism may have been useful to Marshall in his struggle to turn the Constitution into a clear legal text. It was, however, devastating in its consequences for human life and justice.[26]

Seldom discussed, but of greater importance, was the holding that the municipal law of a place—that is, the positive law of a particular city, state, or country—trumps international law and natural rights. When this principle was applied to the positive law permitting the slave trade, and when custom and practice could serve as the basis for that positive law, the result was particularly pernicious. During the War of 1812, the United States successfully defended the principle that British warships could not stop and search American ships on the high seas. After 1815, Great Britain made a great effort to use its naval forces to suppress the African slave trade, but those efforts were often futile. Slave traders quickly realized that they were almost untouchable under the American flag, and so the slave trade continued apace, sheltered under the U.S. flag and often financed from the United States. As John Marshall explained in the *Antelope* opinion:

> The right of visitation and search being strictly a belligerent right, and the slave trade being neither piratical, nor contrary to the law of nations, the principle is asserted and maintained with great strength of reasoning, that it cannot be exercised on the vessels of a foreign power, unless permitted by treaty.[27]

If the Court had ruled that the slave trade violated international law, American navy ships could have stopped and searched any ship suspected of slaving. No more would a quick change to another nation's flag prevent discovery. Were the trade ruled illegal under the law of nations, treaties for the mutual right of search at sea could have been made with Great Britain and other nations. No more would slavers have sailed with impunity under the American flag. The Atlantic Ocean was large and the number of warships small, but the Court's ruling the slave trade illegal under the law of nations would have made a substantial impact. Evidence for this comes from events following the secession crisis in the United States. As war loomed, President Lincoln recalled the American navy squadrons patrolling the Caribbean and the west African coast. The administration worried that without American ships on patrol, the slave trade would increase. Charles Francis Adams, son of John Quincy Adams, was serving as minister to Great Britain. He asked if British ships could take the place of the American vessels patrolling Cuban waters to intercept slavers. The discussions that followed resulted in the Lyons-Seward Treaty of 1862. Each nation granted the other the right of search at sea. Courts of mixed commission were established in New York, Cape Town, and Sierra Leone. The Lincoln administration abandoned one of the cherished principles fought for in the War of 1812, but the results were immediate. By 1863, six Royal Navy steamers cruised the Cuban coast. With this sort of close enforcement by the British, and the treaty right to stop and search American and Cuban vessels, the Royal Navy crushed the slave trade to Cuba within five years. In a burst of enthusiasm, Secretary of State William Seward in Washington wrote Charles Francis Adams, "Had such a treaty been made in 1808, there would have been no sedition here." While such a treaty might not have prevented the American Civil War by destroying slavery, it almost certainly would have diminished the Atlantic slave trade.[28]

Instead, unwittingly, the Court's *Antelope* decision facilitated the Atlantic slave trade's continuance for another forty years. It waxed and waned, but there was no decline. In 1859, more ships brought slaves to Cuba than at any time since the 1820s. As many as 170 of these voyages were financed and organized in New York City alone. The slave trade seemed impossible to control. There were more than 4,000 successful slaving voyages from Africa to the Americas between 1825 and 1866. During this period over 1,700,000 people were loaded aboard slave ships in Africa in documented voyages. At least 1,500,000 of these new slaves arrived in the Americas. More than 10 percent of those embarked died. At least 170,000 people were directly killed by the continuance of the slave trade.[29]

John Marshall wrote in the *Antelope*, "Slavery, then, has its origin in force; but as the world has agreed that it is a legitimate result of force, the state of things which is thus produced by general consent, cannot be pronounced unlawful." Because it was not pronounced unlawful, tens of thousands more would suffer and die.[30]

EPILOGUE

"One step further and the case of the Antelope would have conferred unfading glory on the Supreme Court. One step more, and the heartless sophistry would have been silenced, and the cold blooded apathy to human suffering would have been stung into sensibility."

John Quincy Adams
Argument of John Quincy Adams . . . in the Case of the . . . *Amistad*

On January 14, 1841, John Quincy Adams arrived at the Supreme Court chamber long before the justices. Adams was an early riser; he had been one most of his life. That January he was seventy-three years old, afflicted with eye problems, lumbago, and a palsy of the right hand that forced him to use a wrist rest when he wrote. Undaunted, Adams wrote for hours each day, not just official documents and letters but also his exceptional diary entries. His grandson, Charles Francis Adams Jr., recalled that John Quincy was "a very old-looking gentleman, with a bald head and a white fringe of hair . . . [and] a perpetual inkstain on the forefinger and thumb of his right hand." Despite his age, Adams was an extraordinarily busy man. Most days he woke at five, took a long walk, and then began business. Adams had been a member of Congress for ten years and was deeply involved in the political whirl of Washington, D.C. In some ways he seemed to matter more as a congressman than he had as president. Every evening he wrote, sometimes working as late as midnight, but then he would wake again at five. His grandson's other recollection was that Adams did not have "a holiday temperament." His numerous enemies were harsher. The House of Representative clerk Benjamin French described Adams as "a demon just from hell, with all his passions under the influence of the infernal regions." His incredible skill, wit, and cleverness with parliamentary procedure and debate befuddled his opponents. Adams's visit to the Supreme Court on the morning of the fourteenth was part of another project that would drive his enemies wild: He had agreed to join Roger Baldwin in representing the captives from the slave ship *Amistad* before the Supreme Court. Adams wanted to check the progress of the Court docket, for he was gravely worried that time was short, and that he might not be able to properly prepare for his oral argument in the upcoming case.[1]

While he waited, Francis Scott Key joined him. Now in his sixties, Key was still a leading advocate in the Supreme Court and a leading proponent of the American Colonization Society. Soon the two older men were involved in a discussion of the coming *Amistad* case and the plight of the captives even as the business of the Court began to swirl around them. Adams wrote that Key "said he was afraid there was not any chance for the poor creatures; that the case of the *Antelope* was precisely in point against them." Key reminded Adams that he "had argued the case for the freedom of the negroes," and that he knew the *Antelope* case intimately. The only hope, Key said, was to collect money, purchase the *Amistad* captives, and send them to Liberia. Adams later wrote in his diary:

> I said we hoped to prove that the case of the Antelope would not be conclusive in its bearing on our clients; but he continued very positive in the impression that it would. I went, therefore, into the Supreme Court library-room, and took out the volume of Wheaton's Reports containing the case of the Antelope. I read as much of it as I could, and longed to com-

ment upon it as I could; but I have neither time nor head for it—nothing but the heart.[2]

Francis Scott Key would die just two years later, but he had managed to resurrect the *Antelope* case one last time.

The *Antelope* had been an issue Secretary of State John Quincy Adams had fervently hoped would go away and an issue he had ignored completely while president. He probably did not appreciate the irony of its resurfacing. His disengagement from the case was so complete that he apparently read Marshall's full opinion for the first time in 1841. Of course he knew of the case, and had mentioned it in connection with the *Amistad* when writing abolitionist Ellis Gray Loring in October of 1839, but Adams had convinced himself that the case did not apply. He and his co-counsel, Roger Baldwin, intended to attack the legitimacy of Spanish documents designating the captives as seasoned Cuban slaves, *ladinos*, rather than as new captives, or *bozales*, from Africa. Despite attestation by the highest government officials in Cuba, the documents were obviously false. Under current law and treaties, the Spanish could legitimately transport *ladino* slaves around Cuba, but they could not import *bozales* from Africa. If these were slaves being legally transported by the Cubans, as the documents alleged, then they were Spanish property and had to be returned to their owners. If not, they should be free. After speaking with Key, Adams realized that it was possible the Supreme Court would accept the Spanish documents and rule the captives legal slaves. If so, under the *Antelope* ruling they would be returned to their owners in Cuba. The lower courts had already ordered this for Antonio, a *ladino* slave who had been owned by Captain Ramón Ferrer of the *Amistad*. Adams realized that he had to find a way to attack and discredit the *Antelope* ruling. Over the next five weeks he went to the office of the clerk of the Supreme Court eleven times to read over the record of the case. He had copies made of Judge Davies's decree and all of Justice Johnson's rulings. Adams became obsessed with the *Antelope*; he worried that it was the key to victory or defeat in the *Amistad* case.[3]

Defeat was something Adams knew well. As a minority president more than a decade earlier he had suffered political attacks and legislative defeats. By the time he quietly signed the bill canceling the bond for the Spanish slaves from the *Antelope* in May of 1828, he knew he probably would not be reelected. It turned out much worse than that. Andrew Jackson's popular movement crushed John Quincy Adams in the 1828 election. The campaign became vicious and personal, so personal that President-elect Jackson refused to make a goodwill call on the outgoing president, and Adams refused to attend Jackson's inauguration. Over the next year and a half the challenges of moving into the old family home in Quincy, the suicide of his son George, and his precarious financial situation all led to depression for John Quincy Adams. "I am suffering distress of mind," he wrote, "longing for the capacity to give some value to the remnant of my life." By August of 1830, he wrote, "I have no plausible motive for wishing to live."[4]

Then, in September local leaders asked Adams to stand for Congress. The depression passed quickly, replaced by an eagerness to rejoin politics. Adams handily won election in the fall of 1830 and went to Congress a very different man. He had always been so careful, had always controlled his words and actions, refusing to compromise his chances for political advancement. For what may have been the first time in his life he felt free to speak his mind and support the causes he thought morally right. This was especially true with regard to slavery. Before and during his presidency he had struggled to avoid the issue, to keep silent on the subject, to avoid antagonizing southern slaveholders and politicians whose support he needed and with whom he had to work. Now, in Congress, he felt no need to control his speech. The passionless president became an impassioned advocate for the Bill of Rights and a foe of slavery. After the "gag rule" was imposed in 1836, preventing the presentation of petitions concerning slavery or their debate upon the floor, Adams cleverly found ways to circumvent it. He saw this as a First Amendment issue and humiliated many opponents who dared to debate him on the subject. His confrontational attitude, his wide knowledge of history, and his remarkable career as a diplomat, all enhanced by an astute attention to language, made him a devastating opponent in the House. The aging Adams felt that by openly advocating for what was right, he could redeem his presidency and confound the "slave mongering" enemies who had hounded him from office.

In 1839, another route to redemption appeared. The *Amistad*, a Cuban coastal schooner that had been captured in an uprising by its cargo of slaves, was seized in late August by the revenue cutter *Washington*. The captives of the *Amistad* were imprisoned in Connecticut, and there began a legal journey that ultimately reached the Supreme Court. In September of 1839, Ellis Gray Loring wrote Adams to ask his advice in the case. Over the coming months Adams gladly took up the role of advisor but did his utmost to remain behind the scenes. Then, in November of 1840, with the case scheduled to go before the Supreme Court that winter, Loring and fellow abolitionist Lewis Tappan visited Adams and asked him to work with Roger Baldwin in pleading the case. Explaining that he was old and hadn't argued in the Supreme Court for thirty years, Adams said no. Loring and Tappan would not give up. Finally, "I yielded," Adams wrote, "and told them . . . I would argue the case before the Supreme Court; and I implore the mercy of Almighty God so to control my temper, to enlighten my soul, and to give me utterance, that I may prove myself equal to the task."[5]

Adams struggled to keep up with all of his duties and commitments while he prepared for the case. In December the congressional term began, and Adams was so fully engaged in the House that he feared he was neglecting his preparation. In fact, he worked constantly on the case. A typical day was February 17, 1841. Adams went early in the morning to the office of the Supreme Court clerk, where he read over Judge William Davies's February 1821 district court decision in the *Antelope*. After asking for a copy of the decision, he went to his seat in the House of Representatives, where an argument raged over the question of funding national mints. Among the debaters was "Habersham of Georgia," who with "much snarling" attacked a representative from Rhode Island. Adams did not mention, or even seem to realize, that this was the same man who twenty years before had fought so powerfully for the freedom of the *Antelope* captives. This was the same man whose arguments had been cavalierly dismissed by Judge William Davies in Adams's morning reading. Despite his "snarling," or perhaps because of it, Richard W. Habersham had become a powerful Whig politician in Congress. Like Key, in less than two years Habersham would be dead.[6]

On Monday, February 22, 1841, Adams walked to the Capitol feeling both overwhelmed by the task looming before him and unprepared for his role in it. The Supreme Court chamber was much the same as it had been for the *Antelope* case years before: a dark semicircular room with just three windows behind the justices, who sat at desks on a raised dais. The lawyers sat at tables before the Court and often saw little more of the justices than backlit shapes. Attorney General Henry Gilpin opened for the United States as appellant. "He contended that the *Amistad* was a regularly documented Spanish schooner," wrote Adams, and that the essential documents "were regularly signed by the Governor-General of Cuba, and proved beyond all controversy that the blacks were the property of Ruiz and Montez." "The Court," continued Gilpin, "could not go behind or enquire into the validity of these documents." Gilpin then presented numerous cases to support this argument. Finally, he argued that, as in the *Antelope* case, the slaves had to be returned to their owners.[7]

Roger Baldwin began his argument Monday afternoon and continued for four more hours on Tuesday. Adams silently waited his turn "with increasing agitation of mind, now little short of agony." He was very conscious that the lives of the captives depended upon his performance. If they lost, the captives would be sent back to Cuba to face probable execution. On Wednesday, February 24, Adams went to the Capitol early and stayed in the clerk's office reviewing materials until the moment Court began. He emerged to find the Court "filled to overflowing." Chief Justice Roger B. Taney asked Adams to begin. Later, Adams wrote, "I had been deeply distressed and agitated till the moment I rose." The fear vanished and Adams argued for four and a half hours. One reporter recalled, "Mr. Adams . . . displayed all his extraordinary powers of eloquence and reasoning." Another explained that despite having taken fifty-eight pages of notes on the first day, he could provide only a "meager skeleton" of Adams's argument. Adams expected to complete his argument the next day and spent an "uneasy, restless night." The next morning he arrived early at Court, only to learn that Justice Philip Barbour had died in his sleep. Court adjourned until Monday. Adams had to wait.[8]

On Monday, March 1, 1841, a nor'easter paralyzed the capital, blanketing the ground with snow. Despite this, the Supreme Court chambers were so crowded that the audience drove lawyers from their usual seats and even "encroached on the chairs of the Judges." A more rested Adams argued an additional four hours before the Court; in total he had argued for more than eight hours. On occasion he rambled, he made mistakes and misstatements, and much of his argument was not so much law as a discourse on political philosophy. One correspondent wrote that Adams's "remarks partook somewhat more of the statesman than of the practiced advocate." Other observers didn't care. "Mr. Adams concluded his plea before the Supreme Court yesterday," wrote one, "And such a plea—and such a *close*. What can I say? It was worthy of himself. Can I say more?" During that second day, "he examined the celebrated case of the *Antelope*, and brought forward the records of the District and Circuit Courts." Again and again reporters marveled at the number of documents Adams brought before the Court. Finally, in closing, Adams reflected upon the death of Justice Barbour and the passing of time. He named the men who sat on the Court when he first pled before it in 1804. "Where are they all?" he asked, "Gone! Gone! All gone." Adams began to weep and his voice grew softer and softer as he continued. Some barely heard his final statement. He hoped that all the justices past, he said, and the justices present, would be received at the portals of heaven with the words, "Well done, good and faithful servant; enter thou into the joy of thy Lord."[9]

The printed version of Adams's argument was 135 pages long.

Forty-one pages were devoted to the first full analysis of the *Antelope* decision ever published. Speaking of the *Antelope* captives after they arrived in Savannah, Adams asked, "Why were they not instantly liberated and sent home to Africa by the act of March 3d, 1819." In part, he answered, because the judges "were both holders of slaves, adjudicating in a State where slavery is the law of the land." Adams ridiculed Judge William Davies's district court opinion. He had nothing good to say about William Johnson's rulings either, and even apologized to the Court for speaking so frankly about the failings of a former member. In particular, he decried at length the absurd idea of a lottery to decide freedom. He labeled Johnson's circuit court decision "a chaos of confusion." Then, Adams turned to the Supreme Court opinion itself.[10]

The *Antelope* opinion, Adams said, was built on hypocrisy. Treading carefully and reassuring the Court of his respect for the late chief justice, Adams marveled that John Marshall could "admit that the traffic in slaves is contrary to the law of nature; that it is inhuman, odious, detestable, but that it is not contrary to the law of nations, and therefore must be acknowledged, defended, protected, and carried into execution for other nations by the Courts of the United States, although as abhorrent to our laws as the laws of nature."[11]

Adams called upon the Court for justice, and argued that it could be given by a return to the natural law foundations of the Republic. To some degree this was an old man's rant, but it was also a powerful call for the justices to remember the basic ideals of the Revolution. Several times during his argument Adams approached and pointed to a copy of the Declaration of Independence posted on the wall of the Supreme Court chamber. "In the Declaration of Independence," he said, "the Laws of Nature are announced and appealed to as identical with the laws of nature's God, and as the foundation of all obligatory human laws." This, he said, was the ultimate standard for all law. Adams called upon the Court to do what the *Antelope* Court would not: declare the African slave trade illegal under the law of nations because it violated the basic laws of nature.[12]

The *Antelope* case could not guide the Court in its decision, Adams continued, because it was fatally flawed. The justices had divided equally, so, as John Marshall had written, "no principle is settled." How could a case with no settled principle be determinative? Adams called on the Supreme Court to finally settle the principle, to resolve the question of proof raised in the *Antelope* by adopting the principle of liberty. The Court should always decide in favor of liberty, he argued; liberty should be the first principle. If the Court chose liberty, then the solution to the issue of proof became obvious. Adams contrasted Sir William Grant's opinion in the British admiralty case of the *Amedie* with the Supreme Court's opinion in the *Antelope*. The arguments "of the British Judge glow with the flame of human liberty," Adams observed, while "those of the American Judges are wedged in thrilling regions of thick ribbed ice." American decisions such as the *Antelope* used "a bluster of mental energy to shelter a national crime behind a barrier of national independence."[13]

Adams said that he did not want to speak critically of the justices involved in the *Antelope* decision, but that they had failed in their duty to give justice. They had failed, for with a just decision they could have redeemed the United States. The legal reasons for a just decision were there in the case. Attorney General William Wirt had argued in the *Antelope* that because the captives were human beings, the claimants faced an especially heavy burden of proof. Mere documents showing that the *Antelope* was legally engaged in the slave trade did not constitute sufficient proof that the captives were legally slaves. If only the Supreme Court had required a higher level of proof, Adams lamented, then they could have freed all of the *Antelope* captives. By requiring a higher level of proof they could have protected future victims from enslavement. John Marshall and his fellow justices had failed. They should have required strict proof. They should have found that the slave trade violated the law of nations. They should have freed all of the *Antelope* captives:

One step further and the case of the Antelope would have conferred unfading glory on the Supreme Court. One step

more, and the heartless sophistry would have been silenced,
and the cold blooded apathy to human suffering would have
been stung into sensibility. . . . This step was not taken; there
lacked one voice in a divided court to reverse the whole of
that decree of the Circuit Court.[14]

On March 9, Justice Joseph Story read the opinion in the case.
Adams need not have worried, for the Court rejected the government's assertion that they "could not go behind or enquire into the
validity" of the Spanish documents. The Spanish documents were
clearly fraudulent, the captives were illegally taken from Africa, and
so the captives were free people. Story did not address any of Adams's
wide-ranging arguments on natural law or political philosophy; his
decision focused simply on the clearly legal issues. Nor was there any
suggestion that the slave trade violated the law of nations, it simply
violated the law of some nations. Nonetheless, Adams was elated with
the result. "THE CAPTIVES ARE FREE," he immediately wrote to
Roger Baldwin and Lewis Tappan.

Interestingly, Adams continued his research in the *Antelope* records
after the case had been decided. He used his knowledge as a former
secretary of state to locate documents and records from Cuba and
from Great Britain. He grew ever more absorbed by the issue of the
continuing illegal international slave trade, the financing of that trade
in the United States, and even the documented complicity of the U.S.
consul in Havana, Nicholas Trist. In April, looking over the evidence
he had collected, Adams felt called to do something with it. Perhaps
this could be his next cause? Then, he began to think of the money
and the power that lay behind the continuing trade. He was overwhelmed by the "magnitude, the danger, the insurmountable burden
of labor to be encountered in undertaking to touch upon the slave
trade." In an agonized diary passage, he wondered what he, now age
seventy-four, could possibly do to assist with the suppression of the
African slave trade. In the end he concluded that he had done enough,
and that the cause should be left to others.[15]

"Great cases like hard cases make bad law," Justice Oliver Wendell Holmes Jr. wrote famously in his *Northern Securities Co. v. United States* dissent. The *Antelope* was a hard case, and while the opinions by William Johnson and John Marshall may not have been bad law, they certainly were pernicious. Meanwhile, over the course of eight years the captives had traveled to many dark places: the slave deck of the *Antelope*, Marshal Morel's Cottenham plantation, the streets and squares of Savannah. All the captives suffered, and half of them died during these years of rootlessness. Even for many of the captives sent to Liberia, freedom turned dark. Many of the legacies of the *Antelope* were dark, and the voyage of the *Antelope* led the United States to a darker place as well. The case plunged many Americans more deeply into a commitment to slavery, and entangled the protection of property rights with the suppression of individual rights. John Quincy Adams feared that his nation would pay dearly for this.[16]

There was some hope in this dark place. Richard W. Habersham, William Wirt, and Francis Scott Key called upon Americans' ideals, and on their commitment to natural rights. While they did not win, they caused many to reflect upon those ideals, and those ideals speak to us today. Most importantly, John Quincy Adams was right. With the case of the *Antelope*, the United States Supreme Court stood poised one step from leading the nation into a new world, a world free of the slave trade, perhaps even free of slavery. The Supreme Court could not take that step. That the United States could reach that precipice, however, just one step from revolution, showed that such a transformation might one day be possible. It was a longer and more difficult step than anyone had imagined, but a step that would come nonetheless.

NOTES

Prologue

1 *Niles' Weekly Register*, March 26, 1825, 706; *The Antelope*, 23 U.S. 66, 73 (1825); Edward S. Delaplaine, *Francis Scott Key: Life and Times* (New York: Biography Press, 1937), 191–218.

2 Henry S. Foote, *Casket of Reminiscences* (Washington, D.C.: Chronicle Publishing Co., 1874), 12–15.

3 *Niles' Weekly Register*, March 26, 1825, 706–7; Foote, *Casket of Reminiscences*, 12–15, Michael J. Frank, "Judge Not, Lest Ye Be Judged Unworthy of a Pay Raise," *Marquette Law Review* 87 (2003): 61. If Cuesta Manzanal y Hermano had recovered all the captives, they would have been worth between $60,000 and $100,000.

4 Foote, *Casket of Reminiscences*, 12; John P. Kennedy, *The Life of William Wirt*, Vol. 2 (Philadelphia: Lea and Blanchard, 1850), 373–74. The best biography of John Macpherson Berrien is Royce Coggins McCrary Jr., "John Macpherson Berrien of Georgia (1781–1856): A Political Biography" (PhD diss., University of Georgia, 1971).

5 Julian P. Boyd, *The Papers of Thomas Jefferson*, Vol. 1 (Princeton, NJ: Princeton University Press, 1950), 426.

6 John Quincy Adams, *Argument of John Quincy Adams, Before the Supreme Court of the United States: In the Case of the United States, Appellants, vs. Cinque, and Others, Africans, Captured in the Schooner Amistad* (New York: S. W. Benedict, 1841), 39. Hereafter Adams, *Argument*.

7 Alan Taylor, *The Internal Enemy: Slavery and War in Virginia, 1772–1832* (New York: W. W. Norton, 2013), 21–27; James Madison, *Journal of the Federal Convention*, edited by E. H. Scott (Chicago: Albert, Scott & Co., 1893); James Oakes, *Freedom National: The Destruction of Slavery in the United States, 1861–1865* (New York: W. W. Norton, 2013); U.S. Const. art. III, § 2.

8 Thomas Jefferson to John Holmes, April 22, 1820, Library of Congress, http://www.loc.gov/exhibits/jefferson/159.html (accessed August 3, 2013); *The Antelope*, 23 U.S. 66, 86 (1825).

9 Robin Blackburn, *The Overthrow of Colonial Slavery, 1776–1846*, 286–87, 310–15; Matthew Mason, *Slavery and Politics in the Early American Republic* (Chapel Hill: University of North Carolina Press, 2006); An Act to Prohibit the Importation of Slaves into Any Port or Place Within the Jurisdiction of the United States, From and After the First Day of January, in the Year of Our Lord One Thousand Eight Hundred and Eight, in *The Public Statutes at Large of the United States*

of America, 1789–1845, Vol. 2, edited by Richard Peters (Boston: Little and Brown, 1848), 426–30; An Act for the Abolition of the Slave Trade, 47 Geo III Sess. 1 c. 36. South Carolina reopened the slave trade from 1803 to 1807, but no other state followed suit.

10 Hugh Thomas, *The Slave Trade: The Story of the Atlantic Slave Trade, 1440–1870* (New York: Simon & Schuster, 1997), 537–785; Voyages: The Trans-Atlantic Slave Trade Database (hereafter Voyages Database), http://slavevoyages.org/tast/database/search.faces?yearFrom=1790&yearTo=1825 (accessed August 3, 2014).

11 An excellent and accessible account of the struggle to suppress the slave trade is Siân Rees, *Sweet Water and Bitter: The Ships That Stopped the Slave Trade* (Durham: University of New Hampshire Press, 2011).

12 An Act in Addition to the Acts to Prohibit the Importation of Slaves, March 3, 1819, in *The Public Statutes at Large of the United States of America, 1789–1845*, Vol. 3, edited by Richard Peters (Washington, D.C.: 1845), 532–34. This Act in Addition is hereafter referred to as the 1819 Slave Trade Act.

   An Act to Protect the Commerce of the United States and Punish the Crime of Piracy, March 3, 1819, and An Act to Continue in Force An Act to Protect the Commerce of the United States and Punish the Crime of Piracy, and Also to Make Further Provisions for Punishing the Crime of Piracy, May 15, 1820, in Thomas F. Gordon, *A Collection of Laws of the United States Relating to Revenue, Navigation, and Commerce* (Philadelphia: Isaac Ashmead, 1844), 244–46, 253–55.

13 *Dred Scott v. Sandford*, 60 U.S. 393 (1857); *Prigg v. Pennsylvania*, 41 U.S. 539 (1842); *United States v. Libellants and Claimants of the Schooner Amistad*, 40 U.S. 518 (1841).

14 *The Antelope*, 23 U.S. 66, 114 (1825).

15 Ibid., 81, 86, 87.

16 The problem of finding and using African voices is addressed in Alice Bellagamba, Sandra E. Greene, Martin A. Klein, eds., *African Voices on Slavery and the Slave Trade, Volume 1: The Sources* (Cambridge: Cambridge University Press, 2013).

17 Marcus Rediker, *The Amistad Rebellion: An Atlantic Odyssey of Slavery and Freedom* (New York: Viking, 2012), 11.

18 Joseph Conrad, *Heart of Darkness and The Secret Sharer* (New York: Pocket Books, 2004), 66, 69, 76. The classic postcolonialist critique of Conrad's story is Chinua Achebe, "An Image of Africa: Racism in Conrad's 'Heart of Darkness,'" in *Heart of Darkness, An Authoritative Text, Background, and Sources* (London: W. W Norton, 1988), 251–61.

Chapter 1

1 Translation of Spanish Documents by William Scarbrough, RG 21, District Court of Georgia (hereafter DCG), Box 30, Folder 7, National Archives and Records Administration, Atlanta (hereafter NARA-Atlanta); Martín Martínez, "Santiago de la Cuesta Manzanal, un valuro Conde de la Reunión de Cuba," http://maragato.wordpress.com/2012/06/13/santiago-de-la-cuesta-manzanal-un-valuro-conde-de-la-reunion-de-cuba/ (accessed August 3, 2012); Thomas, *The Slave Trade*, 601.

2 *Letters from the Havana, During the Year 1820* (London: John Miller, 1821), 71, 74–77; J. W. Noire, *Sailing Directions for the Gulf of Florida, the Bahama Banks and Islands, and the Adjacent Coast of Cuba* (London: Charles Wilson, 1860), 7–9; Translation of Spanish Documents by William Scarbrough, RG 21, DCG, Box 30, Folder 7, NARA-Atlanta.

3 Translation of Spanish Documents by William Scarbrough, RG 21, DCG, Box 30, Folder 7, NARA-Atlanta; Richard H. Steckel and Richard A. Jensen, "New Evidence on the Causes of Slave and Crew Mortality in the Atlantic Slave Trade," *Journal of Economic History* 46 (1986): 57–77. It is very difficult to discern the true spelling of the captain's name in the old documents, but it was Vicente de Llovio. John Noonan read this as "Vicente de Slavio." See John Thomas Noonan, *The Antelope: The Ordeal of the Recaptured Africans in the Administrations of James Monroe and John Quincy Adams* (Berkeley: University of California Press, 1990), 167.

4 José A. Piqueras, "La Siempre Fiel Isla de Cuba, o la Lealtad Interesada," *Historia Mexicana* 58, no. 1 (July–September 2008): 427–86, 458–59. Helpful discussions of the Atlantic world and the Atlantic system can be found in Bernard Bailyn, *Atlantic History: Concepts and Contours* (Cambridge, MA: Harvard University Press, 2005); Alison Games, "Atlantic History: Definitions, Challenges, and Opportunities," *American Historical Review* 111, no. 3 (June 2006): 741–57; Jack P. Greene and Philip D. Morgan, *Atlantic History: A Critical Appraisal* (Oxford: Oxford University Press, 2009).

5 David R. Murray, *Odious Commerce: Britain, Spain, and the Abolition of the Cuban Slave Trade* (Cambridge: Cambridge University Press, 1980), 3–79; Matt D. Childs, *The 1812 Aponte Rebellion in Cuba and the Struggle Against Atlantic Slavery* (Chapel Hill: University of North Carolina Press, 2006), 48–61; Anthony Pagden, *The Enlightenment: And Why It Still Matters* (New York: Random House, 2013), 6.

6 Adam Smith, *An Inquiry into the Nature and Causes of the Wealth of*

Nations (Edinburgh: Thomas Nelson, 1843), 258–59; Pagden, *The Enlightenment*, 5–15.

7 Charles Petrie, *King Charles III of Spain: An Enlightened Despot* (London: Constable, 1971). Image of Carlos III at http:// www.museodelprado.es/en/the-collection/online-gallery/on-line-gallery/obra/carlos-iii-1/ (accessed August 3, 2012).

8 Perhaps the best account of Charles III and colonial reform is Stanley J. Stein and Barbara H. Stein, *Apogee of Empire: Spain and New Spain in the Age of Charles III, 1759–1789* (Baltimore and London: Johns Hopkins University Press, 2003). See also Carlos Marichal, *Bankruptcy of Empire: Mexican Silver and the Wars Between Spain, Britain, and France, 1760–1810* (Cambridge and New York: Cambridge University Press, 2007).

9 J. H. Parry, *The Spanish Seaborne Empire* (Berkeley: University of California Press, 1990), 117–35; J. H. Elliott, *Empires of the Atlantic World: Britain and Spain in America, 1492–1830* (New Haven, CT: Yale University Press, 2006), 292–301; Stein and Stein, *Apogee of Empire*, 11–13, 48–56.

10 Murray, *Odious Commerce*, 4; Stein and Stein, *Apogee of Empire*, 55; Franklin W. Knight, *Slave Society in Cuba During the Nineteenth Century* (Madison: University of Wisconsin Press, 1970), 8–22.

11 Elliott, *Empires of the Atlantic World*, 303–94.

12 Stein and Stein, *Apogee of Empire*, 56–57, 147–49; Murray, *Odious Commerce*, 5; Laird W. Bergad, Fe Iglesias García, and María del Carmen Barcia, *The Cuban Slave Market, 1790–1880* (Cambridge: Cambridge University Press, 1995), 24–25.

13 Murray, *Odious Commerce*, 4–10.

14 Stein and Stein, *Apogee of Empire*, 71–77; Thomas, *The Slave Trade*, 532–44; Murray, *Odious Commerce*, 13.

15 Martínez, "Santiago de la Cuesta Manzanal, un valuro Conde de la Reunión de Cuba."

16 Gwendolyn Midlo Hall, *Social Control in Slave Plantation Societies: A Comparison of St. Domingue and Cuba* (Baltimore: Johns Hopkins University Press, 1971), 125–26; Jose Guadalupe Ortega, "The Cuban Sugar Complex in the Age of Revolution" (PhD diss., University of California, Los Angeles, 2007), 64; slave imports to Havana declined from official numbers of 13,832 in 1802 to 1,162 in 1809—see Murray, *Odious Commerce*, 18. See also María Dolores González-Ripoll, Consuelo Naranjo, Ada Ferrer, and Gloria García y Josef Opatrný, *El Rumor de Haití en Cuba: Temor, Raza y Rebeldía, 1789–1844* (Madrid: CSIC, 2004).

17 Thomas, *The Slave Trade*, 578–79; Rees, *Sweet Water and Bitter*, 50–63.

18 Thomas, *The Slave Trade*, 601–3, Murray, *Odious Commerce*, 78–79, Ortega, "The Cuban Sugar Complex," 61; *Niles' Weekly Register*, September 18, 1819, 35. Murray provides the figure of 95,817 to Havana. The Voyages Database produces the figure of 88,063 for the number of slaves brought to Havana during the period 1816–1820.

19 Translation of Spanish Documents by William Scarbrough, RG 21, DCG, Box 30, NARA-Atlanta; Martínez, "Santiago de la Cuesta Manzanal, un valuro Conde de la Reunión de Cuba"; J. R. Harris, "Copper and Shipping in the Eighteenth Century," *Economic History Review* 19, no. 3 (December 1966): 550–68. Voyages No. 14629, 14718, 14809, and 14369 (see Voyages Database) were probably all made by this vessel, giving a total of 1,067 captives loaded in Africa and a total of 961 delivered to Havana, with a better than average loss rate below 10 percent.

20 Crew List for the *Antelope*, RG 21, DCG, Box 31, Folder 2, NARA-Atlanta; Clearance by Nicolas de Torre, Captain of the Port of Havana, RG 21, DCG, Box 30, Folder 1, NARA-Atlanta; Contract for the Crew of the *Antelope*, RG 21, DCG, Box 30, Folder 1, NARA-Atlanta. Spanish silver pesos exchanged one for one with U.S. dollars.

21 Translation of Spanish Documents by William Scarbrough, RG 21, DCG, Box 30, NARA-Atlanta; Robert Harms, *The Diligent: A Voyage Through the Worlds of the Slave Trade* (New York: Basic Books, 2002), 308–10, gives the average water ration on a slave vessel as two quarts per day.

22 Translation of Spanish Documents by William Scarbrough, RG 21, DCG, Box 30, NARA-Atlanta.

23 Ibid.; Joseph C. Miller, *Way of Death: Merchant Capitalism and the Angolan Slave Trade, 1730–1830* (Madison: University of Wisconsin Press, 1988), 273–80; Phyllis M. Martin, *The External Trade of the Loango Coast, 1576–1870* (London: Oxford University Press, 1972), 107–9; Phyllis M. Martin, "Power, Cloth and Currency on the Loango Coast," *African Economic History* 15 (1986): 1–12.

Chapter 2

1 *Savannah Republican*, July 13, 1820; Commission of Don Simeon [Simon] Metcalf of August 10, 1818, RG 21, DCG, Box 30, NARA-Atlanta; David R. MacGregor, *Merchant Sailing Ships, 1775–1815: Sovereignty of Sail* (Annapolis: Naval Institute Press, 1988), 136–38. The *Columbia* may have once been named the *Baltimore*; this is somewhat murky, as is fitting for a privateer.

2 See James E. Lewis Jr., *The American Union and the Problem of Neighborhood: The United States and the Collapse of the Spanish Empire, 1783–1829* (Chapel Hill: University of North Carolina Press, 1998); Philip Coolidge Brooks, *Diplomacy and the Borderlands: The Adams-Onis Treaty of 1819* (New York: Octagon Books, 1970). The United States Supreme Court decided, in *United States v. Palmer*, 16 U.S. 610 (1818), and in *The Divina Pastora: The Spanish Consul*, 17 U.S. 52 (1819), that privateer commissions from the insurrectionary republics of South America would be recognized as valid in federal courts as long as no U.S. laws had been broken by the privateer.

3 Jerome R. Garitee, *The Republic's Private Navy: The American Privateering Business as Practiced by Baltimore During the War of 1812* (Middletown: Wesleyan University Press, 1977), 11–31, 114–18; Karl Heinz Marquardt, *The Global Schooner: Origins, Development, Design and Construction, 1695–1845* (Annapolis: Naval Institute Press, 2003), 40–65.

4 An Act Laying an Embargo on All Ships and Vessels in the Ports and Harbors of the United States, December 22, 1807, in *Public Statutes*, Vol. 2, 451–53; An Act to Prohibit the Importation of Slaves into Any Port or Place Within the Jurisdiction of the United States, From and After the First Day of January, in the Year of Our Lord One Thousand Eight Hundred and Eight, March 2, 1807, in *Public Statutes*, Vol. 2, 426–30; Noonan, *The Antelope*, 13–14.

5 Garitee, *The Republic's Private Navy*, 14–21.

6 Edgar Stanton Maclay, *History of American Privateering* (New York: Appleton, 1899); Donald A. Petrie, *The Prize Game: Lawful Looting on the High Seas in the Days of Fighting Sail* (New York: Berkley, 1999), 47–82.

7 Garitee, *The Republic's Private Navy*, 32–46; Petrie, *The Prize Game*, 1–11, 147–63.

8 See Garitee, *The Republic's Private Navy*, for the best account of privateering in Baltimore.

9 *Niles' Weekly Register*, March 25, 1815, 56, April 29, 1815, 137–38.

10 Garitee, *The Republic's Private Navy*, 210–37; C. Edward Skeen, *1816: American Rising* (Lexington: University Press of Kentucky, 2003), 1–16.

11 David Head, "Sailing for Spanish America: The Atlantic Geopolitics of Foreign Privateering from the United States in the Early Republic" (PhD diss., State University of New York at Buffalo, 2009), 27, 72–80; *Niles' Weekly Register*, December 28, 1816, 289–90.

12 Head, "Sailing for Spanish America," 93; Royce Gordon Shingleton, "David Brydie Mitchell and the African Importation Case of 1820,"

Journal of Negro History 58, no. 3 (July 1973): 327–40; *Niles' Weekly Register*, January 29, 1820; *Governor of Georgia v. Madrazo*, 26 U.S. 110 (1828); *Ex parte Madrazzo*, 32 U.S. 627 (1833).

13 Head, "Sailing for Spanish America," 93, 240 (Appendix D); Petrie, *The Prize Game*, 83–105.

14 *Niles' Weekly Register, September 4, 11, 18, 25, 1819, Oct. 2, 9, 16, 1819*; Garitee, *The Republic's Private Navy*, 230–37.

15 Examination and Deposition of John Morrison, January 19, 1821, RG 21, DCG, Box 32, NARA-Atlanta.

16 Head, "Sailing for Spanish America," 89–95; Crew of the Brig Athenian of Baltimore Whereof Is Master John Smith Bound for Rio de la Plata, RG 21, DCG, Box 31, NARA-Atlanta; Port of Baltimore Clearance for the Athenian under Master John Smith, June 17, 1818, RG 21, DCG, Box 31, NARA-Atlanta. The papers taken from Smith's sea chest all have the notation "Filed July 11, 1820" on the back and are found in RG 21, DCG, Box 31, NARA-Atlanta. His history is constructed from them.

17 *Savannah Republican*, July 8, 1820; Deposition of James D. Knight, January 18, 1821, RG 21, DCG, Box 32, NARA-Atlanta.

18 See Larry Neal, *The Rise of Financial Capitalism: International Capital Markets in the Age of Reason* (Cambridge: Cambridge University Press, 1990), David Hancock, *Citizens of the World: London Merchants and the Integration of the British Atlantic Community, 1735–1785* (Cambridge: Cambridge University Press, 1995), and Philip D. Curtin, *The Rise and Fall of the Plantation Complex: Essays in Atlantic History* (Cambridge: Cambridge University Press, 1998). On the future British-dominated Atlantic-based world trade system see John Darwin, *The Empire Project: The Rise and Fall of the British World-System, 1830–1970* (Cambridge: Cambridge University Press, 2009).

19 *Savannah Republican*, July 13, 1820; Examination of John Morrison, January 19, 1821, RG 21, DCG, Box 32, NARA-Atlanta; Examination of Thomas Bradshaw, February 15, 1821, RG 21, DCG, Box 30, NARA-Atlanta.

20 *Savannah Republican*, July 13, 1820; *Savannah Daily Georgian*, July 15, 1820; Circuit Court of the United States Sixth Circuit, Indictment of John Smith for Piracy from a French Schooner, December 14, 1829, RG 21, DCG, Box 127, NARA-Atlanta.

21 *Savannah Daily Georgian*, July 15, 1820; Examination of John Morrison, January 19, 1821, RG 21, DCG, Box 32, NARA-Atlanta; Attestation of the Artigan Commission by Simon Metcalf, January 21, 1820, RG 21, DCG, Box 30, NARA-Atlanta. Arraganta is spelled

various ways in different documents, from Aragonta to Arrogante. In
the Supreme Court reports it is spelled Arraganta. I suspect Arrogante
is correct, but will use the Supreme Court's spelling for the sake of
consistency.

22 Hydrographic Office of the Admiralty, *Africa Pilot, Part I*, 5th Ed.
(London: J. D. Potter, 1890), 253; *Savannah Republican*, July 13, 1820;
Savannah Daily Georgian, July 15, 1820.

23 *Savannah Republican*, July 13, 1820; *Savannah Daily Georgian*, July 15,
1820; *Papers Presented to Parliament in 1821*, Vol. 3 (London: R. G.
Clark, 1821), 120, 121, 128, 129.

Chapter 3

1 "Sir Henry John Leeke," in William Stewart, *Admirals of the World:
A Biographical Dictionary* (Jefferson, NC: McFarland and Co., 2009),
202; J. K. Laughton, "Leeke, Sir Henry John (1794–1870)," in *Oxford
Dictionary of National Biography* (Oxford: Oxford University Press,
2004), online ed., October 2005, http://www.oxforddnb.com/view/
article/16328 (accessed April 25, 2013).

2 Order Issued by the Lords Commissioners of the Admiralty on the
15th July, 1819, to H. J. Leeke, Esq., Commander of His Majesty's
Sloop Myrmidon, in *Papers Presented to Parliament in 1821*, Vol. 3
(London: R. G. Clarke, 1821), 305–7.

3 Captain Leeke to Sir George Collier, January 13, 1820, quoted in
*Abstract of the Information Recently Laid on the Table of the House of
Commons on the Slave Trade* (London: Ellerton and Henderson, 1821),
162–63; entry for HMS *Myrmidon* in David Lyon and Rif Winfield,
The Sail and Steam Navy List (London: Chatham, 2004), 69. During
this cruise the *Myrmidon* had aboard two future admirals and Knights
of the Bath, Henry J. Leeke and Second Lieutenant Edward Belcher,
who later won fame as an Arctic explorer. The first lieutenant, Richard
Nash, died of fever on the African coast.

4 Order issued by the Lords Commissioners of the Admiralty on the
15th July, 1819, to H. J. Leeke, Esq. Commander of His Majesty's
Sloop Myrmidon, 305–6.

5 James Stephen, *War in Disguise; Or the Frauds of the Neutral Flags*, 3rd
ed. (London: C. Wittingham, 1806), 5–10; Adam Hochschild, *Bury the
Chains: Prophets and Rebels in the Fight to Free an Empire's Slaves* (New
York: Houghton Mifflin, 2005), 301–14; Blackburn, *The Overthrow
of Colonial Slavery*, 295–329. For a nuanced discussion of how the
growing economic warfare between England and France pushed the
United States toward war, see Paul A. Gilje, *Free Trade and Sailors' Rights*

in the War of 1812 (Cambridge: Cambridge University Press, 2013), especially 148–70.

6 Blackburn, *The Overthrow of Colonial Slavery*, 286–87, 310–15; An Act to Prohibit the Importation of Slaves into Any Port or Place Within the Jurisdiction of the United States, From and After the First Day of January, in the Year of Our Lord One Thousand Eight Hundred and Eight, in *Public Statutes*, Vol. 2, 426–30; An Act for the Abolition of the Slave Trade, 47 Geo III Sess. 1 c. 36.

7 Thomas, *The Slave Trade*, 574–75; Rees, *Sweet Water and Bitter*, 8–18.

8 Jenny S. Martinez, *The Slave Trade and the Origins of International Human Rights Law* (Oxford: Oxford University Press, 2012), 16–27, Table 2.1, 26; W. E. F. Ward, *The Royal Navy and the Slavers* (London: George Allen, 1969), 102.

9 Martinez, *The Slave Trade*, 24–26; *The Amedie*, 1 Acton 240.

10 *Charleston City Gazette*, February 2, 1810; *The Amedie*, 1 Acton 240, 250–51. While the case of the *Amedie* is not mentioned, James A. McMillan, *The Final Victims: Foreign Slave Trade to North America, 1783–1810* (Columbia, SC: University of South Carolina Press, 2004), does an excellent job telling the story of the merchants, investors, and slaves in this last period of legal direct trade.

11 *The Africa*, 2 Acton 1; *Nancy*, 2 Acton 4; *Anne*, 2 Acton 6, 10.

12 Rees, *Sweet Water and Bitter*, 20–35.

13 *A Report of the Case of the Louis, Forest, Master, Appealed from the Vice Admiralty Court at Sierra Leone and Determined by the High Court of Admiralty, December 15, 1817* (London: Butterworth and Son, 1817).

14 *A Report of the Case of the Louis*, quotes 38, 48.

15 Martinez, *The Slave Trade*, 30–33; Henry Kissinger, *A World Restored: Metternich, Castlereagh and the Problems of Peace, 1812–1822* (New York: Houghton Mifflin, 1957), is the classic study of this struggle to balance power at Vienna.

16 Rees, *Sweet Water and Bitter*, 47–49; Martinez, *The Slave Trade*, 30–37, 69.

17 Martinez, *The Slave Trade*, 67–98.

18 Henry J. Leeke to Commodore Sir G. R. Collier, December 15, 1819, in *Papers Presented to Parliament*, Vol. 3, 85–86.

19 George R. Collier to J. W. Croker, Esq., February 14, 1820, in *Papers Presented to Parliament*, Vol. 3, 112–14.

20 Henry J. Leeke to Sir George Ralph Collier, January 30, 1820, in *Papers Presented to Parliament*, Vol. 3, 128–29; Edward Belcher to Henry J. Leeke, January 1, 1820; Statement of John Baker and John Evans, January 14, 1820; List of Vessels Detained for Illegally Trafficking in

Slaves; Henry J. Leeke to Sir G. R. Collier, January 25, 1820, all in *Papers Presented to Parliament*, Vol. 3, 102–5, 116–17, 123–27, 235–36; Rees, *Sweet Water and Bitter*, 45.

21 Henry J. Leeke to Sir George Ralph Collier, January 30, 1820, in *Papers Presented to Parliament*, Vol. 3, 128–29; George R. Collier to J. W. Croker, February 14, 1820, in *Papers Presented to Parliament*, Vol. 3, 113–14; *Savannah Republican*, July 13, 1820.

22 George R. Collier to J. W. Croker, February 14, 1820, in *Papers Presented to Parliament*, Vol. 3, 113–14; *British and Foreign State Papers, 1820–1821* (London: J. Harrison and Son, 1830), 932–52; Sir G. R. Collier to J. W. Croker, February 16, 1820, in *Papers Presented to Parliament*, Vol. 3, 122, 123.

23 *Savannah Republican*, July 13, 1820; *Savannah Daily Georgian*, July 15, 1820.

Chapter 4

1 Declaration of Captain Vicente de Llovio, taken at Cabinda, March 30, 1820, RG 21, DCG, Box 30, Folder 1, NARA-Atlanta; Captain W. F. W. Owen, *Narrative of Voyages to Explore the Shores of Africa, Arabia, and Madagascar; Performed in H. M. Ships Leven and Barracouta* (London: Richard Bentley, 1933), Vol. 2, 291–300.

2 Declaration of Captain Vicente de Llovio, taken at Cabinda, March 30, 1820, RG 21, DCG, Box 30, Folder 1, NARA-Atlanta; Phyllis M. Martin, "Family Strategies in Nineteenth-Century Cabinda," *Journal of African History* 28, no. 1 (1987): 65–86.

3 Jan Vansina, *Paths in the Rainforests: Toward a History of Political Tradition in Equatorial Africa* (Madison: University of Wisconsin Press, 1990), 35–46; Martin, "Family Strategies," 71–80. See Ira Berlin, *Many Thousands Gone: The First Two Centuries of Slavery in North American* (Cambridge, MA: Harvard University Press, 1998), for the concept of Atlantic world creoles.

4 Rees, *Sweet Water and Bitter*, 26–49; Martin, "Family Strategies," 71–80.

5 Martin, *External Trade of the Loango Coast*, 33–92.

6 Vansina, *Paths in the Rainforests*, 73–83; Martin, "Family Strategies," 65–86.

7 Owen, *Narrative of Voyages to Explore the Shores of Africa, Arabia, and Madagascar*, Vol. 2, 291–300.

8 Martin, *External Trade of the Loango Coast*, 93–115.

9 Ibid., 33–35, 73–92; Owen, *Narrative of Voyages to Explore the Shores of Africa, Arabia, and Madagascar*, Vol. 2, 297.

10 Martin, *External Trade of the Loango Coast*, 87–90.

11 Ibid., 87–90, 95–105.

12 John Purdy, *The New Sailing Directory for the Ethiopic or Southern Atlantic Ocean* (London: R. H. Laurie, 1844), 401–7; Owen, *Narrative of Voyages to Explore the Shores of Africa, Arabia, and Madagascar,* Vol. 2, 291–300. Contemporary photos taken along the coast can be found at *http://blog.smu.edu/studentadventures/category/earth-sciences-in-angola/* (accessed December 12, 2013).

13 Purdy, *The New Sailing Directory for the Ethiopic or Southern Atlantic Ocean,* 401–7; Owen, *Narrative of Voyages to Explore the Shores of Africa, Arabia, and Madagascar,* Vol. 2, 291–300; Martin, "Family Strategies," 65–86.

14 Vansina, *Paths in the Rainforests,* 35–46; Martin, *External Trade of the Loango Coast,* 117–19.

15 Martin, *External Trade of the Loango Coast,* 93–115, 136–57; Declaration of Captain Vicente de Llovio, taken at Cabinda, March 30, 1820, RG 21, Box 30, Folder 1, NARA-Atlanta.

16 Deposition of Domingo Grondona, taken in Savannah, November 25, 1820, RG 21, Box 30, NARA-Atlanta.

17 Declaration of Captain Vicente de Llovio, taken at Cabinda, March 30, 1820, RG 21, Box 30, Folder 1, NARA-Atlanta; Examination of Domingo Grondona, February 13, 1821, RG 21, Box 30, NARA-Atlanta.

18 Declaration of Captain Vicente de Llovio, taken at Cabinda, March 30, 1820, RG 21, Box 30, Folder 1, NARA-Atlanta; Sworn Statement of Domingo Grondona, taken at Havana, September 6, 1820, RG 21, Box 30, NARA-Atlanta; Sworn Statement of Thomas Ximenes, taken at Havana, September 6, 1820, RG 21, Box 30, NARA-Atlanta.

19 Declaration of Captain Vicente de Llovio, taken at Cabinda, March 30, 1820, RG 21, Box 30, Folder 1, NARA-Atlanta; Examination of Domingo Grondona in Open Court, February 13, 1821, RG 21, Box 30, NARA-Atlanta.

20 Declaration of Captain Vicente de Llovio, taken at Cabinda, March 30, 1820, RG 21, Box 30, Folder 1, NARA-Atlanta; Sworn Statement of Domingo Grondona, taken at Havana, September 6, 1820, RG 21, Box 30, NARA-Atlanta. The actual number of slaves aboard the *Antelope* proved a thorny question for the courts later in this story.

21 Martin, *External Trade of the Loango Coast,* 117–35. Possibly, these three names indicated direction for the source of the captives. Congues could have meant south and east toward the old Kongo kingdom. Majumbas may have come from the North. Madungoes meant from far inland. The *African Repository and Colonial Journal,* the organ of

the American Colonization Society, usually spoke of the *Antelope* "recaptives" as "Congos." See *The African Repository and Colonial Journal* 8 (1833): 200–201.

22 Ibid; Vansina, *Paths in the Rainforest*, 155–225; Miller, *Way of Death*, 3–39; Walter Henry Stapleton, *Comparative Handbook of Congo Languages* (Stanley Falls, Congo Independent State, 1903). The languages spoken by the captives are unknown, and that the language in this case was Kikongo or a related pidgin is only informed speculation.

23 An accessible discussion of this can be found in John K. Thornton, *A Cultural History of the Atlantic World, 1250–1820* (Cambridge: Cambridge University Press, 2012), 63–99.

24 Declaration of Captain Vicente de Llovio, taken at Cabinda, March 30, 1820, RG 21, Box 30, Folder 1, NARA-Atlanta; Sworn Statement of Domingo Grondona, taken at Havana, September 6, 1820, RG 21, Box 30, NARA-Atlanta; Deposition of Domingo Grondona, taken in Savannah, November 25, 1820, RG 21, Box 30, NARA-Atlanta.

25 Examination of Domingo Grondona in Open Court, February 13, 1821, RG 21, Box 30, NARA-Atlanta; Interrogatory of John Smith, Savannah, February 14, 1821, RG 21, Box 32, NARA-Atlanta.

26 Declaration of Captain Vicente de Llovio, taken at Cabinda, March 30, 1820, RG 21, Box 30, Folder 1, NARA-Atlanta; Deposition of Domingo Grondona, taken in Savannah, November 25, 1820, RG 21, Box 30, NARA-Atlanta; Sworn Statement of Domingo Grondona, taken at Havana, September 6, 1820, RG 21, Box 30, NARA-Atlanta; *Savannah Daily Georgian*, July 15, 1820. To limit confusion, the *General Ramirez* will be referred to as the *Antelope* despite the name change.

27 Declaration of Captain Vicente de Llovio, taken at Cabinda, March 30, 1820, RG 21, Box 30, Folder 1, NARA-Atlanta; Deposition of Domingo Grondona, taken in Savannah, November 25, 1820, RG 21, Box 30, NARA-Atlanta.

28 Preface to the Declaration of Captain Vicente de Llovio, taken at Cabinda, March 30, 1820, RG 21, Box 30, Folder 1, NARA-Atlanta; Deposition of Domingo Grondona, taken in Savannah, November 25, 1820, RG 21, Box 30, NARA-Atlanta. At least six of the twenty-three men died at Cabinda, or more than 25 percent of the crew.

Chapter 5

1 *Savannah Republican*, July 13, 1820; *Savannah Daily Georgian*, July 15, 1820.

2 Interrogatory of John Smith, Savannah, February 14, 1821, RG 21, Box 32, NARA-Atlanta; *Savannah Daily Georgian*, July 15,

1820. Relative value calculation from "Measuring Worth," http://www.measuringworth.com/uscompare/.

3 John Street, *Artigas and the Emancipation of Uruguay* (Cambridge: Cambridge University Press, 1959), 227–29; David Brion Davis, *Inhuman Bondage: The Rise and Fall of Slavery in the New World* (Oxford: Oxford University Press, 2006), 149. Emancipation was complicated by war and revolutions in Venezuela and Colombia, and was not complete until the 1850s. See Christopher Schmidt-Nowara, *Slavery, Freedom, and Abolition in Latin America and the Atlantic World* (Albuquerque: University of New Mexico Press, 2011).

4 James Boswell, *Boswell's Life of Johnson*, edited by George Birkbeck Hill, Vol. 5 (New York: Bigelow, Brown and Co., 1887, repr. of the 1799 London 3rd ed.), 156–57; Olaudah Equiano, *The Interesting Narrative of the Life of Olaudah Equiano, or Gustavus Vassa, the African, Written by Himself* (London: 1789), 79.

5 *Savannah Daily Georgian*, July 15, 1820; *Savannah Republican*, July 13, 1820; Examination of John Stephens, January 18, 1821, RG 21, Box 30, NARA-Atlanta.

6 Thomas, *The Slave Trade*, 611–13.

7 *Savannah Republican*, July 13, 1820; *Savannah Daily Georgian*, July 15, 1820; Examination of John Stephens, January 18, 1821, RG 21, Box 30, NARA-Atlanta; Examination of James D. Knight, January 18, 1821, RG 21, Box 32, NARA-Atlanta.

8 *Savannah Republican*, July 13, 1820; *Savannah Daily Georgian*, July 15, 1820; Examination of John Stephens, January 18, 1821, RG 21, Box 30, NARA-Atlanta.

9 *Savannah Republican*, July 13, 1820; *Savannah Daily Georgian*, July 15, 1820; Noire, *Sailing Directions*, 55–59. In late October of 2012, Hurricane Sandy destroyed the Hole in the Wall, leaving it now the "Gap in the Wall." See http://rollingharbour.com/2012/11/03/from-hole-in-the-wall-to-gap-in-the-wall-hurricane-sandy-smashes-abaco-landmark/.

10 *Savannah Republican*, July 13, 1820; *Savannah Daily Georgian*, July 15, 1820; *Charleston Times*, June 19, 1820, quoted in *Savannah Daily Georgian*, June 26, 1820; *Niles' Weekly Register*, July 1, 1820.

11 *Savannah Republican*, July 13, 1820; *Savannah Daily Georgian*, July 15, 1820.

12 M. Rafter, *Memoir of Gregor McGregor* (London: J. J. Stockdale, 1820), 91–113; *Niles' Weekly Register*, July 19, 26, 1817.

13 *Niles' Weekly Register*, July 26, August 9, September 27, October 4, 1817.

14 Ibid., July 26, August 9, September 27, October 4, November 29, December 27, 1817, January 10, 24, 1818; Brooks, *Diplomacy and the Borderlands*, 86–88; William C. Davis, *The Pirates Laffite: The Treacherous World of the Corsairs of the Gulf* (New York: Harcourt, 2005), 349–51.

15 *Charleston Courier*, July 6, 1820; *Savannah Republican*, July 13, 1820: *Savannah Daily Georgian*, July 15, 1820.

16 *Charleston Courier*, July 6, 7, 1820; *Savannah Daily Georgian*, June 26, July 1, 1820; *Baltimore Patriot*, July 15, 22, 1820; *Niles' Weekly Register*, July 1, 8, 1820; *Savannah Republican*, July 13, 1820. Richard Henry Wilde included the story of Coppinger in his clumsy epic poem *Hesperia*. See Richard Henry Wilde, *Hesperia: A Poem* (Boston: Ticknor and Fields, 1867), 28.

17 *Savannah Republican*, July 8, 1820; Examination of John Jackson, January 17, 1821, RG 21, Box 30, NARA-Atlanta; Examination of James D. Knight, January 18, 1821, RG 21, Box 32, NARA-Atlanta. The Revenue Marine was the predecessor to the U.S. Coast Guard.

18 *Savannah Republican*, July 8, 1820; Examination of John Jackson, January 17, 1821, RG 21, Box 30, NARA-Atlanta; Examination of James D. Knight, January 18, 1821, RG 21, Box 32, NARA-Atlanta.

19 Ibid. This loss rate of 15 percent was about average for the Middle Passage. For good estimates of numbers of slaves embarked and slaves who arrived in the New World that produced the 15 percent average of deaths in the Middle Passage, see the Voyages Database, http://www.slavevoyages.org/tast/assessment/estimates.faces.

20 *Savannah Republican*, July 8, 1820; *Savannah Daily Georgian*, July 10, 1820; Examination of John Jackson, January 17, 1821, RG 21, Box 30, NARA-Atlanta; Examination of James D. Knight, January 18, 1821, RG 21, Box 32, NARA-Atlanta.

21 Affidavit of John Jackson, July 10, 1820, RG 21, DCG, Box 30, NARA-Atlanta; Affidavit of James D. Knight, July 10, 1820, RG 21, DCG, Box 30, NARA-Atlanta; Richard W. Habersham to John Quincy Adams, July 19, 1820, RG 59, Miscellaneous Letters, August–October 1820, Department of State, National Archives and Records Administration, Washington, D.C. (hereafter NARA-Washington), Microfilm M-179, Roll 48. Richard W. Habersham's official title was United States District Attorney for Georgia, but rather than risk confusion with the modern connotation of district attorney, I will refer to him as United States Attorney.

22 Examination of John Jackson, January 17, 1821, RG 21, Box 30, NARA-Atlanta; Examination of James D. Knight, January 18, 1821, RG 21, Box 32, NARA-Atlanta.

23 Examination of John Jackson, January 17, 1821, RG 21, Box 30, NARA-Atlanta; Examination of James D. Knight, January 18, 1821, RG 21, Box 32, NARA-Atlanta; John H. Morel to John Quincy Adams, Savannah, July 27, 1820, RG 59, Miscellaneous Letters, August–October 1820, Department of State, NARA-Washington, Microfilm M-179, Roll 48.

24 "Names of Africans cargo of the Brig Ramiriz collected together and delivered to sundry persons whoes names are here with stated," March 24, 1823, RG 21, Box 32, NARA-Atlanta. By the nineteenth century, ever larger numbers of children were exported as slaves from West Central Africa. See Paul Lovejoy, "The Children of Slavery—The Transatlantic Phase," *Slavery and Abolition* 27, no. 2 (August 2006): 197–217.

Chapter 6

1 Joseph Gaston Baillie Bulloch, *A History and Genealogy of the Habersham Family* (Columbia, SC: R. L. Bryan Co., 1901); Kenneth Coleman, *Colonial Georgia: A History* (New York: Charles Scribner's Sons, 1976), 213; Frank Lambert, *James Habersham: Loyalty, Politics, and Commerce in Colonial Georgia* (Athens: University of Georgia Press, 2005).

2 Lambert, *James Habersham*, 169–78; W. Calvin Smith, "The Habershams: The Merchant Experience in Georgia," in *Forty Years of Diversity: Essays on Colonial Georgia*, edited by Harvey H. Jackson and Phinizy Spalding (Athens: University of Georgia Press, 1984), 198–216. Oral tradition in Savannah suggests that James Habersham Jr. committed suicide, perhaps despondent over his wife's death, or perhaps in response to a massive lawsuit faced by his family that began in 1798. See *Savannah Morning News*, October 23, 2008.

3 Lambert, *James Habersham*, 169–78; Smith, "The Habershams: The Merchant Experience in Georgia," 210; William J. Northen, ed., *Men of Mark in Georgia*, Vol. 2 (Atlanta: A. B. Caldwell, 1910), 106; 1819 Savannah Tax Digest, Microfilm, Bull Street Library, Savannah, GA; Richard W. Habersham to John Quincy Adams, April 12, 1819, Miscellaneous Letters of the Department of State, 1789–1906, M-179, Roll 44.

4 *Savannah Republican*, May 22, 1820; *Milledgeville Recorder*, May 16, 1820; *Augusta Chronicle*, May 20, 1820; Thomas Henry Rentz, "The Public Life of David B. Mitchell" (master's thesis, University of Georgia, 1955).

5 *Savannah Republican*, May 22, 1820.

6 Ibid.
7 *Savannah Republican,* July 8, 13, 1820; *Charleston Courier,* July 10, 1820. The full text of An Act to Continue in Force An Act to Protect the Commerce of the United States and Punish the Crime of Piracy can be found in *Public Statutes,* Vol. 3, 600–601.
8 *Niles' Weekly Register,* March 11, 25, April 15, May 27, June 3, 1820; John Quincy Adams, *Memoirs of John Quincy Adams,* edited by Charles Francis Adams (Philadelphia: J. B. Lippincott and Co., 1875), Vol. 5, 19–21; *Charleston Courier,* June 24, 1818, December 23, 1819; *United States v. Klintock,* 18 U.S. 144 (1820); *United States v. Furlong,* 18 U.S. 184 (1820).
9 *Milledgeville Recorder,* May 9, July 4, 1820; John Quincy Adams to James Monroe, August 21, 1820, in *Writings of John Quincy Adams, Vol. 7, 1820–1823,* edited by Worthington Chauncey Ford (New York: Macmillan, 1917), 61–62; Adams, *Memoirs,* Vol. 5, 150–52. After the death of his first wife, James S. Bulloch married his father-in-law's widow. Through a daughter from this marriage he became the grandfather of President Theodore Roosevelt.
10 Jn. H. Morel, Marshal District of Georgia to John Quincy Adams, Secretary of State, July 31, 1820, Miscellaneous Letters of the Department of State, 1789–1906, M-179, Roll 48. Klintock was finally pardoned in the summer of 1821, though how long he survived afterward is unknown.
11 These papers taken from Smith's sea chest all have the notation "Filed July 11, 1820" on the back and are found in RG 21, DCG, Box 31, NARA-Atlanta; Examination of John Jackson, January 17, 1821, RG 21, DCG, Box 30, NARA-Atlanta.
12 Papers Filed July 11, 1820, RG 21, DCG, Box 31, NARA-Atlanta; An Act to Continue in Force An Act to Protect the Commerce of the United States and Punish the Crime of Piracy, in *Public Statutes,* Vol. 3, 600–601.
13 *Savannah Republican,* July 13, 1820, March 12, 1821.
14 *Savannah Daily Georgian,* February 26, 1821; *Savannah Republican,* March 10, 12, 19, 1821; Paul M. Pressly, *On the Rim of the Caribbean: Colonial Georgia and the British Atlantic World* (Athens: University of Georgia Press, 2013), 82–87; Frank Byrne, *Becoming Bourgeois: Merchant Culture in the South, 1820–1865* (Lexington: University of Kentucky Press, 2006), 13–20.
15 *Savannah Daily Georgian,* February 26, 1821; *Savannah Republican,* March 19, 1821. A survey of duels during the early nineteenth century shows a preponderance occurring May through August. See

Thomas Gamble, *Savannah Duels and Duelists, 1733–1877* (1923; repr. Savannah: Oglethorpe Press, 1997), 90–166.

16 John Melish, *Travels in the United States of America in the Years 1806 & 1807, and 1809, 1810 & 1811* (Philadelphia: T & G Palmer, 1812), 35–38, 204–11, 261–68; Adam Hodgson, *Remarks During a Journey Through North America* (New York, 1823), 134–35; Joseph Frederick Waring, *Cerveau's Savannah* (Savannah: Georgia Historical Society, 1973), 21.

17 Jonathan Mason, *Extracts from a Diary kept by the Hon. Jonathan Mason of a Journey from Boston to Savannah in the Year 1804* (Cambridge, MA: John Wilson and Son University Press, 1885), 24–25; John Lambert, *Travels Through Lower Canada and the United States of America* (London, 1810), 251; Frank O. Brayard, *S. S. Savannah, the Elegant Steam Ship* (Athens: University of Georgia Press, 1963, 2008), 24.

18 Savannah City Council Minutes, June 5, 1820; I. Stouf, *Plan of the City & Harbour of Savannah in Chatham County*, hmap1818s7, Hargrett Rare Book & Manuscript Library, University of Georgia Libraries, Athens, GA. Requiring Savannah's free black men to labor on the fortification followed an 1818 state law allowing such forced labor. See Whittington B. Johnson, *Black Savannah, 1788–1864* (Fayetteville, AR: University of Arkansas Press, 1996), 40–41.

19 *Niles' Weekly Register*, July 19, 1817. Lacy K. Ford, *Deliver Us from Evil: The Slavery Question in the Old South* (New York: Oxford University Press, 2009), 192–93. See also Steven Deyle, *Carry Me Back: The Domestic Slave Trade in American Life* (New York: Oxford University Press, 2005). Georgia tried to control the number of slaves entering from other states, fearing they would have a bad influence on local slaves. In 1817 the legislature even imposed a strict ban on new slaves. The ban failed; there was just too much money to be made.

20 Paschal N. Strong Sr., "Glimpses of Savannah, 1780–1825," *Georgia Historical Quarterly* 33, no. 1 (March 1949): 29–31; Walter J. Fraser, *Savannah in the Old South* (Athens: University of Georgia Press, 2003), 190–97; Thomas P. Govan, "Banking and the Credit System in Georgia, 1810–1860," *Journal of Southern History* 4, no. 2 (May 1938): 164–84; Charles C. Jones Jr., *History of Savannah, Georgia* (Syracuse, NY: D. Mason and Co., 1890), 337–40; *Niles' Weekly Register*, December 4, 1819, January 20, 1821.

21 *Savannah Daily Georgian*, January 17, 20, 1820; E. Merton Coulter, "The Great Savannah Fire of 1820," *Georgia Historical Quarterly* 23, no. 1 (March 1939): 1–27.

22 *Savannah Daily Georgian,* January 17, 20, 1820; Coulter, "The Great
  Savannah Fire of 1820," 1–27; Adelaide Wilson, *Historical and Picturesque
  Savannah* (Boston Photogravure Co., 1889), 134–35, 181, 232.

23 Wilson, *Historical and Picturesque Savannah,* 232–33; "Chatham County
  Courthouse," http://georgiainfo.galileo.usg.edu/courthouses/
  chathamCH.htm (accessed September 14, 2012).

24 Libel of John Jackson, RG 21, DCG, Box 30, NARA-Atlanta; Rich.
  W. Habersham to John Quincy Adams, Savannah, July 19, 1820,
  Miscellaneous Letters of the Department of State, 1789–1906, M-179,
  Roll 49, NARA-Atlanta; 1819 Slave Trade Act, in *Public Statutes,* Vol. 3,
  532–34.

25 Rich. W. Habersham to John Quincy Adams, Savannah, July 19, 1820,
  Miscellaneous Letters of the Department of State, 1789–1906, M-179,
  Roll 49, NARA-Atlanta.

26 Libel of John Jackson, RG 21, DCG, Box 30, NARA-Atlanta;
  Robert W. Habersham's Response to the Libel of James Jackson,
  RG 21, DCG, Box 30, NARA-Atlanta; Oliver Sturges Valuation of
  the Negroes, February 27, 1821, RG 21, DCG, Box 32, NARA-
  Atlanta; 1820 Savannah Tax Digests, Microfilm., Bull Street Library,
  Savannah, GA. The Richardson mansion is now the Telfair Museum's
  Owens-Thomas House, and the Scarbrough House is now the Ships
  of the Sea Museum, http://www.shipsofthesea.org/. The Bulloch
  mansion was destroyed to build the City Auditorium. The portico
  of Habersham Hall in Atlanta's Ansley Park Neighborhood was
  modeled on Jay's portico for the Bulloch house. As a share of GDP
  at the time relative to 2012 GDP, the calculator returns a value of
  $52,900,000 for the 258 captives. See "Measuring Worth," http://
  www.measuringworth.com/uscompare/relativevalue.php (accessed
  July 8, 2013).

27 A. S. Bulloch, Collector to William H. Crawford, Secretary of the
  Treasury, November 25, 1817, in *Letter from the Secretary of the Treasury
  in Relation to the Illicit Introduction of Slaves* (Washington, D.C.: Gales
  and Seaton, 1820), 9; *J. H. Elton v. The Slaves of the Politina,* RG 21,
  DCG, Box 25, NARA-Atlanta; *John Elton v. The Slaves of the Tentativa,*
  RG 21, DCG, Box 24, 25, NARA-Atlanta. The best treatment of the
  developing paternalistic ethos is Jeffrey Robert Young, *Domesticating
  Slavery: The Master Class in Georgia and South Carolina, 1670–1837*
  (Chapel Hill: University of North Carolina Press, 1999).

28 Wm. I. M'Intosh to Hon. Wm. H. Crawford, March 14, 1818, *Letter
  from the Secretary of the Treasury in Relation to the Illicit Introduction of
  Slaves,* 8–9; *J. H. Elton v. The Slaves of the Politina,* RG 21, DCG, Box

25, NARA-Atlanta; Order of Judge William Stephens, November 27, 1817, Bond of Thos. U. P. Charlton, December 10, 1817, in *John Elton v. The Slaves of the Tentativa*, RG 21, DCG, Box 24, 25, NARA-Atlanta; Justice William Johnson to John Quincy Adams, Secretary of State, June 12, 1821, in Philadelphia Yearly Meeting of the Religious Society of Friends, *A View of the Present State of the African Slave Trade* (Philadelphia: William Brown, 1824), 44–45.

29 John H. Morel to John Quincy Adams, March 9, 1818, Richard W. Habersham to John Quincy Adams, April 12, 1819, Richard W. Habersham to John Quincy Adams, July 18, 1821, Miscellaneous Letters of the Department of State, 1789–1906, M-179, Roll 40, 44, 51; Expenses, February 8 to August 8, 1820, *John Elton v. The Slaves of the Tentativa*, RG 21, DCG, Box 25, NARA-Atlanta; Adams, *Memoirs*, Vol. 6, 87.

30 Timothy James Lockley, *Lines in the Sand: Race and Class in Lowcountry Georgia, 1750–1860* (Athens: University of Georgia Press, 2001), 45, 191 n. 130; 1819 Slave Trade Act, in *Public Statutes*, Vol. 3, 532–34; Statement of Moses Sheftall concerning the events of July 24, 1820, RG 21, DCG, Box 32, NARA-Atlanta. Bills for the marshal's expenses are scattered throughout the court papers on the *Antelope*. Examples include Bill from David Leon for 259 Blankets and 16 Dozen Caps, July 25, 1820; Brown and Overstreet for Lumber, July 25, 27, 1820, RG 21, DCG, Box 28, NARA-Atlanta.

31 Slave Trade Act, in *Public Statutes*, Vol. 3, 532–34; Libel of John Jackson by Berrien, Proctor, July 25, 1820, RG 21, DCG, Box 30, NARA-Atlanta.

32 Libel of Charles Mulvey, August 1, 1820, RG 21, DCG, Box 30, NARA-Atlanta.

33 Libel of Francis Sorrel, August 12, 1820, RG 21, DCG, Box 30, NARA-Atlanta.

34 Libel of the United States by District Attorney for Georgia Richard W. Habersham, August 16, 1820, RG 21, DCG, Box 30, NARA-Atlanta; Adams, *Memoirs*, Vol. 6, 87. Habersham's libel tried to cover all bases. He referenced, by using the language "hovering off the coast," the 1807 Slave Trade Act, and mentioned specifically the 1818 Slave Trade Act and the 1819 Slave Trade Act. See An Act to Prohibit the Introduction of Slaves, March 2, 1807, in *Public Statutes*, Vol. 2, 426–30; 1819 Slave Trade Act, in *Public Statutes*, Vol. 3, 532–34.

Chapter 7

1 William R. Waring, *Report to the City Council of Savannah on the Epidemic Disease of 1820* (Savannah: Henry P. Russell, 1821), 8–9. Two

weeks is about the incubation period of yellow fever—see Michael A. Johansson, Neysari Arana-Vizcarrondo, Brad J. Biggerstaff, and J. Erin Staples, "Incubation Periods of Yellow Fever Virus," *American Journal of Tropical Medicine* 93, no. 1 (2010): 183–88.

2 See Jacob De La Motta, *An Oration, on the Causes of the Mortality Among Strangers, During the Late Summer and Fall: Pronounced Before the Georgia Medical Society, and Citizens of Savannah, on January 1st, 1820* (Savannah: Kappel and Bartlet, 1820); Waring, *Report to the City Council of Savannah on the Epidemic Disease of 1820*; and W. C. Daniell, *Observations Upon the Autumnal Fevers of Savannah* (Savannah: W. T. Williams, 1826), for accounts by Savannah's best physicians struggling to unravel the puzzle of yellow fever.

3 Margaret Humphries, *Yellow Fever and the South* (Baltimore: Johns Hopkins University Press, 1999), 1–18.

4 Ibid., 17–44. Billy G. Smith, *Ship of Death: A Voyage That Changed the Atlantic World* (New Haven, CT: Yale University Press, 2013), tells the story of the ship that transported yellow fever in 1793 to Philadelphia, where Dr. Benjamin Rush published the first American studies of the disease. These studies were greatly influential in Savannah during the 1820 epidemic.

5 *Savannah Daily Georgian*, May 25, 1820; Daniell, *Observations upon the Autumnal Fevers of Savannah*, 22–34. Many writers commented on the unhealthiness of Savannah; the only question in most cases was whether Savannah was healthier than Charleston or New Orleans. See Mills Lane, ed., *The Rambler in Georgia* (Savannah: Beehive Press, 1973).

6 Waring, *Report to the City Council of Savannah on the Epidemic Disease of 1820*, 20–21; *Savannah Daily Georgian*, July 18, 22, 1820. The 1820 Death Register, City of Savannah, Recapitulation for July, shows a total of fifty-three deaths, with thirty-nine from "fever." The term "yellow fever" was rarely used in 1820 Savannah, usually just the terms "fever" and "malignant fever."

7 Q. K. Philander Doesticks (Mortimer Thomson), *Great Auction and Sale of Slaves at Savannah, Georgia, March 2nd & 3rd, 1859* (New York, 1863), 6–7.

8 Various bills to Marshal Morel, July and August 1820, in RG 21, DCG, Box 28, NARA-Atlanta; Marshal's Report of May 8, 1822, RG 21, DCG, Box 32, NARA-Atlanta.

9 Waring, *Report to the City Council of Savannah on the Epidemic Disease of 1820*, 34–35; Daniell, *Observations upon the Autumnal Fevers of Savannah*, 64–66; "Statement of the Marshal Relating to the Africans from the

Brig Genl. Ramirez," December 15, 1821, RG 21, Box 32, NARA-Atlanta.

10 *Savannah Republican,* August 24, 1820; Johnson, *Black Savannah,* 139; Lockley, *Lines in the Sand,* 118–26.

11 Waring, *Report to the City Council of Savannah on the Epidemic Disease of 1820,* 20–21; Marshal's Report of May 8, 1822, RG 21, DCG, Box 32, NARA-Atlanta; J. H. Morel to John Quincy Adams, September 4, 1820, Miscellaneous Letters of the Department of State, 1789–1906, M-179, Roll 49, NARA-Atlanta; Microfilm of Savannah City Council Minutes, August 9, 1820, Bull Street Library, Savannah, GA.

12 Mayor T. U. P. Charlton to Judge Wm. Davies, August 9, 1820, RG 21, Box 32, NARA-Atlanta; Microfilm of Savannah City Council Minutes, August 9, 1820, Bull Street Library, Savannah, GA; Judge William Davies Order in Chambers, August 9, 1820, RG 21, Box 32, NARA-Atlanta; Resolution of City Council, July 9, 1820 (misdated), RG 21, Box 30, NARA-Atlanta; Official Proceedings of City Council, August 14, 1820, 362, City of Savannah, Clerk of Council's Office, Savannah, GA; Noonan, *The Antelope,* 45–46.

13 Order of Judge Wm. Davies, August 8, 1820, RG 21, DCG, Box 30, NARA-Atlanta; Order of Judge William Davies, August 9, 1820, RG 21, DCG, Box 127, NARA-Atlanta.

14 *Savannah Georgian,* August 15, 1820; *Savannah Republican,* August 15, 1820, Joseph Ioor Waring, "The Yellow Fever Epidemic of Savannah in 1820: with a Sketch of Dr. William Coffee Daniell," *Georgia Historical Quarterly* 52, no. 4 (December 1968): 398–404.

15 *Savannah Georgian,* August 15, 17, 24, 29, September 2, 1820; *Savannah Republican,* August 15, 19, 24, 1820.

16 *Savannah Georgian,* August 15, 17, 24, 29, September 2, 1820; *Savannah Republican,* August 15, 19, 24, 1820; "1820 Register of Deaths, Savannah, Georgia," found at Ancestry.com, Savannah, GA, Vital Records, 1803–1966 (database online at http://www.ancestry.com/). Provo, UT, USA: Ancestry.com Operations, Inc., 2011.

17 Waring, "The Yellow Fever Epidemic of Savannah in 1820," 400–401; *Savannah Republican,* September 14, 1820; "1820 Register of Deaths, Savannah, Georgia," Ancestry.com, Savannah, GA, Vital Records, 1803–1966 (database online); *Niles' Weekly Register,* October 14, 1820.

18 Fraser, *Savannah in the Old South,* 200; "1820 Register of Deaths, Savannah, Georgia," Ancestry.com, Savannah, GA, Vital Records, 1803–1966 (database online); Tim Lockley, "'Like a Clap of Thunder in a Clear Sky': Differential Mortality During Savannah's Yellow Fever Epidemic of 1854," *Social History* 37, no. 2 (May 2012): 166–86.

19 *Niles' Weekly Register,* September 16, 30, October 14, 21, 28, November 4, 11, 1820; "1820 Register of Deaths, Savannah, Georgia," Ancestry.com, Savannah, GA, Vital Records, 1803–1966 (database online).

20 *Savannah Georgian,* August 15, 17, 24, 29, September 2, 1820; *Savannah Republican,* August 15, 19, 24, September 2, 12, 14, 1820; Daniell, *Observations upon the Autumnal Fevers of Savannah,* 23, 24, 32; Waring, "The Yellow Fever Epidemic of Savannah in 1820," 400–401; "1820 Register of Deaths, Savannah, Georgia," Ancestry.com, Savannah, GA, Vital Records, 1803–1966 (database online); *Niles' Weekly Register,* September 16, 30, October 14, 21, 28, November 4, 11, 18, December 26, 1820; Henry P. Russell, *An Official Register of the Deaths Which Occurred Among the White Population in the City of Savannah* (Savannah: Henry P. Russell, 1820), 23, 24.

21 Ric'd W. Habersham to John Quincy Adams, August 31, 1820; J. H. Morel to John Quincy Adams, September 4, 1820, Miscellaneous Letters of the Department of State, 1789–1906, M-179, Roll 48, 49.

22 Margaret Humphries, *Yellow Fever and the South,* 6–7; "Report of the Clerk," February 27, 1821, RG 21, DCG, Box 32, NARA-Atlanta.

23 "Statement of the Marshal," December 15, 1821, RG 21, DCG, Box 32, NARA-Atlanta; "Report of the Clerk," February 27, 1821, RG 21, DCG, Box 32, NARA-Atlanta.

Chapter 8

1 *The Josefa Segunda,* 18 U.S. 338 (1820); Jane Lucas de Grummond, *Renato Beluche: Smuggler, Privateer, and Patriot 1780–1860* (Baton Rouge: Louisiana State University Press, 1983), 157–70.

2 *The Josefa Segunda,* 18 U.S. 338, 357–58 (1820).

3 Slave Trade Act, in *Public Statutes,* Vol. 3, 532–34.

4 Three Grand Jury Indictments Against John Smith for Piracy, December 14, 1820, RG 21, Box 127, NARA-Atlanta; *Savannah Republican,* December 16, 1820; An Act to Protect the Commerce of the United States and Punish the Crime of Piracy, March 3, 1819, and An Act to Continue in Force An Act to Protect the Commerce of the United States and Punish the Crime of Piracy, and Also to Make Further Provisions for Punishing the Crime of Piracy, May 15, 1820, in Gordon, *A Collection of Laws of the United States Relating to Revenue, Navigation, and Commerce,* 244–46, 253–55.

5 *Savannah Republican,* July 8, 1820; James Monroe to John Quincy Adams, August 3, 1820, in Stanislaus Murray Hamilton, *The Writings of James Monroe, Vol. 6, 1817–1823* (New York: AMS Press, 1969), 145–46.

6 Noonan, *The Antelope*, 36–40. *Savannah Republican*, December 16, 1820, reported that the grand jury "found true bills against Capt. John Smith, the officers and crew of the Gen. Ramirez for Piracy." If so, the indictments of all but Smith have vanished.

7 Lucian Lamar Knight, *A Standard History of Georgia and Georgians*, Vol. 2 (Chicago and New York: Lewis Publishing Co., 1917), 663; Resolution of December 19, 1827, Georgia House of Representatives, in William C. Dawson, *Compilation of the Laws of the State of Georgia* (Milledgeville: Grantland and Orme, 1831), 103–4; Rich. W. Habersham to John Quincy Adams, January 8, 1822, Miscellaneous Letters of the Department of State, M-179, Roll 53. A fuller sense of the man can be obtained by reading his letters to his son found in the Bernard Elliott Habersham family papers, MS 36, Hargrett Rare Book and Manuscript Library, University of Georgia Libraries, Athens, GA.

8 Deposition of John Smith, February 13, 1821, RG 21, Box 30, NARA-Atlanta, *Savannah Republican*, December 22, 1820. Craig Robertson, *The Passport in America: The History of a Document* (New York: Oxford University Press, 2010), has an excellent discussion of the issues of identification in the nineteenth century. There was a wealthy merchant family named Smith in Baltimore, but this John Smith had no connection to that family.

9 *Savannah Republican*, December 16, 1820; Alexander A. Lawrence, *James Moore Wayne: Southern Unionist* (Chapel Hill: University of North Carolina Press, 1943); McCrary Jr., "John Macpherson Berrien."

10 Noonan, *The Antelope*, 51–53, 66–68; *Savannah Republican*, December 16, 1820. Noonan suggested that Berrien had acted unethically in this case, and might have suggested more had he known that Berrien defended Smith in the piracy case. Noonan also mistakenly thought that William Law had defended Smith in the piracy trial, because Law served as Smith's proctor in the case at Admiralty, and did not know of Berrien and Wayne's connection.

11 *The Josefa Segunda,* 18 U.S. 338 (1820); Noonan, *The Antelope*, 66–68; "The Claim of John Smith on behalf of himself and others," February 13, 1821, RG 21, DCG Box 30, NARA-Atlanta.

12 Libel of John Smith, February 13, 1821, RG 21, DCG, Box 30, NARA-Atlanta.

13 U.S. Const., art. I, § 8; An Act for the Punishment of Certain Crimes Against the United States, April 30, 1790, ch. 9, sec. 8, 1 stat. 112 (1790); An Act to Protect the Commerce of the United States and Punish the Crime of Piracy, March 3, 1819, ch. 77, sec. 5, 3 stat. 510 (1819); *United States v. Furlong*, 18 U.S. 184 (1820); *United States*

v. Klintock, 18 U.S. 144 (1820); G. Edward White, "The Marshall Court and International Law: The Piracy Cases," *American Journal of International Law* 83, no. 4 (October 1989): 727, 733; *United States v. Smith*, 18 U.S. 153, 161 (1820). As the old circuit courts consisted of two judges, the Judiciary Act of 1802 provided for a certificate of division when the two judges could not agree on the law even if it did not involve a federal question. The Supreme Court would decide what the law was.

14 *Niles' Weekly Register*, March 25, 1820; John Quincy Adams to Habersham, August 10, 1820, quoted in Noonan, *The Antelope*, 40; Rich. W. Habersham to John Quincy Adams, August 31, 1820, M-179, NARA.

15 Indictments of John Smith, December 14, 1820, in RG 21, Box 127, NARA-Atlanta; *Savannah Republican*, December 16, 22, 23, 1820.

16 *Savannah Republican*, December 22, 23, 1820; "Law Case—Piracy," in *Niles' Weekly Register*, January 13, 1821.

17 Lawrence M. Friedman, *A History of American Law* (New York: Simon & Schuster, 1985), 154; *Savannah Republican*, December 23, 1820; *Niles' Weekly Register*, January 13, 1821; *United States v. Smith*, 18 U.S. 153, 161 (1820). Not until 1878 did criminal defendants have the right to testify in federal courts—see An Act to Make Persons Charged with Crimes and Offenses Competent Witnesses in the United States and Territorial Courts, Statutes at Large, Vol. 20, p. 30 (March 16, 1878).

18 *Savannah Republican*, December 23, 1820; *Niles' Weekly Register*, January 13, 1821; *United States v. Smith*, 18 U.S. 153, 161 (1820).

19 *Savannah Republican*, December 22, 23, 1820.

Chapter 9

1 Deposition of James Thompson, December 28, 1820, RG 21, DCG, Box 28, NARA-Atlanta.

2 Deposition of John M. Rupell, December 13, 1821, RG 21, DCG, Box 28, NARA-Atlanta; *Savannah Republican*, December 30, 1820. Death depositions are scattered throughout the district court papers, mostly in Box 28.

3 Slave Trade Act, in *Public Statutes*, Vol. 3, 532–34.

4 *DeLovio v. Boit*, 7 Federal Cases, Vol. 7, p. 418 (1815); Gerald T. Dunne, "Joseph Story: The Lowering Storm," *American Journal of Legal History* 13, no. 1 (January 1969): 5; William W. Adams, "Constitutional History: Development of Admiralty Jurisdiction in the United States, 1789–1857," *Western New England Law Review* 8 (1986): 157–89. In 1825 the

Supreme Court affirmed Justice Story's understanding of the extent of admiralty jurisdiction in *The Thomas Jefferson* 23 U.S. 428 (1825).

5 For a concise summary of nineteenth-century United States Admiralty law see Robert M. Hughes, *A Handbook of Admiralty Law* (St. Paul, MN: West Publishing, 1901), or M. M. Cohen, *Admiralty, Jurisdiction, Law, and Practice* (Boston: Soule and Bugbee, 1883); An Act to Amend the Judicial System of the United States, April 29, 1802, 2 stat. 156.

6 McCrary Jr., "John Macpherson Berrien," 34–40.

7 Appellate Case Files of the Supreme Court of the United States, 1792–1831, Nos 1161–62, *The Antelope*, Microfilm M-214, Roll 59, NARA-Atlanta.

8 Examination of William Richardson, December 1, 1826, RG 21, DCG, Box 32, NARA-Atlanta; Examination of John H. Morel, December 1, 1826, RG 21, DCG, Box 32, NARA-Atlanta.

9 Robert Manson Myers, *The Children of Pride: A True Story of Georgia and the Civil War* (New Haven, CT: Yale University Press, 1972), 1591. Contingency or conditional fees had begun to appear in American courts by this time, but a lawyer could still be accused of "champerty," that is, illegally benefiting from his client's case. See Stephan Landsman, "The History of Contingency and the Contingency of History" *DePaul Law Review* 47, no. 2 (April 1998): 261–86. William Law would astonishingly continue to practice law until 1873.

10 Slave Trade Act, in *Public Statutes*, Vol. 3, 532–34.

11 Examination and Deposition of John Jackson, January 17, 1821, RG 21, DCG, Box 30, NARA-Atlanta; John Jackson Bill for $1245.96, January 18, 1821, RG 21, DCG, Box 28, NARA-Atlanta; list of Revenue Service Officer Commissions, http://semperparatus.com/usrcs_officers.html (accessed November 5, 2013).

12 Examination and Deposition of James D. Knight, January 18, 1821, RG 21, DCG, Box 32, NARA-Atlanta.

13 Examination of John Stephens, a Greek, January 18, 1821, RG 21, DCG, Box 30, NARA-Atlanta; Examination of William Brunton, January 18, 19, 1821, RG 21, DCG, Box 32, NARA-Atlanta.

14 Examination and Deposition of John Morrison, January 19, 1821, RG 21, DCG, Box 32, NARA-Atlanta; *The Brig Alerta, and Cargo v. Blas Moran*, 13 U.S. 359 (1815). While it was decided later, *The Santissima Trinidad*, 20 U.S. 283 (1822), also engaged these issues of neutrality. The Neutrality Law of 1818 is An Act in Addition to the Act for the Punishment of Certain Crimes Against the United States, April 20,

1818, in *Public Statutes at Large of the United States, 1789–1873,* Vol. 3 (Washington, D.C., 1845), 447–50.

15 Examination and Deposition of John Morrison, January 19, 1821, RG 21, DCG, Box 32, NARA-Atlanta.

16 Examination of Thomas Hemanus, January 19, 1821, RD 21, DCG, Box 32, NARA-Atlanta. The court reporter George Glen did not know Spanish, and Ximenes made his mark with an X, so he probably couldn't read—hence the phonetic spelling.

17 John Smith Libel for Restitution, February 13, 1821, RG 21, DCG, Box 30, NARA-Atlanta; Deposition of John Smith, February 13, 1821, RG 21, DCG, Box 30, NARA-Atlanta.

18 Examination of Domingo Grondona, taken in open court, February 13, 1821, RG 21, DCG, Box 30, NARA-Atlanta.

19 Examination and Deposition of Thomas Ximenes, February 13, 1821, RG 21, DCG, Box 30, NARA-Atlanta.

20 Deposition of John Smith, February 13, 1821, RG 21, DCG, Box 30, NARA-Atlanta; John Charles Chasteen, *Americanos: Latin America's Struggle for Independence* (Oxford: Oxford University Press, 2008), 123–36, 162–67.

21 Interrogatories to be propounded to John Smith, February 14, 1821, RG 21, DCG, Box 32, NARA-Atlanta.

22 "We agree to unite," Savannah, February 14, 1821, RG 21, DCG, Box 28, NARA-Atlanta. This document was not filed with the court until December 31, 1825.

23 At a Special Court of Admiralty Held at the Court House in Savannah, February 16, 1821; Judge Davies' Decision in the cases of the *Antelope* or *General Ramirez,* February 21, 1821, in Records of the Supreme Court of the United States, RG 267, microfilm copy, M-214, Roll 59, NARA-Washington.

24 "Heads of the Argument," in Rich. W. Habersham to Honorable Jno. Quincy Adams, March 12, 1821, Miscellaneous Letters, August–October, 1820, Records of the Department of State, RG 59, NARA-Washington, Microfilm M-179, Roll 48.

25 Ibid.

26 Ibid. See above, chapter 3, for a discussion of the British Admiralty cases.

27 "Heads of the Argument."

Chapter 10

1 Judge Davies' Opinion, in Rich. W. Habersham to Honorable Jno. Quincy Adams, March 12, 1821, Miscellaneous Letters, August–October, 1820, Records of the Department of State, RG 59, NARA-

Washington, Microfilm M-179, Roll 48; *The Alerta v. Moran*, 13 U.S.
359 (1815), was the basis of Judge Davies' decision on Smith's claim.
For the Slave Trade Acts, see An Act to Prohibit the Introduction
of Slaves, March 2, 1807, in *Public Statutes*, Vol. 2, 426–30; An Act in
Addition to An Act to Prohibit the Introduction of Slaves, April 20,
1818, in *Public Statutes*, Vol. 3, 450–53; 1819 Slave Trade Act, in *Public
Statutes*, Vol. 3, 532–34.

2 Judge Davies' Opinion; *The Josefa Segunda*, 18 U.S. 338 (1820).

3 Judge Davies' Opinion.

4 Ibid.

5 Ibid.

6 At a Special Court of Admiralty Held at the Exchange in Savannah,
February 23, 1821, in Records of the Supreme Court of the United
States, RG 267, microfilm copy, M-214, Roll 59, NARA-Atlanta.

7 Ibid.; Discharge of Carlos, February 21, 1821, RG 21, DCG, Box 30,
NARA-Atlanta.

8 At a Special Court of Admiralty held at the Exchange in Savannah,
February 23, 1821.

9 Clerk's Report of the Value and Salvage, February 27, 1821, in
Records of the Supreme Court of the United States, RG 267,
microfilm copy, M-214, Roll 59, NARA-Washington.

10 *The Blackwall*, 77 U.S. 1, 13–14 (1869); Clerk's Report of the Value
and Salvage, February 27, 1821; Joshua C. Teitelbaum, "Inside the
Blackwall Box: Explaining U.S. Marine Salvage Awards," Georgetown
Business, Economics and Regulatory Law Research Paper No. 12-
017, *http://scholarship.law.georgetown.edu/facpub/960* (accessed January
25, 2014); Horatio Davis Smith, *Early History of the United States
Revenue Marine Service, 1789–1849* (Washington, D.C.: R. L. Polk
Printing Co., 1932), 18.

11 United States Exceptions, February 21, 1821, Portuguese Vice Consul
Exceptions, February 27, 1821, John Smith's appeal bond, March 13,
1821, in Records of the Supreme Court of the United States, RG
267, microfilm copy, M-214, Roll 59, NARA-Washington.

12 United States Exceptions, February 21, 1821, Portuguese Vice Consul
Exceptions, February 27, 1821, John Smith's appeal bond, March
13, 1821, in Records of the Supreme Court of the United States,
RG 267, microfilm copy, M-214, Roll 59, NARA-Washington;
Rich. W. Habersham to Honorable Jno. Quincy Adams, March 12,
1821, Miscellaneous Letters, January–April, 1821, Records of the
Department of State, RG 59, NARA-Washington, microfilm M-179,
Roll 50, NARA-Washington; Noonan, *The Antelope*, 61.

13 *Milledgeville Southern Recorder*, February 6, 1821; *Savannah Daily Georgian*, February 20, March 13, 1821; Noonan, *The Antelope*, 60; John Jackson's Answer to the Libelants, September 29, 1829, RG 21, DCG, Box 33, NARA-Atlanta.

14 Affidavit of David Polock, March 9, 1821, RG 21, DCG, Box 28, NARA-Atlanta; "In Council, 26 March 1821," RG 21, DCG, Box 32, NARA-Atlanta; *Savannah Daily Georgian*, March 1, 1821.

15 Joshua Glick, "Comment: On the Road: The Supreme Court and the History of Circuit Riding," 24 Cardozo L.Rev.1753 (April 2003); *Savannah Daily Georgian*, June 21, 1821.

16 The best biography of Johnson is Donald G. Morgan, *Justice William Johnson: The First Dissenter* (Columbia, SC: University of South Carolina Press, 1954). See also Herbert A. Johnson, "The Constitutional Thought of William Johnson," *South Carolina Historical Magazine* 89, no. 3 (1988): 132–45.

17 Morgan, *Justice William Johnson*, 135–46.

18 "Reasonings and Holdings of Justice William Johnson," Records of the Supreme Court of the United States, RG 267, microfilm copy, M-214, Roll 59, NARA-Washington.

19 Ibid.

20 Ibid.

21 Ibid.

22 Ibid. Confusingly, later in the decree Johnson ordered that the captives awarded to Spain could be separated out by lot and turned over to them. Because Habersham appealed this decision this did not happen.

23 *The Maria Josepha*, Federal Cases, Vol. 16, p. 733 (May 1819); "Reasonings and Holdings of Justice William Johnson."

24 "Reasonings and Holdings of Justice William Johnson."

Chapter 11

1 Mills Lane, ed., *General Oglethorpe's Georgia: Colonial Letters, 1733–1743* (Savannah: Beehive Press, 1990), 389. The best recent account of Trustee Georgia is Noeleen McIlvenna, *Laborers Were Become Our Masters: The Short Life of Free Georgia*, forthcoming from the University of North Carolina Press.

2 Betty Wood, *Slavery in Colonial Georgia, 1730–1775* (Athens: University of Georgia Press, 1984); see also McIlvenna, *Laborers Were Become Our Masters*.

3 Kenneth Coleman, *Colonial Georgia: A History* (New York: Charles Scribner's Sons, 1976), tells the traditional story of economic success. For more nuanced tellings, see Wood, *Slavery in Colonial Georgia*; Alan

Gallay, *The Formation of a Planter Elite: Jonathan Bryan and the Southern Colonial Frontier* (Athens: University of Georgia Press, 1989); and Pressly, *On the Rim of the Caribbean.*

4 Leslie Hall, *Land and Allegiance in Revolutionary Georgia* (Athens: University of Georgia Press, 2001), 161–63; Sylvia Frey, *Water from the Rock: Black Resistance in a Revolutionary Age* (Princeton, NJ: Princeton University Press, 1991), 81–106. Also see Watson W. Jennison, *Cultivating Race: The Expansion of Slavery in Georgia, 1750–1860* (Lexington: University of Kentucky Press, 2012), 41–69. South Carolina may have lost as many as twenty thousand or more slaves during the Revolution. The desire to replace these lost slaves explains in part why delegates at the Constitutional Convention from Georgia and South Carolina insisted that the international slave trade remain open.

5 Voyages Database, http://slavevoyages.org/tast/database/search.faces?yearFrom=1783&yearTo=1799&mjslptimp=21400 (accessed February 24, 2013); Jennison, *Cultivating Race,* 61–69; Jeffrey Robert Young, "Slavery in Antebellum Georgia." New Georgia Encyclopedia, http://www.georgiaencyclopedia.org/articles/history-archaeology/slavery-antebellum-georgia (accessed December 14, 2013).

6 Kevin Mulroy, *Freedom on the Border: The Seminole Maroons in Florida, the Indian Territory, Coahuila, and Texas* (Lubbock, TX: Texas Tech University Press, 1993), 6–17.

7 John H. McIntosh to James Monroe, July 30, 1812, in *Message from the President of the United States to the Two Houses of Congress, Dec. 6, 1831* (Washington: Duff Green, 1831), 16–18; William C. Davis, *The Rogue Republic: How Would-Be Patriots Waged the Shortest Revolution in American History* (New York: Houghton Mifflin Harcourt, 2011); Rembert W. Patrick, *Florida Fiasco: Rampant Rebels on the Georgia–Florida Border, 1810–1815* (Athens: University of Georgia Press, 1954), 154–55. See also James G. Cusick, *The Other War of 1812: The Patriot War and the American Invasion of Spanish East Florida* (Gainesville: University Press of Florida, 2003).

8 These conflicts are all fascinating stories in their own right. See Mary R. Bullard, *Black Liberation of Cumberland Island* (DeLeon Springs, FL: M. R. Bullard, 1983); Claudio Saunt, *A New Order of Things: Property, Power, and the Transformation of the Creek Indians, 1733–1816* (Cambridge: Cambridge University Press, 1999); Gregory A. Waselkov, *A Conquering Spirit: Fort Mims and the Redstick War of 1813–1814* (Tuscaloosa: University of Alabama Press, 2006); and Kathryn E.

Holland Braund, ed., *Tohopeka: Rethinking the Creek War and the War of 1812* (Tuscaloosa: University of Alabama Press, 2012).

9 James W. Covington, "The Negro Fort," *Gulf Coast Historical Review* 5, no. 2 (January 1990): 78–91; Jane G. Landers, *Black Society in Spanish Florida* (Urbana: University of Illinois Press, 1999); Paul E. Hoffman, *Florida's Frontiers* (Bloomington: Indiana University Press, 2002); Jennison, *Cultivating Race*, 176–88; John Missall and Mary Lou Missall, *The Seminole Wars: America's Longest Indian Conflict* (Gainesville: University Press of Florida, 2004).

10 "William Richardson," Savannah 1821 Tax Digest, microfilm copy, Bull Street Public Library, Savannah, GA; Payment J. H. Morel to Wm. Richardson, August 7, 1821, RG 21, DCG, Box 28, NARA-Atlanta; "Reasonings and Holdings of Justice William Johnson." William Richardson was listed as owning a house and building at Spring Hill, and two lots and buildings in New Leeds nearby.

11 Richard W. Habersham to John Quincy Adams, July 22, 1821, Miscellaneous Letters, May–August, 1821, Records of the Department of State, RG 59, NARA-Washington, Microfilm M-179, Roll 51; "Statement of the Marshal Relating to the Africans from the Brig Ramirez," Circuit Court, May Term, 1822, RG 21, DCG, Box 32, NARA-Atlanta.

12 "For taking four Africans runaway on the 16th July, 1821," RG 21, DCG, Box 28, NARA-Atlanta; Richard W. Habersham to the Secretary of the Navy, August 17, 1821, in Society of Friends, *A View of the Present State of the African Slave Trade*, 47.

13 William Johnson to John Quincy Adams, June 12, 1821, Miscellaneous Letters, May–August, 1821, Records of the Department of State, RG 59, NARA-Washington, Microfilm M-179, Roll 51; "Africans of the Brig Gen. Ramirez," July 15, 1821, RG 21, DCG, Box 28, NARA-Atlanta.

14 Joseph Gaston Bulloch, *A History and Genealogy of the Families of Bellinger and De Veaux and Other Families* (Savannah: Morning News Press, 1895), 81–84, Buddy Sullivan, *From Beautiful Zion to Red Bird Creek: A History of Bryan County, Georgia* (Darien, GA: Bryan County Board of Commissioners, 2000), 58–62. The letter *H* was used by Morel to distinguish himself from his cousin John Morel. A number of historians have conflated the two men.

15 Savannah Tax Digests, 1819, 1820, 1821, 1823, 1824, microfilm copies, Bull Street Library, Savannah GA; Roulhac Toledano, *The National Trust Guide to Savannah* (New York: John Wiley and Sons, 1997), 136–39; Bulloch, *A History and Genealogy of the Families of Bellinger and De*

Veaux and Other Families, 81–84; *Savannah Columbian Museum*, June 15, 1803, November 11, 1812.

16 Chatham County Tax Digest, 1823, Savannah Tax Digest 1821, Microfilm, Bull Street Library, Savannah, GA; Sullivan, *From Beautiful Zion to Red Bird Creek*, 26–27, 98–101, 381, 386.

17 Richard Dwight Porcher and Sarah Fick, *The Story of Sea Island Cotton* (Charleston, SC: Wyrick and Co., 2005), 89–100.

18 Ibid., 154–72.

19 Ibid., 173–218.

20 For overviews of slavery see Davis, *Inhuman Bondage*, and Berlin, *Many Thousands Gone*. For Savannah, consider Betty Wood, *Women's Work, Men's Work: The Informal Slave Economies of Lowcountry Georgia* (Athens: University of Georgia Press, 1995); Lockley, *Lines in the Sand*; and Leslie M. Harris and Daina Ramey Berry, eds., *Slavery and Freedom in Savannah* (Athens: University of Georgia Press, 2014).

21 Whittington B. Johnson, *Black Savannah, 1788–1864* (Fayetteville, AR: University of Arkansas Press, 1996), 7–31.

22 Johnson, *Black Savannah*, 85–106; Susan Eva O'Donovan, "At the Intersection of Cotton and Commerce: Antebellum Savannah and Its Slaves," in *Slavery and Freedom in Savannah*, edited by Harris and Berry, 42–68.

23 Johnson, *Black Savannah*, 107–32; Lockley, *Lines in the Sand*, 29–56.

24 William Grimes, *The Life of William Grimes, the Runaway Slave* (New York: 1825); *Savannah Daily Republican*, March 24, 1820.

25 William Grimes, *Life of William Grimes* (New York: 1825), 46. Archibald S. Bulloch was one of the men John Quincy Adams thought was involved in the illegal slave trade. William Grimes was also owned once by Dr. Lemuel Kollock, the partner of John M. Berrien's brother who died in the 1820 yellow fever epidemic. See *Savannah Daily Georgian*, February 21, 1821.

26 Grimes, *Life*, 35–48.

27 Wood, *Women's Work, Men's Work*, 12–100; Lockley, *Lines in the Sand*, 57–97; *Savannah Republican*, June 17, 1820.

28 "Jeremiah La Touche Cuyler," in the Federal Judicial Center Biographical Directory of Federal Judges, http://www.fjc.gov/servlet/nGetInfo?jid=551&cid=999 (accessed February 18, 2014); "Reasonings and Holdings of Justice William Johnson."

29 "Ordered and Decreed," Circuit Court of Georgia, December 28, 1821, RG 21, DCG, Box 28.

30 Appeal to the Supreme Court, January 2, 1822, RG 21, DCG, Box 30, NARA-Atlanta.

31 Richard W. Habersham to John Quincy Adams, January 8, 1822, Miscellaneous Letters, January–July, 1822, Records of the Department of State, RG 59, NARA-Washington, Microfilm M-179, Roll 53; Noonan, *The Antelope*, 74–75.

32 "Charges of the Marshal," December 15, 1821, RG 21, DCG, Box 32.

Chapter 12

 1 John H. Morel to William Crawford, December 7, 1821, Miscellaneous Letters, September–December 1821, Records of the Department of State, RG 59, NARA-Washington, Microfilm M-179, Roll 52; Adams, *Memoirs*, Vol. 5, 453–55.

 2 Adams, *Memoirs*, Vol. 5, 455.

 3 Stanislaus Murray Hamilton, ed., *The Writing of James Monroe, Vol. 6, 1817–1823* (New York: AMS Press, 1969), 13. A solid biography of Monroe is Harry Ammon, *James Monroe: The Quest for National Identity* (Charlottesville: University of Virginia Press, 1990). Two works that present the political shrewdness of Monroe well are Daniel Walker Howe, *What Hath God Wrought: The Transformation of America, 1815–1848* (Oxford: Oxford University Press, 2007), and Robert Pierce Forbes, *The Missouri Compromise and Its Aftermath* (Chapel Hill: University of North Carolina Press, 2007).

 4 William M. Meigs, *The Life of Charles Jared Ingersoll* (Philadelphia: J. B. Lippincott, 1897), 114.

 5 There are numerous biographies of John Quincy Adams. Two of the best are Paul C. Nagel, *John Quincy Adams: A Public Life, A Private Life* (Cambridge, MA: Harvard University Press, 1997), and William Earl Weeks, *John Quincy Adams and American Global Empire* (Lexington: University Press of Kentucky, 1992).

 6 Galen N. Thorpe, "William Wirt," in *Journal of Supreme Court History* 33, no. 3 (November 2008): 223–303, 234; Noonan, *The Antelope*, 74–77.

 7 John R. Spears, *The American Slave Trade* (New York: Charles Scribner's Sons, 1900), 148–50; Rees, *Sweet Water and Bitter*, 64–74.

 8 James Monroe to Daniel Brent, September 15, 1821, James Monroe to Daniel Brent, September 17, 1821, in Hamilton, *The Writings of James Monroe, Volume 6, 1817–1823*, 193–97; William P. Mason, *A Report on the Jeune Eugenie Determined in the Circuit Court of the United States, First Circuit at Boston, December 1821* (Boston: Wells and Lilly, 1822).

 9 Joseph Story, *A Charge Delivered to the Grand Juries of the Circuit Court at October Term, 1819, in Boston, and at November Term, 1819, in Providence* (Boston, 1819); Adams, *Memoirs*, Vol. 5, 376–98.

10 *The Schooner Exchange v. M'Faddon*, 11 U.S. 116 (1812); Adams,

Memoirs, Vol. 5, 376–98. Interestingly, in 1829, a ship named the *Jeune Eugenie* was captured by the British navy at Old Calabar. It was engaged in the slave trade and was almost certainly the same ship as in the case before Joseph Story. See Thomas, *The Slave Trade*, 597.

11 William P. Mason, *A Report on the Jeune Eugenie*, 48, 71, 76, 85, 86; *Salem Gazette*, December 18, 1821.

12 *Washington Daily National Intelligencer*, December 27, 1821; *Alexandria Gazette*, December 27, 1821, January 2, 1822; William Wirt to President James Madison, January 22, 1822, *Opinions of the Attorneys General* (Washington, D.C., 1851), 348–49; Society of Friends, *A View of the Present State of the African Slave Trade*, 18, 19. Sadly, J. Q. Adam's diary is silent on this case.

13 *Savannah Georgian*, April 20, 1822.

14 *Savannah Georgian*, April 20, 1822; "District Judge John Dick," in United States District Court, Eastern District of Louisiana, "Tracking Louisiana's Legal Heritage: Celebrating 200 Years of the Federal Courts in Louisiana," http://www.laed.uscourts.gov/200th/judges/dick.php (accessed on March 18, 2014).

15 *Savannah Georgian*, April 20, 1822; Serge Dagat, *La répression de la traite des Noirs au XIXè siècle: l'action des croisières françaises sur les côtes occidentales de l'Afrique, 1817–1850* (Paris: Karthala, 1997), 208–9; Donald L. Canney, *Africa Squadron: The U.S. Navy and the Slave Trade, 1842–1861* (Dulles, VA: Potomac Books, 2006).

16 October 26, 1822, Adams, *Memoirs*, Vol. 6, 84–87.

17 October 26, 1822, Adams, *Memoirs*, Vol. 6, 87.

18 Ibid., 86–87; Michael Daly Hawkins, "John Quincy Adams and the Antebellum Maritime Slave Trade: The Politics of Slavery and the Slavery of Politics," *Oklahoma City University Law Review* 25 (Spring and Summer 2000): 1–47.

19 Manifest of Slaves, Passengers on Board the Sloop *Spartan*, R. Gibbs, Master, April 26, 1822, Slave Manifests Microfilm, January–May 1822, Outward, Reel 10, NARA-Atlanta; John H. Morel statement, "The following sixteen Africans decreed to the United States," RG 21, DCG, Box 32, NARA-Atlanta; *Baltimore Patriot*, May 7, 1822.

20 Ralph Randolph Gurley, *The Life of Jehudi Ashmun, Late Colonial Agent in Liberia* (Washington, D.C.: James C. Dunn, 1835), 117–21, Early Lee Fox, *The American Colonization Society, 1817–1840* (New York: AMS Press, 1971), 67, 68.

21 P. J. Staudenraus, "Victims of the African Slave Trade, A Document," *Journal of Negro History* 41, no. 2 (April 1956): 148–51.

22 Staudenraus, "Victims of the African Slave Trade."

23 Gurley, *Life of Jehudi Ashmun*, 117–28; Elwood D. Dunn, Amos J. Beyan, Carl Patrick Burrowes, *Historical Dictionary of Liberia*, 2d ed. (Lanham, MD: Scarecrow Press, 2001), 83.

24 Gurley, *Life of Yehudi Ashmun*, 128–34; Randall M. Packard, *The Making of a Tropical Disease: A Short History of Malaria* (Baltimore: Johns Hopkins University Press, 2007), 7–35.

25 Gurley, *Life of Jehudi Ashmun*, 135–48; Noonan, *The Antelope*, 84.

26 *Savannah Daily Georgian*, April 22, 1822, quoted in the *Baltimore Patriot*, May 7, 1822.

Chapter 13

1 "We are of Opinion that the Marshal is entitled to . . . ," William Johnson, May 13, 1822; "A detailed, statement of the expenditure of the sum appropriated by the, 7th section of the act passed March 3, 1819, in addition to the acts prohibiting the slave trade," 20th Congress, 1st Session, *Senate Documents* No. 340 (Washington, D.C., 1827), 77–79.

2 "A further order of the Honorable William Johnson . . . Made in Washington on the tenth day of March, 1823," RG 21, DCG, Box 28; "Names of Africans cargo of the Brig Ramiriz collected together and delivered to sundry persons whoes names are here with stated," March 24, 1823, RG 21, DCG, Box 32, NARA-Atlanta.

3 "Names of Africans cargo of the Brig Ramiriz collected together and delivered to sundry persons whoes names are here with stated," March 24, 1823, RG 21, DCG, Box 32, NARA-Atlanta; Iman Makeba Laversuch, "Runaway Slave Names Recaptured: An Investigation of the Personal First Names of Fugitive Slaves Advertised in the *Virginia Gazette* Between 1736 and 1776," *Names* 54, no. 4 (December 2006): 331–62; John Thornton, "Central African Names and African-American Naming Patterns," *William & Mary Quarterly* 50, no. 4 (October 1993): 727–44; John C. Inscoe, "Carolina Slave Names: An Index to Acculturation," *Journal of Southern History* 49, no. 4 (November 1983): 527–54.

4 "Names of Africans cargo of the Brig Ramiriz collected together and delivered to sundry persons whoes names are here with stated," March 24, 1823, RG 21, DCG, Box 32, NARA-Atlanta.

5 Ibid.; "George Millen's hire of the slave Dick," May 31, 1823, RG 21, DCG, Box 32, NARA-Atlanta.

6 "Names of Africans cargo of the Brig Ramiriz collected together and delivered to sundry persons whoes names are here with stated," March 24, 1823, RG 21, DCG, Box 32, NARA-Atlanta; Return of Africans

in Possession of Jn. H. Morel, December 16, 1825, RG 21, DCG, Box
32, NARA-Atlanta; William Robert Mitchell Jr, *Classic Savannah:
History, Homes, and Gardens* (Savannah: Martin Publishing, 1991),
32. Interestingly, Richard Richardson's attorney for this process was
Richard W. Habersham. The legal world of Savannah was sometimes
quite small. See *Savannah Republican*, May 28, 1822.

7 "Names of Africans cargo of the Brig Ramiriz collected together
and delivered to sundry persons whoes names are here with
stated," March 24, 1823, RG 21, DCG, Box 32, NARA-Atlanta;
Berrien House Restoration, Savannah, 2012, Savannah Historic
District Review Board Application Supplement, page 10, http://
www.thempc.org/eagenda/x/hrb/2013/JANUARY%20
9,%202013%20HISTORIC%20DISTRICT%20BOARD%20
OF%20REVIEW%20REGULAR%20MEETING%20on%20
Wednesday,%20January%2009,%202013/B93F299D-5BAB-4205-
A285-ED824B50F7D4.pdf (accessed March 2, 2014).

8 McCrary Jr., "John Macpherson Berrien," 4–10.

9 Rev. George White, *Historical Collections of Georgia* (New York: Pudney
and Russell, 1855), 371–79; McCrary Jr., "John Macpherson Berrien,"
5–17.

10 "Joseph Clay, Jr." in Federal Judicial Center Biographical Directory of
Federal Judges, http://www.fjc.gov/public/home.nsf/hisj (accessed
October 17, 2013); McCrary Jr., "John Macpherson Berrien," 17–22.

11 George R. Lamplugh, *Politics on the Periphery: Factions and Parties in
Georgia, 1783–1806* (Newark: University of Delaware Press, 1986);
McCrary Jr., "John Macpherson Berrien," 22–24.

12 McCrary Jr., "John Macpherson Berrien," 22–28; Lamplugh, *Politics on
the Periphery*, 149–50.

13 McCrary Jr., "John Macpherson Berrien," 27–30.

14 George H. Shriver, *Pilgrims Through the Years: A Bicentennial History of
the First Baptist Church, Savannah, Georgia* (Franklin, TN: Providence
House, 1999), 19, 22; "Joseph Clay, Jr." in Federal Judicial Center
Biographical Directory of Federal Judges, http://www.fjc.gov/
public/home.nsf/hisj (accessed October 17, 2013); McCrary Jr., "John
Macpherson Berrien," 32–40. In 1802, Clay was licensed to preach,
and traveled locally as an exhorter for the church. In 1804, he became
the full-time associate pastor of the Savannah Baptist Church, and
in 1807, he accepted the position as pastor of the Baptist Church in
Boston. Clay died there in January of 1811.

15 White, *Historical Collections of Georgia*, 369–71; McCrary Jr., "John
Macpherson Berrien," 32–40.

16 McCrary Jr., "John Macpherson Berrien," 35–40.

17 Ibid., 35–48, 91.

18 Ibid., 64–67. Berrien's first wife, Eliza Anciaux, bore nine children before her death in 1828. Berrien's second wife, Eliza Hunter, bore six more children. That both wives were named Eliza has caused some confusion.

19 White, *Historical Collections of Georgia*, 371–73; McCrary Jr., "John Macpherson Berrien," 72–82.

20 Ibid., 82–84.

21 Robert M. Charlton, *Reports of Decisions Made in the Superior Courts of the Eastern District of Georgia* (Savannah: Thomas Purse and Co., 1838), has seventeen written decisions by Berrien; *Sheftall v. Clay* (1811), in Charlton, *Reports of Decisions made in the Superior Courts of the Eastern District of Georgia*, 9; White, *Historical Collections of Georgia*, 373.

22 *Savannah Republican*, November 25, 1822; Thomas Jefferson, *Notes on the State of Virginia* (Richmond: J. W. Randolph, 1853), 128–30; McCrary Jr., "John Macpherson Berrien," 95–97.

23 McCrary Jr., "John Macpherson Berrien," 92–100; Edward M. Buttimer Jr., "Thomas U. P. Charlton," http://library.armstrong.edu/Charlton_Thomas%20U%20P-1.pdf (accessed September 12, 2013).

24 McCrary Jr., "John Macpherson Berrien," 99–103; Geo. M. Troup to Charles Harris, Oct. 14, 1807, in Edward Jenkins Harden, *The Life of George M. Troup* (Savannah: E. J. Purse, 1859), 39; see also Harden, 11.

Chapter 14

1 Berrien to Governor Troup, June 28, 1825, reprinted in the *Savannah Republican*, September 22, 1825; in 1824 alone, cases included *The Emily and the Caroline*, 22 U.S. 381 (1824); *The Merino*, 22 U.S. 391 (1824); *The Margaret*, 22 U.S. 421 (1824); *The St. Jago de Cuba*, 22 U.S. 409 (1824); *The Plattsburgh*, 23 U.S. 133 (1824); John T. Noonan, *The Antelope*, 74–92. Noonan argued, in part, that John Quincy Adams prevented the case from coming before the Court, and only allowed it to go forward after a political quid pro quo trade with Key that gave Adams Maryland's support for election to the presidency.

2 *Washington Daily National Intelligencer*, December 17, 24, 1816; Claude A. Clegg III, *The Price of Liberty: African Americans and the Making of Liberia* (Chapel Hill: University of North Carolina Press, 2004), 30; Douglas R. Edgerton, "'Its Origin Is Not a Little Curious:' A New Look at the American Colonization Society," *Journal of the Early Republic* 5 (Winter 1985): 463–80.

3 Edward S. Delaplaine, *Francis Scott Key: Life and Times* (New York:

Biography Press, 1937), and Jefferson Morley, *Snow-Storm in August: Washington City, Francis Scott Key, and the Forgotten Race Riot of 1835* (New York: Doubleday, 2012), provide very different views of Key and slavery.

4 Matthew 5–7; Early Lee Fox, *The American Colonization Society, 1817–1840* (Baltimore: Johns Hopkins University Press, 1919), 50–51; Eric Burin, *Slavery and the Peculiar Solution: A History of the American Colonization Society* (Gainesville: University Press of Florida, 2005), 6–19.

5 Slave Trade Act, in *Public Statutes,* Vol. 3, 532–34.

6 Noonan, *The Antelope,* 15–30; Adams, *Memoirs,* Vol. 4, 292; Fox, *The American Colonization Society, 1817–1840.*

7 *Washington Daily National Intelligencer,* March 23, 1825; G. Edward White, *The Marshall Court and Cultural Change, 1815–1835* (Oxford: Oxford University Press, 1988), 158–66.

8 White, *The Marshall Court and Cultural Change,* 158–66; Adams to Wirt, February 7, 1823, in Noonan, *The Antelope,* 84–85; *The Apollon,* 22 U.S. 362 (1824).

9 Berrien to Governor Troup, June 28, 1825, reprinted in the *Savannah Republican,* September 22, 1825; *Washington Daily National Intelligencer,* December 30, 1816; *Albany (NY) Advertiser,* January 18, 1817. See Claude A. Clegg III, *The Price of Liberty,* for a discussion of these continual problems for the ACS. .

10 Delaplaine, *Francis Scott Key,* 232–35. Key's argument in the case called for the Supreme Court to find the law of nations prohibited the international slave trade—see *The Antelope,* 23 U.S. 66, 70–81 (1825).

11 Fox, *The American Colonization Society, 1817–1840*; Eric Burin, *Slavery and the Peculiar Solution: A History of the American Colonization Society*; William M. Meigs, *The Life of Charles Jared Ingersoll* (Philadelphia: J. B. Lippincott, 1897), 130; *Washington Daily National Intelligencer,* February 21, 1825; Edward S. Delaplaine, *Francis Scott Key: Life and Times,* 209.

12 *Charleston City Gazette,* February 15, 1825; *Alexandria (VA) Gazette,* February 24, March 12, 1825; Steven P. Brown, *John McKinley and the Antebellum Supreme Court: Circuit Riding in the Old Southwest* (Tuscaloosa: University of Alabama Press, 2012), 121; Charles Jared Ingersoll, *Inchiquin the Jesuit's Letters, During a Late Residence in the United States* (New York: Riley, 1810), 53; White, *The Marshall Court and Cultural Change, 1815–1835,* 181–83. Justice Todd would die in February of 1826.

13 *Niles' Weekly Register,* April 7, 1821, March 26, 1825; White, *The Marshall Court and Cultural Change, 1815–1835,* 158–59.

14 *Richmond Enquirer*, March 4, 1825; *The Santa Maria*, 23 U.S. 431 (1825).

15 *The Antelope*, 23 U.S. 66, 69–70 (1825).

16 Ibid., 71–73.

17 Ibid., 73–77.

18 Ibid., 77–81.

19 Robert E. Corlew, "Henry S. Foote," http://tennesseeencyclopedia.net/entry.php?rec=475 (accessed March 24, 2014); Henry S. Foote, *Casket of Reminiscences*, 13; *The Antelope*, 23 U.S. 66, 77 (1825).

20 Henry S. Foote, *Casket of Reminiscences*, 13–15; *Savannah Republican*, March 16, 1823.

21 *Alexandria Gazette*, March 3, 1825; *The Antelope*, 23 U.S. 66, 81 (1825).

22 *The Antelope*, 23 U.S. 66, 82–84 (1825).

23 Ibid., 85–86.

24 Ibid., 87–93.

25 Ibid., 93–99; Foote, *Casket of Reminiscences*, 14–15.

26 Biographical Note to the Charles Jared Ingersoll papers (Collection 1812), Historical Society of Pennsylvania, http://www2.hsp.org/collections/manuscripts/i/Ingersoll1812.html#ref7 (accessed April 25, 2014); *The Antelope*, 23 U.S. 66, 99–105 (1825).

27 Three good sources on the jurisprudence of the Marshall Court are White, *The Marshall Court and Cultural Change, 1815–1835*; R. Kent Newmyer, *John Marshall and the Heroic Age of the Supreme Court* (Baton Rouge: Louisiana State University Press, 2001); and Sylvia Snowiss, *Judicial Review and the Law of the Constitution* (New Haven, CT: Yale University Press, 1990).

28 *Washington Daily National Intelligencer*, March 1, 1825.

29 *The Antelope*, 23 U.S. 66, 105–8 (1825).

30 Ibid., 108–10.

31 Ibid., 110–13.

32 Ibid., 113–14.

Chapter Fifteen

1 William P. Mason, *Report of the Case of the Jeune Eugenie* (Boston: Wells and Lilly, 1822); Joseph Story, *A Charge Delivered to the Grand Jury of the Circuit Court of the United States at Its First Maine, May 8, 1820* (Boston: A. Shirley, 1820); Berrien to Harris, March 4, 1825, quoted in Noonan, *The Antelope*, 95–97; *Richmond (VA) Enquirer*, March 25, 1825. See also R. Kent Newmyer, *Supreme Court Justice Joseph*

Story: Statesman of the Old Republic (Chapel Hill: University of North Carolina Press, 1985), 345–50.

2 White, *The Marshall Court and Cultural Change*, 157–200; Newmyer, *John Marshall and the Heroic Age of the Supreme Court*.

3 *Alexandria Gazette*, March 22, 1825; Charles Warren, *The Supreme Court in United States History: Volume Two, 1821–1855* (New York: Little, Brown, 1922, repr. 1999), 69 n. 1; *Gibbons v. Ogden*, 22 U.S. 1 (1824).

4 *The Antelope*, 23 U.S. 66, 114 (1825).

5 Ibid., 116.

6 Snowiss, *Judicial Review and the Law of the Constitution*; *Marbury v. Madison*, 5 U.S. 137 (1803); *McCulloch v. Maryland*, 17 U.S. 316 (1819); *Gibbons v. Ogden*, 22 U.S. 1 (1824).

7 Arthur Nussbaum, *A Concise History of the Law of Nations* (New York: MacMillan, 1947), 102–64; Jean-Jacques Burlamaqui, *The Principles of Natural Law*, translated by Thomas Nugent (Dublin: T.V. Morris, 1838), 119–24; Lynn Hunt, *Inventing Human Rights: A History* (New York: W.W. Norton, 2007), 15–34, 113–45; David Kennedy, "International Law and the Nineteenth Century: History of an Illusion," *Quinnipiac Law Review* 17, (1997): 17.

8 Nussbaum, *A Concise History of the Law of Nations*, 156–250; M.W. Janis, "Jeremy Bentham and the Fashioning of International Law," *American Journal of International Law* 78, no. 2 (April 1984): 405–18; Jeremy Bentham, *Rights, Representation, and Reform: Nonsense upon Stilts and Other Writings on the French Revolution* from *The Collected Works of Jeremy Bentham*, edited by Philip Schofield, Catherine Pease-Watkin, and Cyprian Blamires (Oxford: Oxford University Press, 2002), 317; see also Lynn Hunt *Inventing Human Rights: A History* (New York: W.W. Norton, 2007).

9 *The Antelope*, 23 U.S. 66, 116–19 (1825).

10 Ibid., 119–20.

11 Ibid., 120–21. William Wirt had gestured to the famous Somerset case in his closing before the Court, but Marshall had also read that case closely. In it, Lord Mansfield ruled that slavery was repugnant to the laws of England. The case was popularly understood to say that slavery violated the law of nature and was so "odious" that it could not exist in the English legal system. Mansfield, however, had qualified his ruling, writing, "The state of slavery is of such a nature, that it is incapable of being introduced on any reasons, moral or political; but only positive law, which preserves its force long after the reasons, occasion, and time itself from whence it was created, is erased from

memory: it's so odious, that nothing can be suffered to support it, but positive law." Marshall did not mention the source of his focus on positive law, but Somerset was the most likely culprit. See *Somerset v. Stewart*, 98 ER 499 (1772).

12 *Mima Queen and Child, Petitioners for Freedom, v. Hepburn*, 11 U.S. 290, 295, 299 (1813); Noonan, *The Antelope*, 105–17, provides a convincing and well-supported argument for the votes of the justices in the case. I have depended upon this analysis in my comments, except I believe Duvall was more likely to join Story than Smith Thompson, as Noonan argued.

13 *The Antelope*, 23 U.S. 66, 123–24 (1825).

14 Ibid., 123–27.

15 Ibid., 126–27.

16 Ibid., 126–28.

17 Ibid., 129–30.

18 Ibid., 130.

19 Ibid., 131–32.

Chapter 16

1 Affidavit of William Harrison, May 30, 1825, RG 21, DCG, Box 28, NARA-Atlanta; Affidavit of Thomas Nelson, November 24, 1825, RG 21, DCG, Box 32, NARA-Atlanta; Affidavit of Robert Habersham, December 16, 1825, RG 21, DCG, Box 32, NARA-Atlanta.

2 Michael D. Green, *The Politics of Indian Removal: Creek Government and Society in Crisis* (Lincoln: University of Nebraska Press, 1982), 69–97; Angie Debo, *The Road to Disappearance: A History of the Creek Indians* (Norman: University of Oklahoma Press, 1941, 1979), 72–107.

3 Green, *The Politics of Indian Removal*, 69–97.

4 Edward Harden, *The Life of George M. Troup* (Savannah: E. J. Purse, 1859), 254–99; Jennison, *Cultivating Race*, 189–200.

5 Michael D. Green, *The Politics of Indian Removal*, 69–97; *Journal of the Executive Proceedings of the Senate of the United States, Volume 3* (Washington, D.C.: Duff Green, 1828), 424. Adams did not even mention it in his usually complete *Memoirs*.

6 *Savannah Georgian*, March 19, 1825.

7 McCrary Jr., "John Macpherson Berrien," 108–14; Berrien to Lumpkin, May 31, 1825, Joseph Henry Lumpkin family papers, MS 192, Hargrett Rare Book and Manuscript Library, University of Georgia Libraries.

8 Adams, *Memoirs*, Vol. 7, 3–21.

9 *Savannah Georgian*, May 30, 1825; George M. Troup, *Governor's Message*

to the General Assembly of the State of Georgia at the Opening of the Extra Session, May 23, 1825 (Milledgeville: Camar and Ragland, 1825), 7–8.

10 *Augusta Chronicle,* June 1, 1825; *Charleston City Gazette,* June 1, 1825; *Niles' Weekly Register,* July 2, 1825, 277; McCrary Jr., "John Macpherson Berrien," 109–10.

11 *Washington Daily National Intelligencer,* June 30, 1825.

12 Ibid.; McCrary Jr., "John Macpherson Berrien," 110; *Savannah Georgian,* June 11, 1825.

13 Edward L. Tucker, *Richard Henry Wilde: His Life and Selected Poems* (Athens: University of Georgia Press, 1966).

14 Berrien to Troup, June 25, 1825, in Harden, *The Life of George M. Troup,* 304–6.

15 Ibid., 305.

16 Ibid., 306.

17 Troup to Berrien, July 2, 1825, in Harden, *The Life of George M. Troup,* 307–8; Wilde to Berrien, July 15, 1825, in McCrary Jr., "John Macpherson Berrien," 112.

18 *New York Evening Post,* July 28, 1825.

19 Adams, *Memoirs,* Vol. 7, July 21, 1825, 35; *Savannah Georgian,* September 22, 1825.

20 "Marshal's Office, Savannah Georgia, One Hundred and Seventy Seven African Negroes," December 24, 1825, RG 21, DCG, Box 32, NARA-Atlanta; Mulvey, *Vice Consul of Spain v. The United States,* Records of the Supreme Court of the United States, RG 267, microfilm copy, M-214, Roll 72, NARA; *The Antelope,* 24 U.S. 413 (1826).

21 "We hereby certify to the Supreme Court a division of opinion," Mulvey, *Vice Consul of Spain v. The United States,* Records of the Supreme Court of the United States, RG 267, microfilm copy, M-214, Roll 72, NARA-Washington.

22 There is no record extant of Richard W. Habersham's motion on paying the captives the money they had earned. This motion was described in both Francis Sorrel's answer and Judge Cuyler's ruling. "Francis Sorrel in Answer," December 19, 1825, RG 21, DCG, Box 28, NARA-Atlanta; "In the Matter of the Africans of the *Antelope,*" December 31, 1825, RG 21, DCG, Box 32, NARA-Atlanta. .

23 "Francis Sorrel in Answer," December 19, 1825, RG 21, DCG, Box 28, NARA-Atlanta; "In the Matter of the Africans of the Antelope," December 31, 1825, RG 21, DCG, Box 32, NARA-Atlanta.

24 Adams, *Memoirs,* Vol. 7, 97–111; J. Marshall to Samuel Southard, January 1, 1826, in *The Papers of John Marshall,* Vol. 10, edited by

Charles F. Hobson (Chapel Hill: University of North Carolina Press, 2000), 262.

25 Southard to Habersham, January 3, 1826, "Annual Report of the Secretary of the Navy, 1826," in *American State Papers, Naval Affairs*, Vol. 2 (Washington: Gales and Seaton, 1832): 750; *The Antelope*, 24 U.S. 413 (1826).

26 "On Motion of the District Attorney, May 9, 1826," *The Antelope*, Records of the Supreme Court of the United States, RG 267, microfilm copy, M-214, Roll 75, NARA-Washington; *Savannah Georgian*, May 16, 1826.

27 Southard to Habersham, August 10, 1826, in "Annual Report of the Secretary of the Navy, 1826," in *American State Papers*, Vol. 2, 751.

28 "We shall consider the questions arising on the costs," *The Antelope*, Records of the Supreme Court of the United States, RG 267, microfilm copy, M-214, Roll 75, NARA.

29 Ibid.

30 Ibid. The judges did not reveal which one supported the idea of a lien on the freed captives.

31 Examination of William Richardson, December 1, 1826; Examination of John H. Morel, December 1, 1826; Examination of Henry Haupt, December 1, 1826; Examination of Dr. Berthelot, December 1, 1826, all RG 21, DCG, Box 32, NARA-Atlanta.

32 Examination of William Richardson, December 1, 1826; Examination of John H. Morel, December 1, 1826, RG 21, DCG, Box 32, NARA-Atlanta; "The Court proceeded to take testimony," December 1, 1826, RG 21, DCG, Box 30, NARA-Atlanta.

33 *The Antelope*, Records of the Supreme Court of the United States, RG 267, microfilm copy, M-214, Roll 75, NARA-Atlanta.

Chapter 17

1 *Ogden v. Saunders*, 25 U.S. 213 (1827); *The Antelope*, 25 U.S. 546 (1827).

2 *The Antelope*, 25 U.S. 546 (1827); John Macpherson Berrien to John Morel, December 23, 1826, Historical and Special Collections, Harvard Law School Library, Harvard University.

3 Adams, *Memoirs*, Vol. 7, 235–36; Noonan, *The Antelope*, 128–29; *Savannah Georgian*, March 20, 1827.

4 Melvin I. Urofsky, *Biographical Encyclopedia of the Supreme Court: The Lives and Legal Philosophies of the Justices* (Washington D.C.: CQ Press, 2006), 556–61; *Ogden v. Saunders*, 25 U.S. 213 (1827); *The Antelope*, 25 U.S. 546 (1827).

5 *The Antelope*, 25 U.S. 546, 552 (1827); *Mima Queen v. Hepburn*, 11 U.S. 290 (1813).

6 *The Antelope*, 25 U.S. 546, 552–53 (1827).

7 Ibid.

8 John Marshall to Timothy Pickering, March 20, 1826, in *The Papers of John Marshall*, Vol. 10, 277; Fox, *The American Colonization Society, 1817–1840*, 65–77.

9 "Latest from Liberia," December 6, 1826, in *The African Repository and Colonial Journal*, Vol. 2 (Washington: Way and Gideon, 1827), 377; *Savannah Georgian*, May 24, 25, 1827.

10 Adams, *Memoirs*, Vol. 7, 190–93.

11 Ibid., 192–95, 284–85.

12 Ibid., 284–88; *Washington Daily National Journal*, June 20, 1827.

13 Samuel Southard to John H. Morel, June 11, 1827, RG 21, DCG, Box 33, NARA-Atlanta; George P. Todson to the Secretary of the Navy, August 29, 1827, in *American State Papers, Naval Affairs*, Vol. 3 (Washington, D.C.: Gales and Seaton, 1860), 60–61. See also pages 85 and 119.

14 *American State Papers, Naval Affairs*, Vol. 3, 58–61.

15 Ibid.; Ashmun to the Secretary of the Navy, December 22, 1827, in *American State Papers, Naval Affairs*, Vol. 3, 58–61, 144–46.

16 *American State Papers, Naval Affairs*, Vol. 3, 60–61, 145–46; "Ship Norfolk's Company," in *Public Documents Printed by Order of the Senate*, Vol. 9 (Washington, D.C.: Gales and Seaton, 1845), 175–80.

17 Ibid.; R. Randall to the Board of Managers, December 28, 1828, in *The African Repository and Colonial Journal*, Vol. 5 (Washington, D.C.: James Dunn, 1830), 4; J. B. Taylor, *Biography of Elder Lott Cary, Late Missionary to Africa* (Baltimore, 1837), 10–11, 74–78, 92–93.

18 "Ship Norfolk's Company," in *Public Documents Printed by Order of the Senate*, Vol. 9, 175–80.

19 *Savannah Georgian*, March 20, May 20, 1822, October 20, 1824; *Charleston City Gazette*, May 10, 1822, February 3, 1826. Mutiny account, *Providence Patriot*, March 1, 1823.

20 *American State Papers, Naval Affairs*, Vol. 3, 77–85; *Message from the President*, December 2, 1828 (Washington, D.C.: National Journal, 1828), 127–28..

21 Noonan, *The Antelope*, 138–42; *Savannah Georgian*, May 28, 1827; "Resolution of the Senate of Georgia," in Dawson, *A Compilation of the Laws of Georgia*, 104; "To Thomas U. P. Charlton, Proctor of the Spanish Claim from Richd. W. Habersham, Proctor for John H. Morel, October 27, 1827, RG 21, DCG, Box 28, NARA-Atlanta.

22 "Petition of Richard H. Wilde," 170 H.doc 56 (Washington, D.C.: Gales and Seaton, 1828).

23 Ibid.

24 Wilde to Berrien, May 22, 1827, Series One, Folder Five, in the John MacPherson Berrien Papers, #63, Southern Historical Collection, The Wilson Library, University of North Carolina at Chapel Hill.

25 Ibid.

26 Robert Pierce Forbes, *The Missouri Compromise and Its Aftermath: Slavery and the Meaning of America* (Chapel Hill: University of North Carolina Press, 2007), 37–38, 40, 87–88, 109–10, 125–26, 191; *Gales and Seaton's Register of Debates in Congress,* Vol. 4 (Washington, D.C.: Gales and Seaton, 1828), 915, 955–66.

27 *Gales and Seaton's Register of Debates in Congress,* Vol. 4, 2501–03.

Chapter 18

1 Charles F. Hobson, ed., *The Papers of John Marshall,* Vol. X (Chapel Hill: University of North Carolian Press, 2000), 277.

2 *Memorial of Robert Campbell and Geo. B. Cumming, February 11, 1828* (Washington, D.C.: Gales and Seaton, 1828); *Savannah Georgian,* February 7, May 26, 31, 1828.

3 *Memorial of Robert Campbell and Geo. B. Cumming, February 11, 1828,* 3–4.

4 Ralph B. Flanders, "Farish Carter: A Forgotten Man of the Old South," *Georgia Historical Quarterly* 15, no. 2 (June 1931): 142–72; Edward E. Baptist, *Creating an Old South: Middle Florida's Plantation Frontier Before the Civil War* (Chapel Hill: University of North Carolina Press, 2002), 94–96; R. H. Wilde to Gen. Blackshear, February 20, 1825, in Stephen F. Miller, *The Bench and Bar of Georgia,* Vol. 2 (Philadelphia: J. B. Lippincott, 1858), 479.

5 Richmond County, Georgia, 1827 Tax Digest; Richmond County, Georgia, 1830 Tax Digest; Georgia Department of Archives and History, Atlanta; *Augusta Chronicle,* September 13, October 8, 1820.

6 Richard Henry Wilde, *Hesperia: A Poem* (Boston: Ticknor and Fields, 1867), 175.

7 Edd Winfield Parks, *Ante-Bellum Southern Literary Critics* (Athens: University of Georgia Press, 1962), 52–56; Wilde, *Hesperia,* 175.

8 Names from Examination of Henry Haupt, December 1, 1826; Examination of John H. Morel, December 1, 1826; Examination of William Richardson, December 1, 1826, all RG 21, DCG, Box 32, NARA-Atlanta.

9 Irving H. King, *The Coast Guard Under Sail: The U.S. Revenue Cutter Service, 1789–1865* (Annapolis: Naval Institute Press, 1989), 71–76, 103, 147–49.

10 "Letter to the Secretary of the Treasury Concerning the Obstructions

in the Savannah River," in *Executive Documents of the House of Representatives*, Vol. 3 (Washington, D.C.: Duff Green, 1831), Doc. No. 104, 8–40; Bulloch, *A History and Genealogy of the Habersham Family*. As for Morse's painting, see "Samuel Morse's Other Masterpiece," August 16, 2011, http://www.smithsonianmag.com/arts-culture/samuel-morses-other-masterpiece-52822904/?no-ist (accessed July 28, 2013).

11 John H. Morel, 1832 Chatham County Tax Digest; 1834 Savannah Death Register: City of Savannah, as found at Ancestry.com Savannah, Georgia Vital Records, 1803–1966 (database online, http://www.ancestry.com). Provo, UT, USA: Ancestry.com Operations, Inc., 2011.

12 The biographical discussion is based on McCrary Jr., "John Macpherson Berrien."

13 "Trade with the Cherokees," Berrien to Eaton, December 21, 1830, *Opinions of the Attorneys General* (Washington, 1851), 745–47; *Cherokee Nation v. Georgia*, 30 U.S. 1 (1831).

14 "On the Capture of the Spanish Ship Fenix," January 18, 1831, *American State Papers, Naval Affairs*, Vol. 3, No. 435, 865–71. The telling of the *Fenix* story still awaits an eager archival researcher.

15 McCrary Jr., "John Macpherson Berrien," 126–80. Perhaps the best overview of this period is provided by Robert Pierce Forbes, *The Missouri Compromise and Its Aftermath* (Chapel Hill: University of North Carolina Press, 2007), especially 210–73.

16 Captain W. E. Sherman to Edward Hallowell, May 10, 1830, in *The African Repository and Colonial Journal*, Vol. 6 (Washington, D.C.: James C. Dunn, 1831), 114.

17 Gail Swanson, *Slave Ship Guerrero* (n.p.: Infinity Publishing, 2005), 12–16.

18 Ibid., 16–104.

19 *The African Repository and Colonial Journal*, Vol. 8 (Washington, D.C.: James Dunn, 1833): 129–35.

20 Ibid., 198–201.

21 Ibid., 198–201, 210.

22 *The African Repository and Colonial Journal*, Vol. 9 (Washington, D.C.: James Dunn, 1834), 127, 158.

23 Swanson, *Slave Ship Guerrero*, 117–19, *Public Documents Printed by Order of the Senate of the United States* Vol. 9 (Washington, D.C.: Gales and Seaton, 1845), No. 150, 175–80.

24 *Dred Scott v. Sandford*, 60 U.S. 393, 407.

25 William M. Wiecek, "Slavery and Abolition Before the United States Supreme Court, 1820–1860," *Journal of American History* 65,

no. 1 (June 1976): 34–59; Donald M. Roper, "In Quest of Judicial Objectivity: The Marshall Court and the Legitimation of Slavery," *Stanford Law Review* 21, no. 3 (February 1969): 532–59; Theodore Dwight Weld, *The Power of Congress over the District of Columbia* (New York: J. F. Trow, 1838), 39; *The Antelope*, 23 U.S. 66, 121 (1825). James Oakes does a fabulous job tracing briefly the legal implications of slavery based solely on positive law in *Freedom National: The Destruction of Slavery in the United States, 1861–1865* (New York: W. W. Norton, 2013), 2-48.

26 For a nuanced discussion of this, see Frederick Schauer, "Formalism," *Yale Law Journal* 97, no. 4 (March 1988): 509–48. A legal formalist is someone, particularly a judge, who sees the rules of law as standing completely independent of society and politics. Once a law is made, the social and political content is fixed. The job of judges is to apply the law neutrally to the facts of a case. The personal beliefs of the judge, the ethical and moral issues of a case, the social and political context, were all supposed to be extraneous to the legal decision. Legal formalism can be seen as something other than just a guiding judicial principle. Was such formal application of the law simply a mask used by the justices to disguise their real motives? Perhaps it is hard to imagine these justices consciously hiding behind such a mask, but might their decisions also have been a product of the cultural forces of the day? Just as slaveholders from Marshal Morel to William Johnson openly condemned the slave trade and expressed their concern and care for the captives, could the mask have been related to the growing influence of a paternalistic understanding of slavery? Was the mask used to distance the justices from the results of their decisions in the lives of real people? Did masks provide the distance, the "objectivity," needed to follow such a formalistic path?

27 *The Antelope*, 23 U.S. 66, 119 (1825); see W. E. F. Ward, *The Royal Navy and the Slavers: The Suppression of the Atlantic Slave Trade* (London: Allen and Unwin, 1969); Rees, *Sweet Water and Bitter.*

28 Thomas, *The Slave Trade*, 775–85; A. Taylor Milne, "The Lyons-Seward Treaty of 1862," *American Historical Review* 38, no. 3 (April 1933): 511–25.

29 Thomas, *The Slave Trade*, 773; David Eltis, "A Brief Overview of the Trans-Atlantic Slave Trade," Voyages Database, *http://slavevoyages. org/tast/database/search.faces?yearFrom=1825&yearTo=1866* (accessed March 31, 2013).

30 *The Antelope*, 23 U.S. 66, 121 (1825).

Epilogue

1 Adams, *Memoirs*, Vol. 10, 396, 397; Joseph Wheelan, *Mr. Adams's Last Crusade: John Quincy Adams's Extraordinary Post-Presidential Life in Congress* (New York: Public Affairs, 2008), 236.

2 Adams, *Memoirs*, Vol. 10, 396, 397.

3 Howard Jones, *Mutiny on the Amistad* (New York: Oxford University Press, 1987), 81–84, 132–35. Antonio later escaped, and was never sent to Cuba; see Jones, 199–200. This account and all accounts that follow of John Quincy Adams's personal thoughts and actions from November 27, 1840, to April, 2, 1841, come from Adams, *Memoirs*, Vol. 10, 358–455, and Paul C. Nagel, *John Quincy Adams: A Public Life, A Private Life* (Cambridge, MA: Harvard University Press, 1999).

4 Nagel, *John Quincy Adams*, 301–34.

5 Rediker, *The Amistad Rebellion*, 186–91; Adams, *Memoirs*, Vol. 10, 358; Jones, *Mutiny on the Amistad*, 153–54.

6 Adams, *Memoirs*, Vol. 10, 424–25.

7 Ibid., 429.

8 New York *Commercial Advertiser*, February 26, 1841; *New York Log Cabin*, March 6, 1841.

9 *Portland (ME) Weekly Advertiser*, March 16, 1841; *New York Spectator*, March 1, 1841; *New York Long Cabin*, March 6, 1841; *New York Emancipator*, March 11, 1841.

10 Adams, *Argument*, 94–134, 97, 112.

11 Ibid., 125.

12 Ibid., 126, 131, 134–35; *New York Emancipator*, March 11, 1841.

13 Adams, *Argument*, 94, 110,

14 Ibid., 116.

15 *The Amistad*, 40 U.S. 518 (1841); *Salem (MA) Register*, March 15, 1841; Adams, *Memoirs*, Vol. 10, 441, 453–54.

16 *Northern Securities Co. v. United States*, 93 U.S. 197, 400 (1904).

ACKNOWLEDGMENTS

Three great archives were essential to the research for this book: the National Archives and Records Administration in Washington, D.C., the National Archives at Atlanta, and the Georgia Archives. While I worked on this project, the staffs and budgets of these archives suffered continual cuts, reducing public access to the people's documents. This was particularly true for the Georgia Archives, where in 2010 access was reduced to three days per week. In 2011 it became two days per week. By 2012, the Georgia Archive was essentially closed to the public, and the staff was reduced to five people. Later in 2012, Georgia's Secretary of State, facing even more budget cuts, announced that access to the archive would end completely.

Thankfully, a political groundswell saved the Georgia Archives. Archival organizations, historical societies, genealogists, and other interested persons came together and demanded that it be saved. Georgia Governor Nathan Deal listened to these groups and helped arrange emergency funding for the archives. Ultimately, the archives were made a responsibility of the University System of Georgia. This saved public access to state records, even as it burdened the University System with unexpected expenses and responsibilities. While all three archives continue to struggle with inadequate funding, they are still open to the public.

Thus, I am deeply in debt to the long-suffering directors and staffs of these archives, as well as to the organizations, enlightened politicians, and individuals who fought to provide and maintain public access for citizens and scholars. Without this political movement to support our archives, writing this book would have been impossible.

The librarians at Georgia Southern University's Henderson Library provided significant support throughout the writing of this book. The late Marvin Goss, in particular, made certain I had access to everything I needed among the rare books and special collections. Marvin died in 2012, and he is greatly missed. The City of Savannah Research

Library and Archives, the Bull Street Branch of the Live Oak Public Libraries, and the collections at the Georgia Historical Society were all essential for this book. The University of Georgia Libraries Special Collections, the Southern Historical Collection, the Library of Congress, the Boston Public Library, and the Harvard Law School Historical and Special Collections were all important sources for this story. Thanks to the staffs of all these institutions.

My colleagues in the History Department at Georgia Southern University have created a congenial intellectual environment in which scholarship thrives. Cathy Skidmore-Hess, Christina Abreu, Johnathan O'Neill, and Kathleen Comerford all read and commented on portions of the manuscript. Several colleagues allowed me to rattle on repeatedly about the developing manuscript and gently pointed out errors or logical fallacies. Michael Van Wagenen and his Visual History Workshop brought home the need to think spatially about the story and how best to communicate this tale to the wider public. Shannon Browning-Mullis and Inger Wood helped me organize my extensive notes and photographs. Many thanks to all.

A long list of scholars outside of my department read portions of the manuscript, listened to me talk about my ideas, and offered encouragement and suggestions. Among them were Glenn Eskew, Lee Ann Caldwell, John Inscoe, Stan Deaton, David Parker, Sally Haddon, Leslie Harris, Susan O'Donovan, Bruce Baker, Brian Kelly, Jacqueline Jones, Tim Lockley, and John Harris. I am sure I have omitted someone from this list, and for that I ask forgiveness.

Finally, W. W. Norton & Company proved remarkably open to good ideas. Even though I was an unagented author, Steve Forman at Norton was willing to engage in extended email conversations with me about the book. Once he was convinced, he passed me on to Katie Adams at the Liveright imprint of Norton. I did not realize at the time how fortunate I was. Katie Adams guided me in writing the proposal, advocated for the book's publication, and then began the hard work of teaching me how to write. Her contributions greatly improved the book. Cordelia Calvert assisted with choosing illustrations and forcing me to respect deadlines. Without these two wonderful people this would have been a much poorer book.

Finally, my family, Miriam, Naomi, Eleanor, and Alexander, all patiently supported my seemingly endless work on the book. I missed parties, family travel, and visits to our extended kin. I love you all and can only hope that this book to some degree makes up for my absences.

CREDITS

Part One: *The African slave-trade—slaves taken from a dhow captured by the H.M.S.* Undine, *1884.* Library of Congress.

Part Two: The Savannah Exchange, Rev. George White, *Historical Collections of Georgia.* New York: Pudney and Russell, 1855, 313. From the author's collection.

Part Three: *A slave-coffle passing the Capitol,* 1876–1881. Library of Congress.

Part Four: *John Quincy Adams/taken from a daguerreotype by P. Haas; lith. & publ. by P. Haas Wash. City,* ca. 1843. Library of Congress.

Insert

Plate 1: *The Case of the Vigilante, a ship employed in the Slave Trade.* London: Harvey, Darnton, and Co., 1823. Courtesy of the Trustees of the Boston Public Library.

Plate 2: John MacPherson Berrien, 1781–1856. Library of Congress.

Plate 3: *Plan of the city & harbour of Savannah in Chatham County, state of Georgia: taken in 1818,* drawn & published by I. Stouf; engraved by Hughes Curzon & Co., 1818. Courtesy of Hargrett Rare Book and Manuscript Library/University of Georgia Libraries.

Plate 4: *Carte de l'île de Cuba: redigée sur les observations astronomiques des navigateurs Espagnols et sur celles de Mr. de Humboldt,* 1820. Library of Congress.

Plate 5: From RG 21, District Court of Georgia Records, National Archives and Records Administration, Atlanta, Georgia. Photograph by the author.

Plate 6: Cotton field, Retreat plantation, Port Royal Island, South Carolina. Photographed by Hubbard & Mix, Beaufort, South Carolina. Library of Congress.

Plate 7: *Savannah, Georgia (vicinity). Market Place.* Sam A. (Samuel A.) Cooley, 1865. Library of Congress.

Plate 8: *Capitol Washington D.C. 1826/C. Bullfinch [sic] Architect, delt.; H.&J. Stone fecit,* 1826. Library of Congress.

Plate 9: *Francis Scott Key, 1780–1843.* Library of Congress.

Plate 10: *William Wirt, head-and-shoulders portrait, facing left.* Charles Balthazar Julien Fevret de Saint-Mémin, Richmond, 1807 or 1808. Library of Congress.

Plate 11: From the author's collection.

Plate 12: *Chief Justice John Marshall, half-length portrait.* Robert Matthew Sully, 1900–1912. Library of Congress.

Plate 13: *View of Old Supreme Court Chamber from west—U.S. Capitol, Old Supreme Court Chamber, Intersection of North, South, & East Capitol Streets & Capitol Mall, Washington, District of Columbia, DC.* James W. Rosenthal, 2008. Library of Congress.

Plate 14: *Casa Bianca hunting party wagons—Jefferson County, Florida,* ca. 1900. State Archives of Florida, *Florida Memory,* http://floridamemory.com/items/show/146312.

INDEX

abolition, 33

Act for the Abolition of the Slave Trade (1807), xvi, 33

Act for the Punishment of Certain Crimes Against the United States (1790), 118

Act in Addition to the Acts to Prohibit the Importation of Slaves (1819), *see* Slave Trade Act (1819)

Act to Continue in Force An Act to Protect the Commerce of the United States and Punish the Crime of Piracy, and Also to Make Further Provisions for Punishing the Crime of Piracy (1820), 84, 113–14

Act to Prohibit the Importation of Slaves (1807), xvi, 18, 33

Act to Protect the Commerce of the United States and Punish the Crime of Piracy (1819), 113, 118

Adams, Charles Francis, 293, 294

Adams, Charles Francis, Jr., 295, 296

Adams, David, 176

Adams, George, 298

Adams, John, 178

Adams, John Quincy, xiv, 17, 25, 71, 72, 81, 82, 90, 91, 93–94, 97, 104, 109–10, 114, 115, 128, 145, 147–48, 160, 170–71, 175–77, 179, 184–87, 193, 207, 209, 210–11, 212, 213, 224, 226, 227, 242, 243–44, 245, 247, 248, 251, 258, 265, 269, 273, *275*, 279, 281–82, 293, 295–305

Amistad case and, 299–300

Antelope case and, 187, 296–97

assassination threat against, 261–62

diplomatic skills of, 177–78

Jeune Eugenie case and, 180–82

slavery as viewed by, 178

Adams administration, 268, 284

admiralty law, 77, 90, 179

civil cases in, 125

jurisdiction of, 125–26

Africa, xvi, xvii, 4–5, 6, 11, 13, 14–15, 27, 30, 37, 40, 44, 91, 97, 141, 156, 179, 187–89, 208, 210–11, 221, 234, 251, 260–61, 264–67, 292, 293, 297, 302, 304

as dangerous to Europeans, 31

participation in slave trade of, 54–55

Africa (slave ship), 36

African Baptists, 165

African Repository, 290

aguardiente de caña, 14

Alabama, 158, 242

alcohol, 49

Alexander I, Tsar of Russia, 177

Algiers, 31

Alligator (U.S. navy schooner), 179

Amedie (American slave ship), 35

Amedie case, 35–36, 37, 38, 137, 303

Amelia Island, Fla., 22, 23, 65–67, 69, 79, 83, 92, 157, 288

American Colonization Society (ACS), 97, 115, 187, 188, 208–11, 212, 215, 260, 266, 270, 272, 273, 296

Antelope case and, 213–14

American Indians, 282, 284

American Revolution, xiii–xv, 17, 19, 78, 155–56, 201, 282

Amistad (slave ship), xx, 296, 299, 300

Amistad case, xiv, xviii, xx, 295, 297, 300

anasarca, 124

Anciaux, Nicholas, 201

Andrew Low and Co., 89

Anglo-Dutch Treaty (1817), 39

Angola, 54, 59

see also Cabinda, Angola

animo furandi, 119

Anna Maria (Spanish schooner), 28–29, 41

Anne (American ship), 36

Antelope, xi, xvii, xix–xx, 4–6, 12–14, 17, 18, 30, 39, 44, 51–58, 59–65, 80–81, 82–83, 84, 90–91, 94–97, 98, 128, 129–37, 139–43, 150, 156, 188–89, 193–96, 214, 220, 224, 226, 230, 235–37, 255, 265, 266, 273, 280, 287, 300, 302
 captives' conditions on, 95–96
 crew grievances on, 63, 65
 crew of, 81
 documents of, 83
 Florida landing of, 67–68
 Jackson's capture of, 68–71
 missing captives from, 71–72
 piracy case against, 83
 post-capture deaths aboard, 70–73
 sale of, 219, 267–68
 stores of, 14–15
 in Suriname, 62–63
 value of captives of, 91–92
 water supply on, 67–68

Antelope, captives of, 101–5, 113, 129, 145–46, 167, 185–86, 189, 190, 191–92, 224, 239, 279, 283–85, 288–91
 assimilation of, 160
 average age of, 73
 on Berrien's plantation, 240–41
 bill to cancel bonds of, 270–73, 277
 bonding out of, 194–97
 children of, 241
 claims against, 96
 Colonization Society's interest in, 213–14
 deaths among, 103, 160–61
 designation of, 252–53, 255–56, 259–60
 distribution of, 122, 123–24
 dividing up of, 142–43, 150, 170, 218, 221
 Habersham's closing argument for, 136–37
 as hired out, 250
 identity of, 124
 labor use of, 109
 lots drawn by, 159–60
 lottery to divide, 218, 221, 302
 Marshall's opinion on designation of, 236–39
 Morel's lien on, 254–55, 257–58
 on Morel's plantation, 127, 146, 162, 164–65, 172, 255
 mortality of, 110
 names given to, 194–95
 race track housing of, 101, 109–10
 returned to Africa, 251, 253, 263–64
 runaways from, 103
 Savannah's use of labor of, 104–5, 165–67
 Smith piracy case and, 111–22
 Spanish and Portuguese title to, 140–41, 145, 150–51, 236–39
 termination of Morel's control of, 194
 treated as slaves, 123, 127
 valuation of, 143–44
 venereal disease in, 102
 yellow fever among, 103, 109

Antelope case, xi–xii, xv, xvii, xviii–xx, 3, 16, 30, 33, 43, 44, 77, 89–90, 94–95, 98, 105, 111, 112–13, 114, 122, 123, 126, 139–40, 147, 151, 153, 169–72, 175–77, 178–79, 183, 184, 193–94, 197, 204, 207–8, 211, 213–14, 216–18, 222–29, 240–43, 245, 247–49, 257–59, 261, 269, 278, 282, 291–92, 293, 294, 295, 296–98, 299, 300, 301, 302, 303–5
 appeals in, 148–49
 Berrien's arguments in, 218–22
 captives as party to, 90–91
 costs for, 268
 Davies's decision in, 139–42
 designation of, 249–52
 excitement caused by, 228
 Key and, 212–13, 216–18, 219–20
 Key's arguments in, 216–18, 219–20
 oral testimony in, 127–34
 Portuguese claim in, 137–38, 170, 171, 236–39
 Spanish claim in, 236–39, 252
 Spanish-Portuguese deal in, 134–35
 in Supreme Court, 172, 186–87, 207–26, 229–39, 248–49, 252, 257–58
 Supreme Court opinion in, 229–39, 294
 Wirt's argument in, 224–26

Antonio (*ladino* slave), 297

Apalachicola River, 158

Apollon case, 212

"apprenticeship" contracts, 39

Argentina, 22

Arkansas River, 242
Arraganta (Artigan privateer), 27–29, 30, 41–43, 55–57, 64, 90, 96, 119, 120, 121, 129, 130, 133, 134, 140, 149, 170, 235, 236, 237
    citizenship of crew of, 131–32
    deaths of captives of, 61–62
    Portuguese slaves captured by, 59–60
    wreck of, 61–62
    see also Columbia (Venezuelan privateer)
Arrivas, Raymond "Blake," 25, 64, 126, 127
Articles of Agreement, 20
Artigas, José, 22, 27, 42, 60, 63, 69, 121, 131, 132, 134
Ashmun, Catherine Grey, 188, 191
Asia, 282
Asiento, 8–10
Asiento system, 8–10
Askwith, William, 70, 71–72, 129
Athenian (privateer), 25
Atlantic Ocean, 293
Atlantic trade, 5
Augusta, Ga., 170, 202, 246, 277
Augusta Chronicle, 245, 279
Aury, Louis, 66
Ayers, Eli, 187–88
Azores, 190

Bahamas, 64, 114, 120, 162
Bahamas Bank, 64
Bahia, Brazil, 83
Baldwin, Roger, 296, 297, 300, 304
Baltimore, Md., 16, 18–25, 41, 42, 64, 83, 84, 116, 118, 119, 131, 132, 134, 139, 186–87, 188–90, 192, 209, 235, 268
    privateers from, 20, 25
    yellow fever in, 24
Baltimore clippers, 18, 21
Baltimore Customs House, 20
Banda Oriental (Oriental Republic), 22, 23, 27, 42, 60, 63, 70, 114, 121, 131, 132, 134
Bank of the State of Georgia, 87
Bank of the United States, 196, 277
Bank of the United States v. Bank of Georgia, 229
bankruptcies, 257
Bantu languages, 54
Baptist Church, 200

Barbour, James, 244
Barbour, Philip, 301
Bargello, 280
barracoons, 49
Bath, England, 88
Bella Dora (Spanish schooner), 32, 40
Bentham, Jeremy, 177, 232
Berrien, Eliza Anciaux, 201, 202, 286
Berrien, Eliza Hunter, 286
Berrien, John Macpherson, xi, xii–xiii, xv, xix, 95, 108, 116–17, 118, 120, 128, 135–36, 146, 148, 152, 196–206, 207, 212, 216, 219–22, 227–29, 236, 237, 239, 240, 241, 242, 243, 245–46, 248, 250, 258, 267, 270, 271–72, 278, 291–92
    Antelope case and, 204–5, 218–19
    Antelope case profits of, 283–87
    as attorney general, 285–86
    captives bonded by, 196–97
    childhood and education of, 197–98
    Clay's practice taken over by, 200
    closing argument of, 136
    and direct election of Georgia governor, 205
    early law practice of, 198–99
    as expert on admiralty law, 126
    father defended by, 199–200
    political career of, 205–6
    resignation of, 145
    Savannah law practice of, 200–202
    as superior court judge, 202–4
    Troup and, 246–47, 248
    as U.S. senator, 206
    Wilde's friendship with, 246
Berrien, Major John, 197, 198–200
Berrien, Margaret Macpherson, 197
Berrien, Richard M., 108
Berthelot, John B., 255, 256
Bethesda Orphans Home, 77
Bight of Biafra, 11
Bill of Rights, 298
Billy (*Antelope* captive), 160
Black Seminole, 156
Bladensburg, Battle of, 208
blue Guinea cloth, 14–15, 49
Boatswain (*Antelope* captive), 160
boatswains, 131
Bolívar (Colombian privateer), 281

Bolton, John, 168
Bonny, 35
Boon's livery stable, 88
Bordeaux, France, 184
Boston, Mass., 86, 179–80
Boston Advertiser, 228
Bourbon reforms, 9
bozales, 11
Bradshaw, Thomas, 27, 119
Brazil, xvi, 18, 22, 46–47, 59, 60, 61–62, 67,
    83, 96, 119, 235
    slave trade dominated by, 45–46
Brent, Daniel, 179–80
Brión, Luis, 16, 24
Bristol, R.I., 43
British Guyana, 62
British Midlands, 164
Broken Arrow, 242
brokers, 48
Brown, George, 24
Brunswick, Ga., 92
Brunton, William, 119, 130, 237
Bryan County, Ga., 72, 280, 283
Bryan Neck, Ga., 162
Buenos Aires, Argentina, 60
Bulloch, Archibald S., 82, 89, 91, 92, 168,
    186
Bulloch, James S., 82, 93
Bulloch, William B., 108, 128, 281–82
Bulloch County, Ga., 201, 202
Bulloch family, 162, 171, 186
Bulwer-Lytton, Edward, 280
"bundle," 48–49
Burke County, Ga., 170
Burlamaqui, Jean-Jacques, 232
Bushrod Island, 287
Butler, Pierce, 101

Cabinda, Angola, xxi, 43, 44–51, 53–58, 59,
    67, 110, 119, 133, 134, 167, 195, 255,
    272
    ethnicity of slaves in, 53–54
Cabinda Bay, 44, 50, 51, 57
Cádiz, Spain, 4, 8, 42
Calabar, Nigeria, 11
Caldwell (place), 291
Caldwell, Elias B., 208, 213, 2112
Calhoun, John C., 184–85, 186, 246
Campbell, Robert, 277–78

Canada, 7
Cape Mesurado, 37, 188, 190–91, 251, 260,
    263
Cape Mount, 40, 41
Cape Town, 293
Cape Verde Islands, 26–27, 34
capitalism, finance, 26
Capitol, 214, 300
Caribbean, 7, 18, 21, 22, 27, 60, 63, 64,
    81–82, 120, 163, 293
Carpenter's Row, 86
Carricabura, Arieta & Co., 112
Carter, Farish, 278, 281
Cary, Lott, 266
Casa Bianca, 278–79, 280, 281
Cayenne, 62
Celia (*Antelope* captive), 124
Centinella (privateer), 182, 183–84
Centinella case, 182–84, 186, 281
Central of Georgia Railroad, 287
Charles III, King of Spain, 7–8, 10
    reforms of, 9
Charleston, S.C., 3, 35, 65, 68, 78, 84, 107,
    128, 147, 165, 166, 267, 281
Charleston City Gazette, 245
Charleston Times, 65
Charlton, Emily, 108
Charlton, Thomas U. P., 81, 92–93, 96, 104,
    106, 107, 108, 117, 126–27, 130, 144,
    146–47, 148, 203, 205–6, 212–13, 219,
    249, 255, 267, 268
Charlton, Tippo, 267
Chatham County, Ga., 72, 283
Chatham County Courthouse, 89–90
Chatham County Inferior Court, 161
C. H. Bustamante and Co., 4
Cherokee Nation, Cherokees, 158, 284
Cherokee Nation v. Georgia, 284
Chesapeake Bay, 25, 131
Chesapeake Canal, 262
Chioua, Angola, 46
Christian Gospel, 188
churches, 165
Circuit Court for the District of Georgia,
    U.S., 77, 79, 81, 115, 119, 147, 150,
    169–70, 185, 187, 193, 198, 215, 219,
    236, 248–49, 252, 253, 261, 270, 302,
    304
circuit courts, 146, 125–26

Civil War, U.S., 279, 294
Clark, John, 79–80, 176, 266
Clark, Samuel, 196
Clarkesville, Ga., 282
Clarkson, John, 33
Clay, Henry, 177, 208, 210, 214, 251, 262
Clay, Joseph, Jr., 78, 198, 200, 201
Cobb, Thomas W., 206
coffee, 9, 10
Cohen (*Centinella* owner), 183, 184
Collier, George R., 40–41, 42
Colombia, 182–84
Columbia (Venezuelan privateer), 16–18, 22, 24–27, 63, 84, 118, 119, 134, 139
  see also Arraganta (Artigan privateer)
Columbian Museum and Savannah Gazette, 106
commerce clause, 231, 257
commissioned privateers, 20
compensated emancipation, 60
Condorcet, Marquis de, 6
Congo Basin, 50, 53
Congo people, *see* Kongo people
Congo River, 49, 53
Congress, U.S., xii, xv–xvi, xvii, 33, 81, 89, 91, 118, 144, 177, 210, 223, 269, 270, 272–73, 278, 279, 280, 282–83, 284, 295, 298, 300
  Law Library of, 228
  see also House of Representatives, U.S.; Senate, U.S.
Congress of Vienna (1815), 38
Congues, 53
Connecticut, 167, 299
Conrad, Joseph, xxi
Constantia (privateer), 23
Constitution, U.S., xii, xiv–xvi, xvii, xviii–xix, 118, 220, 222, 223, 257, 292
  as legal text, 231
Constitutional Convention, of 1787, xiv
contract clause, 231
coppering, 13
Coppinger, Cornelio, 64–65, 68, 70, 114–15, 119, 120
Coppinger, José María, 64, 68, 114–15, 119, 120
Cornelius Vanderbilt v. John R. Livingston, 229
Cottenham plantation, 161–62, 187, 280, 283, 305

cotton, 84, 87, 88, 162, 166
Court of Common Pleas, 116
courts of mixed commission, 39–40
Crawford, William, 92, 93, 176, 187, 202, 205–6, 210, 248, 251
Crawford/Troup party, 161, 248
Creek Confederacy, 158
Creek Indian Agency, 79
Creek Nation, 22, 157, 158, 241–42, 243–44, 248, 251, 269
Creek territory, 66
Cuba, xii, xvi, xvii, 3–15, 17, 18, 30, 32, 35, 39, 53, 57, 60, 64, 96, 112, 126, 267, 270, 271, 273, 278, 281, 287, 288, 293, 294, 297, 300, 304
  Charles III's reforms in, 9
  plantation system of, 4
  slave population of, 8–9
  slave trade in, 7–8
  smuggling of slaves into, 10
  Spain and importance of, 8–9
Cuesta, Carlos, 13, 56, 57, 142
Cuesta Manzanal y Hermano, 3–4, 5, 11, 12–13, 15, 18, 96, 126–27, 128, 130, 135, 219, 252, 269, 270, 271
Cuesta y Manzanal, Pedro, 10, 12
Cuesta y Manzanal, Santiago de la, xii, 3–4, 5–6, 10–12, 96, 126, 219, 236
Cumberland Island, 158
Cumberland Sound, 71
Cumming, George B., 277–78
Cumming family, 277
curfew, 166
Customs and Court building, U.S., 89
Cuthbert, Alfred, 186
Cuyler, Jeremiah La Touche, 170, 249, 250, 253, 254, 256
Cuyler, Richard R., 286

Dallas (revenue cutter), 59, 68–71, 80–81, 90, 120, 124, 128, 129, 220, 236, 281
Daniell, William C., 101
Dante Alighieri, 280
Davies, William, 80, 81, 93, 104, 105, 117, 119, 121, 126–27, 136, 139–42, 143, 144, 146, 151, 152, 284, 297, 299, 300, 302
  law partnership of, 201–2, 204
  resignation of, 145

Davis's Hotel, 208
Declaration of Independence, xiii–xiv, 6, 234, 302
Deep South, 155, 157
Dei people, 289
De La Motta, Jacob, 102
Del Carmen (Cuban schooner), 28, 29, 41, 42
Derwent (ship), 34
Deveara, Mary, 102
Dick, John, 183–84
Dick (Antelope captive), 160
Dolphin (Portuguese slave ship), 44, 50–52
Doris (brig), 265
Dover, England, 50
Dred Scott, xviii, 291
Dublin, Ireland, 246
dueling, 85
Duvall, Gabriel, 235, 248
D'Wolf, James, 35
dysentery, 31

Early, Eleazar, 184–85, 186, 193
East Indies, 6
Eaton, John, 286
Eaton, Peggy, 286
Eboe people, 289
Eliza "Clarissa" (Antelope captive), 240
Elliott, John, 82, 205
Elmina, Ghana, 48
Elton, John, 92–93
emancipation, 209
Emanuel (Lucy captive), 188
Embargo Act (1807), 18, 34
endemic diseases, 31
Endymion (American slave ship), 28
England, see Great Britain
Enlightenment, 6–7
Episcopal Church, 282
Eppinger, John, 92, 93
Equiano, Olaudah, 61
Europe, 18, 282
Exchange (American schooner), 43, 62, 114, 119, 129, 130, 141–42, 143, 149–50, 160
Exchange case, 181, 182

Factors, 84
Fanny (Antelope captive), 124

federal court system, 146
Federalist Papers, 205
Federalist Party, 147, 199, 202
Fell's Point, Md., 16, 24
Fenix (Spanish slaver), 285
Fenix de Cádiz, see Antelope (slave ship)
Fernandina, Fla., 22, 65–66, 69, 288
Ferrer, Ramón, 297
finance capitalism, 26
First African Baptist Church, 165
First Amendment, 298
First Seminole War, 158–59
Flint River, 22, 79, 241
flogging, 168
Florence, 280
Florida, xi, 22, 65, 67–68, 92, 120, 154, 156, 158–59, 167, 178, 241, 267, 273, 278–79, 281
Florida, Spanish, xvii, 17, 64, 65, 93, 118, 154, 157, 158, 220
Florida (sloop), 263
Florida Keys, 267, 268, 287
Floridas, Republic of the, 22, 66
Florida Straits, 287
Florida Territory, 175, 271
flour, 18, 21
Foote, Henry S., xii, 218–19, 221, 222
Ford, George, 28, 62–63, 129
Foreign Slave Trade Act (1806), 33
formalism, 235
Fort Jackson, Treaty of, 241
France, xvi, 7, 8, 10, 11, 20–21, 25, 27, 32, 34, 36, 37–38, 39, 40–41, 42, 49, 50, 60, 62, 63, 83, 113, 114, 175, 179–83, 184, 212, 221, 241
  slave trade in, 33
Franque, Francisco "Chico," 45–46, 48, 51
Franque family, 46
Fraser, James, 53
free blacks, 97, 229
  African colony for, 208–11
Freetown, Sierra Leone, 32, 34, 37, 42
French, Benjamin, 296
French Revolution, 21
Furlong, John, 82, 83

gag rule, 298
Gallery of the Louvre (Morse), 282
Gallinas River, 27–28, 32, 179, 287

gang labor, 163
General Arismendi (Venezuelan privateer), 111, 112
General Ramirez, see Antelope
George (*Antelope* captive), 124
Georgetown (Washington, D.C.), 209
Georgia, xiii, xiv, xx, xxi, 22–23, 66, 68–73, 77–97, 98–110, 115, 126, 146–47, 159–71, 175–76, 184–87, 197–206, 212, 240–43, 246, 248, 251, 269, 270, 273, 278, 279, 280, 282, 283, 284, 287, 299
  criminal code of, 203
  direct election of governor in, 205
  history of slavery in, 153–59
  land hunger in, 241–42
  slave population in, 156
Georgia Constitution (1798), 203, 205
Georgia General Assembly, 78, 87, 154, 199, 203, 205, 206, 244, 287
Georgia Governor's Council, 78
Georgia Grand Jury, 176
Georgia House of Representatives, 115
Georgia Judiciary Committee, 205
Georgia Superior Court, 116, 128, 202, 206
Georgia Trustees, 153
Ghent, Treaty of, 178
Gibbons v. Ogden (1824), 178, 229, 231
Gilpin, Henry, 300
gins, 164
Glen, George, 141, 143–44, 150, 254
Glen, John, 82
Grampus (Navy schooner), 285
Gran Colombia, 60
Grant, William, 35–36, 303
Great Abaco Island, 64, 67
Great Awakening, 77
Great Britain, xiii–xiv, xvi, xxi, 7–10, 11, 12, 19, 20–21, 25, 48, 53, 60, 62, 78, 83, 125, 126, 137, 154, 155–56, 157–58, 180, 187, 208–9, 214, 217, 223, 233, 241, 258, 292, 293, 294, 304
  Havana occupied by, 8–10
  slave trade outlawed by, 30–31, 45, 149
  suppression of slave trade by, 30–43
Great Rift Valley, 54
Greene, Nathanael, 156
Grimes, William, 167–68
Grondona, Domingo, 13, 51, 55–58, 126, 127, 133, 135, 162, 170, 236, 255, 256, 259

Grotius, Hugo, 232
Grove, Samuel, 35
Guerrero (Spanish slave ship), 287–88
Gulf of Mexico, 158
gunpowder, 49
guns, 49
Gurley, Ralph, 260
Gustavia, 63

Habersham, Alexander Wylly, 282
Habersham, Bernard Elliott, 282
Habersham, Esther Wylly, 78
Habersham, James, 77–78
Habersham, James, Jr., 78, 79, 87, 115
Habersham, John, 78
Habersham, Joseph (cousin), 159–60
Habersham, Joseph (uncle), 78, 282
Habersham, Richard Wylly, xx, xxii, 71, 77, 78–80, 89, 90–91, 95, 96–97, 109, 139, 140, 141, 143, 144–45, 148–49, 159, 162, 185, 186, 195, 226, 243, 249, 250, 252–53, 254, 255, 256, 259, 260, 267, 268–69, 271, 277–78, 281–83, 299–300, 305
  Antelope case and, 127–38, 170–71
  background of, 115
  investigation of Morel by, 193–94
  Politna and *Tentativa* cases and, 93–94
  Smith piracy case and, 111–22
  U.S. claim on *Antelope* captives filed by, 97
Habersham, Richard Wylly, Jr., 282
Habersham, Robert, 195, 240
Habersham, Stephen Elliott, 282
Habersham County, Ga., 282, 283
Habersham and Harris, 78
Hagan, Robert, 37
Haiti, 9, 11, 111
  see also Saint-Domingue
Halfway Farms, 266
Harris, Charles, 96, 104, 117, 126–27, 128, 130, 144, 148, 219, 227, 268
Harris, Francis, 78
Harrison, William, 240
Harrison, William Henry, 287
Haupt, Henry, 255, 256, 281
Havana, Cuba, 3–4, 5, 10–11, 12–14, 15, 32, 39, 42, 44, 96, 112, 126, 141, 267, 268, 304
  British occupation of, 8–10

hearsay, 129, 259
Heart of Darkness (Conrad), xxi
Heath, John D., 66
Henry, Patrick, 178
Hesperia (Wilde), 280
Hetty (*Antelope* captive), 240
Hibernian Society, 242–43
High Court of Admiralty, 32, 34, 35, 37, 40,
    125
High Court of Chancery, 35
Hill, Henry W., 143–44
Hole in the Wall, 64, 65, 67
Holland, 38–39, 60, 62
Holmes, John, xv
Holmes, Oliver Wendell, Jr., 305
Hope, Despair, 267
Hope (schooner), 26
Horace (*Antelope* captive), 160
Hornet, USS, 182, 183, 184
House of Representatives, U.S., 227, 246,
    251, 272, 277, 279, 280, 296, 299–300
    Judiciary Committee of, 272
    see also Congress, U.S.
Houston, Sam, 284
Huntt, Henry, 261
Hyde de Neuville, Baron, 181

Igbo people, 288, 289
independence movements, 21–22
    Spanish American, 17
Independent Presbyterian Church, 202
Indian Mission, U.S., 22
Indian Springs, 241
Indian Springs, Treaty of (1821), 241, 242,
    243
Indian Springs, Treaty of (1825), 242, 244,
    251, 268–69
individual natural rights, 232
Ingersoll, Charles Jared, 177, 214, 216,
    222–23, 228, 229, 258
international law, 232
Ireland, 243
Isabelita (Spanish Slave ship), 22
Isabelita case, 79–80
Isla de Margarita, 22, 23

Jackson, Andrew, 67, 158, 175, 209, 210, 241,
    251, 284, 286, 298
Jackson, Fort, 241

Jackson, James, 199, 202, 205
Jackson, John, 59, 71–72, 83, 90, 91, 96, 117,
    120, 126, 128–29, 148, 152, 197, 268,
    281, 283, 284
    in capturing of *Antelope*, 68–71
    final salvage award of, 145
    salvage bounty due to, 124–25, 136,
        141–42, 144–45, 151–52
    salvage claim of, 95
Jackson, Rachel, 286
Jackson administration, 284, 285, 286
January (*Antelope* captive), 160, 240
Jay, William, 88, 89, 91
Jay's Treaty (1795), 147
Jefferson, Thomas, xiii–xiv, xv–xvi, 147, 176,
    178, 198, 205
Jefferson County, Fla., 278–79
Jeffersonian Republicans, 161, 187, 199,
    202, 205
Jenckes, Ebenezer, 256
Jenkins, John, 266
Jeune Eugenie (French schooner), 179–80,
    221
Jeune Eugenie case, 179–83, 218, 227, 230,
    235
Jim (*Antelope* captive), 160
Joe (*Antelope* captive), 256
Johns (*Antelope* captives), 160
Johnson, Samuel, 61
Johnson, William, 80, 119, 147–52, 159–60,
    169–70, 171, 187, 193, 194, 215, 218,
    219, 249, 253, 254, 256, 297, 302, 305
Josefa Segunda (Cuban slave ship), 111–12
Josefa Segunda case, 111, 112, 113, 122, 123,
    140
Juan (ship), 11–12
judicial review, 203
Junta Central (ship), 11

Kant, Immanuel, 7
Kentucky, 177, 208
Key, Francis Scott, xi–xii, xiii, xix, 208–10,
    213–14, 215, 216–18, 219–22, 223, 226,
    227, 228, 230, 232, 234, 235, 239, 246,
    258, 259, 260, 261, 292, 296, 297, 300,
    305
    Antelope case and, 212–13, 216–18,
        219–20
    in opposition to slave trade, 212

Key Largo, Fla., 288
Key, Philip Barton, 209
Key West, Fla., 288
Kikongo languages, 54, 127, 159, 195
Kirkland (*Centinella* owner), 183, 184
Kituba language, 54
Klintock, Ralph, 81, 82–83
Knight, James D., 70–71, 83, 120, 129
Kokelo, Franque, 45
Kongo kingdom, 53, 54, 55
Kongo people, 53, 54, 288, 289, 290

labor, task system of, 163
Lafayette, Marquis de, 243
La Pensee (French slave ship), 182, 183, 184
La Pensee case, *see Centinella* case
La Roche, Isaac, 167
La Rochelle, France, 83
Larrinaga, Bonifacio Gonzáles, 11
Latrobe, Benjamin, 215
Law, William, 128, 130, 132, 133, 151
Law Library of Congress, 228
law of nations, 182, 216–17, 221, 230
    slave trade and, 148–49, 171, 182, 183,
        213, 218, 221–23, 224–25, 227, 232–35,
        292–93
    sources for, 231–34
law of nature, 218, 221, 232, 234
Leeke, Augusta Sophia Dashwood, 31
Leeke, Henry John, 30–32, 40, 41–42, 43, 44
Le Louis (French slave ship), 37–38
Le Louis case, 37–38, 42
letter of marque traders, 20
letters of marque, 19–20
libel, 90, 125
Liberia, 97, 190, 191, 211, 213, 251, 260–61,
    264–67, 268, 272, 273, 287, 288,
    290–91, 296, 305
Liberia Herald, 290
Liberty County, Ga., 197
Liddy (*Antelope* captive), 240
Lincoln, Abraham, 262, 293
Lincoln administration, 293–94
Little Mingo (*Antelope* captive), 160, 189
Liverpool, England, 161, 162–63
Livingston, Henry Brockholst, 112
Llovio, Don Vicente de, 5, 13, 44, 51–53, 54,
    56, 57–58
Loango, 11

London, England, 11, 32, 35
Lopez de Castro, Nicolas, 4–5
Lords Commissioners, 35
Loring, Ellis Gray, 297, 299
Louis case, 233
Louisiana, 112
Louisiana (revenue cutter), 281
Louisiana, University of (at New Orleans),
    see Tulane University
Louisiana Purchase, 17, 178
Louisville, Ga., 198, 200
Low, Andrew, 89
Loyalists, 155–56
Luanda, Angola, 5, 48
Lucy (slave ship), 188
Ludlam, Thomas, 34
Lukola River, 50
Lunda, 54, 55
Lyons-Seward Treaty of 1862, 293

Madison, James, xiv, 157, 176
Madrid, Spain, 8
Madungoes, 53–54
Maguibel, Fernando, 13
Major (*Antelope* captive), 160, 189
Majumbas, 53
malaria, 31, 85, 98–99, 124, 191, 265
Malcontents, 154
malignant fever, 99
Malory, Charles, 223–24
mambouk, 45, 49
Manna Point, 28
Manna River, 27, 28, 41
Mansfield, Lord, 204
Marbury v. Madison (1803), 231
Maria (*Antelope* captive), 124
Marion (cutter), 281
Marlow (char.), xxi
maroons, 158, 167
Marshall, John, xviii–xix, 3, 16, 30, 44, 59,
    77, 98, 111, 119, 123, 139, 147, 153,
    175, 193, 198, 207, 212, 214, 216, 218,
    223, 227, 228, 229–31, 232–39, 246,
    247–48, 251, 252, 257, 261, 267, 277,
    291, 292, 293, 294, 302, 303, 305
    on slave trade, 230
Marshall Court, 211, 231
marshal's bill, 260, 270
Martinique, 37

Mary (American schooner), 64, 114

Maryland, 87, 286

Mason, Jonathan, 86

Mason, Lowell, 202

Mason, Mr., 64, 65, 67

Matthews, George, 157

Mayombe, 50

Mayumba, Gabon, 53

McCulloch, James, 25

McCulloch v. Maryland (1819), 178, 231

McGregor, Gregor, 65–66, 83

McHenry, Fort, 209

McIntosh, John H., 157

McIntosh, William, 92, 241, 242, 243–44

McKim, Isaac, 24

Mechlin, Joseph, 289–90

Mekiah/Mariah (*Antelope* captive), 124

Mengs, Anton Raphael, 7

Mercer, Charles Fenton, 272

Mesurado River, 266

Metcalf, Simon, 22–28, 41, 42–43, 56–57, 59–62, 63, 66, 120

Mexico, 7, 17, 212

Mexico City, Mexico, 3

Michael (interpreter), 159

Middle Passage, 264

Middleplace plantation, 161

Milledge, Catherine Elliott Habersham, 282

Milledge, John, Jr., 282

Milledge, John, Sr., 282

Milledgeville, Ga., 79, 80, 115, 147, 242, 248–49, 252

Millen, George, 196

Mima Queen (slave), 235

Mima Queen and Child, Petitioners for Freedom, v. Hepburn, 235, 259

Mingo (*Antelope* captive), 160

Mississippi River, 111

Missouri, xii, xvii, 177, 178, 231, 272

Missouri Compromise, 181

Mitchell, David B., 23, 79–80, 94, 115

Mobile, Ala., 165

Monroe, James, 17, 67, 71, 82, 88, 89, 114, 146, 157, 171, 175–79, 184–87, 193, 198, 207, 210, 211, 212

    Jeune Eugenie case and, 179–83

Monroe administration, 40, 207

Monrovia, Liberia, 211, 264, 287, 288, 291

Montevideo, Uruguay, 22, 23, 60, 83

Morel, Catherine Waldburg, 161–62

Morel, John Henry, 72, 82–83, 90, 91, 93, 94–95, 102, 103–4, 109–10, 123, 124, 127, 129, 146, 151, 159, 160, 161–62, 166, 169, 170, 172, 175–76, 184–87, 195–96, 249, 250, 256, 257, 259, 260, 263, 267, 269, 270, 280, 281, 282, 283, 284, 305

    bill for maintenance of captives submitted by, 161, 193, 253–55, 258

    Habersham's investigation of, 193–94

    reappointment of, 176, 186–87, 207

    slaves owned by, 164

    viciousness of, 185, 207

Morel, Peter Henry, 161

Morel, Sarah Alger, 162

Morel, Tryphenia, 161

Morrison, James, 96, 128, 146

Morrison, John, 24, 130–31, 144

Morrison, Thomas, 27

Morse, Samuel, 282

Morton Hall plantation, 197, 201, 240, 286

Moses (runaway slave), 167

mosquitoes, 99–100, 101

Mubiri traders, 53

Mulvey, Charles, 96, 128, 219, 249

Mulvey, Joseph, 249

Myrmidon, HMS, 31–32, 40, 41–42

Nakata Kolombo family, 45, 46

Nancy (slave ship), 36

Naples, Italy, 7

Napoleon I, Emperor of France, xvi, 11, 31, 32, 33, 34, 45, 62

Napoleonic Wars, xvi, 12, 18, 21, 32, 33, 36, 38, 45, 63

National Intelligencer, 211

natural law, 216–17, 218, 232

Navy, U.S., 34, 66, 129, 182, 188, 193, 210, 260, 268, 283, 285

Navy Department, U.S., 187

Ned (*Antelope* captive), 160, 189–90, 256

Negro Fort, 158

Nelly (*Antelope* captive), 240

Nelson, Thomas, 240

Netherlands, 8, 21, 32, 38–39, 48, 62, 63

Neutrality Acts (1818), 17, 18, 34, 131, 132

neutrality law, 139

New Georgia, Liberia, 266, 287, 288–91

New Jersey, 167

New Jersey, College of, 78, 147, 197
    see also Princeton University
New Leeds, 85
New Orleans, La., 107, 112, 152, 182, 183,
    196, 261, 281, 285
Newton, Ann, 102
Newton, Isaac, 6
New York, N.Y., 3, 18, 83, 84, 294
New York state, 156, 167, 197, 229, 272, 293
New York Tribune, 102
Ngoyo, 45, 46–47
Nicholson (sailor), 130
Nicholson, Thomas, 26
Nicoll, John, 96, 128, 130, 133, 144
Nigeria, 35
Niles, Hezekiah, 25, 66
Niles' Weekly Register, 21, 24, 65, 66, 87, 108
Nimble, HMS, 287–88
Nkata Kolombo, Loemba ("Black Prince of
    Tef") ("King Jack"), 44–46, 47, 51, 57
Norfolk (American ship), 261, 262, 263–64,
    267, 268, 291
Norfolk, Va., 264
Northern Securities Co. v. United States, 305
Notes on the State of Virginia (Jefferson), 205
Nova Scotia, 156
Npuna family, 45, 46

Oakgrove plantation, 286
Oakhill plantation, 179
Ocmulgee River, 241
Odingsells, Anthony, 169
Ogden v. Saunders, 257, 259
Ogeechee plantation, 159, 162, 172
Ogeechee River, 72, 79, 127, 162, 201, 256
Oglethorpe, James, 153
Oglethorpe Ward (Savannah, Ga.), 107, 108,
    166
Ohio Canal, 262
Oklahoma, 284
Old Calabar, 288
Orders of Council, 36
Oregon, 282
O'Reilly, Alejandro, 9
Ossabaw Island, 161
Owen, William Fitz William, 47, 50

Panic of 1819, 23, 88, 89, 91, 162, 196
Paraguay, 134

Parliament, 33, 161
Patriots, 156, 157
Patriot War, 157
Patterson, Joseph, 24
Patterson, William, 19
Paul (*Antelope* captive), 160
Paxaro (Cuban brig), 58
Pay (*Antelope* captive), 240
Peaco, John W., 261, 262
Pendergast, Domino, 4
Pennsylvania, 214
Peru, 7
Pesa people, 289
Peter, King, 188
Philadelphia, Pa., xiv, 3, 83, 107, 177, 189,
    197, 222, 267, 290
Phoenix Fire Company of London, 89
Pickering, Timothy, 277
Pink House, 78
piracy, pirates, 8, 16–17, 19, 26, 37, 41–42,
    43, 52, 64, 77, 105, 111, 112–14, 116,
    118, 130–31, 140, 182, 234
    definitions of, 118–19
    intent requirement for, 119, 121
    punishment for, 81–82
    U.S. law on, xv, 81
    see also privateers, privateering
Piracy Act (1820), xv
"plantation complex," 26
plantations, 154, 155, 156, 163, 164
plantation system, 4, 157, 159
Planter's Bank of the State of Georgia, 87
Point Peter, 71
Politina (slave ship), 92, 94, 123
Poor House and Hospital, 107, 108, 115
Portugal, xiv, 22, 26, 27, 32, 36, 39, 42, 43,
    44, 45–46, 48, 49, 52, 56, 57, 59, 60,
    90, 96, 105, 113, 122, 128, 130, 133,
    134, 135, 137–38, 140–44, 145, 148,
    149, 150, 151, 159, 169, 170, 171, 214,
    216–18, 219, 222, 225, 226, 233, 234,
    235, 236, 237–39, 250, 253, 254, 256,
    258, 267, 269, 270, 292
    slave trade dominated by, 45–46
Price (*Antelope* officer), 129
Prigg v. Pennsylvania, xviii
Prince Regent (British schooner), 192
Princeton University, 78, 117, 206
    see also New Jersey, College of

privateers, privateering, 16–17, 19–20, 21–23, 25, 26–27, 52, 64, 66, 81, 118, 119, 131, 179
    types of, 20
    see also piracy, pirates
Prospect Bluff, 158
Providence, R.I., 267
Providence Channel, 64, 65
public speaking, 214
Puerto Rico, 126
Pulaski Monument Association, 277

Queen Charlotte (Royal Navy schooner), 37–38
Quincy, Mass., 298

Rabun County, Ga., 283
Rae's Hall plantation, 195
raffia cloth, 48–49
Ramirez, Francisco, 134
Randall, Richard, 262, 265, 266
Randolph, John, 208
recaptives, 264
Red Stick Creeks, 158, 241
reform movements, 205
remittent fever, 98–99
Reports of Cases Argued and Adjudged in the Supreme Court, 229
Republican Party, 202, 205, 206
Reuben (slave), 168
Revenue Cutter Service, U.S., 117
Revenue Marine, U.S., xi, 69
Revolutionary War, *see* American Revolution
Rhode Island, 18, 300
rice, 154, 162
Richardson, Richard, 91, 196
Richardson, William, 94–95, 102, 103, 104–5, 124, 127, 146, 159, 160, 195, 255, 256, 260, 281
Richmond, Captain, 43
Richmond, Va., 266
Richmond Baths, 202
Richmond County, Ga., 279
right to search, 37–39, 40–41, 180–81, 233
Rio de Janeiro, Brazil, 45, 51, 60
Río de la Plata, 22
Rochambeau, General, 201
Roche, José Manuel, 4

Roman Empire, xxi
Rousseau, Jean-Jacques, 6
Royal Navy, 30–38, 40, 294
    and slave trade suppression, 34
Rupell, John M., 124
Rush, Richard, 281
Russell, Henry P., 108–9

St. Augustine, Fla., 67, 68, 157, 288
St. Barthélemy, 63–64, 67
St. Catherines Island, 195
Saint-Domingue, 9, 10, 11
    revolution in, 11
    see also Haiti
St. Johns River, 67, 70
St. Martin/St. Maarten, 63, 67, 83
St. Marys, Ga., 68–71, 90, 129
St. Marys River, 66, 69
St. Simons Island, 162
St. Thomas, 83
Salinas River, 27
salt beef, 67
salvage, 90, 151–52
salvage awards, 144, 145
Sambo (*Antelope* captive), 195
Samuel Benjamin (*Lucy* captive), 188
San Carlos, Fort, 65–66
San Juan, Puerto Rico, 58
San Lorenzo el Real, Treaty of (1795), 220
Santa Maria case, 215
Sao Panela (Portuguese slave ship), 44, 51–52
Sao Tiago, 26
Sao Vicente, 26
Saranac, USS, 92
Savannah, Ga., xix, xxi, 3, 65, 70–73, 77–82, 83, 89–96, 98–99, 114–16, 118, 121, 123, 126, 129, 143, 145–46, 150, 155, 156, 159–61, 164–71, 183, 184, 188, 192, 194, 197–98, 200, 202–6, 219, 227, 241, 243, 249–50, 252, 253–54, 255, 261, 262, 263, 264, 267, 268, 269–70, 277, 278, 279, 281, 282, 283, 286–87, 291, 302, 305
    Antelope captive labor used in, 104–5, 165–67
    economic growth of, 87–88
    1820 fire in, 88–89, 91, 101
    exports of, 88
    markets in, 168–69

Oglethorpe Ward in, 107, 108, 166
Orleans Square in, 162, 283
population of, 84–85, 87, 166
race track in, 101–2
runaway slaves in, 103
sand streets of, 86
slaves in, 87
Washington Ward in, 107
yellow fever in, 99–103, 105–10
Savannah City Council, 86, 104, 169
Savannah City Exchange, 81, 85, 89, 106,
    142, 168
Savannah Daily Georgian, 81, 101, 106, 192,
    145, 183
Savannah Literary Association, 202
Savannah Mercury, 279, 280
Savannah-Ogeechee Canal, 256
Savannah Republican, 81, 106, 114, 119, 121
Savannah River, 85, 94, 195, 198, 201, 281,
    286
Savannah Theatre, 85
Sawney (*Antelope* captive), 160
Scarborough, William, 91
Scott, William, 37–38, 233
Sea Island, 162–64
"seasoning," 143
Second African Baptist Church, 165
Second Great Awakening, 200
Secret Service, 262
Seminole, 157, 158–59, 167, 241
Seminole war:
    first, 158-59
    second, 281
Senate, U.S., 223, 269, 270, 272, 284, 287
    see also Congress, U.S.
Seven Years' War, 7
Seville, Spain, 8, 10
Seward, William, 294
Shakespeare, William, 85
Sheftall, Abraham, 102
Sheftall, Moses, 95, 102
Sherbro Island, 187
Sicily, 7
Sierra Leone, 31, 32, 34, 37, 39, 42, 43, 187,
    293
Silk Hope, 79
silver, 7, 8
Simpson Bay, 63
Sitgreaves, Samuel, 189

Sixth Circuit Court, U.S., 142, 144
slave marriages, 278
slave pens, 49
slave rebellion, 212
slaves, slavery, 5–6, 8, 10, 21, 26, 27, 33,
    78, 87, 141, 177, 182, 210, 234, 243,
    244–45
    Adams's views on, 178
    critique of, 7
    cross-border bartering of, 92–93
    disciplining of, 164
    escaped, 167
    gag rule and, 298
    Georgian history with, 153–59
    Johnson's view of, 148–49
    justifications for, 92
    Key's *Antelope* arguments against, 219–20
    largest sale of, 101–2
    plantation, 154, 155, 156, 163, 164
    positive laws on, 222–23, 234–35, 291–92
    racial identification of, 136
    recaptured Africans as, 92–93
    in Savannah, 87
    sectional conflict over, 207
    Story's views on, 180
    violence in, 167–68
slave trade, 3, 4–5, 16, 27, 33, 60, 111, 141,
    167, 171, 180, 216, 217, 223, 231, 261
    African participation in, 54–55
    Amelia Island and, 66–67
    American law as pledge to world on, 216,
        220–21
    Antelope case and, 148–49
    Antelope opinion's impact on, 293–94
    Asiento system in, 8–10
    Baltimorean avoidance of ban on, 18–19
    Brazilian/Portuguese dominance of,
        45–46
    British and American prohibition against,
        11, 12
    British outlawing of, 30–31, 45, 149
    British suppression of, 30–43
    changes in, 11
    in Cuba, 7–8
    dangers of, 5
    Dutch outlawing of, 62
    French, 33
    growth of Cuban participation in, 12
    illegal, 23, 77, 79–80, 81, 82, 115

slave trade (*continued*)
  Key's opposition to, 212
  law of nations and, 148–49, 171, 182,
    183, 213, 218, 221–23, 224–25, 227,
    232–35, 292–93
  law of nature and, 234
  Marshall on, 230
  mongrel vessels in, 12
  privateering in, 22–23, 26–27
  right to search and, 37–39, 180
  shipboard deaths in, 61, 72–73
  smuggling in, 79
  U.S. domestic, 87
  U.S. patrols against, 184
  U.S. prohibition of, 11, 12, 18, 33–34, 35
  U.S. suppression of, 179, 210
Slave Trade Act (1807), 139, 224
Slave Trade Act (1818), 139
Slave Trade Act (1819), xvii, 77, 90–91, 95,
    97, 112, 113, 122, 132, 136–37, 139,
    140, 141, 144, 148, 150, 179, 183, 186,
    193, 210, 216, 260, 285
Slave Trade Law (1819), 213, 268
Slidell, John, 285
Smith, Adam, 6
Smith, Alexander, 34
Smith, John, 24–25, 28–29, 55, 56, 60, 62,
    64–70, 80, 81, 85, 90, 132, 134, 135,
    141, 142, 144, 148, 151, 170, 197, 220,
    226, 237
  Artigan commission of, 131, 132, 134
  citizenship of, 84, 129–30
  as claimant on *Antelope* property, 128,
    132
  claims of, 139–40
  as engaged in slave trade, 136–37
  flight to Baltimore by, 116
  payment for defense of, 117–18
  personal papers of, 83–84
  piracy case against, 105, 111–22, 140
  as privateer, 131
Smith, Samuel, 23
Smith and Buchanan, 23
smuggling, 18, 66, 79
Social Contract (Rousseau), 6
Somerset case, 223
Sophia (*Antelope* captive), 124
Sorrel, Francis, 96, 140–41, 196, 250, 270
Southard, Samuel, 251, 252, 253, 262

South Carolina, xiv, xv, 147, 148, 154–55
South Carolina Circuit Court, 151
sovereignty, as authoritative source of law, 232
Spain, 5, 7–9, 11, 17, 18, 20–21, 22, 27, 32,
    36, 39, 43, 44, 52, 60, 67, 90, 96, 113,
    117, 122, 130, 135, 137, 140–44, 148,
    149, 150, 151, 154, 157, 158–59, 169,
    170, 171, 175, 178, 216–17, 219, 220,
    221, 222, 224–25, 226, 233, 234, 235,
    236, 237, 241, 249, 252, 254, 255, 256,
    258, 259–60, 261, 268, 270, 278, 281,
    285, 292
Spanish American independence move-
    ments, 17
Spanish Main, 18
Spartan (U.S. sloop), 188, 192
Spielberg, Steven, xviii
spoils, 205
Spring Hill, 85, 94, 159
Stanton, Patrick, 99
"Star-Spangled Banner, The," xi, 209
states' rights, 282–83
Stay Law, 203
Steamboat Company of Georgia, 91
Stephens, John, 56–57, 119–20, 130
Stephens, William, 93
Stockton, Robert, 179, 180, 187–88
Stockton Creek, 266, 287, 289
Story, Joseph, 118–19, 120, 125, 180–81,
    182, 183, 215, 218, 227, 228, 230, 232,
    234, 235, 304
  slavery as viewed by, 180
"strict law," 231
Strong (American brig), 188–90, 264, 268, 291
Sturgis, Oliver, 143–44
Successor (privateer), 22
sugar, 9, 10, 21, 62, 63
  price drops of, 21
Superbe (French privateer), 11
Supreme Court, U.S., xi–xiv, xv, xvii–xxi, 23,
    81, 111, 116, 118, 125–26, 135, 146, 147,
    171–72, 177, 178–82, 184, 185, 186, 194,
    203, 243, 245, 246, 249–55, 256, 257–59,
    261, 268, 269, 284, 285–86, 291–93, 294,
    295, 296–98, 299, 300–305
  Antelope case and, 172, 186–87, 207–26,
    229–39, 248–49, 252, 257–58
  Apollon case and, 212
  chamber of, 214–15

Constitutional powers of, 223
demanding case load of, 211-12, 228
oral arguments before, 214
privateering cases before, 179–80
Segunda case and, 112
Suriname, 39, 62–63, 67, 68, 120, 129, 130
Suriname River, 62
Suwannee River, 158
Sweden, 63
Sylvia (runaway slave), 167
Syrina (slave ship), 92

Tafe Point, 46, 51
Talbot, Matthew, 176
Taney, Roger B., 214, 286, 291, 300
Tappan, Lewis, 299, 304
task system of labor, 163
Tattnall, Edward, 186
Tax Digest, 279
Taylor, John W., 272–73
Tennessee, 284
Tentativa (slave ship), 92, 94
Tentativa case, 92–93
Teredo navalis (shipworm), 12–13
Thames River, xxi
Thompson, James, 123
Thompson, Smith, 194, 247
Thompson Town, 190–91
Thomson, Mortimer, 102
Thruston, Buckner, 177
Timolen (Cuban brig), 57–58
Todd, Thomas, 214, 259
Todson, George P., 261–65
Tom (*Antelope* captive), 124, 255, 256
Tombs, Robert, 287
Toney (*Antelope* captive), 160
Tortola, 35
Toulouse, Fort, *see* Jackson, Fort
"Trade and Commerce: As They Were, and As They Will Be," 21
Transcontinental Treaty, 178
Treasury Department, Georgia, 93
Treasury Department, U.S., 260, 268
Treaty of Fort Jackson, 241
Treaty of Ghent, 38
Treaty of Indian Springs (1821), 241, 242, 243
Treaty of Indian Springs (1825), 242, 244, 251, 268–69

Treaty of San Lorenzo el Real (1795), 220
Treaty of Washington, 251, 269
Trimble, Robert, 240, 257, 259–60, 261
Trist, Nicholas, 304
Troup, George, 202, 206, 242–43, 244–45, 247, 248, 251, 258, 269, 284
Troupites, 115
Troup party, 170
Tucker, St. George, 119
Tulane University, 280

Undine, H.M.S., 1
Union Society, 115, 202
United Provinces of La Plata, 21–22
United States, 11, 12, 18, 19, 33–35, 38, 126
domestic slave trade in, 87
Panic of 1819 in, 23, 88
relations with Spain of, 17
suppression of slave trade by, 179, 210
United States v. Charles Mulvey, Vice Consul of Spain, 216
United States v. Francis Sorrel, Vice Consul of Portugal, 216
Uruguay, 22
U.S. Attorney, 284

Val de San Lorenzo, Spain, 10
Van Buren, Martin, 285
Venezuela, 16–17, 22, 23, 24, 27, 42, 52, 60, 63, 111, 112, 114, 139, 151
Virginia, 78, 87, 156, 178, 179, 266
Virginia Capes, 190
volante, 4

Waldburg, Jacob, Sr., 161
Waldburg family, 195
Ware, Nicholas, 206
Waring, William R., 98–99, 101, 103
War of 1812, 19, 20, 25, 35, 36, 38, 40, 83, 86, 118, 157–58, 178, 180, 233, 292–93, 294
Washington, Bushrod, 209, 212, 218, 247–48
Washington, D.C., xii, 40, 81, 177, 179, 182, 184, 186, 207, 208, 209, 227–28, 286, 295
Washington, George, 86, 197, 209
Washington, Treaty of, 251, 269
Washington (revenue cutter), 299
Washington Daily National Intelligencer, 223

Washington Ward (Savannah, Ga.), 86, 98–99, 101, 105–6, 107, 108
Wayne, Anthony, 156
Wayne, Fort, 86
Wayne, James Moore, 116–17, 118, 120, 286
Webster, Daniel, xi, 214, 229
Weekly Register, 25
Weld, Theodore Dwight, 292
West Indies, 6, 10, 11, 18, 156, 188
wheat, 18
Wheaton, Henry, 229, 248
Wheaton's Reports, 296
Whig Party, 115, 282, 287, 300
whippers, 164
White, Joseph, 271, 278, 281
Whitfield, George, 77
Wilberforce, William, 33
Wilde, Richard Henry, 246, 247, 250, 254, 258, 269–71, 272, 273, 277, 278–80, 281, 283
Williams, William, 102
Windward Passage, 9
Wirt, William, xiii, xv, 171, 178–79, 180, 181–83, 184–86, 207–8, 211, 212, 214, 215, 216, 223–24, 227, 228, 230, 235, 239, 243, 245, 247–48, 258, 269, 303, 305
Antelope argument of, 224–26
Woyo people, 45, 46, 48
Wyatt (*Del Carmen* commander), 28
Wylly, Richard, 78
Wythe, George, 198

Ximenes, Thomas, 13, 56, 58, 126, 127, 131–32, 133–34, 135, 170, 236–37

Yamacraw district (Savannah, Ga.), 85, 98, 165, 166
Yazoo Rescinding Act, 199–200
yellow fever, 24, 31, 99–103, 105–10
diagnosis of, 107
immunity to, 109
mortality of, 100, 107–9
Young, Thomas, 195
Young Spartan (smuggling and pirate ship), 81

Zaragoza (ship), 11